Beyond Our Kenneth

The Continued Diaries of
Kenneth Williams

Beyond Our Kenneth

THE CONTINUED DIARIES OF

Kenneth Williams

BILL HOLLAND

fantom
publishing

First published in 2025 by Fantom Publishing, an imprint of Fantom Films
www.fantompublishing.co.uk

Copyright © Bill Holland 2025

Bill Holland has asserted his moral right to be identified as the author of this work in accordance with the Copyright, Designs and Patents Act 1988.

All rights reserved.

A catalogue record for this book is available from the British Library.

Hardback edition ISBN: 978-1-78196-396-8

Typeset by Phil Reynolds Media Services, Leamington Spa
Printed and bound by CPI Group (UK) Ltd, Croydon, CR0 4YY
Cover design by Stuart Manning

Front cover image © Brian Moody
Back cover image © Eric Roberts/Shutterstock

*To Dad,
for indulging my passions
and sharing my dreams*

CONTENTS

Foreword by Wes Butters ix
Carry On, Kenneth… xi
Dramatis Personæ xiii

THE DIARIES

    1988 1
    1989 45
    1990 126
    1991 204
    1992 271

Acknowledgements 357

FOREWORD

Even in death, Kenneth Williams wanted an audience. He quietly regarded his diaries, I'm convinced, as the key to achieving this, looking upon them as his true life's work: a chance to have the last laugh and deliver a monumental performance that could live on forever. Though his half-sister Pat vehemently opposed their publication in 1993, five years after his passing, he had long made clear he expected them to be made public, readily acknowledging to TV interviewer Mavis Nicholson in 1977, 'After I'm gone, one wouldn't mind that at all.'

Day in, day out, he invested in his legacy, tempering a nagging belief that, in his career at least, he was falling short of his own expectations. But, undertaken this way, in the respectable role of diarist, he could orchestrate exactly how he should be remembered. And so it was a serious endeavour, with minimal crossings out and each page completed in exceptionally neat handwriting. Like London's other famed chroniclers, Samuel Pepys and Virginia Woolf, the diaries ensured Kenneth made his own mark, on his own terms, in his own words.

Despite first documenting the year 1942 in a small pocket diary when he was sixteen, his unbroken run of keeping a journal didn't begin until Christmas Eve 1946, while he was serving in Singapore with Combined Services Entertainment. It was his fellow comrade Stanley Baxter who first encouraged him to record work engagements and fees, a practical exercise, though from the outset the entries were amusing and candid snapshots of his life. As Kenneth grew in character, so did his diary, and by the final entry in April 1988, he had filled some forty-three volumes with an estimated four million words. This was his magnum opus – a literary work longer than the *Lord of the Rings* trilogy, *War and Peace*, and the complete works of Shakespeare, combined.

But diaries, too, can be part fiction. Kenneth's morning ritual of writing up the previous day wasn't merely a retelling of what had happened, but a short story, or – better still – a soap opera brought alive by dialogue and observations, faithful or embellished, whichever best enhanced his version of history. This came as a shock to some friends, who found their recollection of events didn't entirely match those portrayed in the published volume, while a few must have realised he wrote them as much to entertain others as he did for personal reflection. After all, sitting in his flat, they had been treated to the author pulling a selection from his bookcase and reading aloud gossipy and outrageous extracts written about people they knew. Just as a writer writes, a performer performs – and Kenneth was both.

While I applaud every effort to perpetuate Kenneth's memory, I must confess to feeling somewhat sceptical when I first heard of Bill Holland's unusual project. How wrong I was. As you will discover, it is a formidable achievement. He has the remarkable ability to recreate not just the preciseness of Kenneth's vocabulary and turns of phrase, but the very spirit of the man. That he could think up such imagined exploits and storylines, perfectly suited to our hero, is extraordinary (so much so, that I spent too much time wondering whether he had found a portal to an alternate reality and unearthed a secret diary nobody knew existed!). Edit together the published diaries and this *conjured coda*, and I defy anyone unfamiliar with the subject to spot the join.

The result is that Kenneth lives, both in the pages that follow, and in our hearts and minds once more. That unmistakable voice, his idiosyncrasies, habits and adventures are born again; they continue.

So, please – carry on, Kenneth…

Wes Butters,
November 2024

CARRY ON, KENNETH...

The incomparably fabulous Kenneth Williams – comic actor, author and raconteur – died during the small hours of Friday, 15 April, 1988, alone in his modest, spartan, North London flat. Having ingested a strong sedative drug, he retired to bed and succumbed to an overdose. An inquest was held, but the coroner couldn't determine whether his demise was attributable to a wilful suicide, an unwitting miscalculation or some other kind of mistake. An open verdict was declared.

For upwards of forty years Williams had kept diaries, which were edited and published following his death. The most remarkable annals of their kind, they constitute a pithily couched chronicle of London life from the Blitz to the zenith of Thatcherism, and present a vivid, revealing self-portrait of a hugely popular, instantly recognisable, yet deeply complicated performer: a gregarious extrovert on the one hand; a disenchanted, profoundly private bachelor on the other.

He pulled no punches. Friends and colleagues were well aware that this infamous journal was updated assiduously and acidly, incidents documented with unequivocal candour. *'You'll be in the diary!'* was the fabled threat, made without ambiguity, a signal that a perceived slight, an impertinent misdeed or a barbed remark was sure to be recorded in tendentious detail for posterity.

All facets of Kenneth's psyche are laid bare. Whether he was writing as the earnest schoolboy, the querulous evacuee, the reluctant soldier, the unfulfilled civvy, the idealist thespian, the camp radio star, the big screen celebrity, the appalled snob, the erudite intellectual, the chat show darling, the razor-tongued miseryguts, the gleeful jester – or the melancholy ponderer of his latter days – the style and substance of the text is wittily blunt and wholly engrossing.

Kenneth Williams, the brilliant, temperamental eccentric, turned sixty-two in 1988. The last few months of his diary expose a sickly, dejected recluse at his wits' end. Professionally, after four decades in showbusiness, he had been reduced to reeling off hackneyed chestnuts on breakfast TV sofas and providing overripe voiceovers for puerile commercials. Personally, he was burdened by the geriatric struggles of next-door neighbour Louie, his octogenarian mother. And privately, behind closed doors, he suffered the incessant agony of longstanding abdominal disorders and the dread of an imminent, speculative operation. Each entry uncovers a mind brimming with morbid thoughts and lonely desperation. Whatever happened that April night, his life came to a conclusion. He left behind a heartbroken old lady, several devastated cohorts, dozens of shocked associates and thousands of saddened fans.

Though the diaries are filled with outrageous dialogue, droll yarns and starry anecdotes, it was actually the gloomy dénouement that motivated me as a storyteller to want to pick up the threads. I craved a different epilogue to this tale, one permeated not with sadness and anguish, but with exuberance and possibility. In my view, Kenneth Williams left us with a final act of the drama unperformed – an unlived period that could well have produced deserved contentment and peace for the man himself, and further joy and laughter for us, his ardent public. I know it's conceited of me to have stepped into his shoes so boldly, and attempted to speak with his voice – but I like to think he would forgive me.

The ensuing pages assume a parallel dimension – a fanciful plane, where this legend of entertainment *didn't* leave the stage that spring morning, but carried on… Carried on into a fresh era, along erstwhile untrod paths, with companions old and new – scribbling extra caustic comments, more sour putdowns; describing a fictive Britain of the early 1990s and reacting to it in a distinct and forthright way.

This is an imagined diary.

It is presented with the addition of explanatory footnotes, the veracity of which is consistent with the illusory universe that has been created, rather than our own reality.

This book finds a lost national treasure enduring in an alternate world. A world that never was – but, with historical tweaks of varying degrees, a world that might've existed, beyond our Kenneth…

DRAMATIS PERSONÆ

A list of persons frequently mentioned in the diary.

Lou/Louie/Louisa – Louisa Alexandra Williams, *née* Morgan (1901-91), KW's mother and greatest fan. From 1972 she lived in the adjacent flat to her son at Marlborough House, Osnaburgh Street, London NW1.

Charlie/Charles – Charles George Williams (1899-1962), KW's father; a Cockney hairdresser with impassive Victorian values. KW rarely saw eye to eye with him, and was essentially unmoved by his accidental poisoning, which proved fatal.

Pat – Alice Patricia Williams (1923-95), KW's half-sister. An imposing, gravel-voiced divorcée, whose illegitimacy caused an underlying friction within the family.

M. – Michael Whittaker (b. 1938), businessman and former chorister at Lichfield Cathedral. KW's best friend; a regular dinner companion, loyal confidant and transport provider.

M.A./Michael/Anderson – Michael Anderson (1929-2019), KW's theatrical agent from 1981.

Paul – Paul Richardson (b. 1944), technical director at Sadler's Wells Theatre; KW's friend and neighbour at Marlborough House.

Gordon/Gording/Nodrog – Gordon Jackson (1923-90), Scottish actor, husband of actress Rona Anderson. KW's colleague and intimate from 1955. Away from the limelight, the Jacksons provided KW with a welcome distraction of conformist domesticity at their Hampstead home.

Stanley – Stanley Baxter (b. 1926), Scottish actor, comedian and impressionist. Combined Services Entertainment comrade of KW in the Far East, and subsequent lifelong friend. The close yet competitive nature of the relationship resulted in intermittent fallings-out.

Mags – Maggie Smith (1934-2024), Oscar-winning English actress. A longstanding friend, who first worked with KW in revue in 1957. She credited him with initiating an understanding of comedic immediacy in her stage work.

Peter – Peter Cook (1937-95), English comedian, actor, satirist and playwright. Wrote sketches for KW's hit West End revue *Pieces of Eight* and its follow-up. Amity between the two became strained in later years.

Rupert/R. – Rupert Peter Jarvis (b. 1952), lifeguard and swimming instructor. Resident of Marlborough House. Engaged in a spasmodic, clandestine relationship with KW from 1988.

Flo – Flordeliza Aquino (b. 1954), domestic cleaner and registered carer. Moving to London from the Philippines in 1986, she was employed by Camden Council as a home help for KW's mother in August 1989.

Rita – Margarita Quinn (1962-2024), a Peterborough native who helped care for Mrs Williams from September 1989, chiefly at weekends.

Gyles – Gyles Brandreth (b. 1948), British broadcaster, writer and politician. Assisted with the collation and editing of KW's books *Acid Drops* and *Back Drops* in the early 1980s.

Also, KW's co-stars in the long-running *Carry On* film series (1958-92):

Joanie – Joan Sims (1930-2001); **Hat** – Hattie Jacques (1922-80); **Kenny C** – Kenneth Connor (1918-93); **Sid** – Sidney James (1913-76); **Bernie** – Bernard Bresslaw (1934-93); **Barbara** – Barbara Windsor (1937-2020); **Charlie** – Charles Hawtrey (1914-88); **Cribbins** – Bernard Cribbins (1928-2022); **June** – June Whitfield (1925-2018); **Frankie** – Frankie Howerd (1917-92); **Jack** – Jack Douglas (1927-2008); **Phillips** – Leslie Phillips (1924-2022).

1988

Friday, 15 April
I'm sick to *death* of this… One hears that expression, wailed despondently or with tart exasperation apropos many an irksome matter. The thuds of a noisy neighbour; the slog of a tedious occupation; the work of Jeremy Beadle – all vexatious enough to rouse its use. The most trivial of predicaments can cause it to be ejaculated, *fortissimo* & with spittle, as an indignant retort to the universe. It's exclaimed with such airy abandon, of course, because it isn't to be taken literally. The utterer is neither sick nor approaching death, yet, as with any phrase, the idiomatic frills underscore the point in the heat of the moment. They don't really mean it… Well, *I mean it.* I mean every sodding syllable.

    I woke at 6 o'c. with those very words resting on my lips. Without hesitation, the pain began, a searing throb about three inches north of the coccyx. The Naproxen doesn't touch the sides now – tho' it is stunningly effective at inducing dizziness and hardening the stools. I had to use the syringe, legs aloft like the Green Goddess.[1] 'Can you see this, Lord?' I cried, excrement on the fingers, '*Thus* hath thou reduced me.' My blasphemy was answered with a button from the pyjama trousers pinging off & rolling under the dresser. Took Bisodol & Libraxin before attempting half a bowl of cornflakes & then had the Zantac. Heard every milligramme squelching through the system. I rang Anderson. Asked him to get me out of this video job on Monday. It's cutting it fine, but I'm in no condition to go anywhere, least of all Swindon.

---

[1] Sobriquet of BBC *Breakfast Time*'s Diana Moran (b. 1939), English model and fitness expert.

Went in to Lou. I'd scarcely set foot in the place before her griping started. 'The toilet's blocked & the deaf aid don't work.' My instinct was to leap headfirst thro' the window, but I meekly counted to ten & fetched the plunger… I think of little else now but putting an end to it. Even the fleeting periods of respite, which once arrived with illusory waves of optimism, have become nothing more than numb interludes, just long enough to give one time to reflect on some other dismal facet of this rotten existence.

After the chiropodist, went to Angell Sound for the Rowntree's voiceover. Incongruous, to sit there gleefully, spouting inane rubbish into the microphone whilst the innards splosh and scream. At the finish the director said 'D'you know, you're looking a bit peaky?' I limped to Marks's for the shopping. Had to ask the girl to fetch me down the cream of chicken owing to the pain. *Shattered* by the time I got back. There was a Dyno-Rod man outside the block, expelling filth from the drain with his nozzle. 'I could've done with you at half-six this morning,' I muttered, but he couldn't hear over the din. I amplified with 'How do you cope with the pong?' He chuckled. 'I don't notice it,' he said, 'but the old lady moans 'cos it does cling to me. Our local Berni Inn always seats us next to the lavs…'

Grilled the fish for Lou, but I had nothing. We sat there in silence, save for her breathing. Despite a fortnight of No Smoking, it remains raspy & terribly irritating. Had a nap but was woken by Murray-Lyon's[2] secretary on the telephone confirming the operation on 27th. Pencilled it in to the appointment book & the palpitations started.

Lou watched *Dynasty* whilst I flailed in the armchair, scarcely able to hold in the tears. Only cowardice is stopping me now.

Saturday, 16 April
Woken at 5.30 by the French queen's car alarm. For one marvellous moment I thought I'd got away with it, but soon as I sat up, bang, there it was, like a machete in the rachis.

Shuffled to Great Portland Street for the papers. Stonehouse[3] has dropped dead, the lucky swine. In earnest on this occasion, too. They don't know they're born, these people who cop it out of the blue, going about their

---

[2] Iain Murray-Lyon (b. 1940), Harley Street gastroenterologist.
[3] John Stonehouse (1925-88), former Labour MP and Postmaster General under Harold Wilson; alleged agent for Czechoslovakian military intelligence. An attempt to stage his own death in 1974 was ultimately foiled.

business, then wallop – goodnight, Vienna. Sooner that than a sad, sickly dwindling... The rhythm of the spinal ache has switched from a metronomic pang to discordant jabs, like Teddy Brown[4] beating the vertebræ with cattle prods, or Lucifer sending marconigrams up the lumbar.

Cornered by the dreaded lurgy on my return. He was fitting draught excluders. 'Ain't seen you on the box lately,' he said. 'I 'spect they go in for younger models nowadays, don't they? Like that "chase me, chase me" feller[5]... He's a *scream*.'

Did a Fray Bentos for the meal, but the top caught & came out black as Newgate's knocker. It took everything I had not to hurl it across the room. Lou turned her nose up, so I finished with a plate of charcoal while she burned her tongue on the filling. Even tinned pies are urging me towards the exit. I put one up & went to bed.

Sunday, 17 April
Considered cancelling *Just a Minute*, but dosed myself up on painkillers & Libraxin and got Lou ready. 'Where are we going?' she asked (as she always does). 'Never you mind,' I said, 'there'll be plenty of old men with big dicks, so you'll be suited,' & she laughed.

M. came at 6.45 and drove us to the Paris. Chris Timothy was on the panel!! I greeted him warmly. 'My mother & I adore your programme.[6] Please say there'll be more.' He said 'We start filming on Thursday, as it happens. I'm sure Bill would be keen to have you on board if you'd like me to put in a word.' Told him I was *born* to shove my arm up a Friesian on Equity rates. He smiled obligingly... The show itself was appalling. The churning belly was inescapable, resulting in v. little engagement.

Monday, 18 April
Death was in the bedroom. I know it sounds barmy, but it was *him* – plain as day, standing by the wardrobe. A hazy Geoff Capes[7] would best describe the form: ample yet ashen. Not that I'd the nerve to look. When I did build

---

[4] Stage name of Abraham Himmelbrand (1900-46), rotund American xylophonist.
[5] Duncan Norvelle (1958-2024), English comedian, whose act was based on appearing to be a stereotypical camp homosexual.
[6] *All Creatures Great and Small*, BBC TV (1978-90), created by Bill Sellars. Drama starring Christopher Timothy as rural veterinarian James Herriot.
[7] British shot-putter and strongman (1949-2024).

up the pluck, he'd moved... but I knew he was still there, a spider lurking in a spout. I held the breath & strained to listen, but he was too cunning for that. After a bit I felt him lean across the quilt; goading me, prodding me – first in the *spine* & then in the *guts*.

I wanted him so much. 'I've been waiting for you,' I whispered. I implored him to take me & do his duty, to not leave the wretched ball in my court any more. I begged to be gone from this place, away from the misery, the failure, the grief & the endless, mangling agony. I pleaded *aloud* for him to take my hand and finish it off.

Heard Holy Trinity strike three. Visions of Lou finding me frigid & blanched, unable to wake me, having to call the porter. Nervous coughing & whispering behind her back; then being turfed out of her flat to some grotty 'home', meanly marched out like a convict. I kept hearing Pat's voice: 'You'll like this place, mum, they have crumble on Tuesdays'... Got up in *desperation* at 4 o'c. Took the Zantac, the belly a writhing mess, the back *throbbing*. A stooped motion seemed to placate it a bit so I lurched up & down, thinking. Shuffled about for ages, just in the pyjamas. Looked out on the street, but all was quiet, bar the milkman's clanks. The pain screamed at me: Do it. Do it. Just *go*...

Stared at myself in the bathroom mirror. Prickly tears accrued on the bottom lid, blurring the reflection. Headlines running through my mind – 'Kenneth Williams is dead... discovered by his elderly mother... the *Carry On* star... the outrageous comic... the fizzled poof...' Got out the pills again & touched them, counted them, arranged them. I thought of Charlie in his hospital bed, convulsing & tortured as the poison did its work, his eyes fixed on mine. Pondered the ineluctability of sons following in their father's footsteps. The mere thought made me retch over the sink.

I've never been so unsure about anything in my entire life. Boarding the troopship at Greenock; posting that first ad to *The Stage*; letting the man on the bus in Bicester put his hand on my knee... all ironclad certainties compared to this. I bit the lip hard & took a breath. One by one, I threw the Sodium Amytal capsules *in the loo*. Felt as tho' I was binning my courage, flinging priceless pearls into a wishing well. Stood pathetically with the empty vial in one hand & the lavatory chain in the other, irresolute and blubbing. Then, *flush*... Got dressed, gingerly. Stripped the sheets... It's a curious sensation. As though I *have* killed myself, but that I've *cheated* Death, fooling him into thinking I've really gone, & that I'm now just a soulless witness to it all. Made the coffee. Went & got papers. The epicene tramp in the doorway of Unwins shouted out 'Good morning, my duck!' & I waved back frugally, like the old King.

It's ludicrous, reely. I've done nothing but chuck some easily replaceable tablets down the carsey. But it's an assertion: that little collection was an insurance policy, my cherished egress. Now it separates, floats off & dissolves, up Bazalgette's canal... The pain gurgled, but I ate dry toast on my return. The *crunch* was reassuring & confident.

It's doubtless disloyal to Murray-Lyon, but *his* only solution is to hack me open & dig around, and I really don't think I can face it. Rang his secretary to cancel op, then 'phoned the specialist that Nimmo[8] recommended, Mr Chatham. Second opinions are always sensible – at least, they are when first opinions are objectionable. Eventually got the receptionist. 'I've had a cancellation at 5.15, would that be alright?'... Bit her arm off.

Went into Lou's flat at 12.30 & prepared lamb chops, chips & tomatoes for lunch. I only picked at it, what with the dull pain & a sense of *apprehension* about what this Chatham will say. Afterwards Lou said 'O! I'm full up now... You are good to me.' I said 'Don't you worry, missus, it's all been added to your bill!' and she laughed. Had a rest, contorted in the chair in a skewed position to appease the vertebræ. Gordon rang. He's been in New York doing the *Upstairs Downstairs* shtick – playing Hudson at *real* dinner parties for wealthy Manhattanites. Sounds ghastly. He said 'I was thinking about you last night... You're always to remember, I'm only ever a 'phone call away,' which of course led to more waterworks.

Slowly lurched to Harley Street, the stabbing in the back replaced by numbness and pins & needles, the stomach inflated & tender... This man, Adrian Chatham, is impressive in his own way. Young, confident, but not pretentious. Bit of a dish to boot. He had my number straitway – 'You're close to the edge, aren't you?'... He listened to my moaning then examined me. Asked what the previous doctors had told me and shook his head & sighed as though he'd heard it all before. He explained that the standard therapies are adequate in temporarily beating back the condition, but the ulcer will *always* recur. He seemed irritated that the same old methods were being applied. Sat me down & told me that the problem is a *bacterial* one –

---

[8] Derek Nimmo (1930-99), English character actor and author. Played upper-class clerical roles in various TV sitcoms.

nothing to do with lifestyle or drinking or smoking or worry. *Campylobacter pylori* is my enemy, if you please, & antibiotics can thwart it... There was no vacillation, he was clear & encouraging. 'It won't be overnight, but we'll get there,' he said – 'Throw away all your Zantac and Bisodol'. I am to come back on Tuesday for the gastroscopy to properly assess the state of the umbles. I shook his hand warmly and on exiting he said 'Is your back alright?'... so I gave him the rundown about that. He asked if I'd tried massage therapy before. Told him I'd had a session with Martita's[9] chiropractor in '56. He smiled & said 'You *could* be due a checkup then,' & gave me the card of an osteopath friend of his who, he insists, works wonders... Talk about the full M.O.T.!

Went in to Lou at 8 o'c. Ate some crisps. She was watching Russ Abbot. I sat in the usual disquiet, but there *was* something different. It's as though the pain's having a final flourish, one last attempt to tip the scale. Fizzing discomfort inside the anus, like a Catherine wheel going off up the rectum. Came back to the flat, exhausted but tranquil. Today feels, rightly or wrongly, like a first step – but towards *what* is anyone's guess.

Tuesday, 19 April
Slept like a log. No ghostly visitors... Didn't wake till *gone 8 o'c.*!! Avoided the dreaded lurgy, who was varnishing the bannisters. Hobbled, Quasimodo-fashion, to get the papers. Had the cornflakes. 'Phoned this physiotherapist, Johnny Johnson, and got an appt. for Thursday. I was advised by the far-too-chirpy nurse to lie on floorboards in the meantime... Getting *to* the floor is alright, but getting up again is agonising & the effort causes the most unpleasant *farting...* O! it's all so revolting. This is the last roll of the dice, I *swear* it... The stitch pain in the left abdomen was a nuisance, so called on Lou and we took a turn in the park as a distraction. It's warmer today with a milky sun. The feeling persists that I've either dodged a bullet or made an awful mistake. We must've looked a frightful pair of old crips, lumbering round the Rose Garden[10] like something out of *Revenge of the Zombies*.

Had moussaka with Lou at 5.30, but I couldn't manage much. Saw the TV news. This bloody Kuwaiti Airways siege continues at Algiers. It's disgusting. 'What's it all in aid of?' said Lou, unable to follow it. 'It's the

---

[9] Martita Hunt (1900-69), Argentine-born British actress. Appeared with KW and Alec Guinness in the Feydeau farce *Hotel Paradiso* at the Winter Garden Theatre in 1956.
[10] Queen Mary's Rose Gardens at Regent's Park.

militant Lebanese,' I said. 'Would never've happened when I was a girl,' she harrumphed. 'Not lesbians, *Lebanese*, you silly cow,' I said... After Uno there was the new Bennett thing.[11] The writing's unsubtle in that broad northern way, & the left-wing digs are tiresome, but it's remarkably effective. It was Alan himself, as a cardiganed homosexual living with the elderly mother. A marvellous still life, but all a bit too close to home for this viewer.

Wednesday, 20 April
M. came at 6.45 & I gave him dinner at the Tent. It's asking for trouble to go out for meals, but there's the rub: one has to *eat*. I had plain cod & green salad & fizzy water with lemon. That Valerio was the waiter, the one with the lopsided arse. Ronnie Barker was in the restaurant!! It was marvellous to see him. Ronnie said 'We're settled in Chipping Norton now. Good air, and it's such a relief not to *have* to make people laugh.' I can believe that! He's running an antique shop now... Intermittent wind on returning. Tried the floorboards again, but it hurts more getting down there than leaving it alone, so I aborted... Can't get Ronnie B out of my head. He looked so contented, & about ten years younger. It proves my theory that *showbiz* is the real disease.

Saw the News. The aeroplane hostages have finally been released & the filthy guerrillas have turned themselves in to the Algerians! O! the horror that is perpetrated, so often in the name of religion. I certainly shan't turn back to *Faith* – it's a filthier habit than the fags were.

Thursday, 21 April
Charming letter from a little boy in Cambridge... he writes enchantingly about my robot voice.[12] 'If computers could tork,' he explains, 'I think they would tork just like you do. Well done on that.' I signed a press photo of myself & SID for him – though it'll probably be a shock to discover that his favourite character is actually a desiccated old man... Lou was on a club outing, so had a tin of oxtail on my own in her flat. Couldn't finish it though. Growling, staccato-like pain, directly behind the navel, as if a zip is being internally opened & closed.

---

[11] *Talking Heads*, BBC TV (1988). A series of six dramatic monologues by English playwright Alan Bennett (b. 1934).
[12] For the BBC children's series *Galloping Galaxies!* (1985-6), created by Bob Block. KW provided the voice of the bog-eyed computer, SID.

Dragged myself to Warren Street tube. The train was rickety to the point of collapse & we travelled in near-darkness. I complained to the stationmaster at Kennington, but got lumbered when he went on & on with 'O! have a heart, sir... that's '38 Stock... they're scrapping 'em tomorrow... end of an era... you'll miss 'em when they're gone...' I beg to differ... Arrived at a grand Georgian building – thinking 'this'll be pricey' – at 2.55... Met this Johnson – bit of a Peter Lorre look about him – & stripped off. *The relief is phenomenal...* Don't know why I didn't go in for this type of treatment years ago. It's more stringent massage than anything else. At one point he had his elbow dug into the small of my back! I laid on a trestle bed, my face shoved through a padded cavity, jammed in like a champion gurner. He announced 'You're full of knots!', as tho' I'd won the sweepstake. I was prostrate as any corpse on the slab – but I *did* feel a few things crack into place & a warm, radiating glow, as if I were a broken clock having my springs mended. I fear I let one go when he was finishing off, which is scant reward for his efforts – I saw him wince. He's given me a list of exercises to do, so we shall see if it lasts. Sailed out of there at 4 o'c., so full of optimism that I barely noticed the belly.

In the evening Louisa said 'You've perked up!' so it must be obvious. I said 'Did you have a nice time in Southend?' 'Not particularly,' she said. 'Winnie was upset 'cos her son's laying down the law & wants to be given power of eternity...' I stifled a laugh... I think of the other morning & I look at Lou. I am wholly ashamed & dazed with guilt.

Friday, 22 April
Was worried in the night that the spell had worn off after a few acute spasms, but got up at 7.15 & all was well. I'm so very grateful for this first step. Considered sending a gift of some sort to Johnny Johnson, but he's had his cheque, I must keep things in proportion. Realised that I couldn't have *anything* to eat in the morning thanks to these bloody tests, so the gut was gurgling, *visibly* – it was like someone was drilling inside. Had a letter from the producer of that video thing: 'We were very disappointed that you pulled out at the eleventh hour... I imagine you must be quite unwell, as I'm sure this isn't your usual practice', etc. – The impertinence is remarkable. Who do these shits think they are? I only agreed to do the job through boredom, it certainly wasn't for the pittance they were offering. Rang ICM to carp, but got Gillian's replacement at the front desk. Mitzie...

not the sharpest tool in the shed. 'Mr Anderson's on his dinnertime,' she said callowly. Told her to blacklist the video firm.

Walked to Mr Chatham. He told me not to worry & that there'd be no pain. Positioning was awkward, he had me leant right back & then bolt upright as if I were having a shampoo & set. He detected a large, penetrating posterior gastric ulcer which is adherent to the pancreas. He sucked air through his teeth, like a builder assessing dry rot & said 'the stomach wall is intensely congested and inflamed,' but he did the biopsy & that was that. Took all of 15 minutes. He was right, it didn't hurt as such, though I feel as if I've been on the gam & the head's ever so woozy. Am to return in a week for results. In the meantime he's given me a bottle of stuff that aims to stabilise the situation. He remains hopeful & certainly bolsters one. He has a lovely sun tan, for April. Though, if his miracles work, I'm quite sure he can afford sunshine holidays.

Prepared steaks for supper. Was ravenous after not having eaten & rather overdid it, the stomach convulsing and angry. Sat with Lou watching the TV, trying to ignore the churning.

Sunday, 24 April
M. drove us to the Paris Theatre for *Just a Minute*. Last in the series, & it surely felt like it! Talk about going through the motions. What it needs is a freshening up – it's incredible that *anyone* still listens to five old crocks like us wittering on every week... Freud[13] and Nimmo arguing about Giotto might be alright around a table at the Reform Club, but the congregation today looked utterly bemused. I tried my best by shouting and screaming the old drivel, but the gut wasn't cooperating & the heart wasn't really in it... Ambushed by the bloody autograph hunters & considered fleeing, but I found a face & signed a few.

Went in to Lou at 5.15 but didn't eat, trying to let the jollop do its work.

Monday, 25 April
Stanley came & gave me dinner at Vecchia Milano. I had soup (a very good Minestrone) and sole, but no wine. Stanley looked marvellous! He's filming this *Mr Majeika* for TVS. Location's down in Tonbridge, which is madly six miles from Tunbridge. He said 'Miriam Margolyes is a hoot and a dream to

---

[13] Clement Freud (1924-2009), German-born British writer and broadcaster; Liberal MP for Isle of Ely, 1973-83.

play with, tho' the tits are more often out than in.' I know what a vivacious creature she is – I asked to be remembered to her. Told him about the potential new treatment and he said it all sounds very positive & that I look more myself. Can't think why, I haven't had the remedy yet, but maybe he's referring to my mood. The back is unquestionably better. I find myself dropping biros in order to bend down & test it.

It's four weeks today of No Smoking and I reckon I've cracked it. Don't miss it reely, except occasionally with the *café matinal*.

Tuesday, 26 April
Met Paul outside after I'd been to the post & he suggested a stroll. Think he was surprised when I accepted. We ended up passing the small Odeon & we were just in time for the 12.50 showing of *Empire of the Sun*.[14] It's overlong but an *extraordinary* piece of work – it really had the feel of the time & the place, & little touches reminded me of being out there. I'd associated Spielberg with horror and science fiction inanity, but there's no denying it, he can really *capture* war & its bleakness on film. Phillips pops up in the picture as well!! He doesn't change… Had to leave Paul expeditiously at the finish, as I could feel a noxious bout of wind coming on, & wanted to be in the flat for the inevitable BM.[15] Briefly worried that the cinema seat had thwarted the spinal progress, but a few stretches and it's alright again.

Went in to Lou. She's had a letter from a Mavis Higgins, daughter of Dolly Hollis who cleaned the lavatories at the Lucas Arms with Lou in '42!! Goodness only knows how this Mavis got the address! Well, the upshot is, the old girl has dropped dead in Presto's aged 90! Lou said 'What's she telling me for?… She never *was* much cop with a J-cloth, and I told her so at the time…'

Wednesday, 27 April
Lousy night. A dull pain in the abdomen (left side) that got worse with every intake of breath. Got up at 7 o'c. and attempted to walk it off but to no avail. Took the medicine, but it's not designed to kill pain & it didn't. Went to M&S to get bits for Lou and tried to take my mind off it. Sat in the park for a while as it's decidedly clement. A fat woman was feeding the horrid *sparrows*, attracting hundreds of the bloody things to the vicinity. Mused on the idea of an avian cull – if I were Minister for Agriculture there'd be a

---

[14] 1987 American war film, directed by Steven Spielberg and starring a young Christian Bale.
[15] Bowel movement.

nationwide poisoning policy, with tax breaks for those who produced the greatest tonnage of defunct birds... Stayed about an hour & got some sun on the pallid cheeks.

Anderson rang at 3.30, ostensibly to see how I am, but I could tell there was some piece of crap he wanted to throw my way. 'The Joan Rivers people have been on again about you going to New York.[16] They're *very* keen. But of course, if you're not well'... I said 'Michael, I'll do whatever you say when this has blown over' to appease him, but I have absolutely no intention of going anywhere.

Thursday, 28 April
Woke at 5.30, fretting about what the results of the biopsy will be. Went into Lou to make bed & she's managed to snap the lid off the Steradent bottle & it's gone *everywhere*. There were floury white footprints all over the flat, as though she'd been entertaining Mr Bun the Baker. Traipsed round with the Ewbank but Lou kept saying 'O! leave it, you can't hardly see it!' so I've probably missed some. Managed to evade the dreaded lurgy & went to the post, with the pain – right side *and* left – thudding with every step I took. If it's bad news, I'll slip away. No one could say I didn't suffer, that's for sure.

Got to Chatham's at 2.45. 'Well, Mr Williams... I think we're going to be alright' he said. This *Campy-basket polari* stuff is present in the digestive tract, & so a combination of *three* antibiotics has been prescribed to kill the bacterium, along with a strong histamine blocker & another tablet to shrink the ulcer as quickly as possible. 'A couple of weeks on this concoction and we'll have you feeling twenty years younger'... Of course, it remains to be seen, & there have been false dawns before, but there's something about this man that makes one inclined to believe. On the way out the receptionist said 'Another victory?'... I asked her if victories were common. 'The man's ahead of his time. He's more interested in results than letters after his name. No wonder the bigwigs aren't keen on him.' I could tell she was damp in the gusset for him – well, who wouldn't be? – but as much for his abilities as his dimples.

Sailed home, grinning at all & sundry. A bus driver shouted from his window 'Carry On Ken!' and I waved – this time last week I'd've wanted to throttle him.

---

[16] KW had been a guest on Joan Rivers' short-lived BBC chat show *Can We Talk?* in 1986.

Beyond Our Kenneth

Played cards with Louisa in the evening. All the old favourites – Rummy, Snip-Snap-Snorem, Beat Your Neighbours... all the while the ulcer nagged away.

All I want to do is count my chickens, but I must hold off.

Friday, 29 April
Swallowing so many tablets is an effort in itself! Takes about ten minutes to get them all down, and that's thrice daily... The French queen has vacated the flat above mine. Met the new chap in the lobby as I was going for the paper. Flash-looking fellow, 30-ish. Butch. Big arms. Little silver chain round the neck. He was shifting boxes & said 'Hi there, I'm Rupert (*I ask you!*). I'm so very pleased to meet you!'... I said 'You don't play loud music, do you?' & he laughed. I suppose he thought I was being nice.

Saturday, 30 April
To Gordon & Rona's for 6 o'c. It was *marvellous* to be up there & Rona did a wonderful spread – alas, I could only pick at the bland stuff. The Kinnears[17] arrived about 6.45. Such a boost to see them all! G. said 'Well, your spark's back, that's for sure.' Told them about the pills & that I was still in pain, but people seem to be noticing a mood change. Shows how low I have been... Rona wanted to watch the Eurovision Song Contest, of all things – her cousin's boy was performing the British 'effort'. So that row was on in the background, tuneless continentals caterwauling for hours on end. I kept saying 'O! turn it off, we'd rather chat,' but she wouldn't have it. Looked like Rona's piece was going to win, but I was inwardly delighted when the Swiss girl pipped him... Left about 11.30, with a dull pain and the dyspepsia.

Sunday, 1 May
'Phoned M. and cancelled lunch. Lou enjoys the trips out, but I must be disciplined food-wise for this fortnight, at least.

Saw Lou in the evening. After the rubbish she wanted to watch, there was *Everyman* concerning the U.S. election, & the advance of moral crusaders trying to combat the rise of crime, drugs, abortion and AIDS, etc... For a country that separates Church from State, there's an astonishing

---

[17] Character actor and comedian Roy Kinnear (1934-88) and his wife, actress Carmel Cryan (b. 1949).

number of Christian zealots in American politics, from Reagan down. Somehow they get elected! Mentioning God would be political suicide over here, and rightly so... I know the Prime Minister is a Wesleyan, no doubt brought up like myself,[18] but those values ought to merely inform personal principles – as for the rest, God and his angels should keep their fucking noses out.

Monday, 2 May
Pat telephoned. 'I just wanted to see if you're feeling any better.' 'Yes, thank you' I said, & replaced the receiver.

Tuesday, 3 May
A lot more energy today. Had the Bran Flakes, as instructed. Went with Louie to get her pension. I *must* be picking up the pace, because her *slowness* was truly infuriating. 'Come on, you silly old cow' I shouted, outside the P.O., much to the astonishment of a black lady traffic warden. But how she tries... even tho' her pace is glacial & she gets easily flustered, she *tries* to adopt the brave face. If I get thro' this and recover, perhaps I'll take her away, one last big holiday whilst either of us can still manage it. I do owe it to her.

First time in ages that I've not felt the need for a catnap. Pain intermittent, & not severe. We saw Mags in *Talking Heads* in the evening. O! the girl can play *anything* – including, it seems, an alcoholic vicar's wife who's knocking off an Asian shopkeeper. She does *everything* with flair, wit, pathos, & it's all dripping with *truth*. I *adore* her to the core, & I always will. Wrote to Alan Bennett to laud the writing, which is the most spare & stylish I've known from him.

Friday, 6 May
Note to Michael saying that I would submit to small jobs if there's anything going, as long as they're in London. Fact is, with Chatham's bill arriving, I could do with the gelt. Lunch Lou: Chicken pie & string beans & a choc ice. No after effects at all!! Walked with Paul. He told me that this Rupert is a lifeguard & kiss of life instructor. 'Well, you can't wet a drip,' I said. We went to C&A for socks and Lou's smalls. Paul picked up a pair of skimpy

---

[18] Raised under this theological tradition, KW later noted (with much chagrin) that he and his fellow Wesleyans had been 'bunged in with the Methodists'.

knickers, looked at the label & said 'Now we know what "C&A" stands for,' & we laughed. I looked at light jackets for Louisa, but they're all spoilt by these ghastly shoulder pads... Feel like I'm going mad with all these pills! They'd better not be calorific, else I'll be waddling down Oxford Street before long.

Sunday, 8 May
Up at 8 o'c. and got paper. Darling George[19] has died in Santo Domingo. On the face of it it's a car accident, but the police are investigating. He'd adopted a teenaged boy in order to 'have an heir'. All sounds a bit sordid. He always had a whiff of the promiscuous about him & I wouldn't be surprised if certain chickens had come home to roost. They always seem to.

There was an old man peeing into the dustbin outside the White House. I saw such a thing when I was in Australia, but never expected to witness it here. I said 'Someone's got to clean that up, you know.' He smiled back at me, shaking the johnson, and said – enigmatically – 'They don't make 'em like *that* any more.'

By 5 o'c. realised I'd had *no pain all day*!! Can't remember the last time I could say that. Bit of wind, but that's alright. Nothing on the television so Louie & I sang old songs. Went through her dresses & removed the ones she's too fat for & bagged them for jumble.

Tuesday, 10 May
Acknowledgement from Bennett inviting me up there for tea, which is kind, if a tad OTT. Walked to Angell Sound for the Oracle Teletext voiceover. Four commercials. Used the Snide voice.[20] The girl was very sweet & seemed pleased. I confess, it wasn't Ibsen, but I was just relieved to feel useful... Bumped into Roy Castle in the foyer! Through it all, that boyish face remains – he's still doing his children's programmes and all the dancing has certainly kept him looking trim. Wanted to chat, but he was called into the studio.

Mitterrand reelected. I suppose it's inevitable these socialists get in. They promise retirement at 40, four-hour dinner breaks *and* the right to strike if the cream in your coffee is off... but when the proverbial hits the fan, as it

---

[19] Singer and actor George Rose (1920-88) had been beaten to death. One of the assailants was the 'heir' KW mentions.
[20] Most famously employed by KW for his 'Stop messin' about!' catchphrase.

surely will, it'll be the Right who have to step in to put things in order. The only surprise is that it hasn't already happened in France. I've never liked them. '*Oui*, it works in *practice* but does it work in *theory*??' It's the obsession with existentialism that wears you out, as opposed to our Anglo-Sax ethos of *getting things done*. We'll see what occurs when they face their own *wintre de discontent*.

Wednesday, 11 May
Harley Street for follow-up endoscopy. Irritation in the waiting room, with the morons' winks & the cretins' nudges and a husband & wife gawping at one. How I *loathe* these people. Asked the receptionist if there was somewhere I could wait without being disturbed, & she put me in their staff room... More uncomfortable this time. Almost flaked out feeling the tube slide through the gullet. However – the ulcer has nearly *gone*. Adrian said 'This is an excellent result. The inflammation has virtually disappeared too, which is more than we could've hoped for...' He seemed delighted with me – and I'm rather delighted myself. *All the years of agony*, all the special diets, all the X-rays, tubes, invasions & treatments. It just needed a pincer of antibiotics to kill off a simple, yet persistent, nasty... I shook the doctor warmly by the hand. I am to complete the course of pills, but he said I don't need to see him again for *six months*!! unless I feel I need to.

Wandered around in a bit of a daze. There's no getting away from it, I do feel well. *Overhauled* is the apt word: as if faulty parts have been recalibrated, oiled & reaffixed. Went to Lunn Poly at Warren Street & was offered two weeks in Minorca for Louisa & myself, 4 to 18 June. It's probably asking for trouble, but, today, I simply don't care.

Friday, 13 May
Walked to Gloucester Crescent. That filthy old woman is *still* parked up outside Alan's house.[21] 'You're another one of those pooves, aren't you?' she said as I squeezed briskly past... Alan gave me tea & talked about the *Prick Up Your Ears* script they want him to write for the theatre.[22] Donovan has demanded that *I* am a character in it!! I told him I didn't want to be

---

[21] The infamous 'lady in the van', Miss Shepherd, an elderly homeless woman who lived in a dilapidated van on Bennett's Camden driveway for fifteen years until her death in 1989.
[22] Based on John Lahr's 1978 biography of playwright (and friend of KW) Joe Orton, and the 1987 film of the same name.

associated with it in any way whatsoever – but I doubt it'll happen at all as Alan seems less than keen… As I left, the woman was hanging sopping wet bedsocks on the wing mirrors.

Saturday, 14 May
M. came at 8 o'c. & we drove up to Peterborough in the blazing sunshine. He avoided the motorway once we were out of town. Some of the villages are positively *chocolate box*, especially around Sawtry. Arrived at the cathedral for the personal tour by Bishop Wise. He insisted on 'Randy', but I stuck with 'Your Reverence'. Chatted to the gang of volunteers who were restoring the High Altar. I said to one utter *vision* 'And what are you, then?' 'I'm a gilder.' 'Cheap at half the price,' I said & it blushed puce with shyness. Purchased a tea towel for Lou, a lovely drawing of the cathedral on it, complete with flying buttocks.[23] Amazing to think that for so many years I would've crossed the threshold of such a place & seen it, truly, as the House of God. So refreshing to view it simply for what it is: a cracking bit of masonry… Then on to the Wheatsheaf at Oakham for lunch – a *superb* Ploughman's – then to Kegworth where we met Bill Tidy the cartoonist. Bill showed us Thomas Moore's house & I recited *Last Rose of Summer*. It was all lovely, even just driving back along the country roads and smelling the freshly cut grass was agreeable. The fact remains, on a sunny day, England *cannot* be topped.

Sunday, 15 May
Saw the news. The Russians have commenced their withdrawal from Afghanistan. It's all very well, but the place has been a political football for so long it's only a matter of time before a different group of maniacs has a go. At least with a Soviet occupation you vaguely know what you're getting – gruel, but *daily* gruel.

Monday, 16 May
Peter Estall 'phoned. 'Will you come on *Wogan* this Friday?' and I said yes. I've nothing to sell, but I suppose it's something to do. Went to the bank, then to Principles (crap), then got shopping for Lou. Stopped & chatted to some navvies who were digging up the road on Triton Street. Stripped to the waist with the shirts tucked in the belts. It never ceases to amaze me how

---

[23] An apparent reference to a malapropism made previously by Louie, when referring to flying buttresses.

big, gruff men like that fall over themselves to converse with me. They're schoolboys, beaming up at one from their trench, eager to hear some impish vulgarity or another. So of course I oblige. The boldest of them was the youngest – 'You can't keep your eyes off me, can you?!'… to be honest, I couldn't! Rushed back to the flat & had the barclays.[24] Took my time & was quite weak at the knees after!! It's *ages* since I've been even remotely in that frame of mind. Suppose the blood flow is returning to the extremities after months devoted to the entrails. I used to think these fellows just delighted in teasing the afflicted, but nowadays I'm not so sure. Went to post a letter at 5 o'c. & deviated thro' Triton Street, but they'd gone.

Thursday, 19 May
Bundle of prints in the post from the shoot I did with Hatch.[25] I am to choose which ones I prefer for the cover of the paperback reprint.[26] I look about ninety in all of them… It's so obvious I'm ill; he might as well have photographed the bum, it's no less appealing. Picked a couple where the grin appears vaguely authentic. Why on earth a further edition of this book is warranted is beyond me; it's been squeezed enough as it is. I'd have thought anyone who was going to read it would've read it by now. One thing's for certain, I'm not lumbering round the country doing signing sessions – not only because it's a hateful task, but the book is a dead horse that has been well & truly flogged. The public can smell that kind of desperation a mile off.

Friday, 20 May
Quite muggy, so decided against lamb cass. and had sardines, salad and bread & butter with Lou. Served it at 12.20. Her breathing is definitely improving, so I'm glad I put my foot down and insisted she stopped the fags too. The flat actually *feels* less filthy.

Car at 6.15 to Shepherd's Bush for *Wogan*. The other guests were Germaine Greer & Rod Stewart. It's as if they pluck names out of a hat. Surely it's not beyond the wit of man to engender some kind of through-line to the proceedings? Luckily I was on first, but when Terry asked what

---

[24] Cockney rhyming slang, i.e. Barclay's Bank = wank.
[25] Oliver Hatch (b. 1950), freelance photographer.
[26] *Acid Drops* (1980), KW's first book. A compendium of his favourite malicious stories and caustic put-downs.

I'm up to, I fell into the trap I'd wanted to avoid, & essentially told all about the ulcer & the treatment. The audience were in stitches of course, which flicked the usual switch within me & I withheld next to nothing. Miming the endoscopy on the chair, blowing off in Mr Chatham's face – O! I was frightful... Expected to get off after my bit, but I'd forgotten that they keep everyone on the sofa now, during the other guests' interviews, so I was stuck for the full half-hour. Terry tried to hold it together, but contriving communal questions for Germaine, a feminist, Rod, a promiscuous pop star, & myself, is a Sisyphean task... Had the drinks afterwards, and the BBC catering. Heaven knows where they get the sandwiches. Rumania judging by the taste. Terry said 'You are looking well. I'm so pleased you're on the mend,' which he clearly meant. 'We'll be tapping you up to be stand-in host again soon!' and I replied with a smile of non-commitment.

Monday, 23 May
One has to marvel at the unflappability of the BBC!! During the News, militant lesbians infiltrated the set, squawking about some injustice or other. Sue Lawley coolly carried on reading the bulletin, as Witchell wrestled the disgruntled Magnuses[27] to the ground just off-screen. It was stoic, quick-thinking professionalism, & it is to be *applauded*.

Tuesday, 24 May
Wanted to paint over the patch of damp in Lou's bathroom, but the contents of the tin in the cupboard were unusable. Walked to Portman's for a replacement. 'Iceberg Blue? 'Fraid not, squire. Dulux don't make it no more. Crown do a similar shade but I'd have to order it.' Was about to leave empty-handed when a scruffy article in splattered overalls took me aside & said 'I can sort you out, if you're in a bind. Iceberg Blue, Dulux. I've got some old stock in my brother's lock-up. £2 a quart.' He glimpsed round nervously as though he were a spiv flogging knocked-off chops. He positively *reeked* of the B.O. – I thanked him but declined.

It was *Talking Heads* in the evening. Thora Hird as an elderly widow who has a fall, can't raise the alarm and dies on the living room floor. Looked at Louisa and thought 'How could I have even *contemplated* leaving you alone?'... Could feel myself tearing up, so bade her a hasty goodnight & returned to the flat.

---

[27] i.e. Magnus Pyke.

1988

Friday, 27 May
Letter from Gerry & Peter.[28] They've wangled the funding for a thirtieth anniversary *Carry On* and want to have dinner with me on Tuesday to discuss it. Apparently there's a script and other survivors are being inveigled too. Frankly it's the last thing in the world I want to do – but I can't see any of these fashionable *alternative* comedians knocking at my door any time soon, so I might have to hold the nose and be brave. If I stay idle the clouds will circle again, functioning viscera or no.

Monday, 30 May
London a bit of a greenhouse, the heat retained by an overcast sky. Will be glad to get to Minorca which, reading the blurb, is the last word in cool breezes… Took Lou on the bus to M&S & Br. Home Stores to look for things for her holiday. These shops presume that women either want to simulate Mrs Thatcher or Linda Lusardi – power-dressing or hardly dressing, & naff all in between. Eventually found a couple of appropriate frocks in Debenhams, but I'll have to alter everything. Got some tan slacks for myself in Marks's. Got caught by the lurgy coming back into the block. It was up a ladder, changing bulbs. 'Warm enough for you, cock?' it said. 'Quite, thank you,' I replied.

Went with Paul to see the Poirot film.[29] It's just as well Agatha Christie's dead, 'cos this picture would've killed her… Gingold[30] shuffling around like a testudinal ghost. Painful.

Tuesday, 31 May
Up at 7.30 and took milk in. Tube to Turnham Green for this Dixons voiceover. Didn't realise until I got there that it was only a test & they were trying lots of other people as well! Sat in a waiting room with a load of deadbeats, didn't recognise any of them. The boy running it obviously didn't know who I was – 'Sorry for the delay, Kevin, they'll be with you soon as poss.' I smiled & when he went away I walked out. *This* is what it's come to! Trundled home feeling utterly worthless.

---

[28] Gerald Thomas (1920-93) and Peter Rogers (1914-2009); director and producer, respectively, of the 32 *Carry On* films.
[29] *Appointment with Death*, directed by Michael Winner, starring Peter Ustinov as Hercule Poirot.
[30] Sir John Gielgud (1904-2000), acclaimed English actor. In 1991 he became only the fourth person to achieve EGOT status, i.e. someone that has received an Emmy, Grammy, Oscar *and* Tony award.

Le Gavroche at 7 o'c. Gerald and Peter embraced me warmly. There was a sense I was being buttered up, but it was delightful to see them. Peter doesn't seem to age. It'll be all that Vitamin D… Some poor, misguided sod has put up the money (£1.5m!!) for this film, *Carry On Again Nurse*. Norman Hudis[31] is making finishing touches to the script and Joanie, Kenny C & Jack have said yes. Gerry says Barbara will do it *if I do it*… So, I've tentatively agreed, provided I can read it before signing anything. Peter said it'll be ready to look at the week I'm back from Spain. They do seem genuinely thrilled at the prospect. The poor fools! Nonetheless, if Michael can negotiate it properly, maybe a late summer at Pinewood with some old chums is what's required.

Thursday, 2 June
In the afternoon walked to St Pauls, but it started spitting so got the bus back. At Russell Sq. a loony got on, a filthy-looking thing, string vest under a hairy sports jacket & a bobble hat. It approached passengers, slurring a rendition of *I Who Have Nothing* into their faces & being generally revolting. I resolutely stared out of the window, & thought I'd been rumbled, but then it shouted at the top of its lungs 'You're all a shower of shit… I was at Goose Green!' before jumping off the platform & staggering down Tott. Ct. Rd!!… The silent tension was broken by the conductor who said 'I bet *he* drinks Carling Black Label!' and they all laughed. Curious how it takes the bizarre, the shocking or the tragic for people to connect with each other *in any way* on London Transport. Blitz spirit, I suppose.

Saturday, 4 June
M. came at 10 o'c. and drove Lou & me to Heathrow. Arrived Mahon 5.40 local time. Brand new terminal, & a girl from Iberian airlines swooped in with a wheelchair for Lou, which was a godsend. Short coach ride to Es Castell. Lou started with the 'Gawd 'elp us! Ain't it *hot?!*', but in actuality it's comfortably warm. Arrived at hotel, the Agamenon at 6.45. Then, *panic stations* – she'd left her handbag on the coach, which I could just see disappearing round the corner. I ran in & told reception. I was furious & didn't conceal my anger as I dragged her inside & checked in. The ingenious girl at the desk 'phoned the hotel towards which the coach was heading &

---

[31] English writer for film, theatre and television (1922-2016); credits include the first six *Carry On*s.

their receptionist intercepted the driver who agreed to stop off here on his way back to the airport... *Thank heavens* the rooms are alright, spacious & clean. We are adjacent with fine views of the little harbour & front. Sorted madam out, then collapsed in a chair for ten minutes. Changed & came down just as the coach driver arrived, bag in hand. Slipped him 500 pesetas... Had Campari & soda in the bar, whisky for Louisa. Met the rabble: Keith & Valerie, Bedfordshire – genial; Trudy & Terry, Chelmsford – urbane; Tony & Jacqui and son Russell, Berkhamsted – delightful; Peter & Daphne and three children, Leeds – overfamiliar & noisy, I foresee trouble; Dieter & Agnetha (I think) and *five* children, Dusseldorf – quiet, but pleasant (very well behaved youngsters); and Hugh & Pauline, Harrogate – sixties, private & shy. There are others, but they seem to be Eyeties and Frogs... Good food (*sublime* gazpacho!!), but too long in between each course, so Lou got quite tight! When her paella arrived she bawled 'About bleedin' time 'n' all!' – no wonder continentals loathe the British... Hugh told me we'd met before, in that he'd been a contestant on *Countdown* when I was doing the Dictionary Corner job! He's a former national Scrabble champion to boot. I've consented to a game one evening – perhaps foolishly. He's brought a special travel set of the game with him – 'I never leave home without it!' he said... 'Poor Pauline,' I thought... Managed to get Lou upstairs & clambered into bed at 11.20. A few touch-and-go moments, but the stomach, back & bum are alright, so blessings must be counted.

Sunday, 5 June
Ambled round Es Castell. It's all English colonial & very appealing. Seems to be free of your typical package holidaymakers, which is marvellous. They weren't kidding with the 'windy island' moniker though, there is a constant current. Coffee at Cales Fonts, the main little harbour. Nice just to sit & watch the boats & fishermen. Settled Lou for forty winks & visited the small castle for which the town is named. Captivating tour guide, Mateo. Nineteen. Took me round. Bright blue eyes, which are rare on your Spaniard. Showed me the battlements etc., & was highly knowledgable. Ruined it at the end when he said 'You like nice boys?', which demolished the didactic purity of it all.

Monday, 6 June
Coffee with Dieter & Anna on the Agamenon terrace at 4 o'c. Karl, their youngest, delighted in showing me his magic card tricks! All of their children are lovely – they all speak perfect English & their politeness is ambrosial.

Tuesday, 7 June
Every morning I have to remind Lou that we're on holiday & she's in Spain. It's all 'That's not *my* bed' or 'These don't feel like *my* towels'… It's bloody exhausting. Pauline said she'd be happy to look after Lou & play cards, so Tony, Jacqui, Russell & myself hired the bicycles & rode to Mahon along the front. The old town is cobbled which didn't do the arse any good, but the sea air is invigorating. Drinks in the bar, but then the Leeds lot started the karaoke contraption so I fled upstairs with Lou at 10.15.

Wednesday, 8 June
Woke up at 6 o'c., stiff from the byke. Walked it off before breakfast. Went up to the fort but couldn't see Mateo. Purchased a snug Panama at Cala Corb as my other one keeps getting blown off!… Daphne said 'I hope our singing didn't scare you off last night!' and I smiled 'O! no, but I have to be careful, my mother needs her beauty sleep' – at which point Louie piped up, 'Don't blame me, I wanted to stay, I was enjoying meself…'

Friday, 10 June
Went into Lou and found she'd had an accident in the bed. Managed to get her up & in the bathroom, but I couldn't face the clean-up operation, it was just too vile. Had a quiet word at reception. Thankfully the girl was very understanding & sorted it. Lou in a bit of a state at the table, but I dismissed it & tried to divert her attention. Pauline's presence is becoming a bit of a gift on this trip!! She took Lou to the front whilst Hugh & I played Scrabble. H. won both games by over 100 points… Sat Lou on the terrace and encouraged her to write postcards to Pat & a couple of her cronies from the club, but she couldn't concentrate so it's obviously on her mind… The Krauts were watching a noisy football match on the TV in the bar after dinner, so I suggested a stroll. She grasped my arm as we ambled *painfully slowly* & said 'I'm so sorry' – I could hardly contain the tears & said 'You silly moo. You've nothing to apologise for.'

Sunday, 12 June
Left Louisa to her nap. Met Mateo at Cales Fonts & we walked to Mahon. We must cut a ludicrous sight, but he oozes vivaciousness. The fact he doesn't know who I am boosts the ego no end. Told him I must get back for Lou & (after checking the coast was clear) he kissed me on the lips!! I recoiled, quite taken aback. Arranged to meet him after work at the fort on Tuesday. It's so perfectly ridiculous. Sailed back to the hotel like an excited schoolgirl. Fool I am.

Monday, 13 June
Leafed through Tony's day-old *News of the World* & saw that Russell Harty[32] is dead. Hepatitis got him, but they're implying something darker, of course. In truth it's gutter journalism that will have cracked him. Rather sad, 'cos I was fond of Russell. He was always v. kind to me & created the most relaxed atmosphere of any of the *chat* people.

Absorbing discussion with Trudy, Terry, Keith & Val, who are all strong Thatcherites, before the Leeds herd arrived & insisted on pop music. Hoisted Lou & led her out, overhearing Daphne's 'They're too good for us' comment... Vulgar north country dross.

Tuesday, 14 June
Louie much brighter! She was up, dressed and singing when I went in at 8 o'c. I was amazed! 'It *is* lovely, isn't it?' she said – 'You can really smell the benefit in the air...' Beautiful sun so got the things together & got cab to the beach at Cala Padera. Luckily it was largely deserted. The bay is sheltered so the wind was lighter. Rolled up the trouser legs and waddled to the water, arm in arm with Lou. Paddled as though we were at Brighton before the war! Quite incredible that either of us are still upright, let alone splashing in the sea. Decided to duck the Mateo & went to buy Lou an ice cream. It went all down her frock but we were almost crippled with laughter, so it couldn't have mattered less. Just as we were packing up Anna & Dieter arrived with the children, so we stayed building sandcastles for another hour until Lou needed the loo.

---

[32] English television presenter (1934-88). In the lead-up to his death, *The Sun* newspaper had published various stories relating to his health and private life. KW had appeared on Harty's chat show in 1974.

Thursday, 16 June
Wrote postcards to Stanley and Gordon. 'You won't remember me, you picked me up in the Balearics & I got right up your nose... Wish you were here, love Spanish Flo.'

Saturday, 18 June
After breakfast, last amble around Es Castell. Bought Lou an ornament of a fish that she'd taken a shine to. Didn't want the risk of the coach steps again so got taxi to airport. Arrived Heathrow at 5.50... M. was there to meet us – he took the cases. Almost had to beg a girl from BA to fetch a wheelchair. Home by 7.30.

There were moments of horror, but the overall sense is one of satisfaction that we went. If I were unwell we'd have been sunk, so a few soiled sheets & crossed words are not the end of the world. It's only when one comes home & looks in the mirror that the sun tan is noticeable! I've gone quite brown!! Well, dark beige.

Monday, 20 June
Up at 8 o'c., got papers from Adonis. Did letters. Walked to Anderson's office to read the draft script of this *Carry On*. Talk about a life going around in circles – whether it's '58, '68, '78 or '88, I'm sitting in a room, reading a script full of cock gags, wondering what I've done to deserve it all. Who should want to pay money to see this stuff, & who could raise a smile whilst watching it, simply boggles the mind... Michael has agreed eleven thousand. *They* are paying for the car. Was offered top billing, but I'd rather share it. Safety in numbers.

Friday, 24 June
Woke up & to my *horror & disgust* found a thick trail of ants marching from the skirting board, across the kitchen floor, up the side of the unit towards the raspberry jam jar. Evidently some had spilled over the edge. Went in to Lou but she had no powder so ran round to Harts. Purchased two huge tubs of the stuff. Spent *all morning* killing the vile things and cleaning them away. Pushed as much of the powder through the tiny hole as I could manage & then used the Polyfilla to cover it. Must've scrubbed the floor & unit a dozen times. How do the disgusting things get *up* here? The jar could only have been there for eight hours... Meal with Lou at 6 o'c. and I was itching all the way through it.

Saturday, 25 June
Maniacally searching for ant remnants in every corner, but think I've cracked it. At least I've a stock of poison now to fend off any further outbreaks. Threw out the jam; I shall breakfast at Lou's from now on.

Monday, 27 June
Letter from Charlie's sister: 'This is your Aunt Phyllis.[33] We are planing (*sic*) a gathering of the freinds (*sic*) and family to celebrate Ivy's birth day. It has been so long since we have all seen you and Louis (*sic*) and we would all love to see you and Louis (*sic*) there...' I expect Lou would like to go, but I don't think I could face it.

Wednesday, 29 June
Car came at 11.15 for Teddington. *What's My Line?* with Penelope Keith. Other guests were Jilly Cooper, Simon Williams and Justin Fashanu. The sense of *tat* is overwhelming. Dressing room felt like one of the less elaborate cells at Pentonville. Penelope said 'You're a lovely colour, Kenneth', to which Justin replied 'You never say that to me, Penny!', which I thought was quite quick for a footballer. At one point I inadvertently said 'shit' and it was heard on the soundtrack, so we had to do it again! The celebrity was Roy Kinnear which I realised straitway, so had to affect ignorance.

Cottage pie with Lou. It was rotten. After *M*A*S*H* returned to flat for the tradiola.[34] Erotic thoughts of Mateo up in the fort, all thoroughly successful.

Monday, 4 July
Watched the final of the Championships. Rain kept interrupting the flow, so my darling Boris lost in the end to a rather dull Swede. The weather has certainly taken a shocking turn. In hindsight, it would've been preferable to have been in Spain *now*.

Thursday, 7 July
Went to the park & sat under the black poplar. There were two creaky Chinese types farting about by the fountain, performing some kind of

---

[33] Phyllis Gidley *née* Williams (1917-2002), youngest sister of KW's father.
[34] A derivation of KW's term 'traditional (i.e. sexual) activity', in this case indicating masturbation. Used interchangeably with 'the barclays'.

Beyond Our Kenneth

synchronised mime. Barmy, but I suppose that's what happens when one has snakes for supper. Still, they seemed suited.

News is all about this oil rig explosion. It sounds ghastly. Gas leak, 150 dead at least.[35] You'd think that after Ixtoc & Chernobyl there'd have been a focus on searching for sustainable energy sources which are *safe*, but as usual too many people are making too much money for anything to change.

Tuesday, 12 July
Mitzie 'phoned and said '*The Mousetrap* is changing its cast after the *fifteen-thousandth* performance in November, and they want to know if you'd be interested in Major Metcalf?'... I said 'On no account whatsoever.' At this stage I'd barely be interested if I were offered Lear at the National, so *why* they imagine I'd be tempted by this kind of crap is baffling. I shall have to speak to Michael. I really have no enthusiasm for the theatre now *at all*, not even a teensy bit of curiosity.

Saturday, 16 July
Spent the afternoon learning lines for this *Carry On*. Could be that the retentive memory is beginning to fail me, or the material is so hackneyed that it leaves no footprints, but either way it didn't want to go in. By my reckoning this is the *fourth* medical entry in the series,[36] so it's no wonder that even Norman Hudis has struggled to flesh out the battered scarecrow of a plot.

Monday, 18 July
To Peter Mario with Paul where I gave him dinner. He's been on holiday in the Canaries & at the finish he presented me with a brown paper bag – 'I picked this up in a little shop in Las Palmas, I thought it was very *you*'... It's an extremely handsome belt, lovely quality calf. It must've been a year or more since I mentioned to him that I needed one! I stammered a grateful riposte, but I'm always awkward when it comes to gifts.

Tuesday, 19 July
Car at 7.45 for Pinewood. Talk about stepping back in time – same decor, same faces, same smell. Kenny Connor came into the dressing room: 'I've

---

[35] The final death toll of the Piper Alpha disaster was 164.
[36] It was actually the fifth, following *Carry On Nurse*, *Carry On Doctor*, *Carry On Again Doctor* and *Carry On Matron*.

known sprightlier crews, I grant you… the best boy's wearing his demob suit!'… Went on to set and met everyone. Gerry proclaimed 'We're back in business!', but looking round the room it suddenly hit me – we are all *old*. A sea of grey hair nestling over a jumble of wizened cadavers. Oh! it's all so depressing! Joanie Sims said 'Lucky there are plenty of hospital beds, I think we might need 'em!'… Did nothing in the morning, except the crossword. Lunch with Bernie & Kenny C… Bernie said Peter went to visit Charlie Hawtrey in Deal to determine the lie of the land but, alas, he's on his last legs – bald, gaunt & sloshed – so any involvement was completely out of the question. Finally turned over at 3 o'c… Nothingy sort of scene. As wonderful as Barbara looks for fifty, she is still *fifty*. They have her clattering around the ward as though she were in the first flush. 'You'll have to bear with me, Gerald,' she said, 'the Bristols are more like Barnstaples these days…'

Friday, 22 July
It's an out-of-body experience, doing this film. Whilst half of me is delivering the banalities of the script & contorting the face accordingly, the other half is thinking 'Why on earth am I *doing* this??'… They introduced Dennis, the stunt double who is to fall down the stairs in my stead. He's pushing six foot & can't be less than 15 stone. The absurdity of it had us all howling, but only to reinforce the truth of the adage 'If you don't laugh you'll cry'. Barbara bumped into me coming out of the lav & said 'Oh! sorry, Dennis…'

Wednesday, 27 July
Andrew somebody from the *News of the World* 'phoned. 'How is it to be back with the gang?'… I said 'It's marvellous & I think it's going to be the funniest one yet!' It's the most convincing bit of acting I've given all week.

Thursday, 28 July
Huge row with Joan. I was *justifiably* having a go at the silly wardrobe girl who'd spilt Ribena all over my powder blue shirt, when madam trudges over & commands that I 'Leave the poor girl alone, they're not paid enough to put up with this kind of abuse,' & 'You never change, Kenny, you've always got to make people feel bad,' & other ugly nonsense… I should've walked away but I said 'That's rich coming from you, you miserable cow. Don't get at me just because the canteen's run out of Cabana bars'… I shouldn't have said that. Nabbed a fag from a runner. Shouldn't have done that either. Oh it's a horrible, hideous mess & I just want to run away.

Friday, 29 July
Put a note on Joan's dressing table. Don't want to speak to her yet but I mustn't let the wound fester. Was barely used so just sat in the corner for most of the day. I should never, ever have assented to this, I *knew* it would be a nightmare... Just looking round the set reminds one of an old folks' home – it is utterly, dishearteningly *bleak*.

Had meal with Lou. Couldn't really keep anything down thanks to a bilious nagging that wouldn't recede. Doesn't feel like a stomach issue, I think it's the result of the altercation. The sooner this ordeal is over, the better.

Monday, 1 August
Looked up the '61 diary: 'What a fantastic paradise to imagine working in nothing but *Carry On*s'... Talk about be careful what you wish for!

Thursday, 4 August
It's as though this production were cursed. We've had Bernie breaking his toe on a door frame, the operating room set catching fire, property going missing from d/rooms (a gold lighter & a wallet) & *today* a light falling from the rig & nearly flattening Barbara! I think it's Sid's ghost trying to tell us something.

They filmed the closing shot of the picture, where Joanie as the Matron picks up a photograph of Hat & says 'Well, did I do alright?'... They were all tearful & choked – whereas I think we all know the answer to the question. Hat is irreplaceable & I don't see the logic in drawing attention to that fact.[37]

Released early so got driver to drop me at Jermyn Street. Found a nice lighter for Paul at Dunhill. His kindness re. belt must be repaid. On the way home I stopped & chatted with a human statue. The grey slap was sliding down his face in the sunshine. 'It must be boiling in that coat on a day such as this?' I said. 'This is nuffink!' he laughed – 'I was in Saudi for two years. It was like living in Satan's airing cupboard.'

---

[37] Hattie Jacques had played the role of the portly matron in all of the previous medical *Carry On* movies.

Sunday, 7 August
'Phone rang at 4 o'c. & a voice said 'Good afternoon, Mr. Williams, I have Peter Brook on the line, would you hold, please?'... 'Uh, yes, alright'... I thought it was Peter Brook (as in Peter Brook the theatre director) & expected to be asked to play the back-half of a cow in *The Winter's Tale* or something – but after a few seconds the penny dropped – it was Peter Brooke, Tory Chairman!! I couldn't believe it! 'Kenneth, we thought you were marvellous on the BBC during the general election[38]... The views of well-known personalities really translate to the public... Would you be willing to take part in Party Political Broadcasts in the future?'... The impertinence & desperation of it is staggering! I've no doubt that *Labour*'s tactics include recruiting celebrities and wheeling them out for the cameras – the fact the Tories are following suit speaks volumes. I said 'I shall, of course, have to think about it, but I'm very flattered to be considered...' – It's madness: the *Chairman* of the Party ringing on a Sunday!! They must've had to pull *some* levers of government just to obtain my 'phone number!

Wednesday, 10 August
Bedpan scene. I said to Gerald, 'This has to be one take, Gerry, I'm not getting pissed on all morning,' which was met with 'One take? It'll have to be one take, we've only got time for one fucking take!'... The atmosphere is atrocious, mainly because it's plain to everyone that the finished product is going to be lousy. No one is up to snuff. We used to get away with it because the uninhibited bonhomie off-camera invariably leached on to the set, but those days are assuredly dead. Everyone knows it too, so professionalism has gone out the window – Bernie was larking about with the prop defibrillator, trying to resuscitate a copy of the script. 'We're too late!!' wailed Barbara, genuflecting.

Thursday, 11 August
Kenny C. looked dreadful. He'd been doing a night shoot in Norfolk for *'Allo 'Allo* & drove straight from Thetford to Pinewood at 6 o'c. in order to film this trash all day. Ken's older than me! Where he gets the stamina – or the willpower – I simply can't fathom.

---

[38] KW had appeared on BBC *News at One* in the run-up to the 1987 general election, speaking in support of the Tories.

Saturday, 13 August
The Rupert dish was in the lobby when we came back from Harts. 'Hi there!' he said (as he always does)... 'Who's that?' asked Lou... 'This is Rupert from upstairs, the lifeguard...' 'Well, I've not seen him before. Looks queer to me.' This flagrant & unedited rudeness is a new streak I've noticed with Lou in public & it can make things terribly uncomfortable. It's no use telling her though.

Tuesday, 16 August
The only person with any enthusiasm is Jack. His energy is boundless. And rather irritating, if truth be told... Broke bread with Joan at lunch. I apologised for any hurt feelings & said 'I'm just fed up with it all'... 'We all are, Ken,' she said. 'But look on the bright side, imagine if you & I *had* got married. We'd have murdered each other long ago!',[39] which is very true. Not certain, but thought I sensed a whiff of gin on the breath... The money men from Hemdale were pacing round the set. They look nervous – as well they might!!

Wednesday, 17 August
Various productions converged in the refectory. We got lumbered with the American lot. Shelley Winters & Ned Beatty got shoved on to our table. I wanted to chat to Ned, but madam was noisily holding court, waxing lyrical about all the "greats" she's worked with. 'Roddy & Gene are pros,' she said, 'but Red Buttons[40] will always be my favourite...' Well, they *do* look nice on a yellow frock, I thought.

Friday, 19 August
Last day on this calamity. A lot of press sniffing around. I kept hearing references to "Licence Revoked" & assumed we'd *finally* been found out & had our permit to produce this tenth-rate drivel repealed – but evidently it's the title of the Bond picture they're making next door. We all had to pretend we were having a marvellous time for the photographers. Cheeks were in *agonies* from all the false grinning. Peter Rogers in his element, posing with the champagne. He announced 'The next one's *Carry On Texas* – so it's Dallas, here we come!'... I think it's rather more 'Houston, we have a problem': We have made the last *Carry On*, I'll put my shirt on it.

---

[39] Joan Sims was one of a handful of women to whom KW had made overtures regarding a potential union, either as a lavender marriage or for mere companionship.

[40] American actor and comedian (1919-2006).

1988

Avoided the drinks do & Kenny C drove me home. Nipped in to Lou, but didn't stay. Came home & put on the Ovalle[41] record. 'Go, little bird, & tell them I'm lonely…'

Monday, 22 August
TV news is all about Andrew & Fergie's baby. They've named her Beatrice Elizabeth Mary. Fifth in line to the throne. Amazing to think that this tiny bundle is destined to spend its life opening office blocks & chewing the cud with lady mayors & cancer sufferers & good samaritans. Poor little bitch. And, if that weren't cruel enough, she's got her mother's colouring!!

Saturday, 27 August
The dreaded lurgy knocked at 10.45. 'A parcel came whilst you was out. I said to leave it with me, as we're pals.' Jesus wept… It's a box of the paperback re-issue from Dent. Twenty copies. Forgot how ghastly the cover picture is, but nothing can be done about it now. The tag line states the book is 'now in paperback again'… That word *again* is rather jarring… 'Yes, we know you've heard it all before, but – spare a copper, guv?'… The publishers attach a note saying 'A potential sequel to your biography would be very popular if you are interested in taking it on, and as the narrative of *Just Williams* concludes in 1975, we are sure there would be plenty of material to furnish a similarly sized volume…' If only they knew! Fifteen years of chat shows, game shows & adverts for cream cakes. Riveting stuff.

Wednesday, 31 August
Cab to Hawley Crescent.[42] Talked about the film. Somehow managed to bluff my way through & make it sound more like fun than fiasco. Coyly mentioned the book. In hospitality I chatted to Frank Bruno (about pantomime) & to Sister Wendy[43] (about Canaletto).

Sunday, 4 September
M. came with Peter[44] & we went to Joe Allen. Seems ages since we saw Peter! The Swiss boy served us. 'Bonjour, Philippe!' I said – 'Have you had a wank

---

[41] Jaime Ovalle (1894-1955), Brazilian composer and poet.
[42] For a *Good Morning Britain* (TV-am) interview with Mike Morris and Kathy Tayler.
[43] Wendy Mary Beckett (1930-2018), religious sister, art historian and television documentarist.
[44] Peter Cadley (b. 1965), employee of Michael Whittaker; a fan who, via Whittaker's introduction, became a friend of KW.

this morning?' He went satisfyingly *purple*. I had fishcakes & Eve's pudding. Lou showed off her ceramic fish & told them about Minorca. I was staggered she could remember any of it! Peter is so good, the way he engages with Louie & indulges her... Coming back from the park at about 2 o'c., we saw a group of scruffy students handing out leaflets and shouting & hollering about the local govt. stuff.[45] When I refused to accept the pamphlet one girl called out 'You of all people should be on our side!'... I want nothing to do with their rotten crusade – if I've learnt *anything* it's that homosexual entanglements lead only to the gutter & promotion of these loose lifestyles will damage the youth irreparably. I've seen too many fingers burned. The schools' province should be the three Rs – meddling with any other sort of *Rs* should be wholly discouraged.

Monday, 5 September
Doubt is an uncomfortable condition, but certainty is a ridiculous one.
– Voltaire

Tuesday, 6 September
These days are very strange to live through. I'm fully aware that I could – & perhaps should – be dead & buried now, & that waking every morning is akin to turning to a superfluous new chapter of an *already* protracted novel. The elation of feeling better, though, has faded. I must remind myself to be thankful for a semblance of ordinariness. I haven't abandoned the *idea* of suicide, I don't think I ever will. But for the moment, a quiet life with a few good chums is enough to keep the wolves at bay. Sent notes to Mags & Sheila Hancock, just keeping things fresh & reminding them of times past. I have, without question, been blessed with the most magnificent friends... they're either saints or fools to bear me, but either way I'm grateful.

Sunday, 11 September
Got papers at Cleveland Street & talked to Mr. Zubarev from the 5th Floor outside the block. He left Russia in '52, but he was decidedly defensive when I criticised recent Soviet activity in Estonia. He said 'They can't expect leniency when they make provocations in such a way'... I'd hardly call staging a singing festival a provocation, but then I've not heard them sing.

---

[45] 'Section 28' – controversial Conservative legislation prohibiting the 'promotion of homosexuality' by local authorities.

Expect it's just the Kremlin flexing some muscles after embarrassments in Afghanistan, but the West will only let them gun down unarmed Baltic crooners for so long before taking some kind of action.

Friday, 16 September
Taxi to TV Centre for *Blankety Blank*. The runner girl said 'I never thought they'd get *you* for this!', which is a nice way of saying 'Christ, you must be struggling'... Met Les Dawson in the foyer. O! he's a wonderful man, bursting with warmth & he raises the spirits instantly. He *knows* the show is a million miles beneath him, so he throws caution to the wind & is completely unrestrained. Met dear Brian Blessed in the Green Room, with Carmen Silvera, Lynsey de Paul & Rustie from TV-AM. There were two other panelists, but I haven't the foggiest who they were... Brian said 'Kenneth, my love, why on earth are you doing this shit?' – Good question!... The cheapness & vulgarity of the operation are bearable when one is in the midst of it, because *everyone* is in on the joke, quite aware that it's total rubbish. It's only afterwards in the cab home that one muses on the absolute pointlessness & tastelessness of it all.

Monday, 19 September
Got papers from Bill & did beds. Took down curtains in Lou's bedroom & took them to dry cleaners. It's as tho' they've been tie-dyed with Typhoo, but it's all nicotine... Letter in the second post from a boy called Oliver at Goldsmiths, a design student. Very funny drawing he's done of me in *Cowboy*! Says he'd love to meet up, so I've suggested the National Gallery next Monday. Goodness knows what possesses these chaps – none of them seem to want money or anything. Still, it fills the appointment book.

Tuesday, 20 September
Michael A. rang at 4.40... 'I thought you'd want to know, Roy Kinnear died today in Spain. He fell from a horse during filming which led to a heart attack...' Rang Gordon to tell him – he was devastated. It's shattering news. I can't imagine a gentler, more absorbing or affable character than Roy. And a talent. Just 54. Nipped to John Menzies to get a condolence card for Lou to fill out. I wrote a letter. They'll be crushed.

Beyond Our Kenneth

Saturday, 24 September
We watched the Olympics from Seoul. Farcical scenes in the 100-metre dash… Lewis & Johnson, who evidently can't stand each other, had words on the start line, followed by fisticuffs! Pushing & shoving like urchins in the schoolyard. They both got disqualified & after *ten minutes* of argument, officials & Korean Old Bill led them out of the arena! In the end, our boy Linford Christie won the gold medal!! Not the most orthodox way to claim victory, but I'm sure that won't bother him. All Louisa could say was 'Glory be! You can see everything he's got to offer in those drawers…'

Monday, 26 September
Arrived at the Gallery at 11.58. Oliver jogged up, perspiring, at 12.03 & apologised. He's an ebullient fellow, & very relaxed, not in awe at all. Puts me in mind of a young Richard Briers – no beauty, but sparky & genial. I showed him *Saint Thomas* & the other Guercino stuff, and he listened enthusiastically… Told me he's the chairman of the Conservative Society at Goldsmiths – but that it's not much to boast about as there are only three other members! Light lunch at the little trattoria on St Martin's Lane (which he insisted we went Dutch on) & we parted about 2.20. At the finish he clasped my hand with both of his & said 'I shall always remember today. Thank you so very much…' I clocked the dirty fingernails, which spoilt things a bit.

Got the tube back to Gt Portland St. Picked up shoes from menders. The man said 'Handsome brogues for a handsome rogue!' as he handed me them, winking. I ask you!

Saturday, 1 October
Went in to Lou & knew immediately what had happened. Once again, she couldn't get to the lavatory in time. It's absolutely disgusting. I was furious & she knew it. The cleaning of it wouldn't be so bad if she didn't fuss around me saying 'Oh leave it, it doesn't show', as if to attenuate the significance of it all. She'd live in squalor if it weren't for me. I retched throughout, but got it done. Not sure how much longer I can cope with all this… I'm rather gung-ho about the notion of retirement homes when I'm down on my knees scrubbing, but when I see that face, I'm six again, and it's *she* who's on all fours, scouring the hearth & singing & taking care of *me*.

Friday, 7 October
Teddington for *Whose Baby?*... Panel was me, Nanette Newman & Bertice Reading.[46] Bertice embraced me in a bear-hug, as she always does, & planted a kiss on my cheek. The lipstick mark must've been there for ages but nobody said a dickie bird – when I sat in the make-up chair I saw it in the mirror & thought I was breaking out in hives... The show was naff as the 'stars' were from *EastEnders* & a pop group, so we'd no chance. Had to pretend we knew who they were. At one point Nanette slid the flailing Bertice a scribbled note of suggestion which she read out in desperation: 'Could it be *Michael A. Strachan*?'... I said to Nanette 'I'm too old for this,' but she's heard me moan about it before, & just said 'Oh, Kenneth!' and invited me to lunch on Sunday with her & Bryan.

Programme in the evening about the oldest woman in the world, who still has the fags & booze & devours truckloads of chocolate. She sold canvasses to Van Gogh in her father's paint shop & was the age I am now in *1937* and is still up and about!! Christ knows what she's being punished for, but then she's lived in Provence for 113 years & has never had to do *Whose Baby?*, so perhaps it's swings & roundabouts.

Saturday, 8 October
Finally found a magnetic soap holder that doesn't require drilling. Should've thought of Superdrug before. This will allow the bar to air dry & I'll avoid the ghastly *jelly*.

Friday, 14 October
We saw Mrs Thatcher's party conference speech. She really *is* a marvel. For all the problems that exist, it's too terrifying to think what state the country would be in without her. She's turned the guns on Europe, however, saying we haven't rolled back socialism at home to have it reintroduced by Brussels... Whilst I concur on that front, our place is in the EEC[47] – we must bring the continentals round to our way of thinking on free markets. And

---

[46] Nanette Newman (b. 1934), English actress and author, appeared in nine films directed by her husband Bryan Forbes (1926-2013) including *The Stepford Wives* and *International Velvet*; Bertice Reading (1933-91), American-born actress, singer and revue artiste, who was based in England for most of her career.

[47] European Economic Community.

there's no doubt about it, if *anyone* can achieve that, it's Margaret Thatcher. Lou said 'She puts all the others to shame,' & I was in complete accord.

Sunday, 16 October
M. took us to lunch at Joe Allen. I had the pea & ham to start which was super. Esta Charkham[48] came to the table & I gave her a glass of wine. She's an effervescent creature, very warm. She said 'What are you up to at the moment?' & I said 'Fuck all'... 'It's a scandal,' she said, 'I saw you with Bergman in *Brassbound*[49] and it was practically *your* show,' which was a kind thing to say, if untrue. Esta said she'd keep me in mind for upcoming projects, but that's a line I've heard so many times I shall have it engraved on my tomb.

Wednesday, 19 October
Spent most of the day reading Fraser's book on Cromwell. She conveys her admiration for him almost perfervidly, & whilst I disagree with some of her conclusions, it's readable as it isn't merely cold criticism. In fleshing out the man's character & displaying him as a complex political operator rather than the cardboard hate-figure known to schoolboys, one becomes sympathetic apropos events which are seen as ghastly today, even Drogheda & the regicide. It's the shoulder-shrugging trust in providence that's difficult to swallow, & further proof, if it were needed, that politicians should lead from the head & not the heart. After all, the king's professed Divine Right implied that at least *some* culpability for dubious actions rested at regal feet, as opposed to the Lord Protector's stance of 'Don't look at me'... Despite the more rounded figure Lady Antonia presents, I would've still fought for King Charles if I'd been around – well, not *fought* perhaps... but I'd've certainly signed up for the Cavalier equivalent of ENSA.[50]

Monday, 24 October
Woke at 3 o'c. needing the lav but found no paper. Silently nipped into Lou's for the Bronco. I'm *certain* I clicked the latch, but after taking a roll

---

[48] Casting director (b. 1949); credits include *Boon*, *Birds of a Feather* and the Oscar-winning *Chariots of Fire*.
[49] *Captain Brassbound's Conversion* by George Bernard Shaw (1900). Starring Ingrid Bergman, Joss Ackland and KW at the Cambridge Theatre, 1971.
[50] Entertainments National Service Association.

1988

from her cupboard I went back & was locked out!! Couldn't find Lou's key to my flat, so had to wake the porter. Mortifying. I implied that *haste* was apt, but he didn't exactly leap into action. Ten more seconds & I'd have been manuring the potted yucca on the landing... I'll wager this a message from on high, telling me not to get complacent with the bum, even when the sun's shining on it. *Planning* & *washing* are essential for every movement.

Thursday, 27 October
Saw the TV news. Charlie Hawtrey is dead. He refused to have his legs off, which would have saved him & he died in hospice this afternoon. Rang Joan Sims & she'd heard... J. said 'He threw a vase at a nurse who wanted an autograph.' Well, I can sympathise with *that*... Ah, Charlie. He'd hounded most of his friends out of his life & drunk away the last twenty years. It's tragic. But mostly, it's pathetic.

Friday, 28 October
Up at 8 o'c. Did all the letters. Running low on 5 by 3½ inch portraits, must ring Mitzie to see if they've got any. Felt a mouth ulcer coming so went to Doug at chemist for Rinsteads. We talked about Charles Hawtrey. I mentioned the seedy lifestyle he'd reduced himself to according to the papers – Doug said 'Well, he was a *real* queer, wasn't he? Not like you.'

Sunday, 30 October
Mouth ulcer continues to irritate! It is right in the fold of gum & lip. Getting through these pastilles like Smarties.
    The TV in the evening was appalling! Firstly the interminable *Summer Wine*, & then *Bread*, a laugh-free sitcom about Liverpudlian layabouts. The licence fee increases to £66 in April! It's a scandal.

Monday, 31 October
In the post an invitation to the premiere of *Carry On Again Nurse*. Threw it in the WPB.
    B.K.[51] 'phoned!! He told me about the woman needling Michael Fish in the street apropos the forecast downpour. 'Well, madam, I think you'll be getting a good three inches, but it won't last very long.' She sighs – 'No change there, then.'

---

[51] Bill Kenwright (1945-2023), West End theatre producer.

Thursday, 3 November
Bright & breezy outside. Went to post office & then to M&S. Took stuff in to Lou. Met Mags at the Tent at 12.20, gave her lunch. She looked wonderful! Rather angular, which suits her. She's finished *Lettice & Lovage*[52] & has agreed to go to America with it. Seems to have enjoyed it. 'Oh you know Shaffer, ducky,' she said, 'the words do all the work.' I apologised for not going to see her & Richard[53] at the Globe & she said 'It seems to me you've fallen out of love with the theatre' & she's right. 'If I were you, I'd write more books,' she said. 'You've got the knack & if you get bored there's always *Crossroads*…!'

Went into Lou at 6 o'c. She was in the lavatory & wasn't aware I'd come in. Heard her gently singing *There's Life in the Old Girl Yet*[54] & it was enchanting & heartbreaking all at once. I poured us each a whisky.

Wednesday, 9 November
News is all about the Democrat victory in America.[55] Evidently no-one saw this coming, *all* the commentators had Bob Dole as a shoe-in. I myself am stunned that the Yanks have turned their backs on the Reaganite form of capitalism, however narrowly. He might've been a buffoon, but when one's purse is full that kind of thing doesn't tend to matter so much. This Dukakis seems stunningly dull from what I've seen of him (they've nicknamed him Zorba the Clerk), but maybe a touch of decorum is what's needed after Ronnie's geriatric antics. Goodness knows what Mrs T. must make of it all… it's like Queen Victoria losing Albert. Or Fanny Cradock losing Johnnie.

Friday, 11 November
Car to Thames for *Give Us A Clue*… Abysmal. There must be more to life than trying to mime "Police Academy 4: Citizens on Patrol" to Victor Spinetti & Bob Holness… And if Parkinson asks me one more time 'What are you working at, Kenneth?', I shall throttle the sanctimonious prig. It

---

[52] By Peter Shaffer.
[53] Richard Pearson (1918-2011), English character actor. Appeared alongside KW and Maggie Smith in Shaffer's *The Private Ear* and *The Public Eye* at the Globe Theatre in 1962. KW maintained a long-lasting friendship with Pearson and his wife Patricia.
[54] From *London Calling!*, a 1923 musical revue by Noël Coward.
[55] Massachusetts governor Michael Dukakis (b. 1933) defeated Kansas senator Bob Dole (1923-2021) by 271 electoral votes to 267.

1988

must be a reflex or his attempt at smalltalk, but it's tantamount to asking an Ethiopian child 'What canapés have you enjoyed recently?'

Tuesday, 15 November
Caught by the lurgy on my way out. 'You off to entertain the masses?' it said. 'Yes, duty calls,' I replied. Ugh! it makes my skin crawl… Went to the Equity council meeting. I've had enough of it. With the Left in charge, getting anything valuable accomplished is nigh on impossible. I shouldn't be in a union in any case: one is a turkey-hen, invited to choose between forcemeat & stuffing.

At 6 o'c. went to the tenants' meeting at Regency House. Asked Mr Saxby if a full-time maintenance man was altogether necessary. It probably *is*, but I can't keep hiding from lurgy, or throwing myself into the lift when I hear it coming… According to Mr Garvin the number of break-ins has skyrocketed, & that's *with* the addition of the new window locks. The area feels as tho' it's in free fall, but with a Labour MP it's not surprising, they're only concerned with Arabs & youth clubs.

Wednesday, 16 November
Walked to Harley Street to see Mr Chatham. Dish. He examined me & said 'You look very well. I can see you've been looking after yourself'… Maybe I have (drinking less & of course No Smoking), but the success is really down to this wonderful fellow. He said 'I'll see you in a year, young man, unless anything else pops up.' Any more talk of that kind, I thought, & *all sorts* might be popping up.

Had meal with Lou at 5.45, moussaka & fruit in meringues. Saw the TV news. More acts of defiance being severely put down in Estonia. Moscow plainly thinks the West isn't going to interfere, at least for the time being. They showed President-elect Dukakis in an achingly awkward interview. Not much for Gorby[56] to worry about there.

Saturday, 19 November
'Phone wouldn't stop ringing. Journalists calling about the *Carry On* and just how atrocious it is. Saw the papers & the headlines are damning. Very cruel about Barbara, 'mutton dressed as lamb', and so on. Various 'unnamed sources' quoted as saying that the mood on set was poisonous &

---

[56] Mikhail Gorbachev (1931-90), Leader of the Soviet Union, 1985-90.

that *I* was the cause of much of the disharmony. It's a disgrace. I was only reacting to the desperate situation in which I found myself, but I suppose it's par for the course that I should get the blame. A reporter from *Today* rang at 12 o'c. & said 'After this, working with Olivier & Orson Welles must feel a *very* long time ago!'… I steered the conversation away. But he's right. It does.

Sunday, 20 November
I shouldn't be so sensitive about this criticism over the film, I don't *care* enough about it, but if I'm not *doing* anything, what am I still here for? In the old days a below par comedy film failing at the box office would've made all the impact of a fart in a typhoon, but they released it with far too much pomp & fanfare, they were asking to be rebuked.

Pondered on ideas for a poetry anthology. Went through the '76-'87 diaries to see if there's enough usable material for an update of the autobiography. There isn't.

Monday, 21 November
When rushing for the ringing 'phone I caught the underside of the cock in the zip. All for some tart from British Gas. Told her to piss off… Liberally applied the Savlon & Vaseline but it stings like the devil. Gingerly walked to pillar box, lallies[57] as divaricate as Gary Cooper's in *High Noon*.

Saturday, 26 November
Took Lou to the surgery as this tickle has turned into a nasty cough. It's irritating me as much as it's irritating her. The reception resembled a triage tent at Bhopal. Clarke is swanning round Somaliland vaccinating babies, so when we did eventually get seen it was Dr Shanmugaratnam. He was very patient with Lou & spoke loudly & clearly… While she was putting her coat on, he took me aside & said 'How are you coping with things, day to day?' His perceptiveness is impressive. I said 'It isn't easy, but I try to keep her mind engaged & keep her as active & fulfilled as possible'… 'You're doing a wonderful job,' he said, 'keep up the good work,' which was rather fortifying.

Bought fish & chips and we watched Kenny C. in *'Allo 'Allo*. That was followed by the Royal Variety, so we switched off that rubbish & got out the Uno.

---

[57] Polari slang, i.e. legs.

Wednesday, 30 November
Outside Foyles a car pulled up & it was the Rupert from upstairs! 'Hi there! Do you want a lift?'... I've altered my opinion: he's a genial cove & not the boob I thought. Huge arms. Back at the block he carried my bags like an errand boy! Asked him to dine with me on Friday & he accepted. Sent a note to Goldsmiths Oliver inviting him too.

Friday, 2 December
Rang Anderson to discuss the dearth of work. He listened, but I could tell his mind was elsewhere. Said he was thinking of taking some time off. He asked 'Would you consider another chat show tour in Australia?' & I said 'No'... When he said 'It's too late to get involved with any of the big pantomimes *this* year,' my insides quaked. I've had it with this lousy business. The truth is I've only stuck at it as I've bills to pay & Louie to keep.

Sat listening to the Fauré[58] record feeling wholly morose. I've three options: keep going & hope for the best, retire into quiet obscurity, or die.

Contemplated cancelling dinner, but Oliver's not on the telephone. Fed & watered Lou, & Rupert knocked at 7.15. We walked to Campana. Oliver was already there. O! it was a marvellous evening! Both diverting from the current malaise & *refreshing* in the sense of feeling engaged with the cadence of these vital young men. Oliver is green in the way most students are, but his true blue convictions are winsome & doubtless he'll go far... Rupert told us about a man he saved from drowning at the baths in Camberwell – a master butcher who remains so grateful for his salvation that every Christmas he sends Rupert a gargantuan side of beef, done up with tinsel. 'I haven't the heart to tell him I've gone vegetarian,' said R.... He's a dishy thing, there's no denying it. I don't imagine he earns much teaching people how to save lives, but one can *tell* that there's money somewhere in the background... We sat like three characters on a Seven Ages of Man print, but I haven't enjoyed a dinner as much in ages.

Thursday, 8 December
It's strangely mild & dry, I really don't need the vest under the shirt, or indeed the cardigan under the jacket. Walked to Gordon & Rona's. Related

---

[58] Gabriel Fauré (1845-1924), French composer. KW selected Fauré's Barcarolle No. 1 in A Minor (Opus 26) as his first record choice on *Desert Island Discs* with Michael Parkinson in 1987.

the idea of a book & out of the options I presented, G. thought a novel would be the best course of action. He's been filming *Campion* for the BBC & thinks a detective story would be a decent métier for me. Rona suggested another children's book as the first was so absorbing,[59] but there's been no talk of a reprint, so I doubt Dent would be keen… Rona served a delicious flan for luncheon & G. played the Jack Benny recordings.

Monday, 12 December
Saw the lunchtime news & the headlines are all about the railway crash at Clapham Junction. I don't know how many more passengers are going to have to die before British Rail is put out of its misery & private companies are brought in. A bit of competition is required… The socialists have managed to turn engine drivers & stationmasters who once took pride in their work into indifferent shirkers who couldn't give a monkey's.

Tuesday, 13 December
Went to Samuels & got a lovely brooch for Lou, silver with a blue topaz (which is her birthstone). Walked to John Wood for the Brooke Bond voiceover. First I tried the Gruntfuttock voice[60] & then an Aylmer version[61] & they went with the latter. It's my second chimp advert for them & I shall be curious to see the finished article. Note from Saxby saying that the dreaded lurgy is gone!! My proposal was approved! It is a great relief, I must say.

Tuesday, 20 December
Went in to Louisa with the brooch & the cards. Of course, she'd forgotten it was her birthday! Pat came at 3 o'c. & we had the sparkling wine… P. said 'Well, mum – 87, that's quite an age'… Lou looked at her & said 'Oh don't you start! It's a bus route & a bingo call, girl. I'm still five-and-twenty in my mind…' – I beg to differ.

---

[59] *I Only Have to Close my Eyes* by KW, 1986. Illustrations by Beverlie Manson. Accompanied by his cat, a small boy dreams up fantastical worlds where he inhabits many roles. Perhaps inspired by experiences during KW's own childhood – he and his sister Pat indulged in 'O.G.' (Our Game), where KW adopted various characters in imaginary scenarios; Pat only ever played herself.

[60] J. Peasmold Gruntfuttock, a lecherous character played by KW in BBC Radio's *Round the Horne*. Described by writers Barry Took and Marty Feldman as 'the walking slum'.

[61] Felix Aylmer (1889-1979), English actor. Frequently impersonated thanks to his lofty and decorous style of delivery.

Asked her *three times* if she needed the lavatory before we left, but as soon as we get her in the cab it's 'I shall want the loo before long' & 'Where are we going?' till I wanted to flee. Got to Lariana at 6.05, the cronies already there, Lou waving regally as she stopped on each step. Paul & M. were there, & a couple from Lou's club; we were 12 in all. The staff made a fuss of her & she enjoyed it, but she soon tired & by 7.30 she was needling me to fetch her home. Had her indoors with Ovaltine by 9.15.

Thursday, 22 December
The front pages are plastered with horrendous pictures of this 'plane crash.[62] All the empty space in Scotland & it had to land on a settlement. Everything points to a terrorist bomb, & the usual loonies have been 'phoning in to claim responsibility – the IRA, Mossad & various Moslem groups… It's a Pan Am 'plane & most of the dead will be Americans, so it's an early chance for Dukakis to prove his mettle. Spent the afternoon doing some low dusting 'cos the skirting boards were caked.

Sunday, 25 December
We had the Riesling that M. had given Lou for the birthday. I served the capon, potatoes, sprouts, carrots & gravy at 12.30. Lou's mince pies after, with some cream. Had a rest, watched the Queen… HM focusing on various centenaries – the discovery of Australia, the Glorious Revolution & the Armada: '400 years after the winds blew & the Spanish ships were scattered…' – Lou said 'We've had quite enough Spanish wind for one year!' & I laughed. It's amazing the things she *does* remember.

Thursday, 29 December
Note from Gordon asking me up there for New Year, but I shall decline. A group of six I can manage, but it'll be a full house & I can't be doing with it.

Did the accounts & despite feeling idle, I'm certainly ticking over. Finished *The Satanic Verses* – didn't do much for me, but it certainly seems to have riled the loopy.

Saturday, 31 December
Did the beds & beat the living room rugs which were filthy.

I'm not sure quite how I got through this year. Luck more than judgment, that's for certain, combined with some medical wizardry & the

---

[62] The Lockerbie disaster, which claimed 270 lives.

firmness of friendships. The fact is I've shifted from the very edge of oblivion & days of desperation to a placid, if slightly prosaic, existence of duty & mellow simplicity. I am thankful.

Went to bed at 10.30 & had the tradiola, visions of strong arms, firm bellies & wet trunks.

1989

Sunday, 1 January
In the afternoon we walked to the Rose Gardens & went round the lake. Don't think we passed anyone, it was as if the city were empty & ours. At 7.45 we watched *Amadeus*. Intoxicating. I don't know the boy who played Mozart, but the manic performance is a real thrill. Lou couldn't follow the film & sat noisily opening toffees & sighing… Came back to the flat & got out the recording that Richard Pearson gave me. Listened to the flute & harp Andantino and wept. Feeling every inch a Salieri.[1]

Thursday, 5 January
To the Paris for *Just a Minute*. Teams were myself, Clement, Peter Jones & Wendy Richard, & in the second show Percival[2] replaced Wendy… The things they get away with these days are nothing short of scandalous. At one point Wendy audibly said 'bollocks' & I sat back expecting to hear 'Cut!' but the call never came & everything continued!! I don't know where standards have gone. Before you know it we'll have *Any bastard Questions?* and *I'm Sorry I Haven't a cunting Clue*.

---

[1] Antonio Salieri (1750-1825). In *Amadeus* (1984 film based on the 1979 play by Peter Shaffer), F. Murray Abraham portrays a fictionalised version of this Italian composer, whose intense jealousy of Mozart leads him to poison the young genius.
[2] Lance Percival (1933-2015), English actor, singer and comedian. In the early sixties he appeared with KW in the Peter Cook revue *One Over the Eight* at the Duke of York's Theatre, as well as *Carry On Cruising*.

Beyond Our Kenneth

Sunday, 8 January
Headlines are about Hirohito dropping dead. Can't imagine *that* will garner too many lamentations from foreign parts. He ought to have been in the dock with Tojo,[3] there's no doubt about that.

Monday, 9 January
Up at 8 o'c. & had the Shredded Wheat. Saw Paul on the landing & he told me about the 'plane crash.[4] They're dropping like flies just lately. It happened at Kegworth of all places!! Started to map out ideas for a detective book. I've a feeling it's best to set it in the past as contemporary stuff ages too swiftly. One concept is to construct the plot around Charlie's poisoning, but it would provoke too many questions – 'Is the book based on your own father's death?', etc. – & could appear crass… Another is to kill off the cast of a low-budget comedy film one-by-one, as per *Ten Little Indians*, but that might raise a few eyebrows too!… In the end I put on the Tchaikovsky Serenade & ate Twiglets.

Friday, 13 January
Loads of mail to answer! Can't think why, I haven't *done* anything. One was a note from Peter Rogers saying that Hemdale have pulled out & *Carry On Texas* won't be going ahead. One didn't need a crystal ball to see *that* coming.

Stanley called at 3 o'c… 'Fancy dinner this evening?' – he *always* 'phones at the right times! Met him at De Quincey's at 7.30. He told me about the flatulent dresser they have on the children's programme: 'He's stone deaf & can't hear himself when he blows off – if there's been eggs for lunch we're sure to get a rendition of Haydn's trumpet concerto…' They call him *John with the Wind*… Told him about Louisa getting more difficult to handle. He asked if Pat could help out, but I know it'd be a disaster: they'd tear each other apart. When I mentioned the book he grimaced & said 'It sounds dour; not your forte. Write about what you know. People love *you*, so you've got to be at the centre of it. You forget how much you're valued…' Honeyed words, but galvanising.

---

[3] Hideki Tojo (1884-1948), Prime Minister of Japan, 1941-4. Hanged after the Tokyo Trial for crimes against humanity.

[4] British Midland flight 092 crashed onto a motorway embankment near Kegworth, Leicestershire. There were 47 fatalities.

Wednesday, 18 January

Got papers, went to post & then cobblers to have the Oxfords stretched. At 10.20 went to the Midland at Russell Sq. I'd finished with the girl & was shoving the notes into the wallet when this man shouted 'Everyone get down!'... I was preoccupied & it took a few seconds to register. I turned & saw two men pulling balaclavas over the faces. The one nearer me had gingery stubble, the other was coloured. The woman at the counter behind me fell to the floor, as did the customers in the queue. I followed suit, inadvertently kicking the woman! We lay under the counter, slightly veiled by its shadow. They clutched objects wrapped in khaki cloth, presumably guns... They didn't take any notice of us, ginger marched towards the two clerks, the other stayed near the entrance. He said 'Get the money in there' in a bland, estuary accent. I faced away & tried to adjust the left leg as the door key was digging into the thigh. The desk girls were audibly terrified & whimpered. Stuff clattering across the desk & to the ground. 'Hurry up, bitch,' barked ginger. The other said 'Come on, Reg' (or Red?), & after more scuffling, they raced out. The alarm started ringing, then the screech of a car pulling away. The manager, plainly shocked, said 'Is everyone alright?'... Hesitantly we started getting up. The girl behind the till was blubbing, the other comforted her. It probably only lasted 90 seconds. It was quite surreal!! The police arrived within two minutes & when they saw me I was led into the office & offered the boss's swivel chair. Sweet tea was brought round while statements were given. I asked the sergeant if there was any chance of keeping me out of it – he pouted & said 'We can hope'. When he turned to his deputy & uttered 'Carry on, constable' & furtively winked, I knew I was doomed. Finally released at 12.35 (after having to sign autographs for the other customers) & a panda car brought me home. Told Lou, then rang Anderson to attempt to divert the onslaught. Rang Gordon & Stanley, knocked at Paul's but he was out. Told Dunthorpe[5] that there *might* be press, etc., so asked him to be vigilant. By 2.15 the 'phone was ringing asking for comment, so I unplugged it.

Louie put a note thro' at 4 o'.c... 'Come in when you're ready, son. I have made cheese straws'... I sat & wept. I'm unscathed, but in hindsight it *was* freetening, & the *anger* about it all flooded out. That these thugs can waltz

---

[5] The porter at Marlborough House.

Beyond Our Kenneth

about instilling terror into ordinary people is maddening. I *detest* this underclass scum & would happily fill Pierrepoint's[6] shoes given the chance.

Went in to Lou at 5.30 & did beans on toast for her. I didn't have anything.

Thursday, 19 January
Slept curiously soundly. Got papers & no surprise, *I've* become the story: 'Ooh! What A Stick-Up'… 'Carry On Ken in Heist Hell'… 'Cop Messing About' (next to a paparazzi picture of me with two policemen). So dispiritingly trite. The actual robbery is totally lost in all the rubbish. Plugged the 'phone back in & it started right away. I just said that the staff behaved impeccably & made no further remark.

Friday, 20 January
'Phone rang at 10.15 & it was Chief Inspector Hewitt from Holborn station, apologising for the disruption. I asked what the likelihood is of apprehending the culprits. 'It seems the main chap wore gloves, so there are no fingerprints, but it's not the first job these boys have done. They got away with £22,000 so we'll put everything into it'… Apparently the security cameras caught some clear images – including ones of me!! – & they're considering involving *Crimewatch U.K.* – I made my opposition to *that* explicit.

With any luck it'll all be next week's chip paper, but didn't fancy venturing out. Paul was kind & got some bits in for Lou.

Saw the News. They showed President Dukakis's inaugural speech. He's no Abe Lincoln, that's a fact. Not even sure he's a Jimmy Carter.

Monday, 23 January
Walked to D'Arblay St for the Cinzano voiceover. They wanted erudite & suave. Did ten or so takes & they seemed happy, but it's all so *boring*. Ambled home & had a tin of mulligatawny alone in Lou's flat – Cecil & Sandra had taken her out to the Mecca at Camden for the bingo… They were back by 3 o'c. When they'd gone it was 'O! I've had my fill of that Sandra. Flouncing round like she's the Queen of Sheba. Silly cow…' It's absurd. Sandra is 72, wears a transparent plastic headscarf & wouldn't say boo to a goose.

---

[6] Albert Pierrepoint (1905-92), English hangman who executed between 435 and 600 people in a 25-year career.

Tuesday, 24 January
Broadcasting House for the radio interview with Darryl Thomas. Thought he was the tea boy when he trolled up – neckties are evidently *démodé* at the BBC nowadays, along with combed hair… All the old anecdotes. One tries to introduce original stuff, but they only seem to want the familiar… 'Tell me about Hancock'… 'What was Sid James like?'… One is almost desperate enough to tell the truth!! That would shatter some illusions… Darryl was good on the robbery, though; 'Presumably you're bemused by the focus being on you rather than the crime?', & he's right – I ought to be a curious postscript, not the central thrust.

Wednesday, 25 January
I've been supplanted in the press by a pair of jessies on *EastEnders* who shared a smooch last evening. All over the tabloids. It was even debated in Parliament!! Huge swathes of the House incandescent with rage that the Great Unwashed – and in particular their *children* – are being subjected to 'yuppie poofs' brazenly canoodling at 7 p.m. on BBC1, just as the darling little innocents are settling down to their fish fingers & *Viennettae*…

Sunday, 29 January
Michael A. came & took us to *Just a Minute*. Marvellous audience! Predictably my first subject was 'bank jobs' & I went on quite a tirade & lasted the full minute to great applause. Derek said 'That was a party political broadcast on behalf of the String 'Em Up Party' which garnered more cheering. He said it to be needling, but the people are clearly on *my* side… Afterwards Michael told me that he and Enzo are going to Australia for a *year*. 'We're not going until March, but I'm telling you first in case you need to make other arrangements.' He says he's burnt out & needs the rest. 'I've blooded Stephen & I know he's entirely capable of looking after you until I get back…' I can't blame him for wanting to escape, of course, but it does rather leave me in the lurch. I am to pop into the office next week to meet this Stephen.

Thursday, 2 February
Walked in the snow to meet Shellard's[7] successor at Dent's, Francis Miller, to discuss autobiography. Took '78, '86 & '88 diaries to peruse. Francis said 'The tone will have to be different to *Just Williams*. More about you than your

---

[7] Peter Shellard, managing director of J M Dent & Sons, publishers, 1978-87.

career, as there's less to work with on that front,' which is a blunt reality. He seems to think a volume based on my view of the world is just what the public want! I agreed to set down a few chapters & we'll go from there.

Friday, 3 February
Went to ICM. Met this Stephen character. Pleasant enough. A bit smarmy, perhaps, but then he's young. If Michael trusts him, then I expect he'll do as a stand-in… it's not as though desperation to employ me is lighting up the 'phones.

Saturday, 4 February
Rupert knocked at 9 o'c. & drove me to Great Missenden where he grew up. R.'s motor is quite luxurious & so quiet! It's very mild & the rain held off. We visited the church of Peter and Paul & started one of the Chiltern walks. Too early for the bluebells but the feel of Spring is in the air. At 2 o'c. to Gipsy House where Roald Dahl & Felicity gave us tea. Roald is a towering figure, not unlike his own friendly giant. Engaging though, I was attracted not only to the Welsh kindliness in him, but that Viking vibrancy in his eyes, as well as the solid Englishness of the demeanour. He told us that his current book is about a mad vicar who says his words back-to-front!… Hughenden Manor at 3.45 to see Disraeli's study & the grounds. Back on the road, R. said he could kill for an omelette & chips & suggested the Happy Eater for supper!! He's a funny one, but curiously pleasing company. He wouldn't accept any money for petrol.

Wednesday, 8 February
Coming out of the post office a tall woman with blue hooped earrings said 'Please let me say how much joy you've brought me & my family over the years'… I was desperate to say 'Piss off' – but I plumped for 'You're too kind'.

Thursday, 9 February
Up at 7 o'c. Did letters. Spent most of the morning writing. Covered *The Undertaking*[8] & directing *Loot* & *Sloane* at the Lyric.[9] Then a chapter I've

---

[8] By Trevor Baxter. KW appeared (as 'the undertaker') during the national tour and its run at the Fortune Theatre, 1979-80.
[9] *Loot* and *Entertaining Mr Sloane*, by KW's friend Joe Orton (1933-67). Long before directing productions at Hammersmith in 1980 and 1981, KW had starred as Inspector Truscott in the initial 1965 tour of *Loot*, to decidedly mixed reviews.

entitled 'Back to Childhood'. That's what the 1980s seem to have been about. What with *Jackanory, Willo the Wisp, Whizzkids, Galloping Galaxies*, the children's book & all the silly parlour games, I've spent the decade in a juvenile state – not to mention dealing with my own infant in the form of Louisa. I'm interspersing bits from my own youth that I've not catalogued before – things Pat & I got up to, evacuation stories from Bicester, etc. – & I think the format of flitting backwards & forwards will work. Rang Gyles Brandreth & he went along with the idea of helping me edit & collate as before.

At 9.30 we watched the *Crimewatch* programme. There was no need for them to include the stills of me from the videos – the culprits' faces are obscured in those frames – but they couldn't help themselves. The ignominy of it all is galling. At the end the boy said 'Don't have nightmares, do sleep well'... Reminds one of a German bedtime story: forty minutes of blood & slaughter & then 'Sweet dreams!' as the lights are extinguished.

Tuesday, 14 February
Walked to Charbonnel et Walker to get Valentine chocolates for Louisa. Purchased a small tub of truffles for Rupert too... The sheer *grubbiness* of the borough is so much more conspicuous in this melting slush. The place has always been dirty, but there's a sense that it's being left to rot. Residents have long since given up attending to their own dwellings (it's years since I've seen anyone scrubbing their front step) & the council hasn't filled the void. The populace has become used to this lack of responsibility & lack of care and it quite literally *stinks*.

Saturday, 18 February
Telephoned Pat. She said 'If a nice rest home can be found, it would take the burden off you,' – but that word *burden* invariably jumps out of these discussions. When I raise the matter with anyone, I'm half hoping to be convinced that putting her away is the right thing to do, but that never occurs. I'm only reminded that I have a duty to perform. And I'm determined to do it... Louie isn't a burden, she's the love of my life.

Went in & we played Scrabble & shared her posh chocolates.

Wednesday, 22 February
Mountains of birthday cards, more than the usual. Browsed, then binned... Went into Lou who had forgotten. 'I'm 63 today,' I said. 'What d'you want, a ribbon?' came the impervious response. I'm *sick* of this surliness.

To the Tent at 7.30 where M. gave Paul, Rupert & myself dinner. We got quite tight! except for Rupert who doesn't really drink. He asked the waiter 'Do you do Arnold Palmers?' – 'Only when the wife's at her mother's!' replied the waiter & we fell about.

Friday, 24 February
Headlines are all about Mandela's murder.[10] It's obviously an inside job but authorities are blaming a crazed inmate. All fingers point to this Van Dijk,[11] Botha's replacement, who comes across like something out of *Colditz*. It's all so horribly tragic, as they were on the cusp of ending this ridiculous racialist separatism, but it won't surprise me if a civil war now ensues. On the news Dukakis kept calling him 'Nelson', which was not only unceremonious, but it also sounded as if he was referring to the Vice Admiral.

Wednesday, 1 March
Finished typing the fourth chapter & walked to Gyles. He seemed to approve, so we spent an hour polishing a few passages. At 2 o'c. went to ICM. Mitzie greeted me as though I were a master bursting in on a daydreaming schoolgirl, the office reeking of inertia. Michael's stuff packed up in boxes. I made it clear to Stephen that I was displeased with the lack of *anything* decent being offered… 'There's talk of some more *Through the Keyhole*s in Leeds,' he said, quite earnestly. I gave him what could only be described as an old-fashioned look, which ended that particular exchange.

Thursday, 2 March
As predicted, the riots have begun in South Africa. The footage is ghastly… Just a further reminder of how devastating the last War was for every corner of the globe. If the effort hadn't bankrupted *us*, the Empire might've survived & all the corruption & bloodshed of the past forty years avoided. Alas, we'll never know now.

---

[10] Nelson Rolihlahla Mandela (1918-89), South African anti-apartheid activist, sentenced to life imprisonment in 1962 for conspiring to overthrow the state. Officially the victim of a knife attack at Robben Island prison by fellow inmate Lindiwe Dube, though this remains highly disputed.

[11] Johannes Van Dijk (b. 1936), President of South Africa, 1989-90. Convicted of murder in 2003, but escaped custody and fled to East Berlin in 2004.

Friday, 3 March
Tube to Kennington for the chirapsia. Johnson away so I saw an assistant, who had all the charm of a splenetic Pol Pot. Flung like a trussed up turkey on the block – but I do feel freer, if not pampered. I shall insist on seeing Johnny next time, he's blest with a gentler touch.

On the news they had Gorbachev, Honecker[12] & Ceaușescu[13] joining western leaders condemning the Cape Town government – if you can make those three wince, it's fair to say you've probably overstepped the mark.

Tuesday, 7 March
After the cereal did beds & vacuumed through. Letter from Paul Ciani at BBC 2 asking if I am interested in the team captain place on *Call My Bluff*, to replace dear Arthur Marshall. 'Interested' would be overstating things, but it's only 14 episodes (7 sessions of two from the 22nd) & in all honesty I could do with the money.

Michael & Enzo's farewell dinner. They got rather emotional. Lovely speaking to John Sessions. He takes people off faultlessly. His Edward Fox is quite something to behold.

Sunday, 12 March
M. came & took Lou & me to Joe Allen. Place was bustling, we had to wait ten minutes for our table. M.'s take on the Johannesburg situation is that this trouble was inevitable, Mandela's murder has only hastened the insanity we're seeing. I disagreed, I think years of international pressure was at last beginning to move hearts & minds in government. Lou's sighing (due to not understanding the conversation) became intolerable, so we had to shift to simpler matters.

Atrocious scenes on the evening news of the slaughter in the townships, LWT actually showing the corpses. They're mostly black Africans, though, so I doubt anything will be done about it.

---

[12] Erich Honecker (1912-94), Chairman of the State Council of the German Democratic Republic, 1976-94.
[13] Nicolae Ceaușescu (1918-90), President of Romania, 1974-90.

Monday, 13 March
Went with Paul to see the Profumo film.[14] Salacious guff for the most part, tho' it does highlight the Establishment figures for the shits they were and *are*, & of course Hurt is as superb as always.

Thursday, 16 March
Walked to Dent. Francis seems happy with the six chapters written, but said 'Don't let the tone get too maudlin, keep the lightness & camp turned up'… I shall do nothing of the kind. This decade has offered very little in the realm of lightness. I'm not going to *invent* things – and Gyles backs me up. They've had the silliness in the *Drops* books, my heyday in *Just Williams* & now they're getting the gritty truth, & if they don't appreciate it, then tough tits.

Friday, 17 March
Quite out-of-the-blue dreams of Minorcan Mateo & woke with the full salute. Had the tradiola there & then as tho' I were 15. Stripped bed then had the coffee, &c.

Saturday, 18 March
To Gordon & Rona's for luncheon. G. had out an album with photos from Summer '55, just after *Moby Dick*,[15] that I'm *certain* I haven't seen before! Down at Brighton with me riding pillion on a Sunbeam motorbyke!!… Gording said the atmosphere in America justifies what the English papers have been saying – Dukakis doesn't appear up to the task. It's as if the Democrats are still in shock that they're in power after so long & don't really know what to do… Rona served duck with cherries & it was simply delectable.

Monday, 20 March
In Boots a man with a jet-black syrup said 'It is Kenneth Williams, isn't it?'… I shammed the Boche vocal & said '*Ich weiß nicht, was soll es bedeuten, daß ich so traurig bin,*'[16] & sauntered away leaving the poor thing eyes agog & baffled.

---

[14] *Scandal*, directed by Michael Caton-Jones, starring Ian McKellen and John Hurt; a fictionalised account of the Profumo affair that rocked the Macmillan government of the early '60s.

[15] *Moby Dick—Rehearsed*, a two-act drama by Orson Welles. A cast including KW, Gordon Jackson, Joan Plowright, Christopher Lee and Welles himself performed on a bare set in contemporary dress.

[16] Opening lines of Heinrich Heine's poem *Die Lorelei* (1824), roughly translated as 'I don't know what it means, that I am so sad'. KW's go-to German phrase, recited at speed when required.

1989

Wednesday, 22 March
TV Centre for *Call My Bluff*. Met Frank Muir in the lobby. 'Kenneth, dear chap, I'm so glad. Arthur would've *preferred* it to be you.' 'I should think he'd've preferred not to be dead,' I said – but confronted with the inexorable gloom of Studio 5, I'm not so sure… The bulk of the budget seems to have gone on mousse to craft Robinson's combover. The quavering 'set' is every shade of brown & it screams *old hat* at the top of its lungs. My team was Peter Lacey (*Daily Mirror*) & Jack someone from *Emmerdale Farm*.[17] After the rehearsal they wheeled in 30 or so macerated carcasses from the local community centre as an audience & we started… The mechanism for changing the words kept jamming, so we had to go *over & over* 'ulotrichous' till I wanted to scream. I don't think I've ever been involved in anything so joyless & funereal – & *I've* been to Clacton.

Came back & did some more writing but couldn't summon anything worthwhile. Sat brooding through the evening, cheered only by the knowledge that nobody's going to see the show now that it's been buried in a daytime slot, so the shame can be contained.

Saturday, 25 March
On getting out of the bath I stubbed the big toe (right) on the edge of the door & split the nail. Blood everywhere, thought I was going to flake out. Held the breath & applied salt water, then Savlon, & bandaged it. Took the Nurofen. Cancelled rummy with Paul, partly because of pain, but also because I can't get shoe on, only the blue slipper.

Monday, 27 March
Found when changing the dressing that it was stuck to the wound which meant another gory mess. Bathroom could've passed for Dennis Nilsen's.[18] Limped to the chemist on Warren St in slippers & overshoes. Asked Doug if there was anything stronger than the pills I had. He offered Solpadeine, but said only a GP could give me the *bona fide* stuff.

Wrote all afternoon. Got the *Standard* and saw Paul outside the block. Told him I was struggling to think of a title for the chapter on the stomach trouble – like a shot he said 'Twenty Four Hours from Ulcer?' & I roared.

---

[17] Clive Hornby (1944-2008), played Jack Sugden from 1980.
[18] Scottish serial killer (1945-2018); had a habit of dismembering his young male victims in the bathroom of his north London flat.

Wednesday, 29 March
Did the two shows, both vapid rubbish. Dosed up on the painkillers so felt a bit dopey. Out as hastily as I could, dodging autograph hunters. Came back for a rest. Woke at 5.10!! with the light nearly gone. Dry mouth & woozy. Went into Lou, but I couldn't stick *Dallas* so beat a hasty retreat.

Tuesday, 4 April
Walked to Marchmont Street & the old haunts... Writing this book is comparable to penning one's own obituary. That ought to be a futile endeavour, but the diary allows objectivity. Once I used it to record events to assess daily progression, then as an ersatz spouse to stave off loneliness, & now it's a tool to make sense of it all – based on catalogued fact, not skewed recollection. I'm sure a careful editor could do just as good a job even if I were six feet under, but as I'm doing little else, I may as well *undertake* the matter. This all feels like time added on, a weird epilogue. A true detachment, but not an unpleasant one. I see men rushing to work, I see the rat race through office windows, I see the despair & I think *good luck to them*. I have as little in common with them as with the boy I read about in the pages of my own journal. Once Louisa is gone, I shall fade away contented, all commitments fulfilled.

Wednesday, 5 April
Letter in the post from the BBC saying that *Round the Horne* and *Hancock's Half Hour* are to be released on audio cassette & that I am due some royalties!! I'll give Fort Knox a bell & ask them to erect another wing for me.

Monday, 10 April
Read the papers. Mostly reports about poll tax riots in Scotland. Doubtless the PM will be as ruthless as Richard the Second, and quite right too... To Broadcasting House for *Quote... Unquote*. Dull as arseholes apart from chatting to Ustinov afterwards. He said 'Kenneth, you're glowing like the vital morn,' & I said 'Percy Bysshe!' straitway.

Wednesday, 12 April
While they were setting up, the Scots electrician was caught smoking & the director bawled 'No fags on set!'... 'Could've fooled me,' chortled the odious beast, much to the delight of the boorish crew. That set the tone for

the day, both shows were miserable. I should've confronted it, instead I stormed out the second it was over & fled home.

Had meal with Lou at 5.45. She keeps complaining about her teeth, the top set, finding it painful to chew. So that's something else to sort out... News is all about the refugees flooding into Zimbabwe. Quite a coup for that absurd Mugabe character, making sure he's being filmed welcoming the exiles into his kingdom out of the goodness of his heart.

Friday, 14 April
13.13 to Leeds to talk to Michael Parkinson.[19] The format is better 'cos you're on for longer and not interrupted by other guests. Afterwards he said 'Those stories always go down well,' so he must've heard 'em multiple times before!

Saturday, 15 April
Gyles commented how curious it was that we were given *German* as a second language at Lyulph Stanley[20] rather than French. He's right of course. 'No wonder you enjoy your lieder!' he said. He's very good at picking up on these kinds of things & linking them together. We worked until 3 o'c. but I'd had enough by then & made excuses.

Evening TV dominated by the disaster at Sheffield. How one can go to a football match & end up dead in this day & age is inconceivable. Of course one expects trouble from these hooligan yobs, but the Police are just as bad. Pitifully useless.

Tuesday, 18 April
Got papers from Adonis & did letters. Collected Lou & got to dentist at 9.57. Went in with her 'cos on the bus I asked 'How's the mouth?' & she said 'What d'you mean? Nothing wrong with *my* mouth, thank you very much'... Tony said that the denture is sound but the palate has contorted & the edge is digging into the gum. He corrected it, took all of five minutes. She tottered out, happy as a sand boy.

Lou hoovered up the pork chops I prepared – she gnawed the bones clean! Left her & met Stanley at Durrants. He related the latest backstage

---

[19] For *Parkinson One to One* (1987-9), ITV's brief revival of the long-running chat show.
[20] The Lyulph Stanley Central School, opened in 1910 by London County Council. LCC central schools were set up to teach commercial or technical subjects to pupils aged 11-15.

rumours about that ghastly Wilkes:[21] 'He's been having it away with a Yugoslavian boy in the Pimlico flat, while the wife's been on dialysis. And then there's the *girlfriend*...' 'Well,' I said, 'his son-in-law's in parliament. That sort always come up smelling of roses.' – 'Smelling of Rose's *what*, though,' muttered Stanley, 'that's what I want to know...'

Saturday, 22 April
Called on Paul & we went to Selfridge's & Boots. Got a few bits for Lou at M&S. On Thayer St there was a chichi woman who watched her Alsatian do its business on the pavement & then casually strolled away. I protested but she didn't flinch. Luckily there was a lady policeman turning out of George St so I informed her & pointed out the assailants. Other people might be tickled pink to live in a litter tray, but I won't have it.

Sunday, 23 April
Telephoned Pat to ask if she remembered the name of the cyclops girl from Cromer Mansions. 'Oh! umm... Irene with an I!' she screamed, & howled with laughter, 'I'd completely forgotten about her!'... She *thinks* it was either Irene Chapman or Chatham. Pat kept coughing on the line & I told her to give up the fags or I shan't allow her to visit again.

Wednesday, 26 April
Did the shows. Wearisome. As I was leaving I saw Ted Rogers in reception. He greeted me but looked thoroughly downcast. 'What are you doing here?' he said – 'I asked myself the same thing just now,' I replied... 'Don't knock it, Ken. Work's work, we're lucky to be offered anything by the Oxbridge lot.' He's evidently still boiling that *3-2-1* got the chop... I'd have seen it as a blessèd release myself.

Bumped into Zubarev outside the block. He said that Jill Sheridan from number 26 had been murdered at her holiday cottage in Yarmouth, battered about the pate, all for the thirty quid in her purse. I'd only met her once at a residents' meeting, but it's still appalling news.

---

[21] John Wilkes (1931-2017), English actor and father-in-law of Labour MP Rob Litany. Best known for the role of Cadger Banks in the ITV sitcom *Getting Down the Banks*, 1981-5.

Thursday, 27 April
Went in to Lou. Found that she'd wet the bed again & I rather overreacted. She cried & I felt monstrous afterwards… The truth is, I'll never turf her out – so I'll have to see if some help can be brought in. It can't go on like this.

Friday, 28 April
Went for a walk with Paul. In the park we held hands & loudly sang *Arf a Pint of Ale* & other Gus Elen numbers. A woman with a pushchair passed us & muttered 'Disgusting' in our direction. I piped up 'How very dare you, madam? This is my long-lost brother-with-arms & he's afflicted with the pox! The pox, d'you hear what I'm saying? Do you deny him a public singsong with his loving sibling before it's too late? Well, do you?!' & hobbled after her. A group of uniformed nurses on a bench laughed & applauded, but Paul looked decidedly embarrassed.

Peter Estall rang at 2 o'c. 'Terry is in Switzerland next week & Sue Lawley has broken her elbow & has had to pull out. We've filled the slots for Monday & Wednesday, but could you present the show next Friday? You can choose one of your own guests…' I said yes & asked him to get Anneka Rice, as I'm rather partial & I've never met her.

Wednesday, 3 May
Did the last two *Call My Bluff*s. Can't remember being so relieved for a job to be over with. The only bright spot was having Matthew Kelly on my side for the second show. Stayed for *one* plastic beaker of sparkling wine afterwards, but had the excuse of needing to get to Shepherd's Bush for the *Wogan* rehearsal, so was able to get away.

Friday, 5 May
Car came & I was at S. Bush for 5 o'c… I've a feeling I used some of this material when I filled in before, but they'll just have to lump it. The new stage manager is a bit of a *Gruppenführer* – the type that instils jitters rather than confidence… Opening went well; some of the audience looked *under* eighty, which is a bit of a departure for *Wogan*. Anton Rodgers went fair, the singing group fair. Then Anneka Rice, superb!! Her vim is infectious & the well-bred fluency & attractiveness are quite enchanting. Drinks afterwards in the pink room. I was practically mobbed by the pop trio, who

seemed bent on posing for pictures with me. All three bold as brass,[22] flirting away with one whilst a hundred screaming girls waited for them in the drizzle outside!! Big Fun, they're called… And rightly so.

Saturday, 6 May
In Marks's the checkout girl said 'You were good on *Wogan*, but I reckon you're better when you're answering the questions,' & when Stanley rang he said 'The trouble is, you're more interesting than the guests,' so I doubt I'll be hearing from BAFTA.

Thursday, 11 May
Up at 8 o'c. Did replies to Eifion in Wrexham, Jeff in France and Jörgen in Sweden before toast & the *St Ivel*, which I shall have from now on… Went to the Social Department on Robert Street. Spoke to a woman called Meghan who put me in mind of an upholstered Yootha Joyce. She said options are available but the council are strict as money's tight, blah blah. I said 'Never mind that, my mother's been paying into the system since Passchendaele, so I trust she's due some service…' There's to be an assessment of Louisa's condition but not till *August 1st*, thanks to the socialists' stellar management of the borough. Endless bloody forms to fill in.

Friday, 12 May
Got the 9.5 to Bristol Temple Meads. Nobody to meet me. Stood waiting like a fart in fantasy-land. I rang the number on the confirmation letter & was told 'Oh dear! Norman is usually very reliable! We're so sorry. Just hang around for a bit…' Ludicrous. It was the last place one would want to hang round for a *bit*. Everyone I saw looked a little *off*. Eventually a breathless young man appeared. 'So sorry! They told me you were coming into Parkway station, so I've been waiting there!'… He drove me to the Somerdale plant. The chocolatey smell hits as soon as you're through the gates. Met Phil, the stuttering producer. He couldn't stop grinning, which was unfortunate, what with his temporary crowns. They had me dressed in your actual striped apron & hat, prancing round like Corporal Jones. Phil kept saying 'Try & make it funny', but the health & safety dialogue didn't allow much scope for comedy… They said they were pleased at the end, but they were lying. Finished at 1.15, thoroughly deflated… 'Phoned Mitzie

---

[22] Bold, i.e. homosexual.

from Temple Meads. I said 'No more of this poxy corporate stuff, under any circumstances.' How they must loathe me.

Sunday, 14 May
M. came & took us to Joe Allen for luncheon. M. said he'll be away in Italy for *four weeks*, so that's the outings gone for a Burton. I said 'I hope you have a shitty time.'

In the evening we saw *Creatures Great & Small* and *Mastermind*. I did rather well on 'Songs of Schubert' – better than the silly fool in the chair at any rate. I said to Lou 'Don't eat all that Whole Nut, you'll be sick'… She said 'I've started, so I'll finish,' & I nearly died.

Wednesday, 17 May
In the paper: 'Carry On Robbing! A violent gang that has committed a series of bank raids in the south east over the past year – including one witnessed by TV funster Kenneth Williams – has struck again in Chelmsford'… Not only am I linked to these crooks for all eternity, I'm a fucking *funster* now.

Thursday, 18 May
As I was walking back from Harts, a voice called out from a car 'Where's it all happening?! Where are all these orgies?! Why haven't we been asked?!…' It was Sheila & John!… I got in the back with the shopping & we drove to Alpino's for coffee. Sheila was glowing & kissed me on both cheeks. She's about to go into rehearsals for *Prin* at the Lyric & said 'You must come to see it, I'll need your support…' I certainly shan't be going, in spite of my fondness for the Lyric, but it was lovely to see the pair of them looking so at ease together. The public evidently love *Morse* – two people came up to John in the caff for his autograph, completely ignoring me and Sheila.

Monday, 22 May
Letter in the second post from Conservative Central Office asking me to appear in a party political for the European elections. Apparently Mrs Thatcher is keen to have me on board!! They're persistent, I'll give them that, so I shall relent. After all, the socialists want us *out* of the EEC, so I ought to do my bit.

Saturday, 27 May
Did beds & took pedestal mats to the cleaners'. Walked to Dent's. 'You're cracking along, this is good stuff,' said Francis. He smokes a Silk Cut in a

holder. 'Remember, though, don't hold back on the funnies…' I smiled & thought 'I'll give *you* funnies, you bearded poof.'

Sunday, 28 May
Took a turn in the park with Lou, but she's so exasperatingly slow that I cut short the route… Saw the TV news. The summit in Helsinki is another disaster for Dukakis, fumbling over the words. If I were Gorby I'd nip across & annex Alaska; this administration probably wouldn't even notice.

Scrabble in the evening, Rupert came into Louisa's for the first time. Lou played 'harris', meaning 'bum'. I said 'It's not harris, it's *Aris* – Aristotle, bottle; bottle & glass, arse…' but she started grousing about it being unfair, so I acquiesced for an easy life.

Wednesday, 31 May
Received a postcard from the T&C in Tangier… 'The Virus has verily slashed the talent pool,' apparently. I knew this comeuppance would come, I told Orton, I told them all. I used to think it was God's punishment for depravity, but that's the same unenlightened drivel they spouted during the Black Death – the truth is that revelling in *filth* & *dirt* of any kind is a precarious business, it's scientifically obvious. Made three attempts at acknowledging the card, but couldn't think of a thing to write; the idea of them lumbering round North Africa on the hunt for trade made me quite nauseous.

Friday, 2 June
Car to Smith Square at 11 o'c. The girl took me upstairs, past the portraits of Peel & Baldwin & Churchill to a meeting room at the front. Met the crew, who were all set up. In came Lord Carrington!![23] & the flunkies. 'As you can imagine, Mr Williams, this is quite a departure for us…' as though I'd forced them into it… Bryan, the press officer, stuck to me like glue. Ran through the text a few times. Had it learnt by the time he said 'We've got the autocue in case you go wrong.' Did the first part alright, cup of tea & a smoked salmon sandwich (bet you don't get *them* at Walworth Road[24]), then the fleet of cars pulled round & took us to Parliament Sq… Baking hot, & the gawping nellies rather got in the way, but we got it in the can. Few

---
[23] Peter Carrington (1919-2018). Defence Secretary, 1970-4; Foreign Secretary, 1979-82; NATO Secretary General, 1984-8.
[24] 144-152 Walworth Road, south London – the Labour Party's headquarters since 1980.

shouts of 'Tory scum' from passing riffraff, but I found that rather more emboldening than disheartening. All done by 2.15.

Monday, 5 June
Read in the paper that the giant grebe has been declared extinct in Guatemala, so I poured myself a large amontillado to celebrate.

Thursday, 8 June
Bus to Gyles. We did three hours but he had to get the train to Leeds at 12 o'c for *Countdown*. Rather him than me… Sardines for lunch. Cab to B.H. for *The News Quiz*. Barry Took is very good, he paces it just right. The *New Faces* chap was extremely nervous beforehand, but Barry Cryer spent some time calming him down & distracting him. Barry's a *gentleman*, from tip to toe… Spent five minutes *signing* for people, quite absurdly. 'I think you're smashing', 'You're our favourite', etc… I was quite the tart!!

Friday, 9 June
Watched my PG Tips advert on Rupert's video recorder. There's no question, I look *marvellous* as a chimp. Then the Party Political. I was actually quite good! Neither too campy nor too grand. 'Warm & succinct,' R. said. Heaven knows whether it'll help or hinder the cause, but it's something different, that cannot be debated.

Tuesday, 13 June
Slept till 8.45! Must end this lethargic trend. Lots of letters about the Tory b'cast. Some offensive, but most in favour… Took Lou to P.O. for pension, then to Marks's for smalls. Luckily the saleswoman was totally practical, took Louie's arm and set to. I sat outside the changing room & read my book.
    Got steaks at the butcher on Greenwell St & served them with *thick* chips at 5.38.

Friday, 16 June
Only a handful of Conservative losses overnight! which for a Party that's been in power for a decade isn't half bad… Rupert wanted to slum it so we went to the Blind Beggar at Whitechapel. Never ceases to amaze me how a bit of glam can seduce the lower orders – irrespective of their tattoos & missing teeth, we were treated charmingly. Bit of a blank expression when I ordered Campari, so I settled for gin & it… In the cab home R. naively

claimed that he'd dropped a cufflink, but it was gold so it was doubtless pinched by some gummy opportunist in the pub.

Saturday, 17 June
Quite a coup for the Russians to locate the remains of Amelia Earhart's aeroplane. The subtext questions *why* Soviet boats were in that part of the Pacific & *what* were they looking for – the official line of 'oceanographic research' strikes as fallacious – but for the moment the needle-in-a-haystack wonder is the chief crux.

Thursday, 22 June
Pat arrived at 11.15. Kept saying to Lou 'You'll have a lovely time & it's only for a week,' but it was all very petulant and resentful.

Waved them off & finished packing… M. came at 3.20 & drove Rupert & me to Gatwick. It's true that Channel Express are economical, but the aircraft had all the comfort of a Vickers Vildebeest. The subaquatic photos of Earhart's mangled monoplane in *Today* didn't provide the cheeriest in-flight reading, neither. Refused the sad, curling comestibles the girl offered. Arrived Funchal 7.20 – 85 degrees but breezy. Cab to the hotel, Reid's Palace. In truth, it evinces the kind of swank that typically makes me uncomfortable… but I must have patience to endure the load. The room is enormous – no wonder he was cagey about the true cost, I shall have to have it out with him… Changed for dinner. The splendour of it is overwhelming. He ordered Krug Grand Cuvée!! it's mad. But quite delightful. Put a Supponeryl up & had *very much* the barclays.

Friday, 23 June
After breakfast we walked into Funchal. R. wanted the Sacred Art museum, then we did the toboggan ride down Monte!! Had the fish lunch with obligatory Madeira wine. Rupert told me that his father was high up in Dunlop Slazenger before the aneurysm, which is why they're so comfortably off… Nap, then read by the pool as R. took a dip. It's all quite lovely – seems somehow less dilapidated than I recall, but that might reflect the company I'm keeping.

Saturday, 24 June
After the botanical gardens we went to the Sé Cathedral (1495) & ended up in the midst of a wedding! We were virtually *dragged* along with the crowd,

R.'s basic Portuguese insufficient to excuse us. In the end we capitulated & joined in!! The un-Englishness of it was all so refreshing & despite the language barrier, to sit & watch them dancing, young & old, in their traditional way, was so moving I nearly wept... We watched the sun go down on the Pontinha & he awkwardly embraced me. Said I was tired & walked back to the hotel alone.

Sunday, 25 June
I'm 63 & he's 36. I'm from St Pancras, he's from Buckinghamshire. I've bare walls, he has a print of Flandrin's *Polytès* over the mantel. Think I am going mad.

Monday, 26 June
Had the afternoon tea in the lounge & was accosted by a ruddy-faced cur with halitosis: 'O! look who it is, matron! Who's this, your toy boy? Come on then, tell us something funny...' I said 'I'm afraid nothing comes to mind at present,' & walked out. Is there nowhere I can evade these vile, repugnant *cunts*?

Tuesday, 27 June
Sweltering. Told R. I was going into Funchal & did a long circuit. Stupidly ate too many custard tarts as I wrote postcards to Lou, Pat & chums. Nearly sick on the way back.

Just had fizzy water with dinner. Rupert said 'Please don't be afraid of me. If we're just pals, then that's A-OK with me...' All quite a relief, it was getting too heavy & foolish. It released the pressure & we played draughts in the *salão* until bedtime. Can't stop thinking about Lou; I hope she's alright.

Wednesday, 28 June
Rupert rang BA from reception & at great cost (the details of which he kept from me) rearranged the flights. 14.30 to Heathrow on BA... Trunk call to M. to tell him of the changes.

Thursday, 29 June
Arrived London 6.25... Wondrous M. met us & got us back to the flats by 7.40. Avoided drawn-out thanks & had a tin of oxtail in Lou's flat. Tons of bloody letters to answer.

Friday, 30 June
Didn't finish replies till gone 11 o'c. Heaven knows what compels these people to write – unless it's down to a sudden fervour for teabag adverts, for they've little else to go on. There were *two* letters from Kirkcaldy, of all places!! Went to post. When I got papers Bill said 'O! glad to see you back. I thought we'd lost you!' as though I'd slipped down the back of a settee… Went to Oxford St with Paul. Told him about the holiday. He agrees it's all ridiculous, but then as a fellow bachelor he's biased.

Sunday, 2 July
Lou said 'O! I can't be doing with this heat,' so put her in a cotton dress. M. collected us & we lunched at Joe Allen. I ordered lobster for Lou but she left most of it. At the restaurant was Joan Rivers!! She was with an LWT exec trying to drum up endeavours over here. 'The U.S. networks don't want me any more,' she said, 'so they can go screw themselves!' I think the husband's suicide has put a dampener on things. 'This business, Kenneth… it's a killer. But it's *everything*.'

Tuesday, 4 July
In the post – Lady Olga Maitland's new book on the PM, signed by the author & Mrs T: 'In recognition of your sterling contribution to the cause. With heartfelt thanks, Margaret Thatcher'… It's an elegant volume & I shall treasure it.

Wednesday, 5 July
Telephone rang & it was Mitzie asking whether I want to do more episodes of that *Password* for UTV, filming in *Belfast*… I replaced the receiver without replying. I'm so tired of this lamentable shit. I just have to think about it & vomit rises in the throat & the heart descends like a crashing boulder… We watched some Wimbledon in the afternoon but it's too muggy so I had a lie down.

It's time to go. I'll finish the book, get Louisa her home help & sign off. I'm well rehearsed. It's the inexorable next move, nothing more… Read and reread *The Garden of Proserpine*[25] & wept – but *not* for the love of living.

---

[25] Poem by Algernon Charles Swinburne, 1866. KW's favourite stanza reads 'From too much love of living, From hope and fear set free, We thank with brief thanksgiving Whatever gods may be That no life lives for ever; That dead men rise up never; That even the weariest river Winds somewhere safe to sea.'

Only that, in point of fact, I ought to have achieved more before my eternal night.

Saturday, 8 July
Went for a walk. Anything to avoid the writing. Sat in the park on one of the deck chairs in the shade & watched the children playing, the lovers lolling. Apart from the sparrows it was quite idyllic. It'll be a question of stockpiling over-the-counter pills as I won't be able to procure anything stronger without inviting queries. A bottle of Croft Original, sixty Embassy & ten boxes of paracetamol. Quite the shopping list.

Monday, 10 July
Note from Stephen inviting me up there for a 'discussion' tomorrow. Never been summoned so formally before… Penned the close of the book: 'Don't let them tell you that life is short. With any luck, we've each thirty-thousand days to fill. Try to say "yes", lest offers aren't repeated. Don't be afraid to make mistakes today as you can try to do better tomorrow. Keep your chin up, smile at the world and, above all – carry on.' Reading it back, of course, one feels distinctly nauseous.

Tuesday, 11 July
Got Lou dressed & prepared. She's going on the club's trip to Felixstowe. The plump West Indian woman said 'Don't you worry, me darlin', we'll take good care o' her… we all very fond o' Miss Louise'. She's just the type I'd seek to get in on a regular basis – she's positive, chatty & practical, and treats the task as more of a hobby than an occupation.

Walked to ICM. Atmosphere icy & forbidding as soon as I arrived. Mitzie displayed an unconvincing smile. 'Come on in, Ken, let's have a chat,' said the Stephen character. Talk about getting his feet under the table. He's made hisself *very* comfortable in Michael's chair, and no mistake. I turned down the offer of that Perrier crap, then it was 'Of course, you're one of our stars, Ken, we all adore you round here'… I said 'Never mind all that rubbish, what are you getting at?'… 'The trouble is, Ken…' I said 'It's Kenneth, if you don't mind…' He said 'Well then – *Kenneth*: we put forward suggestions but you don't seem interested. Mitzie was quite upset when you hung up on her the other day'… In the end I'd had enough & rather blew up. I said 'I don't know who you think you are, talking to me in such a way… I can't imagine what Michael was *thinking* leaving the likes of *you* in charge, but he must want his head testing…' After a few more back & forths he said, sheepishly, 'If you don't want to commit to the projects we offer, then I don't know how much further we can go.' I stood up grandly, my countenance regained. 'Then there is nothing more to say,' I said & left. On the walk home I felt a warm glow of relief. No more false grins into a camera. No more desperation to squeeze laughs out of an indifferent public. No more pounds of flesh to be hacked off, all to scratch a meagre living. There's no more *living* to be done.

Was just about to ring Gordon when the 'phone rang & it was him ringing me!!… 'I don't know if you'd heard, but Olivier passed away this morning…'

Even a level-headed man would admit it's a sign. It is time to leave.

The 'phone went three or four times in the evening but I didn't answer. Heard Louie get back. Put one up and went to bed.

Wednesday, 12 July
Woke at 5 o'c. with the sun. Decided over breakfast not to tell anyone apart from Gordon & Stanley. With so little time remaining there doesn't seem much point.

Friday, 14 July
I am no longer going to reply to fan letters. It's 15p a stamp now & that soon adds up.

Sunday, 16 July
Knocked at Rupert's. 'Would you care to join us for lunch?'… 'I thought you'd gone off me,' he said. M. took us to Zédel for a change, but it was heaving, all the flags were out for this French Revolution nonsense,[26] so we fled to Joe Allen. Huge, black-framed photo of Larry Olivier on an easel in the lobby, as if we were attending a Humanist wake… Getting Lou up & down stairs has shifted from the realm of irritation to that of embarrassment. Abjectly waving disgruntled queuers around the blockage, whilst she blows off & stutters like the unroadworthy wreck she's become, is so *enraging* that one's sympathy saps & I just want to run away. The tongue's in shreds from being bitten. Rupert took her arm & calmly guided her while M. paid & I waded in obsolescence.

---

[26] 14 July 1989, the two-hundredth anniversary of the Storming of the Bastille.

Monday, 17 July
Rang Stanley. He seems to think I'll still crave the limelight, but it's nonsense. I'm the definitive introvert, all the world knows that.

Wednesday, 19 July
Heavy parcel in the post from ICM, containing leftover headshots, headed notepaper & other personalised ephemera. They could've chucked it all, but the postage was £2.49, so some kind of point is being made. I couldn't care in the slightest. Just reaffirms the decision & shows the shyster for what he is. Wrote a note to Michael in Australia, putting my side of the story. I can't believe he was fool enough to install such a shit in his place, but I suppose we're none of us perfect.

Saturday, 22 July
Considered touching up the paintwork in Lou's drawing room, but held off as the odd crack or sign of household neglect might be the difference in obtaining maximum council assistance. Went to Boots, & Harts for food, then to Sue Ryder to get rid of some records as I don't think anyone will want them. I'll leave the clobber & Pat can go through it all & either bin things or donate them, but I think lugging stuff around charity shops myself is unseemly… Just had cold meat salad for lunch. It's still boiling.

Thursday, 27 July
To Gyles to finish the draft. Spent about three hours on it. He said 'Well, contrary to the usual pattern, I think this sequel tops the original,' which was kind, though untrue. Michèle poured us all champagne & we toasted the book's success.

Tuesday, 1 August
Endeavoured to coach Louie in what to say, but abandoned the idea as she'd no clue what I was on about. The woman arrived at 12.30. Couldn't have been more than 21. Asian, but well-spoken & polite. Lots of note-taking & questions to Lou. Her deafness & general lack of understanding (Lou's, that is!) seemed to work in our favour, as did this Sanita not recognising me. We're to hear by letter within a fortnight as to what they can offer.

After the meal I poured us a whisky each. She watched Paul Daniels & I did the crossword.

Friday, 4 August
Went to give blood. They might as well have a drop before the embalmer hoses it down the grate. All change at the Centre. The shrewish blimp on the desk examined me as though I were sticky fingerprint on a window. As I waited it pointedly remarked to the colleague 'Make sure they tick the practising homosexual box if applicable,' ensuring I heard. I said 'Don't worry, ducky, I'm well past practising, I'm a master of the art' & flashed my gold badge.[27] It pouted & plodded into the office. A sweet girl took the blood & said 'I'm sorry about that. She's Pentecostal & recently lost her chow…'

Had salmon steaks with Lou. On the TV they showed Charles & Diana coming out of the Lindo Wing with the new princess. Di looked as if she was stepping out of Vidal Sassoon. They've already named the child Elizabeth,[28] as it's the Queen Mum's birthday today.

Tuesday, 8 August
Perused the will, but I don't think I need alter it again, little has changed since the last crisis. Paul knocked & we went to see the Bond film at the Empire. Overlong, overly violent & 007 was about as suave as Charlie Cairoli.[29]

Wednesday, 9 August
'Phone rang & it was that Parsons.[30] 'What's this I hear about you leaving the business?' It seems that the tongues have inevitably loosened. Told N. that I'm having a break to look after Lou. 'Very noble,' he said. 'I hope you'll be back come January. We really couldn't do the show without you, you know.' He's told me that before, so the call was evidently made to ensure his bread will go on being buttered. Sent note to Peter Plouviez,[31] cancelling my membership.

---

[27] One of KW's proudest possessions, presented by the Blood Donor Centre in 1983, to mark his fiftieth contribution.

[28] Princess Elizabeth Frances (1989-93). Died at Sandringham of Soviet flu.

[29] (1910-80) Anglo-Italian clown, impressionist and musician.

[30] Nicholas Parsons (1923-2020), English actor and broadcaster. Chairman of *Just a Minute*. KW often cruelly ridiculed Parsons when on the airwaves, but this – for the most part – was for comic effect.

[31] Trade union leader. General Secretary of Equity, 1974-91.

Thursday, 10 August
Some lovely lines from Joan Plowright, thanking me for my letter. It's obviously all pretty raw still. She mentioned *Moby Dick* & those mad days at the Duke of York's with Orson. Hard to imagine her as Pip the cabin boy now… It's mercifully quiet in London. Walked up Marchmont St. to Cromer Houses & then Endsleigh as I doubt I'll have the chance again. No ghosts. Just filth & foreigners.

Sunday, 13 August
Caught a glimpse of my nakedness in the mirror after bathing. It was a hideous sight, the grey belly distending obscenely over the basket. I'm almost 10 stone. Moreover, I'm sure the cock is shrinking. If e'er there were a signal to cash in the chips, it's *that*… After the lunch I wrote letters to Gordon, Stanley, M., Paul, Mags & Paul in Sydney. Didn't put stamps on as I'm sure the police or whoever deals with that kind of thing will distribute them appropriately. Placed them in the bedside table drawer so they're easy to find.

Monday, 14 August
Letter from the Council. Lou is to be called on, mornings & evenings, Monday to Friday *and* on Saturday afternoons! Hour-long engagements!! I explained it to Lou but I don't think it will register until the visits start (next Monday). It's such an enormous relief, I never dreamt such provision would be afforded. Rang Pat. She said 'It's marvellous… it'll give you the chance to do other things.' 'Quite,' I said.

'Phoned Stanley & invited him for supper at Vecchia. 'It's like you've won the Pools,' he said, & I admit, it feels comparable. It's batty – I drank Ricard before, Calvados after & devoured a great big sundae *en route*! The level of wind-bound caution-throwing is ludicrous. Could tell in the taxi that the stomach wasn't overly impressed, but it couldn't matter less any more.

Wednesday, 16 August
Didn't rise until 9 o'c!! Did beds. Got food for Louie at Marks's. Went to Boots & purchased the pills. Scanned the 'extra strong' brands, but I imagine there'd be more chance of the body rejecting the stuff if I go down that route, so I favoured the plain.

Briefly considered ringing T. to see if he had the number of a manly Alice for trade, but thought better of it & had very much the barclays in lieu.

Beyond Our Kenneth

Friday, 18 August
Had a rest after the cold haslet salad. Wrote these lines in the afternoon.

> I foiled a feckless father
> As the bombs were raining down;
> I taught myself to learn
> And how to shelter 'neath a clown.
> > I beat shortage and war –
> > But I could've done more.
>
> Dulce et decorum est
> To entertain the troops;
> I square-bashed when the orders
> Came from haughty nincompoops.
> > I endured Singapore –
> > But I could've done more.
>
> I trusted I'd a talent
> And leapt into the blue;
> Provincial cultivation,
> Then a capital debut.
> > I'd opened the door –
> > But I could've done more.
>
> I vowed that I'd be chaste
> In terms of style and of the other;
> Forbidden fruit's more tempting
> When one's living with one's mother.
> > I applied what I swore –
> > But I could've done more.
>
> So very much to offer
> With a mind encyclopædian;
> Yet I made the honchos howl
> And was labelled a comedian.
> > I did one Bernard Shaw –
> > But I could've done more.

A life upon a stage,
The fans become one's other half;
Their warm embrace deceives:
They only want your autograph.
    I'd sign three or four –
    But I could've done more.

The cameras stop rolling,
The flattery ends;
Thank Goodness himself
For the love of true friends.
    They came to the fore –
    But I could've done more.

Crying with laughter or
Crying with dolour?
The tears blur the light and
The sound and the colour.
    I'm approaching the floor –
    And I should've done more.

Saturday, 19 August
Walked to Asprey's & ordered gold cufflinks for Rupert. I'm having them engraved, one with 'KCW~RPJ' & the other '1988~1989'. I'll leave a note attached & they can give them to him when they go through the stuff.

Monday, 21 August
The woman arrived at 9.15 – uselessly late for Lou, who breakfasts at 7.30 as a rule. Sharon she's called, which isn't reassuring. The brogue is nunnish, which Lou won't respond to. The 'hour' visit was over by 9.55, & the place is untidier than before she came. Such a desperately dispiriting outcome. Rang Camden Council, but it was just a recorded message about the fucking *Marchioness*.[32]

    Eventually got thro' to some nance at the council offices.[33] 'It's only the first visit, Mr Williams, these things take time to bed in…' Acquiesced to reevaluate after one week.

---

[32] The pleasure boat *Marchioness* had sunk in the early hours of 20 August, after colliding with a dredger. 51 lives were lost.
[33] See entry for 7 May 1992.

Beyond Our Kenneth

Heard her arrive at 7.30. Lou ravenous. Went in & found her impetuously slopping baked beans into a saucepan. No conversation. Lou looked like a frightened child. I nearly broke down with the shame of it… 'Right, get out,' I said. There was a lot of 'You don't know how difficult this job is' & 'I've seven other ladies to get to tonight,' but I couldn't give a rat's. If needs be I shall *pay* for assistance if this is the local authority's standard of geriatric care.

Got Lou ready for bed. Came back to flat & the fat turd & his foreign floozy were banging about downstairs. Nearly finished it all. I am so wholly & exhaustively depressed.

Tuesday, 22 August
Three quarters of an hour waiting followed by twenty minutes bickering, but the Irishwoman won't be coming again. The girl said she'll arrange for a new help, to begin either on Friday or Monday. I pray it works out alright.

Thursday, 24 August
Headlines are all about East Germany ditching support for the hitherto "suppressed negro comrades" of the ANC & giving passports to *white* South Africans if they relocate to the GDR!! Speaks volumes about the parlous state of both countries, but Honecker is framing it as your actual socialist noble gesture. Quite rightly the Dutch want nothing to do with the fleeing Boers, whereas I expect they'll fit in quite well in Karl-Marx-Stadt or Leipzig.

Friday, 25 August
Publisher rang & is satisfied with the text. Asked me to forward *thirty* never-before-seen photographs to choose from. Looked through a few of Louisa's albums. Spent the evening with her perusing old snaps. She can remember better when the image is in front of her, & seems to hear better too!!… On the TV News it was announced that our MP[34] has been killed in a car crash in York, along with his two passengers. Nasty way to go. Still, I don't suppose we constituents will notice much of a difference.

Monday, 28 August
Got up at 7 o'c. The new girl arrived at 7.20!! I was still in the dressing gown. Filipino, hard to judge the age, but clearly keen to get stuck in. Once again it's clear that the work ethic of these people puts the British to shame. It was obvious that Louisa warmed to her right away!! She's called Flordeliza, but

---

[34] Frank Dobson (1940-89), Labour MP for Holborn & St Pancras, 1979-89.

Lou can't manage that so they've settled on Flo. She learned quickly to up the volume. After twenty minutes I left them to it! O, I hope this is the answer.

Prawn salad for lunch & I asked Lou what she thought of her. 'Who?' 'The foreign girl who came this morning.' 'O! Flo? Oh yeah, she's lovely. What, coming again, is she?'… I walked to Bond St and collected R.'s cufflinks. It's a little cooler & the walk was very pleasant. I had to sign for a window cleaner in Portland Place.

Flo arrived at 6.45, washed the dinner things, turned down Louie's bed & then they played Snap with tea & biscuits. I slipped out & heard her leave at 7.47. Popped in again at 9.30 but Lou had already retired.

Tuesday, 29 August
No reproach for not stopping last night, so she's either forgotten or (fingers crossed) didn't require company thanks to Flo. I pray, prostrate & naked, that it's the latter.

Wednesday, 30 August
Went in at 8 o'c. & Lou was singing *Don't Have Any More, Missus Moore* as Flo was wiping down the sideboard!! Said hello but didn't stay. Wrote letters to Richard Pearson & Andrew[35] & Joanie Sims. Lunch Lou: 'That cleaner come this morning. Let herself in, if you please…' so I had to explain *again*. She's evidently in a musical frame of mind, as we sang old songs for most of the afternoon. She remembers every word, it's remarkable.

Friday, 1 September
Conversed with my pirate friend outside Harts. I could swear his patch used to be on the other eye… He adduced that the weakness of America in the short term spells trouble, but that the Soviet economy is increasingly fragile & essentially doomed… Lou & I watched Mrs Thatcher give her conference speech. *Perestroika* is all very well, but impractical – after all, one wouldn't let a vegetarian run an abattoir, how could a commie successfully run a free market economy?

Spoke to Flo & she agreed to prepare light meals if I happen to be going out. With any luck she can serve breakfast, prepare a sandwich or salad & leave it in the fridge for lunch & then do the main meal when she returns in

---

[35] Andrew Ray (1939-2003), English actor and son of comedian Ted Ray. Worked with KW in the 1962 film *Twice Round the Daffodils*.

the evening. I've written a letter to request three visits a day when I'm dead, but I've a feeling they'll ignore that & put her away somewhere. Pat will have to take up the reins, I've done as much as I can.

Saturday, 2 September
Nearly did it last night. Prepared everything, but postponed as I want to see who they send at weekends. She arrived at 1 o'c. Nice girl, from Peterborough. Rita she's called. 'I feel like I've known you all my life,' she said… 'How nice,' I said. No one knows me. Not even Louisa, properly. I'm unknowable.

Walked round the park in a bit of a daze. Made my peace with God. Thanked Him for all I've been given and the people I've known & loved.

Ambled home & saw the *Gazette* in the lobby. Labour have chosen *John Wilkes* as their candidate in the by-election!! It's a disgrace! As if the borough hasn't sunk low enough without these filthy champagne socialists parachuting a north country "comedian" into a safe London seat… It's this self-righteous Rob Litany,[36] the son-in-law, pulling strings. Shoe-horning famous relatives into the mother of parliaments is *beyond* disrespectful & I reckon it *reeks*. Paul came down & said 'What next? Russ Abbot as Archbishop of Canterbury?'

At 5.45 the 'phone rang. 'Hello, Mr Williams, I do hope I'm not disturbing you – it's John Waterhouse speaking, Tory Central Office…'

Took me a while to cotton on to what he was asking. He actually floated the notion of *me* standing in the election!!! 'If Labour are going to play these kind of games, then we intend to fight fire with fire'… The 'plan', for want of a better word, centres on using my "celebrity" to combat *his*, in an attempt to siphon off as many votes as possible & push sensible Labourites towards the *Liberals*!! It's thoroughly lunatic & I told Mr Water Closet I thought as much. If these are the depths to which politics has plummeted, then I'm certainly better off six feet down. I thanked him for thinking of me, but told him *no* without any ambiguity. I ought never to have got mixed up with these partisans.

Sunday, 3 September
Up at 7 o'c. & got paper. Large picture of Wilkes on the front of *Today*, the ludicrous, plebeian grin plastered across the face. Bill said 'That's all we need! A piss artist Scouser lording it over us…'

---

[36] (b. 1953) Labour MP for South East Durham, 1983-2007.

1989

Knocked up Paul for a walk. Told him about the 'phone call. He said 'Well, it's farcical. What about your career?' Told him I'd packed it in & he fell decidedly schtum.

Couldn't concentrate on the crossword so rang Stanley. He laughed when I mentioned it but concluded with 'Of course – you'd be brilliant at it'... Chops & chips with Lou, I left when Rita appeared.

Buzzer went at 2 o'c. 'Mr Williams, I'm terribly sorry to disrupt your Sunday... It's Kenneth Baker.'[37] I thought '*Who?*...' Then the penny dropped. Went down & there he was, in the flesh, with Mr Hardy, the constituency chairman. Wasn't having them in the flat so I suggested a stroll in the park. After the pleasantries it was 'Now – Holborn & St Pancras. I'll be blunt, we want you'... It turns out there isn't yet a prospective Tory candidate in place & my name came up at CCO[38] as soon as the Wilkes news broke! 'You're local, you're admired & after your tremendous work for us on the box, you're virtually an old hand.' He said 'It'd just be a one off campaign to send this charlatan packing and – with any luck – we'll chip off enough reluctant lefties & give Kinnock[39] a bloody nose...' I was pretty dumbfounded. 'Of course, I know this is out of the blue,' he said, 'but, frankly, we can't have this kind of person in the Commons.' Well, I fervently agree with that. 'The latest poll for Holborn has Labour on 51% & us on 14, but the Alliance are at 34. So the best we can hope for is a poaching job leading to a Liberal gain, coming at Labour from both sides. Only someone with your flair can achieve that, in our opinion'... I thought I was accustomed to this sense of out-of-bodyness, but it was like witnessing the dramatic hiatus of a film, waiting for the actor's response, only to realise that it was *my* turn to speak & I hadn't a clue what the next line was. I cleared the throat & said 'I can't express how flattered I am to be thought of in this light. It's true, the idea of this Wilkes character as our representative at Westminster is grisly, but I've an elderly mother to keep, & I really haven't the experience or the time to donate.' There was a pause & this Hardy chap piped up – 'I urge you to sleep on it. We expect the writ to be issued within the next fortnight & election day to be in mid-October. It's six and a half weeks, that's what we're asking. I implore you to think about it, but, plainly,

---

[37] (b. 1934) Tory MP for Mole Valley, 1983-95. Chairman of the Party.
[38] Conservative Central Office.
[39] Neil Kinnock (b. 1942). MP for Islwyn and Leader of the Labour Party, 1983-95, and Prime Minister, 1991-5.

we must act with some degree of haste.' I yielded to that & said I'd get back to him. He left a number.

I don't need the hassle, it's a foolish proposal & it would disrupt everything. *Everything.*

Monday, 4 September
Heaven knows what made me do it. I was about to 'phone this Hardy to turn them down, but instead I rang Gyles. Just for the final second opinion, to cement the rejection… 'Kenneth! You *must* do it! You'd be marvellous! Can I help in any way?…' I was a bit flummoxed by the enthusiasm. 'I mean, politics is a branch of show business, after all. But it'd be a chance to sink your teeth into something important…' It was that comment that swayed me.

Went into Lou to discuss but she & Flo were playing Connect Four. Walked to Gordon & Rona. They were astonished, but tickled. 'Och, you'll take to it like a duck to water,' said G., 'that gowk won't stand a chance!'

Telephoned Hardy & said yes. Within 20 mins. he rang back & said a car was coming at 1.45 to take me to CCO. Arrived & was whisked up the back stairs to Waterhouse's office. He pushed a scotch into my hand & bellowed 'The battle starts here!' He has a pronounced mole on the left cheek which is hard to take one's eyes off.

A timetable of events was produced & in came the 'campaign team' – spotty interns for the most part, from the double-barrelled surname set, barely out of short trousers. Within an hour I'd joined the Party, signed the nomination papers & (after a brief call) appointed Gyles as my agent!!… Ingham[40] came in & shook my hand. 'The Prime Minister is delighted you've accepted. Now let's give the reds a good kicking.' He's oafish, but amiable, in the manner of many a Yorkshireman. They're going to declare me on Wednesday. I'm to tell only those who need to know in the meantime. WC took me aside & said 'Campaigns aren't for the faint-hearted, but I know you'll have a ball.'

Car brought me back. It'll be the same car & driver throughout. Went into Lou & grilled the steaks & boiled the new potatoes. Explained it to her as simply as I could, but not convinced it went in. When Flo showed I knocked on Rupert & told him. Same face as Gording – shock mingled with mirth.

Sat by the window & watched the passers by. I must be completely loopy.

---

[40] Bernard Ingham (1932-2023). Mrs Thatcher's chief press secretary throughout her time as Prime Minister.

1989

Tuesday, 5 September
Got paper & did letters. One to a woman in Halifax who writes 'We don't see enough of you on the telly these days.' 'Just you wait, ducky,' I thought.

Rang Pat who was incredulous, then Stanley. 'Well, my boy, you never fail to surprise. That must be one of the shortest retirements on record!'

Walked to Francis at Dent. His face lit up & he said he'll put everything on hold. 'This'll make for a fantastic closing chapter!' Tube to Gyles. 'I got up early & started on a few speeches – what issues do you want to focus on?' He's more keyed up than I am! We made a list of priorities & ways to attack Wilkes without libelling. 'Of course, the rumours are all true,' said Gyles, 'but we can't repeat them. We've got to remember where the line is & never step over it.'

M. came & took me to Peter Mario where I gave him supper. He wasn't in the least surprised. 'I think this is the opportunity you've been waiting for. A chance to show them the other side of you…'

Wednesday, 6 September
Up at 7 o'c. Promptly out to get the riah[41] smartened. I said 'You look tired, Nick, were you *at it* last night, with the missus? Going full pelt, were you?' He laughed, uneasily. Lucas turned up with the car at 9.15. At CCO we went over speech, but it's to be pretty loose at this point. Gyles drove me to Camden & we waited in the motor. Listened to the announcement on the wireless in the car at midday. One could almost hear the newsreader rolling her eyes… As planned the press vans started pulling up at 12.20 & we did the interviews outside the Town Hall. It was frantic but all rather pleasant!! Was expecting derision & dismissal but they beamed up at me on the steps, microphones stretched out like proffered 99s. I gave them the guff about not wanting 'the constituency & city I've lived in & loved all my life' to be taken over by 'the Shadow Energy Minister's father-in-law'… One oik shouted 'What makes Willo the Wisp qualified to serve as an MP?' It was all rather gentle & good-humoured, but then with some of the bozos these journalists have to deal with, it must've been a pleasure for them to have me.

To Broadcasting House at 4.30 & recorded the piece with John Cole for the News at Six. He's a Labour sort, this Cole (ex-*Observer*), but said 'I'm astonished Kinnock's given the green light to Wilkes. The Tories have been cunning in sounding you out'… The office at Heath Hurst Rd is the

---
[41] Back slang, i.e. riah = hair.

headquarters. It's adjacent to a butcher's shop & there's a pervading smell of mince. They've a little room set up for me. I detected a few unconvinced purists from the blue-rinse brigade, but overall the reception was warm & we toasted with plastic cups of Pomagne. Whilst chatting to the volunteers, Gyles pulled me aside & said 'Foster's pulled forward the moving of the writ to Friday. Election day will be October 5th!'… It's outrageous, Dobson's barely cold. It's being done so that it's on the same day as the by-election in Fylde South. You'd think Wilkes would be better off standing *there*!! No skin off my nose, it means I'll only be needed for a month. Just as well – Lucas dropped me off *exhausted* at 8 o'c. Folder full of detailed stuff to read. It's futile; they don't want *detail* from me, just silly faces and bum gags. But I'll prove my worth given half the chance.

Went into Lou's flat & she was in her nightgown watching *Tenko*… 'Here's my boy!' she said, 'I thought you'd run away with the circus.' Made her a Horlicks & turned in.

Thursday, 7 September
They took me to Robertson's at Aldgate for photos for the leaflets & posters. The fellow nudged me familiarly & said 'I did the press pics for *Baskervilles*,[42] d'you remember?' 'Of course I do!' I said, 'you've not aged a day!'… I've never set eyes on the man before, but it's good practice for flanneling the electorate.

At Heath Hurst we went through the provisional hustings schedule & TV/radio requests. I imagine it's the calm before the storm.

Friday, 8 September
Got papers. Bill shouted 'You can count on my support, my right honourable friend!' & I waved. *The Times* isn't as impressed: 'Carry On Up The Commons – why are the political parties intent on becoming a laughing stock?'

Dobson's funeral today. The briskness of everything is a bit unseemly, especially having the writ moved on the same day as incumbent's cremation, but that's Labour's choice & blunder, not ours. *The Gazette* & the *Daily Telegraph* rang & I politely, but in no uncertain terms, told them not to ring the home 'phone but the campaign office for statements.

Gyles came & we went through the leisure centre speech. One gets the feeling GB would prefer to be delivering the lines himself, but his zeal is

---

[42] *The Hound of the Baskervilles* (1978), directed by Paul Morrissey. Peter Cook and Dudley Moore starred as Holmes & Watson, with KW as Sir Henry Baskerville.

catching. Went through Lou's tablets with Flo because Newton has upped the dosages. We watched the *Challenge Anneka* programme. The girl is a marvel. We could do with her on the campaign!!

Saturday, 9 September
Loads of letters of support!! Very funny note from Jeremy Swan[43]... Arrived at the hall[44] at 11.10. They gave us a cup of tea in the ladies' changing room while the camera people set up. Gyles bouncing around, loving it. I was cool as a cucumber. Went on at 11.55. Packed house, it was more akin to a rally. They loved the 'Maybe it's because I'm a Londoner' stuff. Less enthused when it came to defending Mrs T's record – might have to leave her out of future addresses and focus solely on local issues & Wilkes' character. Those who love the PM adore her, but there's no grey area – she's clearly *loathed* in equal measure. Mixed up the voice a bit: it's all very well sounding urbane, but it's the common touch that people warm to. Did a quarter of an hour & got off. Gyles said 'We got the level of jokes just about right... but don't be afraid to slow it down – you have the diction, but not everyone thinks at your speed'... A few journalists trying to catch me out – 'What do you *mean* about the Labour candidate's integrity', etc., but I managed not to step in anything. Lots of handshaking afterwards with well-wishers. I don't know if they'd been *told* not to request autographs, but I wasn't asked once! It felt more like a royal walkabout!

Sunday, 10 September
M. came & Rita helped me get Louie into his car. Ken Dodd was at the restaurant! 'It's Rambling Syd!'[45] he shouted & there was an unenthusiastic smattering of applause. 'Pitt the even Elder!' murmured one bright spark... KD came to the table & kissed Lou's hand. 'If your son can stop that pillock from getting in, Mrs Williams, it'll be free drinks for life on Merseyside.' I've never seen Wilkes's programme, *Getting Down the Banks*, but evidently it's made him rather unpopular in Liverpool, so he's been exiled & *we're* stuck with him.

---

[43] Irish director, producer and writer (b. 1943). Worked with KW on *Jackanory, Galloping Galaxies!* and *Aladdin & the Forty Thieves*.
[44] Somers Town community sports centre. Approximately 450 people attended.
[45] Rambling Syd Rumpo, a yokel folk-singer, played by KW in *Round the Horne*. Famous for his suggestive ballads.

Lucas took me to Spencer Rise at 4 o'c. to meet Angela Stevenson.[46] 'I was almost squeezed out,' she said – 'When *you* were confirmed they asked Clement Freud if he wanted to stand, but thankfully he told them where to go!'... Ritzy sort of girl, for a Liberal. We went over plan to surreptitiously funnel people her way, but she looked doubtful. 'The Tories could always step aside completely,' she said. I *think* she was joking.

Monday, 11 September
St Pancras hospital for the walk round. Hateful, with that permeating odour of excrement & death. Half the people I met will be brown bread by polling day, but Hardy insisted we press on as the staff are almost certainly all Labour. Did the Dr Tinkle stuff for the photographers & asked questions here & there, but it felt marvellous to be released.

Tuesday, 12 September
Lou feeling sick after breakfast, but Flo revived her with some hawthorn tea & the distraction of *Crosswits* on the television.

Lovely sunshine so went walking with the leafleters on old stomping grounds in Bloomsbury. Gyles said 'We're preaching to the converted here...' so we went to Camden & they set up a little soapbox, as if it were Speakers' Corner. All quite genial, tho' the spiel about 'having the highest respect for Angela Stevenson' is already sounding forced & unconvincing. Hardy wants that kind of talk dropped altogether, thinking it *disloyal* to the Party. It's madness – confidence is all very well, but he's the type of obstinate Tory who thinks we have the *right* to win everywhere.

Wednesday, 13 September
First *Gazette* poll. Lab 54, Lib 32, Con 12, Others 2... so whatever we're doing, it's not working. Gyles quietly dismayed, but tried not to show it.

Castlehaven day centre was alright (apart from the urine smell) but I refused the King's X flyering & fled to Peter Mario where Gianni gave Rupert & I a quiet table in the corner. He asked if I was enjoying it. The fact is, I am. It's much the same as a book tour, only without all the autographs. There is a downside: the realisation that I'm standing in a decrepit constituency inhabited by the dregs of society – or the *salt of the earth*, as I must remember to call them.

---

[46] Former editor of the *South Devon Gazette* (b. 1949), Liberal Democrat MP for Norwich East, 1995-2007.

Thursday, 14 September
St John's Community School in the morning. O! it was wonderful to be surrounded by such a troop of exuberant & beautiful children! All so well behaved & receptive to my larking about. Shame none of them can vote!!

Indian restaurant in Chalk Farm at lunch, in the face of my objections. Made the right noises, but just ate some of the plain bread for the camera; I'm not risking that spicy crap. Nice to meet the manager though, Mr Anand. There's no doubt about it, the Asians are assiduous & *very* business-minded. 'I came to this country when Mrs Thatcher got in,' he said. 'You tell her – meals are on the house if she wants to come.' I imagine it's the very last place she'd ever wish to dine, but to say that the immigrant classes are all in the Welsh windbag's pocket is clearly a fallacy.

They said I should do some door-knocking, but I put my foot down. I'm not doing it.

Friday, 15 September
Pat came at 8 o'c. She was smoking & I told her to extinguish it before I would let her in. She did but it was all very resentful. Told her not to smoke around Lou at her place 'cos it'll only make her want to pick it up again & she agreed, but I could sense the crossed fingers.

Car to Heath Hurst where Gyles & Andy (the cross-eyed one) were waiting for me. We rehearsed a dry run. 'Remember,' said Andy, 'there are a lot of Europeans in the borough – lay it on *very* thick that only you and Stevenson are pro the EEC.' Gyles suggested I try foreign tongues should the opportunity arise, but I said that'd smack of piss-taking. The practice was worthwhile though, as G. threw in a few questions about JW's reputation for womanising & it's good prep in the art of stealthily *implying* scandal.

Dashed home to change. Lucas arrived at 6.43 & we were at Grafton Rd by 7 o'c. Standing room only!! First time on the hustings that I've felt the butterflies!

This Wilkes is a piece of work. Blimpish, ruddy & plainly on the sauce. Got in a few well-received remarks but Ange didn't pick up the thread or interject at the right times & JW was let off the hook.

Saturday, 16 September
Telegram from Mags! She's in New York & had only just heard. She calls me her 'Bonar Law with bona lallies'… Wrote a reply & included one of the

flyers. Gordon rang & asked how it was going. 'Everyone's asking after you,' he said. Can't imagine who *everyone* is, but the succour is touching; I expected hostility from the profession.

A man shook my hand on York Way, smiled & said 'I'd no sooner vote for you than stick my head between my legs & kiss my own arse…' He strolled away, happy as Larry. When the insults are surreal, they're quite palatable. It's the bluntness of 'fascist dickhead' that is slightly more trying.

Sunday, 17 September
Telephone didn't stop ringing. I shall have to get the P.O. to change the number *again* which is maddening. Unplugged it & read some of the Doyle book on the French Revolution. Not bad if one were a student of the facts, but drier than dust.

Did the fish & potato-in-jacket on my own in Lou's flat & then a rest. Whist at Paul's at 8 o'c. I played with Jeff & Paul with Jean-Jacques. Jeff said 'It's a bit like sex, this game; if you don't have a good partner, you'd better have a good hand…' In point of fact, it was a quote half-pilfered from Mae West (who had been talking about bridge), but I let it go by. Paul related an exchange between two old dears he'd heard in the queue at Littlewood: 'What d'you think of that Kenneth Williams trying to be an MP?' – 'O! it's shocking!' came the reply. 'He should stick to *Treasure Hunt*, if you ask me…'[47]

Monday, 18 September
Camden market, bathed in sunshine. The autograph amnesty has come to an end; all the nellies were pouncing. Chrissie & Marcus had set up the trestle tables with balloons & handed them out to children. That got slightly nasty when a little boy cried as his furious mother forced him to give back the balloon – 'D'you think that bribing my kids is going to make up for that witch shafting the country?' it bellowed. I suppose I've been lucky thus far that there haven't been more incidents of this kind.

3 o'c. – Well, I spoke too soon. A *disgusting* bunch of youths came bounding up, throwing the wads of pamphlets to the pavement, shouting 'dirty queer', 'poncey actor' & other noxious insults. First time I've felt vulnerable during the process. The gang were marvellous, though, instinctively forming a shield wall around me.

---

[47] *Treasure Hunt*, Channel 4 game show (1982-9). Presented by Kenneth *Kendall*.

Put Louisa to bed then went for a night cap at Rupert's. He said 'Well, there's going to be ups and downs. Nevertheless, it's exciting – you must feel so *alive…*' Truthfully, I can't remember the last time I felt this awake. *The public*, whom I generally detest, are asking me *earnest* questions about council rates & vandalism & traffic, & not just making dreary requests for me to say 'stop messin' about'. The mundane honesty of it is quite revivifying. Of course, I ain't got all the answers, but they talk to me as a *man* & not a *cartoon*… O! it was delightful just to sit in silence on R.'s *chaise longue*, sipping Earl Grey with the eyes shut. After the drink he removed the jeans & I took it hard in the throat.

Tuesday, 19 September
Work is much more fun than fun. – Coward.

Wednesday, 20 September
Lou & Flo had *Breakfast Time* on when I went in, with the scrumptious footage of JW throwing a punch at the grinning protestor who chucked the egg at him. The look on Hattersley's[48] face is *priceless*. What a time for *him* to show up!! The offender is flanked by Labour placards – so it's clear that many of his own side are sickened with his selection.

Andy rang HQ with the latest poll at midday. MORI registers Lab 49, Lib 36, Con 13 – so it's moving in Angela's direction.

Thursday, 21 September
'Phone rang & it was Dr Chatham!! 'I've been following events & I just wanted to check you're not pushing things too hard. How are you feeling?'… It's uncommonly kind of him to bother to ring.

Car to Lambs Conduit St where I was given a tour of the new police precinct by Ch. Insp. Hewitt who dealt with me after the heist!! It was good as I was able to bring that into the chat with the reporters at the end: to portray myself as a victim of crime 'along with many of my fellow constituents', yet also to show how the government's investing in the Met locally with such a well-appointed new station… Gyles whispered 'Don't overdo it', as it's an easy goal for the other side to say that crime *levels* rest at Hurd's[49] door, but I think the point was successfully made.

---

[48] Roy Hattersley (b. 1932), Labour MP for Birmingham Sparkbrook, 1964-95; Deputy Labour Leader, 1983-95; Deputy Prime Minister, 1991-5.
[49] Douglas Hurd (b. 1930), Tory MP for Witney, 1983-95; Home Secretary, 1985-9; Foreign Secretary, 1989-91.

Andy sidled up as we were coming out & said 'Message from Number 10: The PM will be joining us for the King's X walkabout on Saturday!'... I won't deny it, I'm rather thrilled by the prospect.

Friday, 22 September
Freud writes & says 'You're the talk of the Liberal conference. You're in danger of becoming their new pin-up boy – that's if you don't count John Cleese, which I don't...'

Speech on *immigration* of all things at the Conservative Club. Lot of blather. If I'm asked to purchase *one more* raffle ticket at a function I shall scream. I can claim the money back on the budget afterwards, according to Marcus, but still.

(2 o'c. – I won a bottle of Estée Lauder Youth Dew in the raffle! Gave it to Lou.)

Saturday, 23 September
Was woken by the telephone at 9.35!! It must be catching up with me. It was Hardy to say car would be arriving at noon. Mrs. Thatcher will be joining us outside Camden T.H. for a chat to the assembled press for *seventeen minutes* at 1.13pm!!! I *know* one should be grateful for any time with the Iron Lady, but really...

Sharpies all over the shop. Andy said 'There are plainclothes officers everywhere.' Heart thudded as the limousine pulled up. Out she leapt, immaculate in cobalt blue. 'Take me to the battle!' she roared as she approached, enveloped by the men in grey. The aura is breathtaking, there's no question about it. She took my hand & fixed my gaze & said 'Kenneth – what a marvellous job you're doing...' And that was it! Toot suite she turned to the crowd & out came the rhetoric – *all* pro-herself rather than pro-me, but that's alright. Not a voter in sight, just cameras, cameramen, notetakers & suits. She dutifully went round the gang, rousing them. She shook my hand again for the photographers & was back in the car quicker than you could say 'Home, James!' – If one can be given as little as that & *still* be made to feel special, it's irrefutable that the woman is made of stardust. Returned to Heath Hurst for sandwiches & coffee.

Sunday, 24 September
TV-AM for chat with Anne Diamond. Gabbled on, but all in all a waste of time.

Monday, 25 September
We saw Angela on the television & she is rather good. Ashdown[50] patently rates her.

Didn't fancy HQ, so asked Gyles to come to the flat. We've planned to go all out on Rob Litany & the 'it's not what you know it's who you know' angle for the debate. G. said 'Have you been burgled?'… Just because one chooses not to plaster cheap prints of the Hay Wain or awful photographs of relatives across the walls, people think you're barmy. He asked to use the lavatory (which he knows I hate), & I *reluctantly* relented.

Library Theatre at 6.40. Sparser audience than before, but it's not surprising that people are getting fed up. Angela turned on me with regards to lack of experience, but I know the trick – she's trying to advance herself as the only serious candidate, & quite right too. Wilkes came out guns blazing, appearing too angry in my opinion, whatever his gripes with capitalism (not that free markets have done him any harm). As we came out, Chrissie handed me a note telling me to ring Paul immediately. Of course I thought *Lou*… I rang from the green room. Paul told me that Rupert had been stabbed as he was getting into his car on Cleveland Place & was at Barts & that it wasn't looking good. Lucas drove me & went with me up to intensive care. They wouldn't let me see him, but the doctor came & spoke with me. He was stabbed in the back below the left kidney & had lost 3½ pints of blood. He'd lain unconscious next to the car for quite a while & is now in a coma. Paul arrived just before Rupert's mother. There's nothing I could do, so we left her with the nurse. Lucas got us home at 10.40.

Tuesday, 26 September
Tried to sleep, but couldn't. Rang Gyles at 7 o'c. & asked him to get me out of everything today. Went into Lou & told her but she didn't know who I was referring to.

Porter let me in to R.'s flat & I got a few of his things together. Got cab to hospital & found Mrs Jarvis asleep in the waiting room. Fetched her a tea & asked what was going on. The matron said they were monitoring his condition, but there'd been no real change since admission. All we can do is wait. Mrs Jarvis said 'He'll be thirty-seven on Sunday.'

---

[50] Jeremy 'Paddy' Ashdown (1941-2018), a former Royal Marine, served as Leader of the Liberal Democrats, 1988-99.

Finally the doctor came & explained that he's stable & there are signs of consciousness, but they're not strong enough to be sure of anything yet. We were allowed in to see him. Ah, the poor boy. Pale like china, almost blue. Wired up to all manner of machines. I held his hand & smothered the waterworks. They wheeled him out for brain scans & we were told to go & get some rest. The nurse got R.'s key out of his trousers & I brought Mrs Jarvis back to Marlborough in the taxi & saw her indoors.

Rang Gyles. He said everything was under control, & they could do without me until 2 o'c. tomorrow. Went into Lou who was watching *Dad's Army*. I sat there, staring at the screen, but thinking only of him.

Wednesday, 27 September
Asked Paul to attend to Mrs Jarvis & he said 'Leave it to me'… Rang Barts but getting decent information is next to impossible. Gave the staff nurse the number of Andy's portable telephone in case anything urgent happens.

Went with Andy & Marcus to Spencer Rise where we waited for the numbers. Could tell Ange was getting a bit peeved by the focus pivoting to me, but then she craves that lark. Call came through at noon, & it's staggering: Lab 40, Lib 40, Con 18!! Angela's eyes were wide as saucers. There was a disbelieving mood of euphoria, which I very nearly got caught up in. Think it's best that I don't come again; they've vetted the need-to-knows, but things tend to slip out, no point in over-egging the pudding.

2 o'c. to the Armitage Shanks factory on St Pancras Way. Ludicrous, like being back on the set of *At Your Convenience* – only even bleaker. Gave the speech & shook the hands, but heart not in it. In any case, half the people there looked as tho' they'd struggle to *write* 'X', even if one did guide their hand towards a ballot paper.

Gyles said 'That's enough for today – go & get some shuteye'… Lucas dropped me at the hospital. He's in a private room & is out of immediate danger. Only stopped for ten minutes due to the frightful odour, but kissed him on the cheek before I left.

Thursday, 28 September
As I came out I heard Lou & Flo laughing hysterically. Heaven knows what they find to talk about, but I ain't complaining… Knocked on Mrs Jarvis but got no answer. Paul already out too, so put a note in, thanking him for yesterday.

Leafleting in the morning. The flyers double as ready-made autograph album pages – never mind collectors' items, you won't be able to *give* them away when this is all over. The reactions are fascinating. There are a few who see their borough being callously used in some mad celebrity experiment & loathe it; there are some who hate me on principle because of the queue element; there are a few who take me seriously; there are a few who don't take me seriously but take to me; & there are loads who couldn't give two hoots.

To HH to prepare for last debate. Message from Paul when I got there that Rupert's being taken down for emergency op to remove a kidney. Said he'd ring again if any news. Couldn't concentrate, but we went through the plan. I'm to criticise Lab *and* Lib policies to put down any rumours of collusion. Not that there's been much of that, *I've* done all the work.

St Pancras Church at 6.40. Wholly inappropriate venue. I started badly & it got worse when Wilkes seemed to get traction by attacking me personally. The fickle louts in the crowd were loving his 'impression' of me. Felt totally out of my depth & just wanted to get away. Looked at Gyles who made the 'breathe deeply' signal, & I'd just about recovered the countenance when JW said 'At the end of the day, it's people like *that* who are ruining the fabric of our community…' Well, it was red rag to a bull.

'First of all, Mr Wilkes, it's not your community,' I said. 'I've lived in this constituency since 1926 – I know these people because I *am* one of them. We're a varied bunch, from all walks of life, & your archaic, intolerant, Victorian values have no place here, in the greatest city in the world. I was up half the night at the hospital bedside of a dear friend, a man who spends all his time guarding the lives of others, but is now fighting for his own after being brutally stabbed in the street, undoubtedly by someone holding views very similar to your own. I've no idea what *you* were doing last night – perhaps it involved punching an elector – but I'm quite sure the people of *my* community can use their imaginations'… I've never heard such applause. I sashayed off the dais in great hauteur, leaving JW with egg all over the face (though he should be used to that by now!) & Ange not knowing what to do… 'By the left,' said Gyles, 'The boy's a natural. It's the greatest turnaround since the second Punic War.'

Friday, 29 September
He's opened his eyes!! Nurse Evans rang at 8 o'c. to say he was groggy but conscious & understood it all. She told me to hold off visiting until the evening. Went up to his mother & the *relief* was etched across the face.

Beyond Our Kenneth

On the way to Smith Sq, Lucas said 'You've set some tongues wagging!' – a full report of the meeting was in the *Daily Mirror* of all papers, & they each carry the image of JW looking thoroughly cheesed off. I come across as very much the virtuous man of the people! It's mad.

Telly afternoon outside CCO. Mostly questions about the 'scourge of personality politics'. As if there has ever really been any other kind. Cole for the Beeb, Brunson for ITN & that awful Crick for Channel 4.[51] They surveyed me with the look of men planning to harangue their bosses for having to stoop so low.

Finally got to Rupert as he was eating something for the first time since Monday lunch. He got quite weepy; I think his mother had told him that I'd been popping in. Ordered him to stop that nonsense & hurry up & get better.

Saturday, 30 September
Sweet letter from Tom Conti.[52] Says he's going to vote for me – not because he knows me, but because my reasoning has convinced him of the socialists' vicious, hostile spirit... Private poll still puts Lab & Lib neck-and-neck – but the opinions were taken before my little outburst, so it's quite obsolete.

Sunday, 1 October
After a brief breakfast to rally the troops, Andy said I could have the rest of the day off. M. came & collected Lou & we drove to Havering-atte-Bower for a lovely lunch at the Royal Oak there. Lou said 'I haven't had lamb as tasty as that since the war' – I doubt the endorsement shall entice Zagat to come a-nibbling, but she was suited.

Back by 4 o'c. Note on the mat from Mrs Jarvis saying he had a full meal today (including some birthday cake) & that someone has come forward with a description of the knifeman. Did Welsh rabbit & we watched *Songs of Praise*. It had some of Lou's favourites – 'Great Is Thy Faithfulness', 'O God Our Help', 'And Can It Be' – and we both belted them out with élan.

---

[51] John Cole, Michael Brunson (b. 1940; former political editor for ITN) and Michael Crick (b. 1958; founding member of the Channel 4 News team in 1982, subsequently the political editor of BBC2's *Newsnight*).

[52] Scottish actor (b. 1941). Friend and neighbour of Gordon Jackson and his family.

Monday, 2 October
Mr Hardy said at the pep-talk meeting that 'I'll come clean & say that there were a fair few members who were appalled at your enforced selection… May I say that many have come up to me since & said they feel thoroughly ashamed. You're the best candidate we've had since Johnson-Smith…'[53] Praise indeed.

The general feeling is that it's going to be very close. The continued chatter about my speech might result in a few votes coming my way, but *at the expense* of Angela, which could ironically see JW home.

At Vecchia, Stanley said 'I've always thought it, but this tops it. You're a brave wee lad.'

Tuesday, 3 October
Thumbs-up-style photos with Lou outside the block for *Gay Times*. Swung by Bart's *en route* to HH. R.'s in a public ward now, so only stayed two minutes. Gave him the chocolates & a belated birthday card from Louie… Collected banners & placards & did the schmoozing at Russell Square. Heard one old dear squawk 'O! for Christ's sake! When will it be *over*?' – I know how she feels!! Andy used his brick to 'phone Lucas to come & get us at Regent St.

Marcus & Sam kept nipping off to make & take calls back at HQ, as there were suggestions that the *Standard* was going to break something big… We only got an hour's notice before press, but the implications are *colossal* – 'My gay affair with Wilkes in £2 million love nest'… The Yugoslavian boy has told Oliver Jackson *everything*.

Within five minutes *all* the 'phones were ringing, pagers bleeping, everyone thrashing about rabidly. I thought 'sod this' & went for a walk.

At 5 o'c. it was decided I should do *one* interview for the BBC, rather than face the pack. They replaced Cole with Jill Dando, which pleased me. I said 'If there is a story here, gender isn't it. Moral judgment *is*.' In the car GB was quiet until he said 'This throws *everything* up in the air… Are you prepared for how the pieces might land?'

Wednesday, 4 October
Last day of the campaign. Saw a bit of *Good Morning Britain* with Lou. JW has denied it, which is all he *can* do I suppose. Saw Paul & he said he would

---

[53] Geoffrey Johnson-Smith (1924-2010). Presenter of the BBC's magazine programme *Tonight* in the late 1950s, and afterwards Tory MP for Holborn & St Pancras South, 1959-64.

accompany me to the count tomorrow; M. is coming too. Pat is going to sit with Louisa. Telephoned the hospital & he is able to stand by the bed unaided, which bucked me up… Lucas arrived at 10 o'c. & we went to CCO. Waterhouse all over me like a cheap suit. The amount of brandy they get through is horrifying.

'Phone call from Gavin at Gallup at 11.48 – Lab 36, Lib 35, Con 27… 'Crikey,' said the boy Hague,[54] which pretty well summed it up. That only represents my gains from the church speech – *goodness knows* what the Yugoslav's allegations will have done. 'Tito's Totty' they call him. Cheers went round the room, but after studying the numbers, the din was reduced to a murmur – the Liberal dip is quite concerning, but all bets are off now.

Back to the flat & had a rest. Gordon rang. 'Rona & I could weep, we're so proud…'

Spoke to Flo. Asked her how she thinks it's going. 'I love to help your mother,' she said. Proposed the idea of her staying on privately if something were to happen to me. I kept it nebulous, and she didn't dismiss it out of hand. Once upon a time the notion of someone coming *between* me & Louie would've been preposterous. Now it's in the order of heavenly manna, and the *only* solution.

GB 'phoned at 9 o'c. 'I shan't get soppy, but I just want to say how much I've enjoyed doing this with you. It's been one of the most thrilling experiences of my life…' I thanked him & told him he was a natural, because he is – in truth he's *far* more suited to the cut-and-thrust of it than me.

Thursday, 5 October
Did beds whilst Louie watched & we played 'I spy'. I howled when her little eye spied something beginning with 'f' & it turned out to be the *fermostat*!!

At 10 o'c. Brandreth arrived & collected us. Cameras outside the polling station & we had to do the grins. I shan't miss that! Idiotic questions. 'How are you feeling?', 'Do you feel nervous?' – No one seems concerned with what one *thinks* nowadays, only how one *feels*… At 10.22 I voted for the Liberals. Reflected in the booth that I may be the only candidate in history not to vote for himself. Typically, Lou forgot the plan & cast her vote for me. She said to the *London Plus* girl 'It was lovely to see my Ken's name on the whatsitcalled…' 'Ballots,' said Gyles. 'Same to you!' came her retort –

---

[54] William Hague (b. 1961). Tory MP for Richmond (Yorks), 1989-2015. Conservative Leader and Prime Minister, 1999-2014.

1989

straight out of a Tolly Rothwell[55] script. She can still turn it on for the cameras, the daffy old moo.

Had the lamb cass., then had a rest. Buzzer at 2 o'c: flowers & a card from Barbara & the dish husband!... Pat arrived at 4 o'c. & we had sparkling wine in Lou's flat. Flo arrived & had a glass with us.

Lucas brought me to Heath Hurst at 6 o'c. Slipped him twenty pounds in an envelope with a signed snap as he has been faultless... Did the thank you speech in the office & Hardy presented me with a lovely group portrait of the team in a silver frame. Tellers kept popping in reporting that turnout seems to be high for a by-election & that we are getting out the vote.

Returned to telegrams from dear Jeremy and Richard & Patricia Pearson. Mrs J. had put a beautiful note from Rupert through the door. Pat served the Scotch broth & rolls as I'd requested at 8.15.

Cleaned the shoes & dressed in the blue suit. Paul knocked at 9.30 precisely. Said goodnight to Lou & Pat pinned on my rosette. M. arrived just as Paul & I reached the street & we were welcomed by one lone photographer.

Arrived at the town hall amidst the well-wishers & ill-wishers as they were bringing in the boxes. The verification process under way. Our group was congregated near the fire escape at the back, presumably chosen by Hardy so he could nip out for fags. The boys swarmed the tables with their clipboards. Little Tom came over, eyes wide: 'It's bloody close.' I perused the process, but couldn't really follow it. Gyles flying round, every bit the excited little boy. As they stacked the piles of votes, it became clear that we are virtually neck & neck – & *neck*: the Lab, Lib & Con piles looking identical. Wilkes was nowhere to be seen until about midnight, dodging the journalists & heading for the anteroom with the awful Litany & the entourage in ill-fitting polyester suits. Ange furiously biting the fingernails every time I looked.

Andy brought us into the library at 1 o'c. & gave us corned beef & pickle sandwiches. M. plonked himself in a wingbacked recliner & had a nap. At 1.45 Gyles was invited to the returning officer's bench. Saw them poring over figures, GB gesticulating & shaking his head profusely. Chrissie casually sidled up to them to try & earwig the conference. She scuttled back grinning from ear to ear. The upshot is that JW leads by *eleven* votes – over

---

[55] Talbot Rothwell (1916-81), English screenwriter. His credits include seven *Carry On* films. The quip delivered by KW in *Carry On Cleo* ("Infamy! Infamy! They've all got it in for me!") was voted the greatest one-liner in film history in a poll by Sky Movies in 2007.

me. Without my authorisation, GB demanded a recount, which was approved. 'What about Angela?' I said. 'She's about five hundred behind. I don't know what to say. It's as close as it can possibly be.' Before the cameras could descend, I fled to the lav & was v. nearly sick.

Composed myself & came back. The counters looked thoroughly cheesed off as the recount was announced, the activists from all sides scampering about feverishly. Caught Ange's eye. A broken woman.

Paul told me to sit in the library, but I couldn't keep still. The R.O. showed us the spoiled ballots. Gyles argued for every single one... Cadged a fag from Hardy & frantically puffed on it in the yard. The condemned man. Tried to hold in the tears but couldn't. At 3.17 we were called again. A Conservative lead of *eighteen* votes. GB nearly keeled over. JW's agent, the one with the Bullen-esque sixth finger, demanded a further recount, much to the R.O.'s displeasure. At half past he announced it from the stage – for everyone to go home & return at 11 a.m. So after *all that*, we're back in square one.

M. drove Paul & me home in silence. Made some warm milk in Lou's flat as the dawn broke.

Friday, 6 October
It started at the crack of dawn, so I unplugged the 'phone. Saw the boat in the bathroom mirror: unalloyed Macmillan, all puffy & droopy, a veritable collapsing soufflé.

Gyles came at 9.30. 'Unless it's a dead heat, this will be the last count... I know we didn't plan for this outcome. But you're duty bound if you get over the line.' I didn't say anything. Just took the Andrews & he followed me out.

The whole lot outside, even RTBF from *Belgium*! It's exhausting, looking happy...

Wilkes appeared about as fresh & rested as me. They unstacked the neat bundles & began again from scratch. The familiar suspect slips laid out like exhibits at a trial. The Labour constituency chap looked about ready to have a coronary. I think the team thought I was just nervous & hopeful, rather than desperate & nauseous. I left them to their illusions.

The cheesed-off R.O. gathered us round & told us that was that, *this* was the result. Wilkes stormed out & Ange stood shell-shocked, the face a proverbial smacked arse.

Assembled, *sans* Wilkes, on the stage.

>Alton, John Dennis (Revolutionary Communist) – 26
>Bourne, Eric Antony (Liberal) – 230
>Forest, Sherwood (Monster Raving Loony) – 30
>Hilton, Rachael Anne (Save the Whales) – 0
>Hoyle, Barbara Genevieve (National Front) – 99
>Jackson, Ernest Peter (Green) – 43
>King, Patricia Ann (Christian Alliance) – 21
>Matters, Leonard (Fellowship) – 19
>Morton, Ian (Raving Loony Green Giant) – 8
>Singh, Baljit (The Chicken Party) – 37
>Stevenson, Angela Louise (Social & Liberal Democrats) – 12,735
>Wilkes, John Timothy (Labour) – 13,246
>Williams, Kenneth Charles (Conservative) – 13,250
>>Majority – 4
>>Turnout – 39,744 (56.3%)

I'm not sure how I got through the speech. Short and sweet, but it was so drowned out by the din that it didn't matter reely.[56]

Gyles immediately roaring into Andy's telephone, & I was diverted into the robing room before the press could get near. Labour will *appeal*, citing "monstrous irregularities". Andy said 'We'll do Auntie & ITN, then floor it to Smith Square...'

Met by the bewildered faces at CCO, as the chars hurriedly dusted off champagne flutes. Haven't felt so alone since that first night at Carlisle Castle.[57] Got through the stilted welcomes & congratulations alright, for the

---

[56] KW's victory speech: 'Mr Returning Officer, ladies and gentlemen... As you might imagine, this sensational result, as marvellous as it is, will take some time to penetrate, if you'll pardon the expression. I can't pretend not to be shocked, despite my conviction that I have the best team and put forward the best plan of action for the constituency, and I think that sense of surprise is shared by many here this morning. I should like to thank all of those that have dedicated themselves to getting the votes counted in as orderly a fashion as possible, despite the late night and the recounts, and that includes the police and all the officials here today. All I can promise is that I'll do my level best for you. Thank you to all those that have supported me.'

[57] In 1944, following assessment by an Armed Forces medical board, KW was sent to Carlisle Castle for military training.

newsmen. Then into the bowels of the building. Waterhouse looking perplexed. 'I've spoken to Edmonds. They're livid & think they've got a case.' It concerns *five* spoiled papers counted for me which they contest.

Gyles pulled me into the lavatory. 'You must try to enjoy it. You may only have a few weeks, who can say? But if I know you – you'll leave your mark.' Lucas drove me home to tell Louisa… Had a long soak and went to bed.

Saturday, 7 October
I suppose, in the end, it was always a possibility. Pretending it was a typical campaign, following the tried & tested measures, is ludicrous. But the look on the faces at Central Office confirmed to me that *no-one* saw this coming.

Gordon & Rona arrived at midday & fussed over Lou. Rang Rita & told her not to bother coming. Gordon gave me the new Hennessy book *Whitehall* & said 'That should explain who to avoid & who to charm…' Paul met us at Peter Mario at 12.45. They all charged the glasses to me, apart from Louisa, who was annoyed at missing her bloody Arthur Negus programme on the television. I wouldn't mind, but the man's dead. Rona distracted her from that, god love her. Embarrassingly, instead of the gateau, they brought over a cake in the shape of the door of Number 10 & the whole place sang 'For he's a jolly good fellow' – all Paul's doing, the rotter. Revolting inch-thick icing, so told the waiter to have it cut up & distributed among the staff.

At 4 o'c. the buzzer went & it was Mrs Jarvis back with Rupert. The ambulance men slowly got him up the stairs & into bed. Whilst mother was making the tea he said 'I'm so very proud of you. I know you don't really want it, but it's yours now. I'll be stuck here for weeks, so let's do it together, alright?' I haven't felt such unalloyed gratefulness for years & years. And they keep calling *me* brave! Went & got the cufflinks from my bedside drawer, discarded the note, & presented them to him.

Sunday, 8 October
Gyles rang. 'It's back to real life for me… Don't worry, they'll match you up with the right people, there are some very good eggs in parliament…' 'Yes,' I said, 'most of 'em pickled.'

It's mild so walked to the Rose Gardens & sat on a bench. Hardly anyone about, just an elderly couple who smiled as they passed. Told Lou that I'll be very busy & *out* a lot of the time. 'I don't mind, as long as I've got my

Flo.' I ought to be thankful & not jealous, but I can't help it. The indifference of the comment was severely cutting.

I'm terrified, of course, but I shall embrace it. I was never a beauty & never allowed to be clever, not properly – they'd crack the gates ajar but then demand a bum-gag. But this is different & fresh. I have to remind myself: Death was standing there, holding open the door & beckoning me through – but the truth is, I haven't thought about Him for ages. I've not had the time.

Monday, 9 October
Woke at 5.30 & attempted the Weetabix, but the *fluttering* wouldn't permit more than a few spoonfuls… Caught the 88 to Westminster. Empty satchel on my lap, like an urchin on the first day of term. Renton's[58] secretary met me at the Carriage Gates, took me past the police officers & into the members' entrance. Handed me my badge – 'Temporary Pass', which speaks volumes. Then her pager thing bleeped, so I was left alone in the members' lobby, feeling very small & *very* out of place. Winston's statue peered down at me, hands on hips in the famous pose, looking decidedly unimpressed. Gatiss,[59] the winner in Fylde, sidled up & said 'Ah, my fellow new boy! What *have* we let ourselves in for?' – it's a salient point: I've not the first *clue* what I'm doing here. 'Shall we make a pair?' he said. Told him I didn't follow, & he explained that it's best to pair up with an opponent early on, so votes can be ducked. Seemed pointless to make enemies on the first morning, even socialist ones, so I agreed.

Eventually Bob Dunn[60] appeared. 'It's my job to find you an office. Which isn't an easy task,' he said. 'But Peterson's[61] got a desk for you. He's a fan of your *(long pause!)*… work. But he's very wet – so, word of advice, don't cock your leg at the first lamppost.' He took me through a maze of corridors & staircases to this Peterson's office. The place changes from gothic & majestical to beige & humdrum in just a few turns. Eyes glaring

---

[58] Timothy Renton (1932-2020), Tory MP for Mid Sussex, 1974-95. Conservative Chief Whip, 1989-91.
[59] Leonard Gatiss (1947-2001), Labour MP for Fylde South, 1989-2001. Killed on Flight 93 during the September 11 attacks.
[60] Robert Dunn (1946-2003), Tory MP for Dartford, 1979-91.
[61] Maurice Peterson (b. 1939), Tory MP for Eskdale, 1970-99. Shadow Home Secretary, 1991-5.

from every window… *he's* arrived. The imposter. The trivial nance. All gut-wrenchingly uncomfortable.

Maurice is amiable. Omi-polone I'd say. 'My dear Mr Williams, you're most welcome!' he said. Showed me the space set aside for me & then gave me the tour of important places – the vote office, the Post Office, the message board, the tea-room, the smoking room, the members' dining room & Annie's Bar (to be avoided at all costs, apparently). 'Don't fret,' he said. 'Until further notice, ask Sarah, & she'll sort you out. She knows everything & I've told her to give you anything you want.' Sarah has hints of a young Fenella Fielding – but I'm glad of an ally, eek[62] notwithstanding.

Renton came in & introduced himself. 'I am the Chief Whip' he said, in a very John-chapter-8-verse-12[63] kind of way. Ushered me down to the Public Bill Office & told me about the procedure. Collected the certificate confirming my election, thence to the Commons. Gatiss was there, apprehensive. In I went, with a suitably grand & solemn expression. All the beady eyes looked on as Renton & Dunn walked me from the Bar (the white line on the floor) to the table clerk who handed me the bible & the card: *I Kenneth Charles Williams do swear that I will be faithful and bear true allegiance to Her Majesty Queen Elizabeth, her heirs & successors, according to law. So help me God.* I signed the Test Roll & then the Clerk of the House introduced me to Bernard Weatherill.[64] He extended the hand, & I reciprocated, expecting a mere pleasantry… 'We have met before,' he said. 'Burma '46, just before I was demobbed. You gave your Felix Aylmer to us in Rangoon.' I couldn't believe it!! Threw me a bit, & I think my cackle threw the Clerk, but he guided me behind the Speaker's chair & they took my signature again. The snooty old fart secretary said 'May I ask how you wish to be known in House documents? Not Rambling Syd, I hope.' The contempt dripped from every syllable. 'Just call me Kenneth Williams,' I said, 'and I shall try & think of something to call you.' Foolish perhaps, but I refuse to be awed by the *place* or the Establishment hangers-on. O! I don't know, the whole thing is so wacky… Escaped to Sarah who told me the basics of what to do & when. She's a dab hand & is going to be invaluable. Maurice has been here donkey's years, so with any luck he won't mind me

---

[62] Contraction of back slang; i.e. eek – ecaf = face.
[63] John 8:12 – 'Again Jesus spoke to them, saying, "I am the light of the world…"'
[64] (1920-2007) Tory MP for Croydon North East, 1964-91; Speaker of the House of Commons, 1983-91.

commandeering her until I get my own Sarah, if I'm here long enough to require one.

Renton came in with a handwritten note for me. 'Welcome to the team. Margaret.' I resent teams, and I've no desire to be on one.

Tuesday, 10 October
It's all a bit meet & greet. Various members coming to introduce themselves, but mainly to have a gawp. The instantly obvious thing to notice is how many of them *despise* each other – as in dodging people in corridors & avoiding eye contact. Peterson's only too happy to acquaint me with friends (fruits, mainly), whereas enemies have to advance themselves. Sarah handed me a recent Erskine May – I'm expected to wade through all the rules quicksticks.

First hurdle was Prime Minister's Questions. Didn't know about the prayer cards which act as seat reservers, so in the event I was awkwardly shoved up the back next to other nonentities. The clamour is abominable, like a borstal assembly before the warden appears. Lots of pointing at one from the opposite benches. I blew one of them a kiss, which they seemed to enjoy. The noise & proximity to others is frightful… The frisson when *she* entered was palpable. Akin to when Ingrid came into the rehearsal room that first time for *Brassbound*. Felt so very out-of-place – an unwelcome curiosity, erroneously taking up a seat. But, for all that, I freely admit: it is *exciting*. The green benches v uncomfortable though, the bum benumbed & cold after only half an hour.

Portaloo[65] came up to me in the lobby. Eminently graceful & absorbing. He's Enfield. 'Anything you want to know, or any help you need, my door is open,' he said.

More induction in the afternoon, & getting in with some of the clerks. Torrence, the fat one with the Chaplin moustache is a Hancock buff, so evidently I can do no wrong. He instructed me with 'If you're addressing an ex-soldier you should say the *gallant* member, for a lawyer it's the *learnèd* member, and for a churchman it's the *reverend* member.' 'And for an actor?' I asked. 'Oh, I dunno,' he said, '…the male member?'

My whip is Townend.[66] Think I shall find it difficult to take orders from such a man.

---

[65] Michael Portillo (b. 1953), Tory MP for Enfield Southgate, 1984-99. Leader of the Opposition, 1991-5. Latterly a broadcaster and journalist.

[66] John Townend (1946-2019), Tory MP for Howden, 1983-99. Assistant government whip, 1988-91.

Home at 6 o'c. Went in to Rupert. Coming on leaps & bounds, but still a bit wobbly & the tablets make him giddy. I related the events of the day. He's started a list of colleagues we esteem & those we don't, ones who could be useful &c. His sister is coming to stay until the weekend, so I said I'd pop in again on Sunday.

Wednesday, 11 October
Breakfasted with Lou. Spoke to Flo & she accepted the figure I suggested. She will come Mondays to Fridays from 10 o'c. to 6 o'c. Lou can still manage her own breakfast, so that should work out for the time being. I'm to tell Flo in advance or by 'phoning if I'm to be back in time to dine. It's a wrench & I'm far from sure about it, but if it prevents Louisa going in to an OPH, then this is the compromise.

Letter from Gatiss confirming the 'pairing' agreement, so at least I won't be stuck in Parliament at nights voting – though even this has to be approved by a whip!! I *know* I'm going to come a cropper with all this control lark.

It's as though I'm late to the ball – one I wasn't invited to in the first place. The other new recruits learnt the ropes in '87; I'm so far behind that there doesn't seem much point in trying to catch up, not on their terms anyway. I shall have to plough my own furrow.

Friday, 13 October
Up at 6 o'c. & got paper. Wilkes is determined to get the revote, though the cat's out of the bag re. his private life, & the tabloids aren't holding back. Lots of lurid details.

The sheer amount of mail is mystifying. Huge bundles of it. Endless invitations to events, receptions & functions, as well as the begging letters for TV appearances. They must think I have power! *Power*?! I keep having to be reminded where the lavatories are!!

Lunched in the over-the-top Churchill Room with Sir Hugh Simons.[67] It's outrageous that I should be invited to break bread with a Minister of the Crown so soon, but the place is manifestly *crawling* with irons. The self-loathing types, generally. Wilkes would certainly fit in. I'm taken with Sir Hugh, though. Lots of flattery. 'The place is *crying out* for someone who can deliver a message the way you do,' he said – 'Here, have another!', filling my

---

[67] Sir Hugh Fortescue Simons (1925-96). Tory MP for North Essex, 1966-91. Secretary of State for Social Security, 1988-90.

glass. It's no wonder so little gets done; they're all pissed as farts most of the time.

Went & sat in on the race relations debate. Only about 30 people in there, all white. Some of them don't half love the sound of their own voice. Slowly learning the flow of the procedure & the giving way decorum & so on. Peterson says that it's conventional to leave a bit of time before making one's maiden speech, but that mightn't be viable in my case, so I pondered on themes as they droned on about minorities… Lots of workmen in the lobby carting equipment about – televising the House starts next week. Townend said 'I dare say *you'll* be right at home with all this?' – evidently he doesn't approve. With *his* alopecia, neither would I.

Met Stanley at Peter Mario at 7 o'c. He wanted to hear all the details, but I just wanted him to talk about anything *but*. He's rehearsing for panto at the King's. The moaning about his director & the trudging around a field he has to do was tremendously comforting.

Saturday, 14 October
Letter from Aunt Phyllis. Usual illiterate scrawl, ostensibly congratulating me but in reality entreating me to budge her up the housing list. Straight in the bin… After lunch Rita helped me get Louie downstairs & we attempted a stroll to the park, but it was hopeless, even with two sticks. She tried, bless her, but I think the time for a wheelchair has come. It makes sense as she won't have to look at the feet all the time, & she can be moved ten times quicker.

Waterhouse rang. 'How was the first week?' he asked. I said 'I feel like Lady Jane Grey… proclaimed to the people, but now waiting for everyone to realise their mistake, switch sides & grind their choppers.'

Sunday, 15 October
Papers all reporting the Zimbabwean tanks pouring into Limpopo *en route* to Pretoria. Endless images of dead white farmers on the roadsides. All backed by Moscow, of course. Gorby just the mouthpiece now, this Vladimir Vstavlyat[68] seems to be holding the reins. Honecker has been ordered to revoke the passports of the newly resettled Boers & deport them all!! Heaven knows what Mandela would've thought of it all, he must be turning over in his grave.

---

[68] Vladimir Vladimirovich Vstavlyat (b. 1952). Leader of the Soviet Union, 1990-7. Tried at the Hague for war crimes, 2002.

Beyond Our Kenneth

Went up to Rupert & we played Scrabble, ate naff chocolates & went over maiden speech draft.

Monday, 16 October
Sarah gave me a list of potentials for staff. Recommends this chap Harry Boardman as a P.A., apparently did good work for Brittan.[69]

Talked to Townend & set next Tuesday afternoon for the speech, if the Speaker is in accord. Just after PMQs, so hopefully there'll be a good few people hanging around to hear it, & Sarah said she'll tell Sky & ITN who, with any luck, will stick around.

The Prime Minister & the entourage passed through the Commons corridor, everyone turning and facing her like flowers towards the sun. Some worship her (the swains). Some pretend to worship her (the gold diggers). Some clearly *detest* her (the rest).

Wednesday, 18 October
Nightmare getting in, thanks to this protest about S. Africa… But what can *we* do? Europe won't act as they're basically sympathetic to the coloured population, as is the Commonwealth, *we* can't do anything alone & Dukakis is too busy bumbling through the aftermath of Black Friday… Maurice thinks we should offer the white refugees asylum. Another reason – together with the halitosis – that I hope Dunn can find me my own office as soon as possible.

Thursday, 19 October
Stacks of post from constituents. They're going to be a pain in the arse, I can tell. How are you meant to *achieve* anything if all you're doing is writing replies to begging letters? Went to Portillo & he gave me tea. 'Don't worry about the voters,' he said, 'you're here now. Let your staff take care of that.' ('What fucking staff?' I thought)… 'May I offer some advice? You'll attract the limelight because of who you are. Words are your passion, everyone knows it. *Use* them to your full advantage. And be selective – being *busy* isn't the same as being *productive*.' He's right. Bugger the detail, bugger Mrs Jones with the noisy neighbour, bugger Mr Smith with the subsidence problem; my strengths can paint much wider strokes – if the telly people want me, they can have me, on *my* terms, and at the taxpayers' expense.

---

[69] Leon Brittan (1939-2015). Tory MP for Richmond (Yorks), 1983-8. European Commissioner, 1989-99.

Friday, 20 October
To Heath Hurst. Hardy not there (he's having a false knee put in), but the welcome was warm. This Harry Boardman chap arrived for the interview. Can't be much more than twenty-five, very much the plum in the mouth, but obviously v. capable. Think it's best to get someone who knows more than me, as I can leave a lot of the dull stuff for them. He's off to a well-paid "think tank" job in Washington next August, but said 'If I can declutter your path in the meantime, I'm ready to get stuck in.' In point of fact, he was immediately useful: Carole sought to offload a pile of grievances on to me, but HB masterfully deflected her with his achingly syrupy charm & I escaped... At the House, memo from Dunn saying my office will be ready on Monday morning – enclosed a *map* of how to reach it!! First proper division in the afternoon. I supported the government on lowering student grants. Should be done away with altogether – people don't pay their taxes so these scruffy layabouts can spend all day with their arses in the marmalade whilst little old ladies go without.

Faulds[70] came up & talked to me. We talked about Tony, but the conversation felt forced & somewhat unfriendly.

Saturday, 21 October
Came out of the post office & bumped into Hugh Paddick[71] & partner!! HP looked marvellous – scarcely believed it when he said he's 74! 'What are you doing for lunch?' he asked. I said 'Nothing', so we went to Montebianco & luckily they had a table... 'Next year will be my last in the business,' said Hugh. 'I've had enough, & we prefer just to potter in the garden nowadays.' I suppose that's what *I* should be doing, not that I've ever had a garden. The boyfriend said 'Isn't it *exhausting*, being an MP?' – I said 'Not thus far, I haven't *done* anything. Still feels as tho' I'm on bob-a-job week... Though half of them are queue; it's like the Spartan[72] in there.' HP said 'All the Wilkes stuff is true.' Evidently he used to bring the Yugoslav trade with him *on location* – Sally Douglas once caught him getting the plate of ham in the

---

[70] Andrew Faulds (1923-2000), Labour MP for Warley East, 1974-95; former actor – a key member of Ken Russell's repertory company in the 1970s, also appeared in the TV version of *Hancock* in the episode 'The Radio Ham' (1961).
[71] English actor (1915-2000). Worked with KW on *Round the Horne*, performing the part of Julian in the 'Julian & Sandy' sketches.
[72] The Spartan, a gay club on Tachbrook Street, SW1.

back seat of his Austin Montego… A girl came over asking me to sign. 'Who's it to?' I said… When she went away, HP said 'Blimey, you've changed. Once upon a time you'd have told her to piss off!' & he's right!! I must be slipping!

Sunday, 22 October
M. came & drove us to Vecchia Milano. Rita catered for Louisa… Roads jammed because these African protests drag on, so we got out at Mansfield Street & walked. Told M. about the speech & the focus on crime. He was in favour but said 'Won't Hurd's people come down on you like a ton of bricks for upsetting the apple cart?'… I explained that I didn't care if they did. I really don't. The beauty of all this is that I'm *not* a politician. It wouldn't matter to me if I were ousted tomorrow. The whole *point* is to upset the apple cart. To severely damage the apple cart, to blow the bloody thing up, whilst I've the chance.

Sat with Lou in the evening. She watched snooker as I fiddled with the speech. She says 'I must get Flo to clean this,' & 'I must get Flo to mend that.' I nearly told her off – but at the end of the day, Flo *is* getting paid… & if *she* wasn't being nagged about various trivialities, it would be *me* getting it in the earhole, so I bit my tongue.

Monday, 23 October
New office. Difficult to find, pokey, no view, but *mine*. Harry started bringing in the files & boxes from Heath Hurst. Belinda arrived from the agency, as the temporary secretary. Timid little thing, but she types as tho' it were going out of fashion. Sarah brought a kettle & some crockery so we are rather self-sufficient!… Various people popped in, the first-footers. Ian[73] came!! I said 'I don't think Townend rates me.' 'Wouldn't worry about that,' he said. 'Probably wary of your exuberance. Or the Welsh surname. He's a 92 Group bod. About as enlightened as Il Duce.'

Tuesday, 24 October
Waterhouse came to the office. Labour have put in the electoral petition & the High Court will now decide!! They're saying that Mayweather, the returning officer, was 'swayed by unsubstantiated press reports about Mr Wilkes's private life which made him *biased* when interpreting the marks

---

[73] Ian Gow (1937-90). Tory MP for Eastbourne, 1974-90.

made on the ballot papers in question'… Waterhouse thinks the court will throw it out, but we won't know until the new year.

Sarah came up. Said 'ITN & Sky will show you live, but the Beeb won't delay *Neighbours.*' Typical. Belinda finished typing the speech & I joined the mêlée to PMQs… It thinned out fleetly after *she* withdrew, but the debate started & Weatherill called me right away – & a lot of the departing members sat down again to listen!

It was as if I were in full flow on *Just a Minute* – only no buzzers, just 'hear, hears' as interruption. Hurd's face was a picture – well, they *all* sat aghast.

Pasted in:

> I wish to thank you most cordially, Mr Speaker, for calling me to make my first contribution to the discourse of this historic place. In divers ways, dubbing this address my Maiden Speech is apt & proper. Indeed I feel queasy as a maiden in days of yore, plunged unprepared from the comforts of home into a maelstrom of responsibility & duty; my green eyes opened, my innocence briskly squashed. I can only promise that I shall listen & learn, & that with my Honourable & Right Honourable friends' help, my endowments will ripen, & my capacities blossom, however long or short the time I am privileged to sit in this chamber.
>
> It has to be said, Mr Speaker, that I am only here at all due to the incidence of various improbable events – some glorious, some preposterous, some controversial, & one acutely tragic. I only stand here today because Frank Dobson can't. I know that the late Member for Holborn & St Pancras will be deeply missed in this House, for his commitment to his constituents, the keen comradeship with his colleagues, & the deep love he felt for his country. It is a mere two months since his heartbreaking demise, too brief a time to fully come to terms with such a loss, but long enough to know that I have distinguished, virtuous & accomplished shoes to fill. Mr Speaker, I will endeavour to meet that challenge in reverence to my gifted predecessor.
>
> I know that many of those listening to me are expecting an Oooh Matron Speech, instead of a Maiden one. It's true that my life's work has been in a field not often ploughed when candidates for the Mother of Parliaments are being harvested. Hitherto, my expertise – if one can call it that – has been in the realm of entertainment, often a quite specific outpost of that realm. I am well aware that the public know more about the condition of my bowels than my position on the Community Charge or race relations. I appreciate that my career in theatre, radio, television & film has made me a 'personality', to use a vulgar modern term. I hope I don't sound conceited when I say that

my nostrils are perhaps the most recognisable nostrils ever to have sniffed the breath of history that whispers through this place, at least as bona fide elected nostrils. I'm mindful of the fact that my face, my voice, & what my constituents know of me as an actor have very much played their part in allowing me to stand before you today. Whilst I accept this, I flatter myself that it is what I said during the recent campaign, & not just how I said it, that also goes a long way to explaining my improbable election.

When all is said & done, I am a product of Holborn & St Pancras. I was born in King's Cross, grew up in Bloomsbury, & after demobilisation, finally settled near Great Portland Street, where I live today. I can say in all honesty, Mr Speaker, that as this tumultuous century of ours has progressed, I have seen it all in Holborn & St Pancras. From every level of society, I have experienced the wonder & dismay, the talent & trickery, the heroism & dereliction of the place, & its people. The constituency is a part of me, as much as is my wit, my erudite flow & my undeniable humility. I expressed to the voters how I feel about our plot, how I see the problems therein, & what I wish to do about them. My victory was narrow – & still angrily contested as I speak – but by increasing my Party's share of the vote to the extent I did, I like to think that my words hit home, & that the people of Holborn & St Pancras have faith in me when it comes to realising their aspirations & addressing their concerns. It was the biggest shock of my life – but if they want me to Carry On Representing them, I will strain every nerve & sinew in their service.

Some assert, Mr Speaker, perhaps justly, that the main thrust of my life has centred on messing about, & lots of it. Well, to coin a phrase, it's time to stop messing about. If my luck runs out & my time here is brief, I am determined not to look back with any regrets. Whilst I respect the atavistic traditions & conventions of this place – & as the new boy I have no right to abuse them – I will not shy away from using my distinctive voice if things need to be said. Confrontation is fundamental to the smooth running of this House, which is why the builders made sure the front benches are more than two sword lengths apart. The days of steel blades are gone, but my tongue can be cutting, & can reach further than a rapier, be in no doubt about that. I don't shirk from infamy, even if they've all got it in for me. That might make me unpopular – perhaps intensely so, even on my own side. But, as Sir Winston said, "You have enemies? Good. That means you've stood up for something, sometime in your life."

As a Conservative, Mr Speaker, my guiding principles are to conserve what is good about our culture and the society our forefathers have built. Trolling around my constituency, as I often do, I marvel at the grand Victorian buildings that line our streets and avenues, their sturdy brick facades embellished with the ornamentation of a confident, robust nation.

Sadly, many of these edifices have seen better days, and their faded glories are increasingly becoming the target of the demolition man and his wrecking ball. Great glass monstrosities, the fancies of industrial modernisers and architectural charlatans are taking the place of our most beautiful buildings. As a Member of Parliament I shall unashamedly oppose these egregious projects, and throw my weight behind the conservation of the beautiful structures we already have. Another area of specific interest for me concerns an issue which was brought close to home only in recent days. I said a moment ago that the days of steel blades are gone – unfortunately, that isn't the case for a close friend & constituent of mine, who at this moment is clinging to life after being mindlessly stabbed in the street in broad daylight. Just another senseless attack to add to the statistics. Increasingly, I find that notions of honesty & individual integrity are becoming alien to our people, particularly in the Labour-run cities of this land. Spoon-fed citizens are repeatedly told by their socialist overlords that it's the capitalists' fault that their rations are thin this year – whilst the trade union leaders' tables groan with pheasant & claret. But, they say, don't for heaven's sake do anything about it – lay the blame at the Prime Minister's door & put your trust in us. As our third general election victory in a row proved, that trust has long-since been extinguished, & moral fortitude thinned to such an extent, that crime has become a way of life in parts of this metropolis & many other cities. The solution isn't a youth club, or a snooker hall, or an arm around the shoulder. It's harsh medicine, appropriate sanctions, followed by education & work. The solution for the Yorkshire Ripper, or Irish bombers, or my constituent's attacker, isn't three square meals & a private television – it's the hangman's noose. As my mother always said, the only good terrorist is a well-hung terrorist.

Mr Speaker, tough words are needed at the moment, & in point of fact are rather overdue. The respectable people of this country are sick to the back teeth with the lily-livered treatment of offenders, the lack of policing & the breakdown of common decency, as they & I see it. As the ambassador of the people of Holborn & St Pancras in this House, I will strive to highlight the scourge of criminality in this kingdom, & exhaustively bend the ears of anyone in power who has the ability to get something done. I shan't hesitate, I shan't deviate, but I shall repeat myself, over & over again. Only good, Conservative governance can provide what my constituents require – that has been illustrated in the miraculous economic turnaround and the improvement in our international standing over the past decade; it is essential that this advancement spreads into all other areas of public life, so that we can all enjoy a safe, disciplined and sensible future.

I thank the House for the indulgence which they have shown me.

When I came out Harry rushed up. '*The Times* want to do a double-page spread & a Peter Estall has rung twice about you doing *Wogan* tomorrow...' I said yes to both.

Wednesday, 25 October
Note from Francis at Dent. He wants a draft chapter about the campaign by the end of next week so they can get the book in the shops for Christmas. Belinda got Gyles on the 'phone for me, & he said he'll put something together.

Lots of funny looks today. It's as though I'd stood up in the middle of evensong & shouted '*Bollocks*'... They all think I've overstepped the mark. Renton came in. Not happy. I don't know why they can't understand that I couldn't care *less* about their rules or hierarchy. It's only people that care about *power* who are afraid to *use* it for fear of *losing* it. I don't care either way... Saw Ian Gow in the tea-room. 'And there's me thinking you were a bit of a leftie,' he said. 'For what it's worth, I side with you. But don't become the pantomime villain with a flailing sledgehammer – there's more than one way to skin a cat.'

After the EEC debate got the cab to Wapping for interview with this Stothard. It was as expected. 'What *methods* of capital punishment do you favour?'... all the focus on the criminal rather than the victim... To Shepherds Bush at 6.40, I was on first with Terry. Same tack from him, but I was prepared so turned the tables a bit. Got a few laughs about getting lost in Westminster & office being the size of broom cupboard, &c. For the most part it was similar to the old days & coming on to promote a book or film. Chatted with Pauline Collins after, who was on plugging this *Shirley Valentine* thing. She said 'You've swapped one stage for another. Which is better?'

Thursday, 26 October
Lawson[74] has resigned!! *Major*[75] has been shoved from the Foreign Off. & is now Chancellor... I've clearly arrived just in time.

---

[74] Nigel Lawson (1932-2023), Tory MP for Blaby, 1974-91. Chancellor of the Exchequer, 1983-89.
[75] John Major (b. 1943), Tory MP for Huntingdon, 1979-99. Foreign Secretary, 1989; Chancellor of the Exchequer, 1989-91.

Friday, 27 October
Up early for walk round the block with Rupert. It's virtually a full recovery & he looks marvellous. In fact, I think the dishiness has even been upped. The baths have given him leave until 8th Jan., so he suggested a holiday somewhere when I break for Christmas. Said I'd think about it. Bumped into Paul when coming back in. Think he's feeling a tad cut off, so arranged dinner this evening.

Harry doing his best to get me within earshot of the PM & Waddington[76] (new Home Sec.), but no luck. 'I think we should stick with the media campaign,' he said. Sat on the 'phone all morning with *News of the World*, *Sunday Times* & *Observer*. Tiresome, but it keeps the spotlight on the issue… Went into the chamber. Discussion about inviting Gorby to London for a bells & whistles state visit. Ventured to catch the Speaker's eye, but I dare say I won't be chosen for a good while yet… Chatted to a boy called Duncan in the queue at the post room. He's under Admiral Kerr at Defence. Said that today they'd decoded *proof* that the Soviets are developing a range of biological weapons. Must say, for someone who works on the fabled *third floor* of the Metropole Building, his lips were decidedly loose.

Met Paul at Vecchia at 8 o'c. Oaf on the next table kept interjecting. 'You've got the right idea, Ken. String 'em up, I say'… Must be careful not to become the mouthpiece for the great unwashed. 'Elegance & wit are the keys to the castle,' said Paul. 'You got in using the common touch; now you can scratch their eyes with manicured nails.'

Saturday, 28 October
Got Lou in the wheelchair alright & pushed her all the way to Cromer St! The chilly air certainly got some colour in her cheeks. Only trouble is, she can't hear me when I'm behind her so I have to shout, but that's no real bother.

Cooked the plaice & served it at noon. Rita arrived & Lou went for the nap. Once upon a time I'd have needed a snooze too, but I've no time for that! Went through a few 'pressing' constituency letters. Harry seems to think that receiving a handwritten note from *me* takes the edge off a grievance & negates the need for surgeries – he even suggested that I include a signed photo, but I think he was being facetious.

---

[76] David Waddington (1929-2017), Tory MP for Ribble Valley, 1983-91. Home Secretary, 1989-91.

Beyond Our Kenneth

Went in to Lou & she sat & watched *Hearts of Gold*[77] while I went through the draft that Gyles posted. He obviously keeps a diary too, as he's captured the campaign in detail & perfectly. Scribbled a few additions, but overall he's done a superb job.

Sunday, 29 October
Got papers. Adonis has shaved all his hair off, the fool. Read the articles & *Observer* is surprisingly good, but the others have stock images of nooses & electric chairs, so they've chosen the sensationalist route, as expected… M. came & took Rupert & me to Joe Allen. R. played it safe with blander selections & mineral water to drink, but he was very much himself. M. said he'd heard Wilkes on the radio on his high horse over my 'unenlightened outburst' in the House. The interviewer asked 'Has your wife accepted the relationship between you & your Bosnian boyfriend?' & the fat clod stormed out *à la* John Nott!![78]

Monday, 30 October
The thought of being *salaried* rather than self-employed is lunatic after all these years – especially in the service of the *state*! Harry gave me the spreadsheet & I'm on £25,701!! The people should take to the streets on that score alone.

Sat in on the debate. To make a point of order during the vote, I had to wear that infernal hat!! The serjeant-at-arms threw a collapsible topper at me & I sat there, asking a serious question of Weatherill, looking like Max Linder[79] on sabbatical. These daft conventions are too toe-curling for words.

Tuesday, 31 October
Urgent question in the chamber about S. African/E. German nationals & possible asylum in Britain. Bonn has rejected them, & I can't see the point in taking them in. Sainsbury spoke well on the matter & I think he's right; since they left the Commonwealth, we have no moral responsibility

---

[77] BBC TV (1988-96), presented by Esther Rantzen. The programme commended members of the public for their good deeds.

[78] John Nott (b. 1932), Secretary of State for Defence during the Falklands War, had discontinued a television interview in 1982 when Sir Robin Day referred to him as a 'here-today, gone-tomorrow politician'.

[79] French comedian (1883-1925); with his trademark silk hat, stick and moustache, was an influential pioneer of silent film.

whatever… Perhaps they should give Australia a try – they take a lot of rubbish, & the climate would suit.

Francis rang from the publisher. Pleased with chapter, but wants *Williams Carries On* as the title, following the *Just Williams* theme. I don't think the reference will click with people, but I'm not overly fussed.

Wednesday, 1 November
Peterson popped in to check up on me. Told me that Sir Hugh had been seen coming out of the Reading Room looking rather flustered, closely followed by the butch number from the Opposition Whips' office. The story, and the concomitant glee with which it was told, made me feel utterly sick.

Cab to Teddington for *Des O'Connor Tonight*. ITV has adopted the corporate feel, all glass tables & water coolers. Nice spread in hospitality though, so I sat with an ebullient Olympic runner called Kriss Akabusi & had egg & cress sandwiches & Aqua Libra… Marvellous audience!! Des was good 'cos he didn't want the old stories. I'm just grateful there are new stories to tell… Mentioned the book, which will please Francis… Harry was excellent afterwards in implying to autograph hunters that I was needed at the House so couldn't stop to sign!!

Thursday, 2 November
Complaint from the W.I. that I've sent them two identical letters within a week, turning down invitations to their lousy luncheon. 'We can only infer, thanks to this carbon copy form of correspondence, that our organisation is not particularly high on your list of priorities…' & more in that dreary vein. They're right, they're not.

Harry managed to wangle a one-month 'consultant' pass for Rupert from the 13th, so he's going to come in & help out in the office to keep him out of mischief.

Hague came up to me in the Commons Library. He's 28 & has only been here nine months, but he might as well have 'crawler' tattooed on his forehead. There's certainly enough room. He follows Lamont[80] around like a faithful pug. He said 'The Chief Secretary is a big fan of Peter Cook(!!). I don't suppose there's any chance you could set up a face-to-face?'… I stuttered a vague 'Perhaps', but wasn't very convincing. When I told Harry

---
[80] Norman Lamont (b. 1942), Tory MP for Kingston-upon-Thames, 1972-95; Chief Secretary to the Treasury, 1989-90.

he said 'Ooh, I'd not thought of that angle. You wouldn't be the first to rent out friends to climb the ladder. Soames[81] used to hawk Prince Charles about non-stop to get selected for Crawley…'

Friday, 3 November
Meeting on consumer rights, bore, then upstairs to European scrutiny meeting, desperate, but *then* to Room 16 for the All Party Parliamentary Group's report launch on suicide. Bizarrely they seem to want levels *lowered* rather than raised, but I wasn't bothered with that, it was the *process* that interested me. It's certainly a platform I should consider, if it's possible to get a foot in the door, as it's so broad base – lots of opportunities to appear dignified & serious amidst the shiny polyester shirts of the Labourites & the vegetarian woolliness of the Liberals.

Townend summoned us & laid down how we're to vote on various divisions. Belinda rang Gatiss's girl & agreed that we cancelled each other out, so I sacked it off. Released.

Came back to flat & had tea with Lou. The balance is better – not Lou's, she's as wobbly as a newborn foal – no, the balance in the *relationship*. Flo gets the moaning & the froth, I get the 'Here's my Ken!' – so absence is currently making the heart grow fonder.

Dressed & got to St John-Stevas'[82] party at 8 o'c. Put me in mind of a scene from the Hundred Guineas Club – balding, overweight queens surrounded by reluctant, disgusted youths, false grins fixed solid. Sir Hugh clocked me: 'Darling! Come & have a drink! And meet Ricky, isn't he just fabulous?'… Didn't even take the coat off – turned right around & got a cab from the corner of Cadogan Place. Had the barclays, &c.

Saturday, 4 November
This recess has come at the right time. Feel as if I've not sat down since Lammas… Went in to Rupert. To see him now, compared to the limp, ashen mannequin I saw in the hospital, is a real wonder. I am grateful – but angrier than ever at the bastard scum that put us through it. I want to see them swing… We watched the fireworks from his window, drank ginger ale

---

[81] Nicholas Soames (b. 1948), Tory MP for Crawley, 1983-95. Grandson of Sir Winston Churchill.
[82] Norman St John-Stevas (1929-2012), Tory MP for Chelmsford, 1964-87. Leader of the House of Commons, 1979-81.

& bitters; then he embraced me, knelt down & jarried the cartes[83] with Wagner on in the background.

Tuesday, 7 November
Walked to Dent & went over the proof of the book. They've cobbled together a cover where I'm done up as Kitchener, pointing ('Your Country Needs You'). I said 'I think something less bellicose would be preferable', but he insisted. Volume itself seems exiguous, but if they're satisfied, I shan't quarrel... Vecchia with the boy Oliver from Goldsmiths at 12.15, drab, then to H.H. at 2.30 for my first surgery. A Mrs Hepplewhite complaining about fly-tipping in her cul-de-sac, a Miss Phat (very much living up to the name) going on & on about dog mess & a Mr Donald Brady who, whilst officially present to petition for disability ramps, seemed more keen on boring the arse off me on the subject of his dead cocker. Pulled the right faces & *strained* to sympathise, but I won't be putting myself thro' *that* again in a hurry.

Thursday, 9 November
Size of the postbag has doubled, much to the disgruntlement of the postman. Even replying to one-in-ten is a chore, but I persevere... No papers at tube, had to go to Cleveland Street. Focus entirely on Gorbachev's state visit. *Today* reports that John Major 'will announce on Monday the introduction of several prominent British brands into the Soviet bloc marketplace... however, it must be deduced that flogging Wall's to Berlin and Mini Kievs to Kiev oughtn't necessarily be seen as a precursor to nuclear disarmament...' I'll say! It's all a pretence!! Gorby may be the nominal emperor, but Vstavlyat is the shogun, & he's the sort that'd make Stalin cower... On the news they showed the *Grenztruppen* permanently sealing the Bornholmer Straße crossing by dismantling the Bösebrücke & installing dozens of security cameras. Still, I'm sure the East Berliners are looking forward to their Findus Crispy Pancakes.

Friday, 10 November
Overcoat needed as it's *freezing*. Walked with Paul to Selfridge's. It's remarkable how the riffraff's manner towards one has altered – gone are the nudges & winks & the 'Carry On, Ken!'; it's been replaced with bold & stony-faced 'When are you gonna sort out the bleeding dustmen?'... M.

---

[83] Polari, meaning fellatio; from the Italian, i.e. 'mangiare il cazzo' = 'to eat dick'.

arrived at noon & helped me & Flo get Lou into the car. Flo seemed delighted to have the afternoon off! I don't blame her!... We were at Rodney Street within ten minutes. Wheeled Lou in to see Marge & knew immediately it was a bad idea. Marge like a husk. Couldn't have weighed more than five stone wet through, & the mind gone. I could tell Lou was shocked. We had refreshments, but it was the most melancholic cup of tea I've ever sat thro'. Marge kept saying 'Fourpence ha'penny they charge 'ere for collops', but there's no real answer to that... Got out hurriedly & took Lou to Joe Allen & gave her lobster & Soave, which I think she deserved. It's clear that having someone around Lou all the time is priceless & that Flo is a *godsend*.

Saturday, 11 November
Went to Marks's & purchased a suit. 34" pants, but they'll still need letting out. I resent having to fork out, but I concede that more regular formal occasions will require it. Lazed around in the afternoon, read Larkin, listened to *Rückert-Lieder* & ate Twiglets. Grab it while you can, I say.

Monday, 13 November
Got the 88 in with Rupert. He said 'The last time I was on a bus was a school trip to Zermatt in the lower sixth'... Showed him the lobbies, & whilst he was clearly agog, he feigned the nonchalants – until the *Prime Minister* passed by with the courtiers... R. visibly stooped!! It's a wonder he didn't do a Raleigh & lay his trench coat on the deck for her there & then. Got him upstairs & ensconced with Belinda. Of course, the flits trolled by to eye him up... Went with Brandon-Bravo[84] to the briefing room & we watched Major give the speech on the television. The top lip resembles grey Bakelite, v. curious. Gorby is coming on the 30th, with all the razzmatazz... Harry ran up afterwards & curtsied. It seems *I* am to be invited to the state dinner, & shall meet old Mikhail *& the Queen!* It's beyond daft, & I should feel totally out of place, but H. thinks there's no way out of it.

Wednesday, 15 November
Questions in the House about Honecker's border antics. *Finally* I got called!! 'Does the Minister opine that the Leader of the Opposition's silence regarding the German Democratic Republic's actions last week amount to substantive *support* for these manœuvres, or simply a reluctance to reveal

---
[84] Martin Brandon-Bravo (1932-2018), Tory MP for Nottingham South, 1983-91.

1989

to his comrades in the politburo that he is in unison with the *Prime Minister*, that they are, in point of fact, vile, heinous, repugnant deeds?'… Should win me a few brownie points.

Thursday, 16 November
Townend hovered in the corridor. 'Can I have a word, Kenneth?' Clocked Rupert, who rolled the eyes… 'We run a tight ship here, Kenneth. Of course you're going to do interviews, you're marvellous at it, but it has to be the Party line guiding what you say…' I said 'This isn't the *Volkskammer*. My brain shall guide what I say, & nothing else.' I could see in that split second that no-one had ever thought to answer back to him before. I half-expected a raging bum's rush, but he just cleared the throat, straightened the tie & limply sodded off.

Friday, 17 November
They are baffled by me. They can't understand that I don't mind the idea of the whip being removed, or being sacked or overthrown. *Their* Heaven is re-election, for the very sake of it… Went to see the Father of the House.[85] Very quiet & elegant, yet concerned with legacy as he's stepping down at the election. Read in *Who's Who* that he's anti-abortion, so I think he's sound. In my experience, those who are desperate to see unwanted fœtuses live are just as keen on seeing unwanted grown-ups dispatched… He says a Private Member's Bill is the only way ahead, as the government will never raise the subject again if left to its own devices. The ballot is my best bet & keep the fingers crossed, but if I cause enough ruckus & perhaps get influential people on side, the Ten Minute Rule option is open. He said 'You know, you could lose a lot of fans in the country over this…' – They're a funny lot. They think I care. I don't care. That's why I admire the Prime Minister – she doesn't give a damn about being *loved*.

Saturday, 18 November
Wheeled Lou to Clinton's to choose card for Flo's birthday. She picked one with a ghastly badge stuck to it. £1.75, outrageous… When Rita arrived I got cab & met Gordon at the Tent. Such a fillip to see him, though he did look awfully drawn. When we were leaving he took my arm & said 'Justice is righteous, Ken. But revenge isn't. Just promise me you'll be careful.'

---

[85] Sir Bernard Braine (1914-2000), Tory MP for Castle Point, 1983-91.

Monday, 20 November
This intern, Ethan, is quite the dish of the day. Almost a Moroccan colouring, but with your *boner fidey* Norfolk accent!! Its smile sends the back of the knees to jelly... Belinda handed me the usual packet of 'urgent' letters. One of interest, a real heartbreaker from a Godfrey Pennington of Starcross St, about how his wife was stabbed to death with a breadknife during a burglary & how the assailant got off on a technicality. It wasn't angry in tone, just desperate & completely tragic. It's *these* people I want to be helping.

Met Cecil Franks & Tim Raison.[86] Talked about America & Dukakis's complete *absence* from international discourse. Cecil said Duke's approval ratings are at 19%, which is unprecedented. 'Un-*presidented*, if he's not careful,' said Tim, guffawing at his – for want of a better word – wit.

Tuesday, 21 November
State Opening. Black Rod & all that hullabaloo. We filed out of the chamber in a slow huddle, as one would queue for the January sales. Fabulous loyal address from Gow!! After lunch, a lot of commotion & bleeping pagers. Sir Anthony Meyer, a complete unknown to me, has challenged for the leadership!! We piled into Gorst's office & heard this Meyer on the radio, grousing on about the poll tax & the PM's "style". Lots of dashing about & 'phones ringing... I knew there was an air of discontent, but never expected this. Spoke to Body,[87] who was fuming. 'It'll be Heseltine putting him up to it,' he said. 'Testing the waters. Bloody *Judas*...' But then Richard thinks that anyone who prefers French cheeses to English is a Judas. The vote will be in a fortnight.

Harry grabbed me as Rupert & I were leaving & said 'Will you do Channel 4 News out on College Green in five?' & I said yes. Went on camera with Crick & pooh-poohed the whole thing.

Wednesday, 22 November
Ian Gow will lead the PM's campaign. He came through discreetly checking numbers. 'The thing she's concerned about,' he said, 'is the number of abstentions... If you encounter a waverer, can I rely on you to knock some

---

[86] (1929-2011) Tory MP for Aylesbury, 1970-95; Secretary of State for Transport, 1990-1.
[87] Richard Body (1927-2018), Tory MP for Holland with Boston, 1966-99. President of the Anti-Common Market League.

sense into them?' & I said yes. Not that any cajoling should be necessary; she's won them three victories, the record should stand for itself... It's inconvenient, though. What with East Germany, South Africa, the Soviet visit & now this fool's errand, my little crusade doesn't stand a chance... Meyer keeps referring to Mrs T's *Euroscepticism*, but it's bilge – being against a superstate & a unified currency isn't *anti* the Community, it's just common sense. The worry is, however, that Thatcherism & Euroscepticism are *perceived* to be one & the same, and that is dangerous.

Went in to Lou. Gave her a brandy & we watched Michael Palin complete his Phileas Fogg routine. Louisa unimpressed – 'Who's *paying* for all these 'olidays, that's what I want to know...'

Friday, 24 November
After the NHS debate got cab to Euston & met Barbara off the train. She curtsied lowly & squawked 'O! what a lovely Member!' & kissed my hand. She looked radiant with her Tunisian tan... Cab to the Waldorf for the Association Dance. All the blokes swarmed Barbara like flies round honey, the wives pursing the lips & tutting... Got quite tight! & so the speech was ragged & the raffle underwhelming, but the advantage of that is not being asked again... Escaped for supper at Biagi's. Barbara is doing panto in Hemel Hempstead, so it's no wonder she was knocking back the Sazeracs.

Saturday, 25 November
Letter from the BBC asking whether I wish to be involved in the next series of *Just a Minute*. Rang Clement & he said it never caused any hassle when he was in the House, so I wrote back asking for the contract to be sent direct as I've no representation.

Stopped raining after Rita had gone, so called on Paul & we wheeled Lou to the duck pond & back. A girl with a Labrador shouted 'Tory ass', but I pretended not to hear.

Monday, 27 November
Portaloo knocked. 'Kenneth, I'm off to Marsham Street for drinks, do you want to come?' – I've not been to the Transport Dept (or any Dept, for that matter), so I accepted. Whiskies galore in celebration of quashing British Rail's request to close some line up north. Cecil Parkinson[88] said a few words

---

[88] (1931-2016) Tory MP for Hertsmere, 1983-91; Secretary of State for Transport, 1989-90.

& clearly it's all down to Miguel.[89] He's an able boy, there's no doubt about it, and people seem to respect him, undeterred by the plummy voice & the haircut. The foreign name signals that he's self-made rather than landed gentry, and as a result folk feel less reticent in warming to him.

Tuesday, 28 November
Townend came & handed me the invitation & protocol sheet for Thursday. My M&S garb won't cut the mustard apparently – the Party are paying for suit hire! Got Rupert to measure me & Belinda 'phoned the sizes through to Gieves & Hawkes. Pondered on what Charlie would've thought of it all – the incredulity at his son wearing Savile Row togs to meet the Queen, conveyed via cruel remarks of self-hatred rather than the dewy pride of 'my boy done good'… PMQs. I'm surprised at how quickly the act of entering the chamber has come to feel commonplace. I've a notion it's because it's quite a *small* room, in point of fact, & wildly uncomfortable when full. Odd ambience today, with much whispering. I was one in front & 3 along from Meyer. Labour backbenchers broke into a chorus of *'Hey there Anthony boy, why you in such a rush?'*… A smirking Lyell turned to me & said 'Chuck Berry.' – 'They harmonise rather well,' I said, 'it must be the Bolshevik in them.' Weatherill calmed it down, but Maggie wasn't on top form, seemed to have a frog in the throat.

Wednesday, 29 November
Received a *handwritten* note from Dickie Attenborough!! Raises concerns about 'a potential bill in your name advocating the return of capital punishment'… He bangs on & on about Timothy Evans[90] & 'miscarriages of justice'. This sort of thing makes me sick – patrician thesps with letters after their name who reckon to be *experts* just 'cos they've donned the greasepaint & learnt the lines. Poor man must be coming unglued.

Thursday, 30 November
Saw the PM on the television standing on the tarmac at a windswept Heathrow to welcome Gorby. Despite the gale, she looked marvellous, not a hair out of place. Lovely fur coat… Went in & listened to the East Europe debate. Lots of the commies calling our guest a puppet – they'd rather

---

[89] Michael Portillo.
[90] Wrongly hanged in 1950 for the murders of his wife and child, committed by John Christie at 10 Rillington Place, W11.

1989

Vstavlyat were here; *he's* their new pin-up. It's idiotic, none of them would last five minutes in Bucharest or Perm. Heffer spoke about Ceaușescu as though he were the Dalai effing Lama… Afterwards Townend chasséd up, that awkward simper plastered across the face. Said an opening on the *charities* select committee could become available. 'They're very sought-after positions,' he insisted. Why he thinks I'd give a shiny shit about charity boggles the mind – I suppose it's a diversion tactic, or a preemptive "reward" for toeing the line. I smiled & said 'I shall give it very careful consideration'… Collected suit from Belinda & taxied home to change. Lou sulking because I wouldn't take *her* as the plus-one!! Thank God for Flo, who distracted her with whist… Rupert delighted to display the EIIR sticker behind his windshield!! Arrived Windsor at 6.40. Left R. (who went off in search of a pub!) & a blond *vision* escorted me to the holding pen – Norman Wisdom was there! Apparently his fame has spread east from Albania & he's taking the Warsaw Pact by storm (he was on *Mrs Gorbacheva*'s wish-list!). Chatted to Hurd & Beaumont-Dark[91] (*langweilig*[92]), then to Joanna Lumley, delightful, & Stephen Fry, gargantuan. Inspected seating plan & found, to my relief, I was between Myfanwy Talog[93] & Emma Nicholson!![94] Eventually we were herded through. Not unlike being in the queue at the Midland, waiting for a free window. Mrs T, in purple velvet, introduced me to the President & Raisa – 'Ah, this is Mr Williams, a new member of parliament & previously a very gifted film actor.' The stolid interpreter translated. Mikhail had the fixed grin, clearly eager to get on with it – more of a hand-touch than a handshake. HM glowing radiantly – 'Oh!' she said blithely, 'We're well orf for entertainers tonight!'… Couldn't hear the speeches, we were sat about a mile from the action. Scallops, lamb & white chocolate mousse, & of course the liquor flowed. Myfanwy made me howl – 'When polled about whether they would have intercourse with John Wilkes, 69% of Yugoslavians said "Not again"'… All in all, it was further proof that – even in the most sumptuous of surroundings – a surplus of *people* can ruin any occasion. Pinched a monogrammed teaspoon for Louie, & Rupert had us home for 11 o'c.

---

[91] Sir Anthony Beaumont-Dark (1932-2006), Tory backbench MP for Birmingham Selly Oak, 1979-91.
[92] German, 'boring'.
[93] Welsh actress (1944-95). Long-term partner of David Jason.
[94] Latterly Baroness Nicholson of Winterbourne (b. 1941). Tory MP for Torridge & West Devon, 1987-95.

Friday, 1 December
Shepherded in to the Royal Gallery for the speech. Sat next to Cecil Franks, moping cos he'd not been at the banquet. Incredible how thin-skinned some of them are... Dull address, essentially unlistenable as Mick had to stop after every paragraph for the monotone translation. Even in Russian, it's clear that he didn't *write* the speech – 'glasnost' & 'perestroika' notable by their absence from the script. I reckon *I* wield more power than this poor sod. Clocked the PM & she looked thoroughly disappointed – the "man she could do business with" reduced to this. Kept looking at the birthmark. I dare say he was teased for it as a boy, but it really does suit him.

Albemarle Street at 6.30 for the book launch. Joanie Sims, Kenny C, Barbara, Sheila & John, all greeted me warmly. Rona came without Gordon, he's got a bug. Signed about 60 books, but in truth, apart from cronies, it was a poor turnout.

Sunday, 3 December
Rita prepared the moussaka for Louie & me and then left us to it. Seems *ages* since we've lunched together alone. She chattered away about this & that – mainly the plot of *Home & Away* & Flo's relatives in Manila – & as trivial as it was, there's a brightness in her eyes. I do feel the guilt for not being here, but it's offset by the fact that she's in a better frame of mind than she otherwise would have been. After the trifle she touched my hand & said 'I'm ever so proud of you' & I was so moved I had to change the subject immediately.

Monday, 4 December
Went through strategy with Harry. Next week we've got *Wogan, Daytime Live, Aspel*, LBC & *Any Questions?*, so we formulated a game plan... H. is good with the 'segueing' technique, as he calls it, the craft of pivoting to a question one wants to answer from the one that's asked. We wrote a list of letters we've had from grieving relatives. H. said 'You'll flow as you usually do – statistics won't win the debate, but they're a useful backup.'

Spoke in the chamber. Asked Waddington about police numbers. Pleased with the mealymouthed reply – I think he'll be more of a pushover than Hurd would've been.

Tuesday, 5 December
Saw the Prime Minister in the corridor outside the Commons' Library, broadly smiling & looking determined as ever. Everyone treading water for

most of the day. Chapman circulating the tea room, obscenely taking bets on the outcome... Eventually filed through to vote. Gow's secretary asked me to go out on to the Green to give the cameras an immediate response. Got the result via the ITN chap's tranny – *Thatcher 315, Meyer 33, Abstentions 3, Spoilt ballots 24 – Majority 282*. I waffled on for half an hour about the crushing victory to the reporters... The devil's in the detail, though – *sixty* colleagues didn't support her... Chatted to Portillo, & we saw Heseltine sweep through the lobby, a pronounced spring in his step.

Wednesday, 6 December
Belinda spread out the invitations for December – all 27 of them!! Rupert & I sorted them into groups: *Unavoidable, Letter of apology & Waste paper basket.*

Watched the News & saw the protesters in America re. the white South African arrivals. The posed photographs of the smiling Boer children embracing Dukakis are repulsive. Meanwhile Mugabe is in East Berlin, signing treaties & shaking hands with Honecker & Gorbachev, as they carve up the veldts between them. Not a dicky-bird said about it while he was here, in public anyway, & the banner-wavers kept at arm's length. Shameful reely... Had lovely minute steak in Members' dining room, better than restaurant standard.

Friday, 8 December
Up at 6 o'c. Got to Chatham at 8.05. 'Any problems?' he asked. He gave the anus a cursory check & had a poke about. Said everything looks sound. Talked about workload. He said 'Your body's a good barometer, you must listen to it – if you're feeling tired, just stop.' *Vis-à-vis* Lou, he thought that there might be parliamentary expenses due regarding care costs – evidently mine isn't the only elected bumhole he's fingered. I shall make enquiries.

Tory Association Xmas party at 8 o'c. I find Conservative *voters* agreeable (in general), but the members are something else. I've known *wakes* with more lighthearted pep. Made excuses at 9.25 & escaped to Paul's for gin rummy.

Saturday, 9 December
Huge stack of neglected fan letters, so spent morning replying. Sending them from the House should result in a large saving on stamps in the long run, if I keep it on the QT.

Sunday, 10 December
M. collected me & I gave him lunch at Joe Allen. Bob Monkhouse was there, that vast face freshly Ronsealed. He's smitten with Mrs T & asked all the 'what's she like *in person*?' questions. Told him I hadn't the faintest clue.

Tuesday, 12 December
Economic news is bad. A slide towards recession feels inevitable, & the leadership win hasn't pacified the doubters. The only comfort lies in looking across the floor at the official opposition – if the country has half the scruples I hope it has, we're safe for a good while yet.

Ridley's dinner in the evening. Spoke to Foster, Waddington's PPS – surprised to learn that they *have* talked about me! Many of them back what I say to the hilt, they're just worried about perceptions. The last vote on the subject in '83 was defeated 361-245, & they expect that margin will have since grown. Foster said 'You're a backbencher, you're free to give it a try. Just don't set your heart on securing ministerial support...'

Wednesday, 13 December
9.33 from Euston to Birmingham New Street. Cab to Pebble Mill. Make-up woman exclaimed 'I did you on *Carry On Dick*!' – 'Alas,' I said, 'a touch more Polyfilla's required these days.' 'Yes,' she replied, bluntly... Went on with Sue Cook,[95] whom I respect. She's the only serious *chat* person they have. Plainly not a supporter of the cause, but I slyly used her other job to trap her: 'I'm sure that many of the heartbroken victims you feature on your *Crimewatch* programme would agree with me', et cetera... Back in London at 3.30. Harry met me & drove me to Heath Hurst. Had coffee in the office & Olivia brought M&S sandwiches. Home to change, went in to Louie. She was teaching Flo the foxtrot, which isn't easy with a walking frame between your legs... *Wogan* at 7 o'c. Other guest was Diana Rigg. Terry went on & on about the book, thanking me for mentioning him so favourably in it.

Thursday, 14 December
Of course, the reason they let me get away with it is that I've been in films. That's all. If I'd been an accountant or an estate agent or a lay preacher they'd've had my guts for garters by now. The 'media' terrifies them. For the

---

[95] English TV presenter and author (b. 1949). Hosted BBC1's *Crimewatch U.K.* with Nick Ross between 1984 and 1995.

moment, at least, column inches about *Hangman Ken*'s outbursts are a useful distraction from the true crises that are brewing. Yet there's no grey area – those that think well of me show it. The rest either loathe or ignore me. 'Twas ever thus.

Friday, 15 December
Belinda showed me how to use the photocopying machine. Went to spend a penny & walked in on Sir Hugh giving the postboy the J. Arthur… 'Darling!' he said, 'don't mind us!' The red-faced boy scurried out sheepishly. The brazenness is vile, I shall have nothing more to do with him.

The boy is called Chris. Greek Cypriot, I think. Lovely teeth.

Saturday, 16 December
Foyle's at 10 o'c. Signing session. Did about 125 copies. Wrist agony afterwards.

Remarkable to think that in a few weeks it could all be over. I can imagine the judge now – the powdered wig, the crumpled face, the bags under the eyes. Wilkes, fat & smug, posing for the photographers, exonerated… I wouldn't really mind. I could sell up, take Lou to a cottage by the seaside & while away the remaining days reading & penning poems. It'd be more productive than all this crap.

Tuesday, 19 December
Harry showed me that my first PMQs question was on the tabled list!! I was up third. Not a plant, either, but a real question about longer sentencing. Dennis Skinner[96] piped up with 'Carry on hanging!' as I got to my feet, but it didn't put me off my stride… Lunched with Body (who is the only true 'eurosceptic' I get on well with) & Cecil Franks. Cecil surmised that, as an election is due before June '92, next year will be crammed with all the *difficult* reforms, to give the government – & hopefully the economy – time to recover before going to the country. The poll tax has been a complete disaster in Scotland, but rumours abound that she's *determined* to push it through nationwide. 'She never was much of a listener,' said Body, 'but she's trying to run things singlehanded. No one can manage that, not even her…'

---

[96] (b. 1932) Labour MP for Bolsover, 1970-2019. Parliament's most infamous heckler, suspended from the House on at least ten occasions during his career for using unparliamentary language when attacking opponents.

Wednesday, 20 December

Up at 6 o'c. Woke Lou & gave her the perfume. 'How old am I?' she asked. 'You're 88.' 'Gawd 'elp us,' she said, 'that's two fat ladies.' When I was going, she dropped one. 'Pardon you!' I said – 'Don't look at me,' she smiled, 'that was the other fat lady!'

Thursday, 21 December

Collected chocolates from Prestat & dispensed them along the corridor. Released. Rupert gave me lunch at Rules as a thank you for having him around. 'On the contrary,' I said, 'you've been essential.'

Had a nap. In the afternoon walked round to Gordon & Rona's to give them the Viognier. Rona opened the door. She'd been crying. Gording was in bed, she let me up to see him. It's bone cancer, & they're too late to do anything about it. G. very stoic & brave, which doesn't surprise me a bit. I couldn't look him in the eye, let alone say what I wanted to; I shall have to write it in a letter. Kissed Rona & came away, weeping all the way home. I'd had a feeling some rotten news was coming, but I never thought it would be *this*.

Monday, 25 December

Gave Lou the presents. Lovely carriage clock from Barry[97] & Giovanni, must've cost them a fortune. Wrote a note of thanks on her behalf. Had the duck, but I overcooked it so it was quite unpleasant. Rang the Jacksons. Roddy answered & said G. had been up & had some lunch, but was back in bed by 3 o'c… Left Lou watching *Miss Marple* at 8.30. I can't get Gordon from my mind.

Thursday, 28 December

Letter from George Borwick[98] to say that Lennox Berkeley has died. G. must be losing the marbles, as I have no interest in Lennox Berkeley: I was barely *aware* of the man… Trudged through the snow & met Stanley at Vecchia Milano at 12.45. 'I shan't miss the eighties,' he said. 'I mean, the seventies weren't much cop, but at least we had our youth.' As we were leaving I shouted loudly to Pierre (waiter) 'Keep applying the cream to the affected

---

[97] Barry Wade, Australian actor. Holidayed in Morocco in the 1960s at the same time as KW, Joe Orton, etc.

[98] Hon. George Borwick (1922-94), loyal friend of KW, particularly during the early years of his theatrical career.

area, my love, twice a day, and it'll clear up in no time!' and he laughed uncomfortably.

Friday, 29 December
Gave Flo a cheque for a hundred as a kind of bonus. Wish I could do more for her. She's no real life of her own, but she's certainly saved mine this year, there's no doubt at all about that... Walked to Menzies to buy a card for Mags. Got one with a gold envelope & spent ages writing the address below *Dame Margaret Smith DBE* in blue-black roundhand. Lou wrote the card congratulating her, & I inserted a letter telling her that, although she's well aware of my opinions apropos *gongs*, the fact is it'll suit her & I'm immensely proud.

Sunday, 31 December
Saw the news about the earthquake in Wuppertal. 'Phoned Gyles, as that's where he was born. 'I'm shaken, Kenneth,' he said, '...tho' admittedly not quite as shaken as my fellow Wuppertallers'... Watched Richter play the Mozart sonatas on BBC 2. Norman Stone[99] was good in the discussion bit; his tone encourages one that he offers sound advice to the PM on Europe – he's evidently in step with the old guard, those who have been around since the War, the pro-Europeans... alas, the newcomers seem far more critical of the continentals... Looked for the recording I had of the Mozart sonatas, but realised that I'd given them to the Spastics when I was going to kill myself. Silly fool. Had a mug of mulligatawny & turned in at 10 o'c.

---

[99] Scottish historian and author (1941-2019); Cambridge University lecturer and advisor to Margaret Thatcher.

1990

Monday, 1 January
Tooth is fucking agony. Don't know what I've done, but can't bite down on the left side or jets of pain shoot through the jaw. Tried ringing Tony Newton, but nothing doing – & of course, I've not a single pain killer in the flat. Went to Doug's & found him open!! He gave me the Nurofen & a gel for the gum.

Thursday, 4 January
Up at 7 o'c. & got papers. Headlines are all about Panama joining Comecon & the Warsaw pact. Evidently Dukakis waited too long to slap down Noriega & now Vstavlyat's got his feet under the table. The PM is furious – Cecil rang & said 'She's threatening to go to Washington to publicly ask what the heck's going on'… Dentist at noon. Tony has flu, so it was the one with the acne. It was a reenactment of the scene from *Marathon Man*:[1] he was digging around like a navvy with a shovel. There was a cavity which – eventually – he filled, but I feel as tho' I've gone ten rounds with Kid Lewis[2]… Came back & Flo was on her knees mopping up piss again. No reproach, bless her, she just gets on with it. Perhaps she's partial to piss, I don't know.

Sunday, 7 January
M. came & took me to Joe Allen where he gave me lunch. Spoke about Gordon. M. told me his uncle had the same condition, & that it would be a

---

[1] 1976 thriller, starring Olivier as a sadistic Nazi war criminal with a penchant for performing dentistry without anaesthesia. Directed by John Schlesinger, who had been seconded to the Combined Services Entertainment unit with KW in 1946.
[2] Ted "Kid" Lewis (1894-1970), English professional boxer; twice winner of the World Welterweight Championship.

mercy if things didn't drag on. We discussed *Just a Minute*, and he is going to do the transport, which is a godsend... Looked in on Rupert; he's back to work tomorrow. Said he'll wear the cufflinks I gave him as a talisman. Went into Lou & had soup & toast. We watched *You Rang, M'Lord?* – in essence, the rotting corpse of *Hi-de-Hi!*, stuffed into plus fours & doused in cheap sherry.

Monday, 8 January
Back to the mad house. Lots of 'If I don't see you again, best of luck' type chatter – they must know something I don't, but it ain't exactly comforting... Found myself in the Strangers Bar, that den of iniquity. The overwhelming sense around the place is that we're buggered. There's an uneasy feeling that no-one's in control of anything: the Soviets are on the rise, America silent, the PM paranoid & distant, and the *people* naffed off, what with the Community Charge, unemployment & crime levels. They discuss the issues, over their subsidised brandies, but noticeably in the abstract; all that really matters to them is the effect events are having on the *party*, and consequently on their own jobs... Saw Gatiss in the Lower Waiting Hall. He said 'The top brass seem buoyant. An election can't come soon enough.' Of course, Labour isn't the answer – to anything – but a 10-point deficit in the polls can swiftly become 20 or 30 & before you know it, there'll be no way back.

We saw the news & Terry-Thomas[3] has popped his clogs, destitute & senile. I never warmed to him, but it's a poor show all the same.

Tuesday, 9 January
Raucous house, droning on about some nonsense or other. Literally going through the motions. Nice to see Foot[4] on his feet. He was a hopeless leader, of course, but he is one of the few impressive *communicators* when it comes to making points of order.

Wednesday, 10 January
Discussed High Court possible outcomes with Waterhouse & Baker. If it's thrown out Wilkes *could* appeal, but that's unlikely to succeed. Other options

---

[3] English actor and comedian (1911-90), famous for his upper-class, caddish characters and a distinctive gap between his front teeth. Appeared with KW in *The Hound of the Baskervilles* (1978).
[4] Michael Foot (1913-2010), Labour MP for Blaenau Gwent, 1983-91; Leader of the Labour Party, 1980-3.

are another by-election or, if the ballot papers are reassessed & are counted for Labour, Wilkes could be sworn in as early as next Thursday, & me out on my arse. They're keeping very tight-lipped, but there's no air of confidence… Went to Townend & turned down the select committee offer. I despise charity. I said 'The situation is in such flux that I oughtn't deprive another candidate from getting their teeth into the work.' I think he bought it.

Lou's new deaf aid has arrived! It'll take an *age* for her to get to grips with it, but that's Flo's province.

Thursday, 11 January
Straight from the House to the Paris for *Just a Minute.* Clocked M. & Lou & Flo in the front row before coming on. Parsons said 'I can't tell you how marvellous it is to see you… we were certain you'd not be coming back.' The audience were fabulous!! O! it was just nice to be frivolous & show off, but for that not to be the *raison d'être*. Panel was me, Clement, Nimmo & Paul Merton. Paul is good at the game, but there were a few digs – 'I'm sure Kenneth would let 'em hang' & 'Nine o'clock Noose' – which were uncalled for… After, Clement asked 'What's the mood in the House?' 'Funereal,' I replied. 'Well,' he said, 'you ought to be putting the fun in the funereal: that's your job, to shake things up a bit.' Everybody seems to think I've got the ammunition to *shake things up*, but in truth I'm one rung up from the Teasmade.

Friday, 12 January
Got away & walked to Gordon & Rona. She looked sad & beautiful. She led me upstairs. He was sleeping & looked comfortable. I sat by the bed & held his hand – I'm sure I felt him squeeze mine, so I think he knew I was there. Left the letter for Rona to read to him when he wakes up. I don't want him to die, but I *certainly* don't want him to suffer. He is the sweetest of men, he doesn't deserve the cruelty of pain.

Saturday, 13 January
Rona called. They've taken him into the Cromwell. She didn't want it, but the fart of a 'specialist' insisted.

Monday, 15 January
Nipped back to office after 'Acid House' debate. Note from Belinda on the desk: 'Ring Rona'… He's gone. He didn't open his eyes again, but Rona read

him my letter. Said the end was peaceful & quiet, in a pleasant private room. The boys were there... I went to table an EDM – this House mourns the death of, etc. Galloway[5] signed it straight away. Had to go to bloody strategy meeting of Tory London MPs. Took my mind off it a bit. Belinda kept getting calls from BBC & ITN for comment, but I declined. Went to vote, but got out & went to tell Louisa. I'm just so grateful that I got to see him.

Wednesday, 17 January
Harry pacing nervously round the office! He feels it deeper than me!! Lots of Good Luck cards & other rubbish. Nice letter from Jeremy Swan. Car came at 1 o'c. & took me, Harry, Baker & the flunkies to the Strand. Mass of press, etc. All very undignified. Saw Wilkes, looking redder & fatter than ever. Quite clinical & charmless inside the chamber, as though I were an African dictator answering charges of genocide at the Hague. A lot of technical chat, but when the verdict came, it was all very succinct: the vote is upheld & the result stands!! JW has sixty days to appeal, but according to Baker no comparable ruling has *ever* been overturned. To CCO for a small drinks reception, but I could tell they were keen to get it over with... Don't quite know *how* I feel about it. If I can't *achieve* any change, the victory today is pyrrhic. Still, it's always pleasant to win – it's certainly jollier than the alternative.

Saw Paul outside the block & he congratulated me. I asked if he'd come with me to Gordon's funeral, & he said yes... Sat by the window for a bit. Watched the trickles of rain uniting on the glass.

Thursday, 18 January
Paul knocked & we got a cab to Actors' Church. Rona looked tired & elegant. I sat next to David Langton & Claire, and behind John Alderton[6] (who spoke *superbly*). They played the Mozart piano concerto, the No. 23 – I gave G. the recording of it in 1960. Rona caught my eye & smiled and I just wept in the pew. I never had a purer, warmer or more uncomplicated friendship than the one I shared with Gordon. The heart actually *aches* at the thought of never being in his company again.

---

[5] George Galloway (b. 1954), Labour MP for Glasgow Hillhead, 1987-99.
[6] David Langton (1912-94) and John Alderton (b. 1940) starred alongside Gordon Jackson in *Upstairs, Downstairs*.

Beyond Our Kenneth

Friday, 19 January
The wonderful Tebbit[7] approached me in the Library!! He might not be in favour any more, but his loyalty to the PM is unswerving. 'We mustn't let the toffs get their feet back under the table,' he said, 'if we lose Basildon man we're done for.' The bluebloods try to gloss over the fact that she won us three elections by bringing in all these Keiths and Normans, rather than leaving them at the mercy of the reds.

Tuesday, 23 January
Headlines are about the Manchester strangler. They're linking it to 3 other prostitute deaths. With any luck, it'll be a serial killer & the hanging agenda can be pushed again.

Wednesday, 24 January
Mrs T flies off to Washington today. I wouldn't want to be Dukakis when she arrives: his scolding is sure to be public & uncomfortable… The atmosphere changes when she's out of the country; very much 'when the cat's away…' Heseltine flounces about like King John, with the bootlickers bowing & scraping. Renton came up & said 'I'm surprised you didn't want the select committee position.' I flanneled him with stuff about not knowing the brief well enough, reckon my talents lie in other fields, etc. I think they're a bit annoyed that I'm still here, & rather stumped as to what to *do* with me.

Friday, 26 January
That's two nights in a row where the dreams have been intense & erotic. I'm at the Fleet Club[8] overlooking Kowloon, spreadeagled on the top bunk, hands & ankles tied to the posts; brigadiers & generals surrounding me, getting up to all sorts. Heaven knows what's sparked this *now*… Dinner at Corrigan's at 8 o'c. Portillo had a private room. It was me, Miguel, Simon Jenkins, Seb Coe, Malcolm Fraser,[9] Jane Seymour, Jan Leeming & a couple of business types. Possibly the most curious guest list I've ever been on. JS couldn't stress enough how let down the Democrats feel by Dukakis.

---

[7] Norman Tebbit (b. 1931), Tory MP for Chingford, 1974-91. Assumed various cabinet roles under Margaret Thatcher.

[8] The China Fleet Club, a major rest and recreation centre for British and allied servicemen, and a haunt of KW's during his time in Hong Kong.

[9] (1930-2015) Prime Minister of Australia, 1975-83.

Jenkins said his *Times* bods at Camp David are reporting back that Duke is *terrified* of Mrs T & avoids eye contact with her!! It's true, she can be blunt, and rude – but only ever to people who can fight back. If they do retaliate, she's in her element… but there's seemingly little likelihood of Zorba engaging with her. Coe said 'There's no doubt he'll be ousted by whomever it is the Republicans stand next time round.'

Saturday, 27 January
Wrapped Lou snugly & Rita got her in the chair. I wheeled her to Biagi for lunch. I know she'd prefer Flo to come seven days, but I can't ask that of her. Lou treats Rita like she's scum, but she just laughs it off! – 'O! Mrs Williams, you are a *one*…'

Tuesday, 30 January
Lots of commotion. Ceauşescu has had a heart attack & dropped down dead, & now Vstavlyat is moving to bring Rumania into the Union, wholesale. Hurd is flying off to Brussels tonight to discuss what to do. The planted puppet in Bucharest will rubber stamp it, so it won't officially be an invasion, but that's very much what it *is*. One has to say, this Vstavlyat has got some front.

To the Paris for *Just a Minute*. Victoria Wood was the guest. I thought we'd hit it off well last time, but she was markedly frosty. During the subject 'deadheading the roses', she pointedly remarked, 'Of course, Kenneth would prefer to *be*-head the roses… though I'm sure he's a fan of hanging baskets – at least I think that's what he said…' They forget that I'm well aware of the squeamish views advocated by actors – I've been around them all my life. What's astonishing is they can't fathom that *their* position is the minority in the country, by a very wide margin.[10]

Wednesday, 31 January
We saw Duke's first State of the Union speech, received in abashed silence by Congress. He wished good luck to 'the Roman people' – presumably meaning the *Rumanian* people – & assured them of the United States' perpetual support. I'm sure that'll be a great comfort to them as they line up for the monthly cabbage ration.

---

[10] The British Social Attitudes poll (1990) found that 70% of respondents supported the death penalty for some crimes, 9% were opposed, and 21% were undecided.

Thursday, 1 February
Spent morning replying to letters. The team do their best to manage correspondence, but some require a personal response. In many cases a social worker would be more apt, but because they've *heard* of me, they assume I have an inside track to help them!!

First PMQs since her return from America. She seemed irritable & said things I think she'll live to regret: 'I spoke at length with the President, Mr Speaker… I merely regret that he seemed ill-equipped to speak at length with me…' I saw Whittingdale[11] outside. 'My advice was to infer the strength of the Special Relationship,' he said, 'which clearly went in one ear and out the other.'

Friday, 2 February
The news came through that Gorbachev has "resigned" & Vstavlyat is the new General Secretary of the Communist Party & Chairman of the Supreme Soviet… Gorby has been sent 'for his security & recreation' to a safe house 'near Tolyatti', which doesn't sound particularly restful… Listened to Hurd in the Chamber, & the EEC's solution is to 'closely observe the situation', which means they'll do sod all.

Argument with the Laughton[12] look-alike at Camden council. They want to erect a "rooftop conservatory" at the old town hall, inside which the affluent can quaff Tattinger whiles the peasantry freeze to death on the pavement. I said I'd fight them all the way, but I don't expect I shall.

Saturday, 3 February
Went to get papers. Another strangled polone found on a waste tip in Stockport. They've dubbed the assailant 'Jack the Gripper'. That's five bodies now. The Chief Constable has just received his knighthood, so we'll see if he's worthy of the honour.

Went to the masseur off Maple Street that Sir Hugh recommended. Don't know if it helped the lumbago, but the libido was satisfied. He said he was called Mario, from Naples, but he had Muhammadan written all over him. In any case, the cat's out of the bag now. Booked another session for next month.

---

[11] John Whittingdale (b. 1959), Political Secretary to the Prime Minister, 1988-91.
[12] Charles Laughton (1899-1962), portly English actor; best known for his grotesque performances as King Henry VIII.

Sunday, 4 February
Couldn't sleep. Rather disgusted with myself. Will cancel massage appt. & tell Rupert things must be platonic if we are to see each other. I am only viable when chaste. In any case, I am an old man. That sphere of life has never reaped much reward and now must be closed for good. Faith has gone, but there's no excuse for Filth to take its place… It is bloody freezing in the flat. Went into Lou & we watched *Bergerac*. Had to change the fuse on her electric blanket.

Tuesday, 6 February
Lousy night. Dreamt of Gordon coming to Marchmont St & making me laugh, then saying 'Och Kenneth, you're far better than this'… Saw Paul who was going for breakfast at Harris's so joined him. I said 'Who am I trying to kid? A spot of altruism after a life of selfishness – it just doesn't wash. And the hours are dreadful.' 'It's healthy to doubt yourself,' he said. 'Whether you're making up for something or not, you seem happier now than I can remember.' Of course, he's right. And it's good to be busy.

H.H. for surgery. Got through ten people. Took Adam from the office to play caseworker. Whilst some of their predicaments require action, most of them just want to talk – or rather they want to be heard. One coiffured virago, a Mrs Gulliver, obstreperously petitioning on behalf of her painfully coy daughter, said 'My Wincey *won't settle* unless we get it all out in the open…' I was furiously nudging Adam under the desk, but he held it in admirably.

Thursday, 8 February
Piers from the Foreign Office came through with a first Bucharest edition of *Pravda* – '*Noi suntem uniti!*' cries the headline: 'We are united!'… Flags are being resewn as we speak. Zhivkov in Bulgaria is expected to fold too – as his ministers hate him – so now the *Greeks* are panicking. PM off to an emergency summit in West Berlin tomorrow.

I sat in on European Communities debate in the chamber. Aitken[13] is rather attractive.

Friday, 9 February
It's curious that, in spite of all the problems at home, the Tea Room chatter universally concerns Eastern Europe. It's worrying, of course, but – as I said

---

[13] Jonathan Aitken (b. 1942). Tory MP for South Thanet, 1983-95. Pleaded guilty to charges of perjury and perverting the course of justice; jailed in 1999.

Beyond Our Kenneth

to Bernard Braine – eventually Vstavlyat will have to rein it in: for all the bluster, the last thing Moscow needs is a war… Eye contact with Rob Litany in the lobby. The smarm oozes from him. If he were a blue he'd probably be headed for the top, but lined up with Hattersley & co., the oleaginous polish is rather otiose.

Escaped early & had meal with Louie. Think she's finally mastered the hearing aid & its fiddly battery. During the peaches & meringue she said 'I wonder what Charlie would've made of me having a *Flipperino* in the 'ouse…'

Sunday, 11 February
Saw Paul & invited him to Joe Allen. M. collected us & I gave everyone luncheon. Peter & Dudley appeared!! They were meeting an Amnesty wallah but came over for a drink. PC did his *Whoops Apocalypse* routine. It's clear that I'm a great disappointment to him. 'Hark! it's the anti-establishment rebel!' he scoffed. I laughed it off & told him Norman Lamont is a fan of his & wants to meet him, & he said 'Excuse me, waiter, do you have any strychnine?'

Old Maid in the evening with Lou. Saw the News. The black communists have arrested Van Dijk & shoved him in the *exact* cell on Robben Island that Mandela occupied. So the fools have chosen revenge & suffering over reconciliation & democracy. Very sad.

Monday, 12 February
Broke wind loudly during a lull in the briefing. It really rang out & vibrated off the oxblood leather. After a pause, Spicer went on: 'Yes… Well… better out than in, as any Eurosceptic would attest…'

Wednesday, 14 February
Two-line whip. Voted *against* the government on the housing bill. Renton furious. I couldn't give less of a toss if I tried… Note from Baker: 'Wilkes has thrown in the towel & won't challenge. Many congratulations.'

Thursday, 15 February
Today we restored diplomatic relations with Argentina. A couple of half-arsed flags flying outside in recognition. Utterly risible. All these little islands should be handed over to whoever wants them – the Falklands, Pitcairn, Gibraltar… the Empire has *gone*; pretending it hasn't makes us look patently puny.

Friday, 16 February
Talked with Winston Churchill,[14] & in doing so he rather proved the theory about the diminishing quality of sequels – the man is an unctuous *bore*… Told him that I'd had it out with Vlad the Impaler. The whole *point* of this place is that it's filled with people from all backgrounds & professions, & the Tory Party is doomed if it fails to come to terms with that. If the chamber is crammed solely with landed gentry, trade union scrubs & Oxbridge politics graduates then we're finished.

Monday, 19 February
Went to apply for the Adjournment debate. Harry & I started composing the speech. We've referenced the *seven* relevant constituency cases re. formerly capital crimes that have gone unpunished or under-punished. With this sort of thing one gives the polemic after the day's business & a government minister *has* to respond.

Dinner with Sheila Hancock at Biagi. John's away doing *Morse*. She'd been up in Banbury all day filming something called *Three Men & a Little Lady*. Sounds appalling. 'The trouble with these bloody Yanks,' she said, 'is they think *we* all live like the Marlboroughs… All they want to talk about is money.'

Thursday, 22 February
Sixty-four. There's no question, that is a venerable age. Lovely letter from Rona, along with the mountain of cards. Popped next door. On Lou's behalf Flo had bought a card & necktie & Lou remembered to give them to me!!… Loads more crap at the office. Belinda had already been on to Smythson's to order acknowledgement stationery! Then in came Harry with Portaloo, Sir Hugh, the McNair-Wilsons, Gilmour, Body & Franks, with the cake & champagne. All very embarrassing. Saved by the division bell!!

One-line whip, so I was in time for Alfredo's at 8 o'c. with M., Paul & Rupert. We raised a glass to Gordon. I complained about the cigar smoke coming from an obese article on the next table. I said 'We asked for No Smoking…' The boy looked puzzled & said 'Well, I did put you in the non-smoking section, sir. The boundary is the red rope.' These places are run by idiots.

---

[14] (1940-2010) Tory MP for Davyhulme, 1983-95. Grandson of former Prime Minister Sir Winston Churchill.

Beyond Our Kenneth

Sunday, 25 February
LWT for the Dimbleby programme. Defending the poll tax is nigh on impossible, especially as I don't believe in it, but I gave it a faint stab. Much firmer footing when Jonathan moved on to crime. Best part was chatting to Janet Brown[15] in the green room. There's one person, at least, who *explicitly* benefits from Mrs T staying at Number 10!!

Tuesday, 27 February
Bulgaria has gone. That dominated PMQs. Hurd is furious, Brussels doesn't have a plan & America seems bizarrely indifferent – or, more accurately, distracted… Finishing touches to speech. Rose at 7.37 to speak. Only about twenty there to listen. Waddington's reply was full of platitudes but it boiled down to 'the government agrees that killers & terrorists should hang, but there are too many invertebrates in the Commons to push it through & there are currently bigger dragons to slay.' A few supportive interjections, but it was a decidedly damp squib.

Wednesday, 28 February
Outside St Margaret's a scruffy man came up & announced 'I'm just the same as you.' 'I'm sure you are,' I said, hurriedly trying to cross the road & escape. 'You see, I'm also a mouthy sod,' it said, before waving & ambling away down Broad Sanctuary.

Friday, 2 March
Whenever I see the Prime Minister, I still get that frisson of excitement. She's not a classic beauty – or, indeed, an unclassic one – but she's one of those creatures with *presence*. She was with the favourites, returning to Downing St, & the smile she gave me would've consoled the most doubting of Thomases. But then I'm safe, I suppose – not a threat, just a court jester… Whether she survives or not, by my reckoning there'll be a general election in a year. Even if I did choose to stand again I wouldn't win, so I've got twelve months to actually *do* something.

Sunday, 4 March
To the Paris at 5.30 for the final *J.A.M.* of the series. O dear! Talk about gloomy, what with Merton going off on one about the poll tax & Dickie

---

[15] Scottish actress and impressionist (1923-2011). Widow of KW's *Carry On* colleague Peter Butterworth. Gained fame for her impersonations of Mrs Thatcher.

Murdoch[16] looking ill & confused. Stanley mentioned that he'd seemed a bit peaky when he did the *Majeika* thing, but he was all over the shop tonight. I practically sprinted out when it was finished.

Tuesday, 6 March
If *Spitting Image* was accurate satire, one would deduce that this place is filled with fascinating 'characters' whose idiosyncratic traits – both physical & temperamental – have some *effect* on how they shape the nation… whereas *in fact*, apart from a very few exceptions, there are no *personalities* here at all – just a herd of rather dull, balding men & the occasional frumpy woman, attempting to undertake a grindingly frustrating job whilst drowning in paperwork & flabby, prolix speeches.

Wednesday, 7 March
Spotted Eric Welsh in the Tea Room. He brought the last cap. punishment bill in '83. Picked his brains a bit. 'The Party's full of "politically correct" wankers,' he said. 'Only a fraction truly believe in their heart that execution is murder – the rest are just afraid of *The Guardian*…' He advised me to be a Robert Catesby,[17] sound people out & pounce when the moment is right – an IRA bomb or the unjustifiably early release of a villain.

3 o'c. to St Joseph's primary school to open their new library. Looked more like a Verner Panton[18] showroom to me, not a straight line to be seen – & not many *books* either. Still, the children were enchanting. One little lad, with the finger lodged in the nose, said 'I've seen'd you on the telly when I was younger…' He couldn't have been more than five… Released & went to the Odeon with Paul for *Driving Miss Daisy*. Rubbish.

Friday, 9 March
Barmy letter from a constituent who wants me to raise an "important" issue in the House – 'I purchased a Ferguson VHS player in good faith in November 1982 for £599 and *now* I read that they're going to stop making the tapes for it! I mean, *surely* I'm entitled to some sort of compensation??' Madly, the very next letter was from Peter Rogers asking me to go on *Breakfast News* to 'promote the Betamax & Laserdisc releases of *Carry On*

---

[16] Richard Murdoch (1907-90), English actor, star of multiple radio comedy series from the 1930s to the 1970s.
[17] English conspirator (c.1572-1605), leader of the Gunpowder Plot of 1605.
[18] Danish furniture designer (1926-98).

Again Nurse.' Dictated a *per pro* letter to Belinda, which concluded 'Whilst the most Honourable Member for Holborn & St Pancras deeply appreciates your correspondence, he feels his commitments in the Palace of Westminster must force him to abrogate any duties related to your recent request. In other words, on yer bike.'

Saturday, 10 March
Lou's got a dicky tummy & the results are unspeakable. I won't go there until it's over.

Sunday, 11 March
Gyles 'phoned. He was quite dismissive of the plans – 'I can't really see the merit in returning to those days.' It's disheartening. One hopes that progressive Toryism is possible, but it can't entail ditching *every* unfashionable parcel of the status quo for the sake of it. The *conserve* bit of *conservative* must mean retaining sensible policies in the face of criticism – & having the courage to revoke old errors… Went in to Louisa. She was sleeping & Rita was soaking sheets. It's only a touch of the runs, but even the slightest ailment floors her nowadays.

Thursday, 15 March
With Harry & Adam to Chancery Court to oversee the refurbishment. Pearl Assurance have pissed off to Peterborough, so they're turning it into an hotel. Soon enough London will be one large hotel, existing wholly for Japanese tourists, as the daily Relocation Buses evacuate Londoners to their new jerry-built prefabs in Stevenage & Runcorn… I refused to wear the mandatory builders' hat, much to the foreman's bewilderment: I'm not messing up the riah & looking idiotic for the cameras, falling masonry be buggered. Gave it 20 mins, then we escaped to Kettner's for lunch.

Friday, 16 March
It's galling to ask Townend for anything, as he plainly loathes me, but as he's on the Selection Committee one has to occasionally brownnose in the hope of better things to come. I've managed to reword the phrase 'I want to be on the Justice Select Committee' about seven different ways since the turn of the year, but the man is a master of changing the subject. Looks like biding the time & a Private Members' Bill is the only way forward… Torrence the clerk tapped me on the shoulder & pointed out a tear in the

elbow of my jacket. 'Slip it off & I'll sort it, sir' he said. Within five minutes he was back & it was repaired!!

Supper in the Strangers Dining Room with Brooke, droning on about Ulster, & Gummer,[19] droning on about fish. It really is a dull cabinet; no wonder the PM feels she has to pull all the strings herself... Made excuses & fled home for cocoa with Louisa. The trots have abated, thank goodness, & she seems more herself.

Sunday, 18 March
Up early. Replied to some fan mail & got papers from Bill. Another strangled body found on wasteland in Manchester. Though how one distinguishes between wasteland & normal land in Manchester is anyone's guess.

Tuesday, 20 March
Budget. I sat comfortably with Major's delicate voice gently nuzzling my cochleas. I didn't pay much attention to *what* he was saying, until he got to the stuff for savers, which was encouraging.

Thursday, 22 March
After Question Time they gathered around the TV in the Bishop's bar & watched them raising the bow of the *Titanic*. Lots of oohing & aahing as the rusting hulk reluctantly surfaced. Legions of Americans on the deck of the recovery vessel, going wild & waving the baseball caps – all quite inappropriate, of course, for a gravesite. Gerry Bowden[20] said 'They'd better get some Jenolite on that, quick.'

To Broadcasting House at 4 o'c. to record some Coward for *Poetry Please*. It's rather nice, dipping back in from time to time. Went for a pee & a West Indian man recognised me at the urinal. He actually held out the hand, mid-flow, wishing to shake mine (the *hand*, that is). 'Another time, perhaps, when we're less occupied,' I said.

Friday, 23 March
Flo 'phoned at 6 o'c. – she's got a bug & can't come. As she probably picked it up from Lou I couldn't sound annoyed, but I was inwardly furious. Paul is on a sabbatical & *thank heavens* came to the rescue... Michael Brunson

---

[19] John Selwyn Gummer (b. 1939), Tory MP for Suffolk Coastal, 1983-2010. Responsible for food safety during the 'mad cow disease' epidemic. See entry for 20 May 1990.
[20] Gerald Bowden (1935-2020), Tory MP for Dulwich, 1983-91.

Beyond Our Kenneth

nabbed me in the Lobby for a poll tax quote. Got away with denigrating the rates rather than lauding the changes, but that in itself is a criticism. Briefing in Committee Room 12, where Renton reiterated the decree to refer to it as the *Community Charge* in interviews, on pain of death… The bigwigs noticeably gloomy as we lost Mid Staffs to Labour overnight.

Saturday, 24 March
Got the 27 to Hammersmith. Woman behind me, to her friend: 'Of course, it's the *shade* that worried me. I haven't seen that kind of colour since Mandy's eldest had gastritis.'

Sunday, 25 March
Got papers. Robert Runcie[21] is stepping down. 'Maybe you should have a crack at that next?' joked Paul. 'Don't you have to believe in God?' I asked. 'Doesn't seem to bother most Anglicans,' he said… M. took us to Joe Allen's. We discussed Namibia. Typical, that a country should be so near to independence & a future on its own terms, & now *this* happens. We really should be doing something, but I'll wager it's a long way down the to-do list.

Wednesday, 28 March
Loads of letters to dictate. The stuff people write about beggars belief! Things nobody would've admitted even to *themselves* in the old days – 'Dear Mr Williams, I suffer from an inflamed vulva & can't bend down to dust…', 'Dear Mr Williams, my lavatory is broken, so I've had to start using milk bottles…' – yet now they shamelessly scribble down the facts in biro in the hope someone else (muggins) will clean up their mess or allay their incompetence. Well, I shan't. If they want sympathy, they can ask *Kilroy*.[22] If our people don't relearn *self-sufficiency* then we're sunk.

Saturday, 31 March
Was meant to be going to the National Gallery with Rupert, but he cried off & thank goodness he did… Watched the riots with Lou.[23] Reminiscent of the Battle of Cable Street. Huge swathes of disgruntled yobs, smashing windows & starting fires. We saw the woman trampled *à la* Emily Davison,

---

[21] (1921-2000) Archbishop of Canterbury, 1980-90. Previously Bishop of St Albans.
[22] BBC1 daytime chat show (1986-2004), presented by former Labour MP Robert Kilroy-Silk.
[23] The poll tax riots, centred on Trafalgar Square, resulted in 339 arrests and 113 injuries.

the Police completely out of control. It was monstrous, quite commensurate with the footage from Johannesburg. Harry 'phoned. 'This is bad,' he said. 'Not many governments survive this kind of thing.' Saw some of the walking wounded pass by the flat. It is a stupid tax, the PM must realise that. It may be a kamikaze mission, i.e. if *she's* finished, so are the rest of us… Had crumpets for tea – the Gateway ones are *extraordinarily* good.

Sunday, 1 April
Poll tax is introduced *today*, April Fool's Day.

Monday, 2 April
There's a leak in Gilmour's office so he's been shifted to the Cloisters. 'It's not always like this, you know.' 'Beg pardon?' I said. 'I don't want you thinking this is typical… I mean, we've had our shaky moments over the years, but you've walked in during an earthquake.' There is a sense of the last days of Rome. The Empress Margaret flits about, former ministers sharpening their knives behind her back with stony contempt on their faces – or worse: sickly smiles. Baker going round extinguishing fires – 'This is the Conservative Party, we don't bow down to agitators or rabble-rousers – the policy remains intact!'… Saw Howe[24] in the Commons' corridor & he looks forlorn & frustrated. I can sympathise in as much as he *believes* in Europe, as do many in the cabinet, but her bellicose attitude is wearing rather thin in Brussels.

Tuesday, 3 April
Patten[25] said to me 'I'm surprised you're so black & white on such a complicated issue,' referring to execution. It's ludicrous. Only intellectuals have the *capacity* to be black & white, legitimately – one collates the facts, evaluates the evidence & comes to a conclusion. It's the uninformed & inept who drown in the quicksand of compromise… The only danger is that enlightened certainty can sometimes be mistaken for 'faith'.

Fax from Francis saying that, despite the lack of promotion, sales of the book have been extremely good!! Says 'I really must insist on a proper publicity tour for the release of the paperback,' but he can go whistle – these figures prove that such expeditions are superfluous.

---

[24] Sir Geoffrey Howe (1926-2015), Tory MP for East Surrey, 1974-91. Chancellor of the Exchequer, 1979-83; Foreign Secretary, 1983-9; Deputy Prime Minister, 1989-90.

[25] Chris Patten (b. 1944), Tory MP for Bath, 1979-91; Environment Secretary, 1989-90.

Thursday, 5 April
Dreamt that I was being forced to stand down as a Member, on the discovery that I was in fact Duke of Connaught & therefore not a commoner. Portillo was there saying 'It's for the best, Your Grace…'

Friday, 6 April
Arrived Tangé at 2 o'c. precisely. Cab to the Rembrandt & unpacked. O! it's marvellous to be out of London!! It's warm here, but bearable. Rupert unimpressed with his room, so he's paid the extra & is in their honeymoon suite!!!

    6 o'c. – regretting everything already. I swore I'd never come back to this dump.

Saturday, 7 April
Took him to the Grande Mosquée & the Casbah. Passed through Petit Socco. Hardly a Moroccan to be seen, just obese American tourists, awful. Eventually met the boys at the Grenouille & Rupert gave us dinner. Fed up with all the English & Yanks, so a vision called Rafiq took us to a filthy café deep in the Medina. Black African boys sat around the edges of the room, sipping mint tea & chewing leaf tobacco. Disgusting pornography playing on an ancient television in the corner. Rupert whispered 'Is it safe?' – I must have a higher tolerance for that kind of thing, but I suppose his caution is understandable… Nothing doing, so went to Ibn Maaq for drinks. Got talking to a Lufthansa steward called Arnie. 'I am shaving the pubic hairs before coming to Morocco,' he said, 'as the guys here are all having the louses.' 'Don't I know it, ducky,' I thought[26]… There's no doubt about it – the thrilling *allure* of this place is long gone.

Sunday, 8 April
Met the boys at the beach & they went swimming – rather them than me; the water brought to mind frothy Bisto. I sat & read the Ishiguro,[27] then chatted to some Mauritanians who were fishing from the jetty. Gave them 30 dirham to share out between them… Went to Ibn Maaq & had the drinks with Derek Jarman.[28] He's preparing to film *Edward the Second*. 'Of course,

---

[26] KW had been infested with pubic lice on a trip to Morocco in August 1969.

[27] *The Remains of the Day* (1989) by Kazuo Ishiguro.

[28] (1942-94) British filmmaker, artist and gay rights activist.

I expect *your* government will try to ban it,' he said. 'Just think of all the *good* you could've done.' Yawn... Returned to Rembrandt for nap.

Monday, 9 April
O! it was daft madness to come away. Distraction is all very well, but I no longer feel free here. It's just a noisy, smelly Southend... well, it's Southend.

Tuesday, 10 April
At breakfast Rupert said 'That fellow keeps looking over... I'm sure I saw him yesterday,' referring to a bearded thing in a shell suit at the bar. Saw it again outside the Librairie des Colonnes. We got out of eyesight & hid behind a column – within seconds, there he was. I saw the camera & the penny dropped. *News of the World*, trying to catch me out. Rupert made sure he was in-between me & the camera as we darted for a cab, but the arse carried on snapping away. 'On your 'olidays, Mr Williams? Who's this, your *friend*??' Snap snap. It was frightful. Straight back to Rembrandt, sat in the room. Went over & over *who* could've told them I'd be here – & *why*... Rupert booked us on the 5.20 Air France to Lyon & the 9.55 British Midland to Stansted. Never so glad to be home.

Wednesday, 11 April
Telephoned Harry. He reckons the check-in girls at London airports have the numbers of the tabloid gossip desks & drop them a line when 'people of interest' go abroad. He must be right. Anyone who knew we'd be in Tangier would have no reason to let on... The tabloid press are *scum*.

Friday, 13 April
Wrote a condoling letter to Nick Lewis[29] & went to post. Grinning girl in a peach cardigan behind the window said 'It's Friday the thirteenth today, so watch yourself!' 'Don't talk such tripe,' I said & walked out. Guilty twinge as I reached the door. Turned round & said 'May I apologise, that was quite wrong of me. Thank you for the warning, I shall watch my step.' I have never done this before, backtracked that is, but there was no need to be impolite to the poor girl. She has a miserable job, yet faces it with enthusiasm. There was a tramp outside Great Portland Street station, and I put 80p in his cup.

---

[29] A student at Warwick University, with whom KW maintained an epistolary friendship. The condoling letter was in response to the death of Lewis's father.

Sunday, 15 April
Went & got papers. One small picture in the *News of the World*: me next to the coloured fisherman on the pier, under the heading 'Black Rod! MP Ken codding locals on African hols'. So horribly dispiriting to think that the cur was watching me throughout the trip, via a long lens... M. is in Switzerland, so had lunch with Louie & Rita in the flat. The way Lou talks, it's a wonder Rita hasn't throttled her – 'O! this lamb ain't 'alf chewy', 'Where'd you put my glasses?', 'D'you call *that* washing-up?'... but Rita's not perturbed! She laughs it all off: 'Oh, Mrs Williams, you are a hoot!'... When she'd gone, Lou said 'That girl is a marvel. She has me on & off the loo before you can say Jack Robinson.'

Monday, 16 April
We saw the television. It was me in *Carry On Teacher*, looking about fifteen. Astounding to think that that kind of junk sustained me for so long. I should've *demanded* better from Eade[30]... Still, it beats sitting up at Heath Hurst listening to old biddies drone on about broken paving slabs.

Wednesday, 18 April
I find John Major rather agreeable. He is quietly engaging, eminently polite & a real listener. You can tell he *wasn't* raised with the silver spoon, a far cry from these born-to-rule loafers. His TESSA[31] plan is admirable, people should be *incentivised* to save. I don't think the idea had occurred to previous chancellors; it was all very much 'let them eat cake'... Went through some constituency stuff with Belinda, rather trying, then car to Banner Street to meet the Victim Support team. Almost choked at the éclat of these marvellous people – when the police have washed their hands of you, thank *heavens* for concerned shoulders to cry on & *practical* advice... They gave me coffee & biscuits in their little office.

Thursday, 19 April
Seems that the rising in Plovdiv has been put down. The new pro-western government in Yugoslavia has already applied for EEC membership, so a frit Belgrade can clearly see which way the wind is blowing... In the tearoom

---

[30] Peter Eade (1919-79), KW's theatrical agent, 1951-79. He also represented Ronnie Barker and Joan Sims.

[31] Tax-exempt special savings account.

after PMQs I overheard a coven of deadbeat peers discussing 'disgusting queers' & 'filthy arse-bandits', egging each other on like playground bullies. AIDS has really bolstered this kind of flagrant nastiness & emboldened the bigoted to air such views. Considered confronting them, but decided to clock who they were & hold off for use at a later date.

Saturday, 21 April
Woken at 6 o'c. by sodding *birds*. Walked to Texas & purchased pigeon spikes for £2.79. Spent the afternoon attaching them to the ledge. A youth shouted from the pavement 'Don't do it, mister!' as I was dangling out of the window.

Tuesday, 24 April
One never sees the Prime Minister without Charles Powell[32] nowadays. I know she feels she can't trust anyone, but narrowing one's clique so drastically can't be astute. Favourites are either in it for themselves, or so devoted to their master that they only offer advice they know will be welcome: this PM requires honesty from aides, *especially* when their guidance is hard to swallow… Dinner in the MDR with Hugh, Cecil & Kenneth Clarke.[33] KC said that persuading the PM to accept his recommendations on the NHS is *exhausting*. His assessments seem perfectly self-evident to me – keep the unions at arm's length & let the doctors spend the money. It'll make him unpopular with the BMA – it already has, what with posters & pamphlets denigrating him – but he's got a thick skin. During coffee, the waiter asked for an autograph. 'Not now,' I said, 'we're talking.' 'Actually,' he muttered, 'I meant Mr Clarke,' & I was left with the ego round the ankles.

Wednesday, 25 April
At long last, the madness at Strangeways is over.[34] Vile. The police should've shot them down off the roof one by one.

Friday, 27 April
Lousy night. Keep dreaming of Gordon & these lines he repeats & repeats – 'Justice is righteous' & 'Without Rona I'm nothing.' It's driving me round the bloody twist.

---

[32] British diplomat and businessman (b. 1941), key foreign policy advisor to Mrs Thatcher.
[33] (b. 1940) Tory MP for Rushcliffe, 1970-2019. Secretary of State for Health, 1988-91.
[34] The 25-day prison riot and rooftop protest at HMP Strangeways in Manchester was the longest in British penal history, leaving one dead and 194 injured.

Sunday, 29 April
Did my bit for the local elections (as little as I could get away with), flyering at Camden. Made sure the *Gazette* photographer caught me in as many shots as possible. Home by lunchtime.

Tuesday, 1 May
Didn't finish voting till gone midnight, so bleary-eyed this morning. Decided to forgo the blood sports meeting – I couldn't care less about foxes. Strove to catch up on the constituency case backlog. Interesting letter from a couple in Gospel Oak. Both aged 80, have been together since 1956 – one is dying of lung cancer & is terrified the other won't be provided for. It *is* a nonsense. A newlywed man & wife who despise each other have more rights than two adoring blueboys who've been together since Suez. Bizarre misconception at the close, though: 'We are sure that you will understand our problem more keenly than anyone else in parliament…' I should've thought my confirmed bachelorhood was more widely acknowledged than that.

Wednesday, 2 May
Belinda in tears, Harry doling out the Kleenex. It seems that vile clod Dennis Chambers[35] *caressed her bottom* by the Public Bill Office & made some remark about her being a 'game filly'. Went immediately to Renton to complain, undeterred by her protestations about me making a fuss… He tried to play it down, but I kicked up enough of a stink for him to 'have a quiet word' – 'Fuck the quiet words,' I said, 'have some loud ones,' which sent him berry-red in the cheeks. It's lunatic – this lot are meant to be men of the world, but the slightest bit of language gives them fits of embarrassment… Lunched with Rifkind.[36] He's convinced the Scots would turn down devolution. Don't know what planet he's on – if Vstavlyat floated the idea, I reckon they'd opt for *that* union over this one… Sat in on the Gulf debate. I counted *four* members who were soundo. It's a disgrace. One expects it in the other place, but not here. I farted & wafted the residue towards Dykes, which had the desired *rousing* effect.

---

[35] (1939-2009) Downing Street Chief of Staff, 1985-91.
[36] Malcolm Rifkind (b. 1946), Tory MP for Edinburgh Pentlands, 1974-95. Secretary of State for Scotland, 1986-91.

1990

Thursday, 3 May
Letter of sincere apology from Chambers. Belinda read it aloud & acted it out, doing the lisp & twitch. So, evidently she's not particularly scarred by the event, but at least the old duffer's had his wings clipped... Came back from committee to memo from Flo. Lou's fallen & bruised the bum. Fled back. She's alright, though the arse looks like Yves Klein's had a go at it. 'I don't know how it happened, I was just watching *Matchpoint* & then I was on the floor...' Flo said 'She were trying to get Club biscuits off top shelf without me & she slip.' Thought about telling her off, but the pain in the backside should be enough of a chiding... Walked to Heath Hurst. Got the file of Mr Pearson & Mr Stride, the Gospel Oak pair. They've written five times & deserve a considered response.

Friday, 4 May
Results are as expected – we lost 222 councillors, with only a third of the vote share. Still, we actually *gained* 2 seats (net) in Camden! All down to my flyering, I should think.

Saturday, 5 May
'Phone rang at 7 o'c. & it was Austin! 'Are you busy today?'... 'Not particularly, why?'... 'We're filming our cookery programme at Maidstone... Edwina Currie[37] was meant to be a judge, but she's had to pull out at the last minute. Could you fill in?'... Got the 10.10 from Victoria & was there in an hour. Straight through into make-up, then on to the set. Three amateurs each produce a meal & a celebrity, a proper chef & the host (Loyd Grossman – the boy from that *Keyhole* rubbish) have to assess the results. The poor saps take it so seriously!! *Quenelling* this & *julienning* that... O! it's such pretentious muck. I asked helpful questions such as 'Do you enjoy dipping them in batter?' and 'What's your technique for spreading & filling?', much to everyone's discomfiture. Briskly out after, declining the drinks. I was indoors by 5 o'c. Went in to Lou & gave her some whisky. Load of foreign types singing on the television, so I switched off & dug out the backgammon.

Sunday, 6 May
M. arrived on crutches!! He's twisted his ankle playing croquet, of all things. I shouldn't have thought that was possible. He gingerly drove us to Joe

---

[37] Writer and broadcaster (b. 1946), Tory MP for South Derbyshire, 1983-99.

Beyond Our Kenneth

Allen's... Joan Sims was there!! She was with Sam Kelly;[38] they're filming something called *On the Up* for the BBC. Sounds yuppyish & ghastly. Joan went to kiss Louie, who bellowed 'Blimey, girl, ain't you a *size* now?', which Joanie laughed off, but I could see the dagger piercing deep. In fairness, she *has* ballooned, but Lou didn't need to broadcast the fact... After, we wheeled her round the park – M. insisted, saying he needed the exercise. We could've passed for day-trippers from the cripples' ward. Lou wanted a 99 from the van – that's *on top* of the soup, salmon & strudel she'd just golloped – but I refused it. 'You don't want to go down the same road as Joan,' I said. 'Joan who?' she replied. There was scowling, & moaning about the bum, but I held firm.

Tuesday, 8 May
There's always lethargy after a recess here. Place like a ghost town till noon. The date's been set for Dukakis's visit: he'll be in London for *one night* on the 22nd, before spending *three days* in Bonn. So much for the 'special relationship'... Telephoned Geoffrey Stride. The boyfriend, Eric, has taken a turn for the worse & hasn't got much longer to go. I was frank. Told him that the law is what it is & there's very little I can do. Gave him the number of Orrin who might be able to give some financial advice. Before replacing the receiver, I said 'I am on your side, Mr Stride. But I am only one man.' 'One famous, *elected* man,' he murmured.

Thursday, 10 May
Gow took me to the Lords Record Office in Victoria Tower... I was staggered!! All the Acts of Parliament going back to the conquest, giant vellum Swiss rolls stacked high on miles of shelving. The Clerk showed us King Charles' death warrant, the Bill of Rights & the Great Reform Act. Some of the penmanship is exquisite, especially for being on calf... O! to have an Act of one's own & actually *accomplish* something!

Friday, 11 May
Spoke in the chamber about longstanding cohabitation, & it having no legal status. Risible to think that *I* should be the standard bearer for such a cause – I've never shared anything... Tagged along with Ryder to the Treasury. A

---

[38] English actor (1943-2014), best known for playing Captain Hans Geering in *'Allo 'Allo!* and Warren in *Porridge*.

Soviet asylum came to mind – white tiles & eerie echoes. Lots of hushed groaning about the inflation figures. Got lumbered with a glum civil servant who went on & on about 'storm clouds brewing' & 'the gloomy outlook'. Kept thinking of Twain: 'I've lived through some terrible things in my life, some of which actually happened...' I agree with Ustinov: pessimism is a romantic indulgence. There's so much that *can* go wrong, optimism is the only way forward, especially for natural melancholics of my ilk.

Saturday, 12 May
Rita on holiday, so I stopped in with Lou. If I hear one more thing about *Home & Away* I shall put a brick through the television screen.

Monday, 14 May
Harry is a rock. He spends virtually all his time getting me *out* of things, mainly corporate invitations. Businesses with bank accounts in Zurich & offices in Hong Kong *do not* deserve my time. 'Here's the list of unavoidables,' he said... In the afternoon we went to St John's hospice. One can rapidly lugubriate in such places, but it was clear they didn't want my sympathy – I sailed round telling the dirty jokes & camping it up & the mood lightened straight away. The dying need laughter at the end... it is *not* frivolous – it girds the loins & puts the whole farce of life into perspective.

Thursday, 17 May
Letter from Mr Stride in the second post. Eric passed on yesterday teatime. He thanked me for the Get Well Soon card & the 'help' I'd given. Felt wretched, so went to talk to Sir Hugh, but he just carped on about the Corsican waiter from Claridge's he's knocking off, so escaped to the library... Was reading an article in *The Times*, about the WHO finally removing homosexuality from its list of *diseases*, when Tony Tichet-Sweeting[39] came & talked. 'About time too,' he said, referring to the article. 'Yes, indeed,' I replied. He sat down &, in hushed tones, said 'Did you know that 76% of the public support the return of hanging, & 76% believe that homosexuality is inherently wrong? Latest polling data.' 'What a time to be alive!' I joshed, but he didn't smile. 'The remnants of our glorious Judæo-Christian traditions,' he remarked, bitterly. 'It can't be right, Kenneth,' he muttered,

---

[39] Antony Tichet Sweeting (b. 1947), Tory MP for Ilkeston, 1983-2010. Wed Rupert Jarvis (sometime partner of KW) on 29 March 2014, the day same-sex marriages were legalised in England and Wales.

shaking his head. 'It can't be *just*...'... Thought of Gordon. Wrote a long reply to Mr Stride.

'Phoned Stanley. Met him at the Tent at 8 o'c. He was in a rather tetchy mood. Told him about the quandary. 'I know you think the country's thrown the baby out with the bathwater,' he said, 'but have a look through your diaries – the past wasn't the paradise it's cracked up to be.' In part, he's right. People miss certainty and order, but they fear change & the unknown. In which case, I shall spin two plates: one v. v. conservative & one v. v. liberal. In a way, that's v. v. *me*.

Friday, 18 May
Irving's[40] party. Greeted me with the usual 'O! it's Dr Soaper!'... He says this *every sodding time* he sees me, so I blanked him & chatted to Matthew Parris,[41] who is a sweetheart... The hired help was sent down to the cellar to get more ice & never came back! Eventually he was found, spread-eagled on the basement floor, a huge welt on the bonce from the doorjamb. They got him to his feet & Ashby shuffled him out to the ambulance, still clutching a bag of melted ice cubes as though he'd won a goldfish at the fair. 'You want some ice on that!' yawped Amos, & they all laughed.

Saturday, 19 May
M. came at 8 o'c., limping, but off the crutches. Collected Rupert & Paul & we drove to Cambridge... Met Simon (the student at Gonville & Caius) & we did the Fitzwilliam & the punting before luncheon at Brown's. Rupert stood in a dog turd &, instead of finding a facility to clean the brogues, went into Cheaney's & simply *bought* a new pair. Mad extravagance. Then to the botanic gardens where a vagrant was getting arrested for peeing in public. Overheard the gardener giving a statement & the charge was 'urinating on an amaryllis in broad daylight'.

Sunday, 20 May
News is all about Gummer force-feeding his little girl beef burgers to prove they don't send you doolally. Footage of the child recoiling in disgust is simply *delicious*.

---

[40] Sir Charles Irving (1924-95), Tory MP for Cheltenham, 1974-91.
[41] South Africa-born British political writer and broadcaster (b. 1949), Tory MP for West Derbyshire, 1979-86. Co-founder of the gay rights charity Stonewall.

Monday, 21 May

Papers are bad. Lots of 'Maggie to give Mick a piece of her mind', re the American visit, which I'm sure the PM & Ingham will lap up, but it's all fantasy. In truth, her influence is slipping: with Reagan she had an ally & with Gorbachev she had a cordial adversary – Dukakis ostensibly resents her & Vstavlyat is about as amenable as Uncle Joe. Helmut Kohl is a tart at heart, & will *love* the attention coming to him… It's going to be gruesome viewing.

Tuesday, 22 May

After Questions, raced round to Richard Body's office where we watched the arrival on television. The American flag flying above Downing Street was noticeably *smaller* than the Union Jack beside it: no doubt on purpose. It's this kind of feeble pettiness that leaves such a nasty taste in the mouth. The smiles were awkward, the handshakes brief. Denis & Kitty seemed to get on well, but then they've got playing the second-fiddle in common… Sneaked off for supper with Kenny Connor. He's in town filming that Croft/Perry thing. O! it was a delight to see him. He told me a wonderful story about a conversation he'd had with the set painter on *Hi-de-Hi!*… Kenny: 'Did you vote in the election?' Painter: 'No fear, they're all the same I reckon.' Kenny: 'Don't you like Mrs Thatcher?' Painter: 'She's alright, I suppose. But, as my missus says, where's the *Realpolitik*?'… The voices Kenny did it in had me howling! The English working classes never fail to disappoint. If only they knew their power.

Wednesday, 23 May

'Where has America gone, Mister President?' screams *Today*. This is apparently what she asked him. The tea room chatter is that the evening was as acrimonious & chilly as expected. He popped in briefly to see the Queen at noon, & is already on Air Force One out of here… *Of course* Dukakis is hopeless, but it doesn't do to alienate the States *and* Europe at the same time. The sharks are already circling again, briefing against her & rebuking her off-the-record to the press. I saw Michael[42] pacing restlessly. 'I know she'll just say "compromise didn't get me where I am today", but someone needs to sit her down & explain the dangers.' But I don't think there's anyone she listens to any more.

---

[42] Michael Mates (b. 1934), Tory MP for East Hampshire, 1983-2010.

Friday, 25 May
Flo put Lou in the mauve dress with the dragonfly brooch & I wheeled her to the Boot. Phyllis & the cousins arrived at 12.04. It was a bit inimical to begin with, but after the sherries kicked in they were alright. Surprisingly, Charlie was never mentioned. Probably because they both hated him… Phyllis was putting it away & when she said 'What's Shanghai Lil' doing 'ere?', referring to Flo, I thought it was probably time to make tracks. Never again.

Saturday, 26 May
Walked to Hackney for *Gay Times* interview. The attitude was initially hostile, but I suppose their defensiveness is understandable – they *feel* attacked, even if 90% of it is imagined. I think Oscar (the one with blue hair) was surprised at my optimism. 'There'll be hurdles,' I said, 'but we're moving in the right direction.'

Sunday, 27 May
We were in the car *en route* to Joe Allen's when Radio 3 cut Brahms short to announce the assassination attempt. It seems Dukakis was getting back in his car after meeting Wałęsa when three shots rang out. Shoddy marksmanship, however, & he's only been clipped – one bullet in the backside. 'The cheek of it!' said Lou, & we fell about… We saw the TV news & he's fine. Trust him to get shot in an embarrassing place! (the bum, I mean, not Poland). It won't even garner much sympathy, just more scope for the punning headline writers… The other side was that ghastly charity crap.[43] If people just paid their taxes we could do away with this ostentatious "giving" nonsense once & for all. I returned to the flat and read *The Buddha of Suburbia*.[44]

Monday, 28 May
Went to St John's Wood for this portrait sitting. The artist, Michael Noakes,[45] has only just finished painting the PM; it's mad that Rupert managed to engage him to do *me*. His wife, Vivien, brought tea into the studio & the atmosphere was very convivial. I am to return on Friday.

---

[43] ITV's *Telethon '90*, presented by Michael Aspel.
[44] By Hanif Kureishi.
[45] English portrait painter (1933-2018). Other sitters included Queen Elizabeth II, President Clinton and Pope Benedict XVI.

Tuesday, 29 May
Got papers from tube. Sir Hugh has been arrested for public lewdness at Hampstead Heath – caught *in flagrante* with two exchange students. The *Mirror* is steaming in, of course. 'Phoned him at home – they'd bailed him. He was whimpering & full of regret, of course. 'My dear, I thought we were quite secluded…' I've no sympathy & I told him so. The real crime is that *homosexuality* will be chalked up as the cause of his behaviour, rather than the simple truth that he's a dirty old man. If the companions had been female, no doubt he'd've been up for a youth employment award.

Thursday, 31 May
Walked with Paul to Selfridge's where he purchased a laserdisc player for £600!! I pity people who are duped into shelling out over these ridiculous fads. I won't even have an electric typewriter in the house… Flo has requested two weeks off in August to visit the wretched family in Manila. It really is too bad of her.

Friday, 1 June
After the sitting I rushed to HH for advice surgery. Usual dross. One woman in a plastic mack complaining that the council want to remove ten of her *thirteen* Alsatians. The only question in my mind was 'what's so special about the other three?' – Her file showed endless complaints from other tenants regarding the *smell*, so I told her to pull herself together. She started snivelling, so I asked 'Have you considered a goldfish?' – which went down about as well as Sir Hugh in a copse.

Saturday, 2 June
It's Rita's birthday so after lunch Lou gave her the champagne (it's only Gateway's, but quite good enough for the purpose) & the card from us both. She broke down – even her mother had forgotten to 'phone – so it got a trifle awkward. Told her to buck up & fetch some glasses & we toasted her health… On the news they showed Duke thanking the Polish doctors & shuffling uncomfortably up the aeroplane stairs. It was *painful* to watch. They might as well elect Emmett Kelly & be done with it.

Sunday, 3 June
Went to get papers. Bill said 'Rex Harrison went during the night. His pancreas'd gone south.' I envisaged a nutant gland taking the sleeper to

Penzance... He'd been doing *The Circle* on Broadway when the cancer struck.

Tuesday, 5 June
Oppenheim[46] is a real dish. I drifted off during his speech at the economic meeting & imagined us entwined, breakfasting *au lit*, the monogrammed silk of his pyjamas & the flawless enunciation. Alas, even in my fantasies it was a non-starter... he's an animal rights proponent, so I expect he's in favour of *birds*.

Wednesday, 6 June
I've an idea that Belinda & Harry are having it off. They think I don't notice the glances & the gestures, but I do... Townend came sniffing round, still trying to palm off this fabricated position of Parliamentary Under-Secretary of State for Culture, to serve under Speller.[47] It's madness to have a department for *culture* – the very *last* realm of life that requires government involvement. I've made it quite clear that I'll only roll up my sleeves for something worthwhile... of course, I get the disapproving looks & the tutting, but I don't care a jot. 'Watch it,' Harry grinned, 'or he'll make you a PPS...' 'He can PPS off,' I said.

Thursday, 7 June
I performed rather well in the House. One of the advantages of not being one of *them* is that even the most politically hostile warm to one. There are some fine minds in parliament, it's true, but many suffer desperately from not being able to deliver a speech, or even a line. I managed to get *four* laughs, from all sides, during *one* short question about British beef, which must be a record[48]... Decided to put Ethan on the payroll – he's too good to be slaving away on expenses. He welled up when I told him. 'That'll be a relief,' said Belinda. 'He's been running on fumes.' I don't know why they don't come to me if they're in trouble, I'm very approachable.

---

[46] Phillip Oppenheim (b. 1956), Tory MP for Amber Valley, 1983-99. Latterly a *Sunday Times* columnist and businessman.

[47] Tony Speller (1929-2013), Tory MP for North Devon, 1979-91. Defeated Jeremy Thorpe at the 1979 general election.

[48] One of KW's quips (from Hansard): "Notwithstanding that, Mr Speaker, it would appear that the honourable lady from Sowerby [Labour MP Daphne Bridges] has a further vested interest in the government's handling of mad cows, a concern doubtless stiffened whenever she looks in the glass..."

Saturday, 9 June
Association luncheon at the Montague. Hardy kept pushing Mainbraces into my hand, so I was three sheets by 2 o'c. The toasts went on & on... one for the Queen, one for the PM, one for me, & when they'd exhausted sentient beings, we were charging glasses to England, London & then the boroughs. Melon balls & cutlets were never going to soak that lot up, so the speeches descended into slurred nonsense. Mrs Hardy was swanning round like Edna Everage, a Craven 'A' dangling from the lips. 'Go on, Kenneth, have a *large one*,' she squawked, cackling shrilly, much to the palpable disgust of her husband.

Sunday, 10 June
Another streetwalker found dead on a tip, this time in Didsbury. The papers are loving it: 'Full throttle – Gripper bags eighth', 'Jack the Tipper – should landfill security be boosted?', 'Smother nature – psychology of the Gripper'... Walked to the park with Paul. Sam & Helene were there, and Sam Sugar. A Rumanian refugee with a baby swaddled across its breast came over & shook thruppence at us, evidently wanting change. We waved it away, but the tragicness of this pitiable figure did give me a start. It's lovely to get some colour in the cheeks, but I got quite red!! Still, it suits me better than the customary chalkiness, & seems to camouflage the creases a bit too.

Monday, 11 June
Ian Gilmour's party at Syon. Starry affair, but the weather's taken a turn, so we all stood around on the patio, freezing our tits off. Lots of people wanting to talk to me, especially the journalists, which visibly annoyed Alan Clark.[49] A wizened Whitelaw[50] came & chatted, as did the Duke of Beaufort, banging on about fox hunting. Escaped early, using Lou as an excuse. It was a bit out-of-body-ish at times – these celebrated Establishment figures round about one, the sort of people I've spent a lifetime loathing... Dinner at Vecchia Milano with Stanley. He told a lovely story about a man who had binned a Gutenberg Bible to the horror of the auctioneer: 'Are you mad? That might've fetched a million pounds!' – 'No, I reckon my copy was

---

[49] Flamboyant and irreverent author and diarist (1928-99), Tory MP for Plymouth Sutton, 1974-91; Minister of State for Defence Procurement, 1989-91.
[50] William Whitelaw (1918-99), Tory MP for Penrith & the Border, 1955-83; Leader of the House of Lords, 1983-8; *de facto* Deputy Prime Minister, 1979-88.

worthless. Some idiot called Luther had signed his name in it & scribbled all over the fucking margins…'

Wednesday, 13 June
Fascinating discussion with Portillo. He's anti-Europe, which one expects from a second generation immigrant, but the head's screwed on. We laughed about Duke's approval ratings soaring in the States since the shooting – if you've had a vision of God or take a bullet, the Americans will *love* you for it. 'If it's *that* foolproof, maybe we should take a shot at the PM,' chortled Dunn – 'Nothing serious, just graze a shoulder pad or something'… I argued that Major's hard ecu was a sensible compromise with respect to currency, but they were horrified. 'Hard or not,' said Dunn, 'an ecu's an ecu, & it's not replacing my pound, thank you…'

Friday, 15 June
Another avalanche of post. More & more I keep thinking that *people* are the problem. There are hundreds of square pegs & just as many round holes: the desire for clean air but the indispensability of cars, the scourge of waste but the demand for asparagus in November, the insistence on tough policing but the assumption of freedoms… they know they can't have it all, they feel *guilt* for that knowledge, so they lay the blame on the filthy politicians – we're just a receptacle for public self-disgust… Richard came & showed me the pictures of Gorbachev in the *Standard*, waving & smiling. Clearly doctored. It's the Princes in the Tower all over again – the long-lens glimpses will be briefer & more seldom, until one day he disappears.

Sunday, 17 June
Rupert knocked & presented me with the Noakes portrait. I look dreadful in it, very gaunt & drawn. So I dare say it's a good likeness. Lord knows how much it set him back – I tried to appear grateful & delighted, but he could see through it. Showed it to Louie; her verdict: 'I wouldn't give you a thank you for it.' So I wrapped it in newspapers & shoved it behind the wardrobe.

Wednesday, 20 June
Put my head round the door of this culture committee, just to confirm my suspicions. Speller gabbing on about 'England's thriving traditions'… It's hogwash. England hasn't had its own traditions since Cabot docked in Bristol: our culture is bound up in that of the Empire – we have taken bits

& pieces from wherever we've landed, & these exotic novelties expunged the status quo. Reciprocally, we've transmitted our own rituals, pastimes & practices to other lands, where they've been internalised & – in many cases – improved upon... It's a trade-off. The only old countries which retain 'thriving traditions' are either insignificant, intractable or isolated.

In the House, Bowden proposed the idea of halving the number of councillors & doubling their responsibilities. I applaud the recommendation; there are far too many people in public life achieving far too little.

Thursday, 21 June
On the way out I saw Rhodri Morgan[51] in the lobby. 'My mother's a Morgan, you know,' I said, 'from Pontnewydd.' He smiled & said 'Ah, then we might be distant cousins!'... He's an affable chap – a Welsh patriot rather than a nationalist: he sings the songs with passion rather than defiance.

Friday, 22 June
She's furious about these murders. Richard said 'It was the same with Sutcliffe. She wanted to go to Leeds to take charge and catch him herself.' The commissioner is coming to Parliament for a dressing down. Ever the cynic, Dennis said 'She ought to be delighted – it takes the riots off the front pages.'

Watson, who's on the petitions committee, told me they've had *eight* public submissions – all with at least 25,000 signatures – calling for us to hang the killer when he's captured.

Saturday, 23 June
Telephone rang & it was Ch Insp Hewitt! They've caught the Midland robbers!! Suffolk Constabulary raided a house in Ipswich & found £525,000 in used notes. Why they should choose to remain in Ipswich with all that cash on the hip is beyond me, but the ginger one, the West Indian & two accomplices have all been apprehended. There'll be a trial, of course, but Hewitt said 'We've got 'em bang to rights.'

Monday, 25 June
I was shaving when Rupert knocked. 'Can you get the day off? Orlando's nabbed Centre Court tickets...' Rang Belinda & she cleared the decks. The 'friend' arrived in a white Bentley & drove us to Wimbledon. He hadn't just got tickets – we were given chitties as royal box guests!! Such swank... I met

---

[51] (1939-2017) Labour MP for Cardiff West, 1987-2001.

Beyond Our Kenneth

Bunny Austin, Rod Laver, Ken Rosewall, not to mention the Duchess of Kent. We saw the marvellous McEnroe play, but he got beat by a swarthy boy called Derek something[52]… I ought to feel guilty for sitting in the hazy sunshine watching tennis & supping Pimm's at the taxpayers' expense – but it's a treat I feel I deserved.

Tuesday, 26 June
Class war during Fowler's[53] questions session. That Jerry McBoyne[54] getting on his high horse about the Tories not understanding the plight of the working man, & 'enlisting celebrities to mask the stench of their cruelty'. These Islington ninnies are all the same, grandstanding on behalf of the poor from their Grade II listed balconies. He reluctantly gave way to me… 'As the target of the honourable gentleman's critique, Mr Speaker, I would ask him whether it's my *celebrity* that irks him so much, or the fact that I was born into poverty under the Labour government, growing up in two rooms off the Caledonian Road, the son of a hairdresser & charwoman, with no formal qualifications & yet I chose *not* to join his crusade, or look to Moscow for my politics? Hardship is regrettable from any distance, Mr Speaker, whether it's from one's own bedroom window, from the Prime Minister's father's corner shop, or from the croquet lawns of Shropshire, with which the honourable member will doubtless be familiar. The question is how do we tackle hardship? With rhetoric from the sidelines or with practical support? Maybe he could consult with Labour's prospective parliamentary candidate for Hampstead & Highgate, Mr Speaker – a Miss Glenda Jackson – but, ultimately, I suppose she's just a *celebrity*…' Went down rather well.

Wednesday, 27 June
The things young girls talk about in public these days!! I was waiting for the photocopier, & in the queue I overheard Goodlad & Couchman's interns chatting: 'I'm all for towels, I don't feel so bunged up.' 'O! really? I prefer the cup. Can't get on with those winged things. Feels like you're sitting on a lilo.' The blonde one noticed me. 'O! hi… didn't see you there.' 'So it would seem,' I said.

---

[52] Derrick Rostagno beat John McEnroe 7-5 6-4 6-4.
[53] Norman Fowler (b. 1938), Tory MP for Sutton Coldfield, 1974-2001. Secretary of State for Employment, 1987-91.
[54] Founder of the Manhole Cover Study Group (b. 1949), Labour MP for Angel, 1983-2019.

1990

Thursday, 28 June
Letter from the BBC inviting me to do a five-episode *Jackanory* entitled *The Twits*. Later – another letter from the Beeb in the second post, withdrawing the offer! Some rubbish about a scheduling mix up. It's bunkum, of course – some Marxist higher up the food chain has got wind of the proposal & blocked it. Would never have happened were Jeremy still at the helm. Whatever the ins & outs, it's an *outrage*, & is a politically motivated action.

Saturday, 30 June
The truth is I've been neglecting Louie. I know she's looked after & the girls do their best, but other than the TV & plebeian chatter, her world has shrunk since I started sodding about with this stuff. It's only me challenging her that keeps her stimulated & the cogs whirring… It was an effort, but Rita & I got her in the chair & to the Rose Garden where we sat & played I-spy & flung some Hovis at the mallards.

Harry rang at 3 o'c. Rumour that Orbell is standing down thanks to the stroke & his place on the justice committee will be up for grabs. We went through the list of possible candidates – all higher up the pecking order in conventional terms, but on the dull side, so muscling in might be possible. We agreed to form a plan of action on Monday, but there's plenty of time as the by-election won't be until after the summer.

Sunday, 1 July
Skin has split at the top of the crack of the bum & it's bloody agony. Washed it & applied the Savlon but it stings something dreadful… Clive drove from Eltham & took Paul & me to Joe Allen's. We had a pleasant time. The waitress was Czechoslovakian – a bonnie face, but the red knuckles & offish mien of a woman annealed by a hard life. She gave Clive the option of 'Grin bins or piss' to go with his steak. 'I'll have the grin bins,' he said, 'I had the piss before I come out'… Paul & I laughed. She *emphatically* didn't.

Monday, 2 July
Bum still murder. The breach is in a place you can't keep static for long, so it's not given time to heal. Spoke to Townend re. committee. 'We'll see' was the condescending response. Not v. encouraging… Overheard more 'backs to the walls' type chat in the team room when I entered. The joke is, I've no doubt every last one of them spent half their schooldays on their knees in the dormitories of Charterhouse, or fagging for preferment up at Oxford.

Beyond Our Kenneth

They abhor me, that's the crux of the matter – *I* get invited to dinner with cabinet ministers & *they* don't. They resent it. I feel increasingly that I'm in the right party in fiscal terms but very much the wrong one when it comes to personnel.

Tuesday, 3 July
Sir Hugh came, looking thin. He's got off with a slapped wrist but they're forcing him out without the accustomed peerage. He was seeking solace but didn't receive any from me... After PMQs I called in the team & we sketched out plans for my Westminster Hall debate. It won't be until November, but I want to cast the net as wide as possible. Finding Tories to speak will be easy, but favourable Labour voices might be another matter... Taxi to LBC to speak with Anna Raeburn.[55] The theme was changing careers, so it was apt. Anna said my paperback is being released on 1st October (which was news to me!!), so she did the plugging for me! Chatted to Charlie Williams[56] in hospitality. 'You've the same name as my late father,' I told him, 'The heart always skips a beat when you're mentioned on the television.' 'Tha's'll not've been mithered for a long while since, then,' he laughed. 'Last time I were on't box I were paid in silver tanners!'... He said how work has dried up & I condoled. 'Nay, flower,' he grinned, 'that's life. No sense getting mardy. 'Appen I should give thy game a whirl – the Bernie Grant of Barnsley... eeh, it's got a ring to it, has that!'

Dined with Cecil in the House, but the bum was itching & driving me up the wall so I didn't stay for coffee. Slapped on more Savlon. Went in to Lou. I made Horlicks & we saw *Fools & Horses*. Lou said 'I do like that Burgess Meredith...' She meant Buster Merryfield.

Wednesday, 4 July
Had the raisin Splitz as they seem to keep me sated best through the mornings. Saw the chaps in the lobby who are installing the new intercoms. It's an outrageous indulgence, but if the tenants are fools enough to shell out, that's their business... Lots of muted chattering in the House thanks to more *sleaze* – Ogilvy's been outed by *The Sun* for frequenting a bawdy house in Walthamstow, of all places. A lot of sanctimonious cant from his friends,

---

[55] Journalist and broadcaster (b. 1944), best known for giving advice as an 'agony aunt'.
[56] Professional footballer and entertainer (1927-2006), Britain's first well-known black stand-up comedian.

1990

Lipton & Mew in particular, outraged at the 'invasion of privacy'... these are the same people who leaked details of Sir Hugh's misdemeanours to the press, for indulging in the *wrong kind* of harlotry... Came out of the library at 7 o'c. & the place was deserted. Saw Torrence & asked where everyone was. 'It's England against Germany, sir,' he said. He elaborated that we weren't at war – there was a football match taking place.

Friday, 6 July
In the afternoon I went to see James Ford at Wells Street on Stanley's advice. He understands the situation, & has consented to be my literary agent & to deal with any other kind of contracts, radio or TV, as & when. He wears an ill-fitting syrup, but was very friendly. Asked him to liaise with Dent's & get me out of any paperback book tour should they make overtures.

Sunday, 8 July
Taxi to Mags. Talk about a sight for sore eyes. O! it was *fabulous* to see her, looking ravishing in deep purple. She talked about playing the Shaffer on Broadway. 'It's a romp, darling... some nights we're atrocious, but one whiff of the accent & they're putty in the hands.' I remarked on how we both have formidable Maggie Ts in our lives[57] & Mags said 'Yes, but mine wins Tonys & yours skins Tories,' which I thought was very quick!! She leaves again for New York tomorrow. Getting into her cab she kissed me & said 'Give my love to Louie. And be a good boy.'

Got quiche & salad, let Rita leave early. Served it for Louisa at 5 o'c. We were playing Scrabble when we heard cheering & a great ruckus on the street with drunken hooligans streaming out of the Queen's Head. Put the News on & saw that England have won the world championship. Means nothing to me, but it should keep the masses appeased for the time being.

Monday, 9 July
Bumped into Orlando on the stairs, tugging his collar to conceal a love-bite. I feigned indifference... Saw Gow, with a spring in his step. 'Thank the Lord for Gazza!' he said, with his thumbs up.

Went in to Lou & she was watching the cooking programme I was on. 'When did you do that?' she asked. 'It was weeks ago,' I said, 'when you had the bruised bum.' '*Oh!*' she said, '...I don't remember.'

---

[57] Smith was appearing with Margaret Tyzack (1931-2011) in *Lettice and Lovage*.

Beyond Our Kenneth

Tuesday, 10 July
Norman Tebbit came & said that Stokes has been earmarked for the committee position when Orbell leaves. So I am to be overlooked again. So be it. The game plan in the autumn will be shit-stirring & unauthorised interviews.

Arranged Harry's leaving do & Belinda is going to book Rules. Walked to Marsham Street & spoke to Portaloo. He said a boy called Cameron at the Tory Research Dept. would be an able replacement for Harry & that he would make enquiries.

Thursday, 12 July
Everyone flocking to have their photographs taken with "Gazza" & "Digger" & "Psycho". Very few are soccer fans, they just want the warm glow of success & to be seen standing next to winners. I sat in the library & read *The Spectator*... The votes in the evening were *endless* & all pretty trivial. I was in such a daze I've a feeling I went through the wrong lobby at one point. Closed my eyes for a while in the smoking room. I'm glad I've packed up, but sometimes it's a luxury to absorb some secondhand smog. Gill[58] tapped my hand. 'Are you there, dear?' she said, as tho' she were trying to rouse a care home resident who'd snuffed it in the night.

Saturday, 14 July
Up at 7 o'c. as it's too warm to sleep any later. Car came at 9.20 to Wardour Street. Photo shoot for the paperback cover. The woman had me holding a *papier-mâché* Yorick skull in one hand & a ceremonial mace in the other. The mace was painted with golden gunk & half of it came off in the hands. Two or three times she said 'Can the nostrils go any wider?'... Walked to Thomas Cook for brochures & to Langfords to order tankard for Harry & then Wheeler's for lunch with this Cameron chap. He looks all of eighteen. Bit of a toff, & a high-flyer. Made the offer, but he seemed distinctly underwhelmed.

Sunday, 15 July
Headlines are all about Ridley's resignation.[59] I, for one, am glad. Comparing the EEC to Nazi Germany is not only inaccurate, it's *facile*, & the cabinet's better off without him.

---

[58] Gillian Shephard (b. 1940), Tory MP for South West Norfolk, 1987-2005.
[59] Nicholas Ridley (1929-93), Tory MP for Cirencester & Tewkesbury, 1959-91; Secretary of State for Trade and Industry, 1989-90. Forced to resign after comments made in an interview

Monday, 16 July
Feeling quite buoyant of late. It's not just that term time is nearly over, but it's the sense of being occupied & at the centre of things. I suppose it's the *theatre* of it that is so appealing – the architecture, the Commons chamber, the cast of characters, & of course the fact that it's all being recorded & commented on by the hacks & critics... Belinda instructed me in the use of her new Acorn R260, but I was hopeless! The typing was alright but it kept beeping at me obnoxiously. I said 'I wonder if the Computer Misuse Act covers throwing one down the effing stairs.' They're British machines & the Treasury are doling them out every which way, thanks to the Ankara deal going the way of all flesh. Well, it's their own stupid fault – *never* do business on 'sale or return' with a Turk.

Tuesday, 17 July
Cecil showed me *Today* with the statue of Vstavlyat they've erected in Red Square. A white marble adonis with bulging muscles atop an Orlov trotter. It's both laughable & chilling at once. 'Ivan the Inerrable' is the tagline – the Russian people *adore* him: they might subsist on rye bread & beetroot, but he's expanding their territory & sticking two fingers up to the West, & that's good enough for them.

At 2 o'c. hosted a meeting of Camden market traders. A lot of concern about the new indoor edifice which is under construction, but I think fears were allayed. A woman with a ring through her nose like a prize heifer said 'I thought you were going to be useless but you know your stuff, I'll give you that...' She's wrong, of course, I don't know the first thing about it, but I was delighted that they thought I did, & that they could readily disassociate me from the government, which they universally scorn.

Friday, 20 July
Everything winding down & inertia has set in – for the worker bees, that is. Ministers will be on hand throughout the break. I hope one or two get the call to return to London just as their private jets set down in Barbados or wherever... I feel the public needs this pause just as much as the politicians – it has been an horrific year for the government & an unnerving period for the country as a whole.

---

with *The Spectator*, where he described the relinquishment of sovereignty to the EEC as tantamount to surrendering it to Hitler.

We gathered at Rules at 7 o'c. I ordered the Bollinger '83 which H. appreciated. Presented the tankard & sang 'Jolly Good Fellow', &c. I got squiffy & then it all came out – 'Ooh! you are lovely, Hal... It's your last chance, run away to the stationery cupboard with me! What's Washington got that I haven't?!' It went on & on. He was embarrassed enough with all the attention, let alone my behaviour. Belinda hailed cabs & pointed us in the right direction. Fell into bed at 12.30.

Saturday, 21 July
Wrote a note to Harry apologising for last night. I feel awful for making him uncomfortable & showing myself up... Heard on the radio that Carr[60] has died of a stroke, so there's to be *another* by-election in Bootle! The poor man was only 43. Walked with Paul to the Renoir for *Cyrano de Bergerac*. O! it was a feast for the senses! Depardieu is so good one almost forgets how unsightly he is.

Monday, 23 July
After coffee & papers walked to Argos & acquired two 16" Micromark 90°-oscillating fans at £10.99 apiece. 'You must be *hot stuff* to need these!' said the Mary on the till. Lugged them home. They don't exactly emit an arctic blast, but at least the air is circulating a bit. Lou seemed more comfortable. I served tinned Vichyssoise cold at 2.30, followed by ham salad & then tinned peaches & cream... Rupert knocked & asked if I wanted to join him & Orlando for *Miss Saigon* at Drury Lane, but the thought of playing third wheel was nauseating so I declined. Had enough of that caper with T. & C.

Tuesday, 24 July
Bus to HH to thank the staff for their work & to wish them pleasant holidays. 'Some of us are here all summer,' said Camilla, the bowlegged one. 'Courage, Camille!' I replied with a grin, but the baffled moue she produced implied more dumbarse than Dumas.

Wednesday, 25 July
O! it's heavenly to wake up & know the day ahead is one's own... Went to Nick for haircut. There's more white than grey now, so it's best kept *short*.

---

[60] Michael Carr (1947-90), Labour MP for Bootle, May-July 1990. Actually succumbed to a heart attack.

Pottered about & did some low dusting. Read a bit of the new Bryson.[61] He asserts that without the United States, English would be no more eminent or utilised than Portuguese or Russian – at once he denounces the expansion of the language through British imperialism & lauds its spread via American "culture". The writing is entertaining enough, but it's hard not to dismiss someone who earnestly tries to make the case for *maneuver* over *manœuvre*.

Thursday, 26 July
We saw the TV news & the new Archbishop's enthronement. It's a curious move by HM to appoint a black African[62] – especially as, according to Michael Alison, the PM preferred the Bishop of Bath & Wells – but it'll have them going wild in the aisles in the townships. Still, the CofE is on a par with the Co-op, membership-wise, so whoever wields the crosier will have all the impact of a piss in the Potomac.

Friday, 27 July
James Ford rang & asked if I would go on *Wogan* on Monday to talk to Jonathan Ross & I said yes.

Saturday, 28 July
Had coffee outside Dino's with Paul then we walked to Somerstown for their summer fête. It was a glorified street party in truth, but they had the Morris men & Indian dancers & the hog roast, that kind of affair. The organiser, Arabella Gittings – a horsy type with a bit of an Adam's apple – nigh on broke my wrist with the overzealous greeting. I signed for some children, then they got me on stage to present the prizes for best costume. First place went to a little boy done up as a ladybird! In this heat!! The child was non-plussed at the reward of a £5 book token, but the mother leapt about like Saint Vitus on a hot tin roof. Had the photographs taken with them, &c… Paul tugged my arm & said 'Here, come in Smith's, it's air conditioned,' & we cooled off in there for a bit before walking home.

Sunday, 29 July
Pat rang to complain about her knee. 'It's agony, I don't know what to do with myself, I don't think I can go on much longer…' 'Oh, really?' I said.

---

[61] *The Mother Tongue: English and How It Got That Way.*
[62] Emmanuel Mwangi (b. 1944), Archbishop of Canterbury, 1990-8.

Beyond Our Kenneth

Monday, 30 July
Was just helping Flo with the beds when the 'phone went. It was Cecil. 'Have you seen the television?' he said. 'No.' There was a pause. 'They've got Gow. Outside his house just after breakfast.' Went in to Lou & turned on the News at One. IRA bomb, under his car. He took the full force & died instantly.

Went & sat in the bedroom. Ian was extremely kind to me, devoted to the job & to the Prime Minister. I thought about her, & Brighton, & Airey[63]... What's it all for? Surely these Irish bastards know that this kind of act will only solidify the government's resolve? I dare say that's their aim, to entrench hatreds. Well, it's worked. I *hate* them. Playing mediæval games, warping the minds of gullible youths, pouring fanatic rot into their ears & turning them into brainwashed crusaders. It's all so very pointless.

Harry rang. 'Are you alright?'... Told him about *Wogan* & he said 'Do it, but be measured. Revenge-talk will be what they want to hear, but that's for another day.'

Got to Shepherd's Bush at 6.10. Struck me that the world continues to turn – I met the American pop group & the football manager Graham Taylor, & Magnus Magnusson. Terry's stand-in, Jonathan Ross, greeted me warmly. 'This must've been a wotten day for you,' he said... I was on last. Got through it alright. At the finish I said 'I'm still the new boy, still learning the ropes... but events such as those which occurred today, & Strangeways, & the Manchester murders, I am not blasé about them, & I'll try to ensure that members of the government aren't either.' Didn't die the death, but the response was decidedly muted.

Thursday, 2 August
We saw Hurd's TV address regarding Saddam Hussein's assassination. Pretty certain that Soviet-backed fingers were on the trigger. Of course everyone is officially condemning it. I think we should be kissing Vstavlyat's jackboots – after all, the only good tyrant is a dead one.

Friday, 3 August
It's absolutely *boiling*. People keep going on about '76, but I don't remember it being as bad as *this*. Put on the tan slacks & rolled up the sleeves. Collected Flo in a cab & helped her with the luggage at Heathrow. I'd the look of a

---

[63] Airey Neave (1916-79), Tory MP for Abingdon, 1953-79. Assassinated by a car bomb outside the House of Commons.

brewer's drayman, lugging those lousy cases, sodden with sweat. Got some sweets for her to give to the nieces & nephews. Did the 'bon voyage' bit & got taxi home again.

Too hot to eat. We just sat listening to *Proms '90* on the wireless, drinking bitter lemon with ice, the fans on full blast. Louisa said 'Gawd 'elp us! It's probably cooler than this in *Vanilla!*', meaning Manila.

Sunday, 5 August
Rita arrived at 8 o'c., the grin from ear to ear. 'I couldn't sleep I was so excited,' she said. Lou being difficult. 'Where are we going again?' If I didn't know better I'd think she does it just to annoy me… M. came at 9.10 & we just about got it all in his car. He was a saint, as usual – the train would've been too much hassle, what with all the bags *and* Louisa's bladder. We had to stop at Fleet services, Winchester services & a pub at Eastleigh so she could have a pee… Boarded the *Livonia* at 12.15. Cunard should win a Pulitzer for the brochure snaps: 'faded grandeur' is one thing, but I'll wager the décor on the *Lusitania* is in better shape. The cabins are on the same passageway, but ten or so apart. Berths are narrow, & you could crack walnuts on the mattresses. The saving grace is Rita! She seems happy as Larry cooped up with Louisa – it'd be a death sentence to a lesser mortal… Got up on deck & we cast off at 2.32.

O! it's marvellous to be at sea & feel the *breeze*. I'd forgotten what it was to be chilly. Dressed & went for drinks. It's mainly retired couples, matching knitwear types. L&R played the bingo & I got stuck with Mary & Leonard, on their ruby anniversary cruise. 'You see, Ken, where Leonard & I think you're going wrong…' etc. etc. I can do without overfamiliarity & advice on an empty stomach, so I cut the girls' game short & we went up for the meal. Was yawning all through the trifle, so I left L&R to it, put one up & turned in.

Monday, 6 August
Rough seas in the night, but it's mercifully calm this morning… Knocked for the girls but got no reply – eventually found them having coffee in the Berengaria Lounge. 'We thought we'd leave you to your beauty sleep,' said Rita. After breakfast we took a turn on the deck. Rita was taking a snap of Louisa when a stout, uniformed woman came bounding up. 'Hello Mr Williams, I'm Veronica, your *holiday enjoyment facilitator*… Sorry to intrude on yourself in this way, but we've got a little problemo – Denise, who was meant to be giving a lecture on origami this afternoon, has come

Beyond Our Kenneth

down with a little something, so she's had to cancel herself... Is there *any* way you could fill in for a little talk today at three?' Ugh. Was about to let her down gently when Rita piped up – 'O! brilliant!', as though it were a privilege to have been asked. This emboldened Veronica, and gave her the chance to add the 'We'd only need twenty minutes from yourself' caveat. Reluctantly resigned myself to it.

Barely civil through lunch. Left them playing Ludo & returned to the cabin to scribble a few notes... Veronica introduced me to a muted smattering of applause at 3.05. They're either anti-Thatcher or pro-origami, but they clearly didn't want *me*. Scraped through with a few gags & reminiscences from *Sailing*,[64] but it was all rather ignominious. The "reward" was an invitation to the captain's table for dinner. Sadly, the captain – ludicrously named Stern Helm – had all the charisma one would expect of a fagged Danish commander counting down the days to retirement, so by the time the dessert was finished, so was I.

Tuesday, 7 August
Palled up with Nobby & Janice for shuffleboard. I was no good at it, but the weather is marvellous!! Sunny, but with a constant flow of Nordic cool. We had spritzers on the poop. Went to find L&R, and they were in the Berengaria, listening to a girl done up as Vera Lynn, mangling a few wartime classics. Louie wanted to join in the waltz, & whilst her sticks aren't strictly *Come Dancing*-approved, she camouflaged them admirably.

We docked in Stavanger at noon. O! it's remarkably quaint & lovely. The old quarter is filled with pleasingly puritanical wooden cottages, mostly white-washed, but interspersed with madly coloured ones at odd intervals. And oh! how beautiful the people are, especially the children. The riah buttery yellow, & all immaculately turned out in sober, sensible woollens... Pushed Louie to the Skagen, a restaurant overlooking the harbour. Ordered her a lobster, which she enjoyed. Rita & I shared the *gravlaks*. I'd imagined Rita demanding chips at every mealtime during this trip, but she was bolting the salmon as though she were on the meter... They went back to the ship for Lou's nap & I met with Nobby & Janice for the Museum of Archæology. It was interesting, but the curator turned out to be Norway's lone *Round the Horne* fan, so instead of seeing the Viking relics I had to sign

---

[64] Presumably a misremembering of the title of *Carry On Cruising*.

& pose for photographs… Wrote postcards to Rupert, Paul & Stanley, & we were steaming away again by 5 o'c.

Wednesday, 8 August
Into the fiords to the village of *Olden*. I thought 'We've come to the right place, with this lot', but oh! the landscape is stunning!! I imagine it's quite forbidding in the wintertime, but with the sun beating down, the greens & blues are inviting, fresh & lovely… When Lou was sleeping, Rita & I toured the bridge & R. was invited to sound the horn. She did it with an air of great self-importance, as though she were opening the day's trading on Wall Street… In the evening they showed *The Killing Fields*,[65] which seemed wholly inappropriate. I said to Nobby, 'These people don't want to see mass death. They could've at least picked something boat-themed…' 'Yes,' nodded Nobby, '*The Poseidon Adventure…*'

Thursday, 9 August
Louisa being irritable. When we got to Geiranger, I said 'Don't you want to see the views?' 'I ain't bothered,' she said, feebly. 'Once you've seen one *fiord* you've seen 'em all.' It's nonsense, the variety in landscape is astounding.
   5 o'c. – I take it back. I've a feeling she might be right.

Friday, 10 August
After breakfast we put on the waterproofs & wheeled Lou into drizzly Bergen. It's nice enough, but I'm sick of this holiday now. The incessant small talk with withered snobs, the countless games of crib, the endless plates of fish… Saw the ink version of Munch's *Scream*. Never mind its depiction of the 'universal anxiety of modern man', what about its uncanny depiction of any poor sod who's spent a week in Norway?

Saturday, 11 August
Louie had an accident in the night, but Rita's practicality & good humour is remarkable. She brushed it off as nothing & Lou soon forgot about it. Their porthole will need to remain open, though. Rita had used a full can of Haze… After breakfast we entered the quiz, with Nob & Janice joining the team. Janice is getting on my wick – there's a lot of 'O! Ken, you are *funny!*' and 'O! Ken, you *do* come out with some things!'… I know I fucking do, the whole

---

[65] 1984 British biographical drama film about the Khmer Rouge regime in Cambodia, directed by Roland Joffé.

world knows I do, we don't need to labour the point. Quiz was evidently written by a fan of Bolton Wanderers, as *three* questions revolved around that subject, as if anyone cared. Escaped to the library to write a few letters.

Sunday, 12 August
Of all the places to be in a traffic jam!! They shoved us in a kind of holding pattern of boats going into Southampton. We watched from about a thousand yards as the tugs piloted the low loader carrying the remains of the *Titanic*'s bow into the dock. It's little more than a jagged heap of greyish-brown rust. They'd hung out the bunting & bowed the cranes, but scrap iron is scrap iron. Rita was wetting herself (as was Lou, I shouldn't wonder), but I found it most unseemly. With the *Mary Rose* it was different – that was King Harry's flagship – but there are living survivors of the *Titanic* whose loved ones drowned, & here they are winching the remnants of their resting place up a conveyor belt, as they would prizes on some ghastly gameshow… Eventually we docked at 2 o'c. Wonderful M. was waiting for us. Had one more picture standing in front of the *Livonia*. I shan't be sad to say goodbye, to the ship *or* our fellow passengers… Inside by 5.15. Rita sorted Lou out & then got weepy: 'Thank you so much, I've had the most wonderful time,' & more in that vein. She was indispensable, & it would've been unthinkable without her. Left the pile of letters, had a tin of Minestrone & went to bed.

Wednesday, 15 August
9.34 to Maidstone for *Tell the Truth*. The show itself was the predictable crap, but I took to Fred Dinenage[66] enormously. One of those types with a little knowledge about lots of things, & in ten minutes we'd covered Caligula, diphtheria & the Trans-Siberian Railway. He introduced his teenaged daughter who is politically minded & wanted to know how to go about getting involved, but I told her she was far too attractive for a life in Whitehall.

Friday, 17 August
Cecil rang. Lots of gnashing of teeth re. the MORI poll. Cecil had been at the Monday Club dinner last night where Boyson[67] was mouthing off about homosexuality again, & how we could wipe out AIDS if we could wipe out

---

[66] English author, broadcaster and news anchor (b. 1942), presented the long-running children's educational programme *How* (1966-2022).
[67] Sir Rhodes Boyson (1925-2012), Tory MP for Brent North, 1974-95.

'unnatural practices'… Stupid man. They might be *unconventional* practices, but it's no more unnatural than growing those ridiculous muttonchops… Rupert drove me to Heathrow. Flo's 'plane landed at 6.58. She is about three shades darker, & looking & sounding refreshed. Took her in to see Lou & then Rupert fetched her home.

Sunday, 19 August
M. came & ran myself, Paul, Lou & Rita to Joe Allen's. Rita wore the 't-shirt' she'd picked up in Bergen (which even for J.A.'s was inappropriate). It has 'My friend went to Oslo & all I got was this lousy t-shirt!' plastered across it. I'd pointed out at the time the multiple inaccuracies in that statement, but apparently she lives & dies in the thing!

Monday, 20 August
HH. Interview with this Tom Staplehurst[68] to fill Harry's place. Young and Northern, but a smart cookie. Bold, but not obviously so. Thought the barnet was a rug at first, but it's just maniacally neat. McCrindle spoke highly, so I shall engage him.

Thursday, 23 August
In the paper they had photos of the gaudy 'inauguration' of the new Soviet puppet in Baghdad, Kareem Kassis.[69] 'Never mind *crème de cassis*,' says Tony Lyle in *Today*, 'this wallah's the Fakir Royale, espousing communist ideals whilst donning an immense golden crown…' The Ba'athists will hate it, but Saddam was their glue, & without him they're washy.

Friday, 24 August
James 'phoned. Dent's have confirmed Oct. 1st release date for p/b, & will acquiesce re. signing tour if I troll it round the chat shows. JF said he'd work on getting me booked on a select few programmes the week before conference.

Saturday, 25 August
Walked to Safeway with Paul & did a big shop for Louisa, cos it's easier that way. P. helped me with the bags… Lunch at 1 o'c. at Sweetings at Nimmo's invitation. It was myself, Derek, Joan Sims, Kate O'Mara, Ian Lavender &

---

[68] (b. 1961) KW's assistant at parliament, 1990-1; Tory MP for Charnwood since 1991.
[69] Karim Kassis (1947-94), President of Iraq, 1990-4. Shot dead by Baathist gunmen at Basra.

Beyond Our Kenneth

Toyah Willcox. They'd all just filmed some rubbish for Granada,[70] which sounded horrific. Went to spend a penny & broke the zip!! Tiptoed back to the table circumspectly, & nudged Kate – 'Have you got a safety pin?' Nothing doing. Then Joanie piped up, 'What's the matter, Ken?' Was about to play it down when Kate announced to the world 'He's bust his zipper & can't do his flies up…' Cue peals of laughter. Joanie dug around in the handbag & produced a pin. 'Now you mind what you're doing,' she warned, 'I shan't be held responsible for any nasty pricks.'

Tuesday, 28 August
Tube to St Pauls where I met Tom & we walked to the Old Bailey. I thought of Andrew Ray & our excited visits all those years ago. A few photographers about, but mercifully no queue. Sat in the public gallery next to a thickset woman in a carmine boiler suit. 'D'you come here often?' I asked. 'Oh aye,' she said in broad Glaswegian, 'It's great to see the crims get their just deserts…' Knew as soon as they marched the suspects up the steps that it was the Midland bunch. Our case was *ninth* on the list to trawl through, but the prosecuting barrister weaved a compelling story.

Sunday, 2 September
Gyles rang. 'Happy anniversary, dear heart!' he bellowed. 'Beg pardon?' I said… I hadn't realised, but it's a *year* since Water Closet telephoned to float the idea of me standing. It feels about five minutes. After lunch I wrote these lines, encapsulating it:

> Autumn leaves were tumbling,
> My perseverance crumbling.
> Appellants came a-knocking
> To interrupt the stumbling.
>
> Though fully contradictory,
> The wintry chill of victory
> Annealed the flagging will
> To offer speeches benedictory.
>
> So slowly gaining traction,
> Avoiding clique or faction,

---

[70] *Cluedo* (1990-3), a game show based on the famous whodunnit board game.

I was springing into something,
Though I wouldn't call it action.

I serve the grocer's daughter,
Defy those who would thwart her.
But the forecast isn't calm:
Summer storms and choppy water.

Monday, 3 September
Bumped into Kenny Everett[71] in Selfridge's. 'O! you gorgeous creature!' he cried & kissed me on the cheeks!! Terribly embarrassing. A pug-faced mare in faux-chinchilla shoved past us – 'Excuse me, some of us are trying to do some shopping…' Kenny dropped to the floor & crawled behind her, grovelling: 'I am so sorry, madam, please forgive me!' he howled, shuffling after her & wailing. 'I was just keeping the British end up, m'lady, nothing more, you simply *must* believe me…' A baffled crowd – including myself – watched on, slack-jawed. He rose, grasped my elbow & said softly 'So, how is the Prime Minister coping?', as though nothing had happened. It was quite bizarre!

Tuesday, 4 September
Le Caprice at 1 o'c. with Tom. Ethan arrived at 1.07. Tom hasn't got Harry's allure, but I trust his instincts & he's clearly a 'details' man. We went through the list of cases for the debate. The most important thing is the *question* we pose – 'hanging for an adult who has committed murder' won't butter any parsnips – nor will loose terms such as 'evil'. Tom had reams of stuff about where Griffiths & Gardner went wrong in the last parliament. We agreed the fundamental points: (i) The age of the assailant, (ii) The severity & cruelty of the crime, (iii) The number of victims, in spree murder or terrorism, & (iv) the degree of premeditation. Tom said 'If the Westminster Hall goes well, there should be time before Christmas to amend the Justice Bill & get it voted on.' Ethan was more interested in the fare. Examining his treacle tart, he greenly remarked 'Pastry's a bit thin… I prefer a nice thick base,' & Tom & I caught eyes, knowingly.

---

[71] English radio DJ and comedian (1944-95). Appeared at many rallies in support of the Conservatives, though – like KW – received criticism for this 'hypocrisy' as a homosexual Tory, in light of the government's enacting of 'Section 28'.

Thursday, 6 September
Was napping when Flo banged on the door. 'Kennit! Mrs William she is fainted!'... Hurried in & Lou was slumped in the armchair, eyes closed & mouth ajar. Couldn't rouse her. Told Flo to get the Mackenzie's from the bathroom cabinet & I 'phoned the ambulance. They were here in four minutes. Paramedics checked her over & quickly posited hypoglycæmia. Flo poured some neat cordial & retrieved a half-eaten Marathon bar from her tabard. After a minute or so, she came round, bemused but aware. They got her in the chair, went down in the lift & took us round to the Cruciform. A Dr Abbas gave her the once over. He suspects diabetes, but they're to run tests. Flo looked thunderstruck. 'She was quiet, but I was think she was just tired...' They're keeping her in for a day or two. Flo ran back to the block to get nighties, etc. She thinks it's her fault. It isn't, & I told her so, but if darting about running errands makes her feel better, I shan't stop her... Louisa was asleep by 5 o'c., so I took Flo to The Dell at Hyde Park for supper. I know I should be touched by how much she cares for Lou, but it was all I could do to hold in my *own* tears – of panic, of relief, of fatigue. Came home & it flooded out. I fear today was a dress rehearsal.

Friday, 7 September
Walked up to UCH. She's on a quiet ward, but in between two Asians, so she looked bored stiff when I arrived. 'What am I doing here?' she asked. Went through it eight or nine times, but it hasn't stuck. Still, she seems bright enough. Spoke to Abbas. It is diabetes, so it'll mean more tablets & a strict diet, which she will *loathe*... Will have to have a word with Clarke about this hospital, though. It's primeval. Filth everywhere. Flo arrived with flowers, grapes & a card, so I left them to it... Read in the *Standard* that the Midland Bank boys received 6 years apiece. It is a *derisory* sentence.

Saturday, 8 September
They finally released Lou at 3 o'c. Glad to get her out of that place. It's the sitting around *waiting* that drags the spirits down. Flo got her comfortable in front of *Fifteen to One*[72] & we went through the bumph – what she can eat, what she can't eat, etc... She ain't gonna like it, that's for sure.

---

[72] Channel 4 quiz show hosted by William G. Stewart, 1988-2003.

Monday, 10 September
Knocked on Rupert to fill him in. The Orlando answered, *déshabillé*. 'He's in the bath,' he said snootily, 'I'd rather not disturb him, he's had a long day…' Door practically slammed in my face. Later, Rupert rang the bell & attempted an apology. 'I know it makes you uncomfortable to see us together,' he said. I told him not to flatter himself. I couldn't care less who he chooses to associate with. The hubris is outrageous. Great conceited fool, I certainly shan't bother with him again. I might be a mushy fruit, but I'm no gooseberry.

Friday, 14 September
Spent the evening at Goodhart's[73] party. Lots of talk about the inevitability of recession – but all quite gossipy, as though it were happening in some far-off former colony. Amery[74] was the worst: 'They showed Bradford on the news. O! it's ghastly! One wonders what they find to do… This beluga is sensational, Petra. What is it, Urbani?'

Saturday, 15 September
Up at 6 o'c. & did letters. Crossed the Terrace to what I'd *assumed* was a new post box, but it turns out to be a bin for dog excrement!! All done out in Royal Mail red. Who makes these decisions? It's an accident waiting to happen.

Monday, 17 September
M. came at 8 o'c. & we drove to Rochester. Looked round the cathedral, learned about bishops Gundulf & Ernulf, then to the reopened Lyons' for tea, sandwiches & Bakewell pudding. Then to the castle where a pleasantly pale girl called Sally showed us round diligently in return for a donation. Scuttling up some steps in the Round Tower, M. said 'I can hardly keep up with you! I don't know where you find the oomph!', which I found very gratifying.

Tuesday, 18 September
Went in to Louisa. She was sulking because Flo has said No Sweets… It *is* rotten. I took away her fags & now her Fruit & Nut. At this age, I wonder if the misery is worth it. She was watching *Carry On Cleo* on the television. I

---

[73] Sir Philip Goodhart (1925-2015), Tory MP for Beckenham, 1957-91.
[74] Julian Amery (1919-96), Tory MP for Brighton Pavilion, 1969-91. Son-in-law of former Prime Minister Harold Macmillan.

looked manic in it, but undeniably beautiful. Joanie Sims & Charlie being wonderful. The past truly is another country... After, they cut to Tokyo & announced that Manchester will stage the Olympic Games in 1996!! I thought he must've got it wrong at first, but it turns out we beat submissions from Athens, Atlanta & *Belgrade* – so it's on par with awarding the Knobbly Knees crown to a cripple ahead of three amputees.

Wednesday, 19 September
Manchester joy didn't last for long. This morning, another body on a rubbish tip in Broadheath, & this afternoon a bomb outside Trafford Magistrates' Court. Provisional IRA. Six grownups & a baby dead. We saw the TV news & they showed Montgomery,[75] looking utterly crestfallen. Both events occurred within his boundaries. I've only chatted to him once, but wrote a supportive note & rang Belinda for his constituency office address. This kind of thing can't be allowed to stand – be it in the name of religion or nationalism, it is *terrorism*, unjustifiable & wicked. They need to be found, punished & put down.

Friday, 21 September
More and more I feel things crashing down around me. Lou is fading fast, friends are either dead or avoiding me, & I've discarded my life's work for this unyielding, powerless, preposterous *game* of lies & backstabbing. Curiously, however, I'm as fit as a fiddle! Feel as though I could conquer the Three Peaks challenge before breakfast.

Tuesday, 25 September
In the queue at Foyle's the chintzy woman in front ordering *Humboldt's Gift* gave her name as Jenny Taylor-Wright. The poor boy's brow furrowed & he said 'Genitalia *who*?'... I held in the laugh, but it was no trivial task.

Wednesday, 26 September
Up early & did letters. Incredible that more than half the stuff I get is still *Carry On* or *Jackanory* related. Shows I've made all the impact of a ton of feathers politically... Went & sat with Lou. She was quiet. The usual tactic would be to offer her some chocolates or a whisky, but both are denied her now. Watched the News. Vstavlyat is to halve his air-launched missile

---

[75] Sir Fergus Montgomery (1927-2013), Tory MP for Altrincham & Sale, 1974-95; PPS to Mrs Thatcher when she was Leader of the Opposition.

arsenal – down to 30,000 warheads. It's a cunning ploy, because it *sounds* like a benevolent move, an extension of INF – whereas in truth a mere fraction of the remaining bombs, if deployed, could flatten Europe in seconds. Hurd is worried that instead of dismantling the arms, they'll be given to China in exchange for grub, so the Soviet people can have full bellies this Christmas.

Saturday, 29 September
Walked to Wiltons & lunched with Patten & Speed.[76] Jeffrey Archer[77] was a few tables away – I smiled obligingly, though I know he detests me. Chris is worried about the mood of the Party. 'The summer has provided time for wounds to heal or to fester, & I'm afraid it's the latter,' he said. Rather put me off my Dover sole… Butchers will be cock-a-hoop though: the lifting of the beef ban, the pesticides warning & the DoH report have convinced the government to announce the Five-A-Day scheme at conference. How anyone is meant to *afford* five portions of meat per day (lean or otherwise), let alone force 'em down, is beyond me.

Monday, 1 October
Shepherd's Bush for *Wogan*. It was Benazir Bhutto,[78] Whoopi Goldberg & then me. I was the light relief – no-one wants Pakistani politics at 7 o'c. in the evening, & American stars are always more interested in aggressively *promoting* their film than telling stories. I prattled on about the lavatories in parliament & Kenny Everett in Selfridge's, but Terry did mention the book, so I did my duty.

Tuesday, 2 October
Bus to Broadcasting House for the interview with John Humphrys. Caught me quite off-balance. He was full of the joys in the lobby, but the gentleness evaporated in the booth: 'You're just playing at politics, aren't you?'… 'Can you name anything you've achieved as an MP?'… Of course, I *am* just playing & I *can't* name anything I've done. I felt punctured & downcast all afternoon.

---

[76] Keith Speed (1934-2018), Tory MP for Ashford, 1974-95.
[77] English novelist (b. 1940), Deputy Chairman of the Conservative Party, 1985-6.
[78] Pakistani politician and stateswoman (1953-2007), Prime Minister of Pakistan, 1988-90 and 1993-6.

Beyond Our Kenneth

Wednesday, 3 October
We saw the new Attenborough, *Trials of Life*. Impressively shot, but it was chiefly a cavalcade of mucus-slathered offspring, oozing unceremoniously from assorted gaping cavities. Felt quite queasy by the end.

Thursday, 4 October
Tom 'phoned, confirming schedule for conference. He's kept things light, thankfully, except for the odd speech. My main job will be casual press interviews, supporting the PM and boosting morale. Famous last words… Tom mentioned this chap Berners-Lee[79] that the Russians have kidnapped – or 'delayed the departure' of. He's a computer boffin & it seems they want what's in his head. Remains to be seen how far they'll go to get it.

Friday, 5 October
6.36 from Euston to Liverpool. Was expecting hostility but not a bit of it! They might loathe the Tories, but they loathe Wilkes more – they think him a class traitor. Cab to Albert Docks for *This Morning*. It's essentially *Pebble Mill* with ad breaks, and the gimmick of a married couple presenting it – at least I think they were married.[80] In any case, I was on for all of ten minutes, spouting the same old claptrap. At the finish they handed out slices of cheese & tomato pizza. I politely declined, images of an Intercity lavatory flashing before my eyes.

Saturday, 6 October
Read in the paper that Alyn Ainsworth[81] is dead. Took him with me to Tangé after *Int. Cabaret*, I recall. Come to think of it, he was a crashing bore.

Monday, 8 October
Pat arrived at 8.15. She tried coming it with notions of using my flat for the week, but I put paid to *that*. I'm not having her sticking her oar in & sleeping in my bed. She can make do with the foldout. I told her: no fags & no sugar, but I suspect there'll be both.

Met Tom, Ethan & Belinda at Waterloo. Arrived Bournemouth at 11.53. Tom managed to get me in at the Highcliff, but I've no sea view. I'm shoved

---

[79] Tim Berners-Lee (1955-?), English computer scientist. Kidnapped by the KGB in 1990 and not heard from since.
[80] TV presenters Richard Madeley (b. 1956) and Judy Finnigan (b. 1948) were married in 1986.
[81] (1924-90) English musician and conductor.

up in the eaves next to Douglas Hogg & Neville Trotter, so the room allocator certainly has a sense of humour.

Lunched with Cecil, Dick Body & dear Matthew Parris. The gossip is unsettling. Worries about ERM membership abound. Heseltine's cronies are putting it about that the last thing the Party needs is another leadership election – which almost guarantees one; they just need the trigger. Dick said the PM can barely *look* at Geoffrey Howe now, let alone speak to him, which isn't wildly encouraging. Squeezed the team into my room & we went through the crime/punishment speech & outlined ideas for the Homosexual Equality group debate. They insist on having ladies present, which is unfortunate.

Drinks with Peter Hitchens,[82] of whom I'm enormously fond. People tend to praise the brother, but I enjoy Peter's world-weariness. He seems not to like himself very much, which always gets my vote too. We spoke about Russia & his quiet admiration for Vstavlyat... Then into the Hall to listen to Gummer announce the five-a-day initiative to half-arsed applause, except for the portly members of the Meat Processors Association, who howled with delight... It's a madhouse: white perms & combovers as far as the eye can see, yuppies swigging Veuve Clicquot & sucking on pulpy Montecristos, smirking ministers avoiding the hoi polloi, & harassed flunkies darting in all directions. Had a slice of quiche & a glass of Châteauneuf-du-Pape with Ian Grist[83] & Robin Oakley.[84] Put one up & went to bed at 9.30.

Tuesday, 9 October
Tom appeared, worse for wear, at 8 o'c. He reeked of booze, so I made him splash on some *Les Plus Belles Lavendes* to take the edge off it & gave him a bit of a dressing down. Big herd of photographers around Maggie at the Purbeck Foyer so thought I'd got away with it, but a couple at the back broke off & cornered me – Imogen from the *Bournemouth Echo* & Rick from the *Western Morning News*!! Heaven preserve us! Grinned for a few snaps, then Belinda rescued me. Delivered the speech to about two dozen of the faithful in a dingy side room. The smattering who *were* there seemed to approve, but the sound of sparse applause is so unbearably disheartening that I got out v. briskly. I know 8.45 on a Tuesday morning isn't 'prime time', but one

---

[82] English conservative broadcaster and author (b. 1951).
[83] (1938-2002) Tory MP for Cardiff Central, 1983-91.
[84] English journalist (b. 1941), political editor at *The Times*.

would've thought a few *Just a Minute* fans might've turned up to swell the numbers... Alas, my star is waning.

John Sergeant[85] nabbed me for a Six O'Clock News piece. Ingham briefed me. The usual guff: forecasts of recession are overstated (they're not), the Party is unified on Europe (it isn't), & there will *not* be another leadership race in this parliament (there will). I've no qualms about lying to journalists when they're not my lies, but I'd so much rather be onscreen giving my *own* opinion, rather than spewing the official line. Despondent, so went for lunch with the Bottomleys.[86] Peter sounds delighted to be out of Ulster – who can blame him? – but fed up now he's been practically dumped. Virginia snowed under at Health. The chablis was flowing. When I referred to Heseltine as a dick, you'd've thought I'd dropped the kecks & exposed meself: Peter nearly choked to death on his chateaubriand. Then I said to Virginia 'Adley[87] told me that your name is an anagram of *I'm an evil Tory bigot...*' In hindsight, I can see that was a little brusque. Heigh-ho.

Wednesday, 10 October
The fact remains, this is all just a barmy distraction. I could be resting now in some picturesque garden of remembrance – the blond-tipped leaves of creeping fig, which frame a plain initialled stone, pruned dutifully by some wistful volunteer... Three times yesterday the girl from the local rag used the phrase 'your change of career'... What *change*? I used to do funny voices to flog baby wipes for a living, now I do funny voices to flog lunatic policies... 'Phoned Pat & she says they're alright. Sent a dirty postcard to Paul – it's a nurse with the hand under the patient's blanket: 'Your pulse is a bit fast today...' 'That's not my *wrist* you're holding, sister...' Should perk him up while he convalesces from the hernia repair.

Thursday, 11 October
Can't sleep in this beastly bed, it's too soft & makes the back ache... Went & listened to Major. What he says is impressive, but the man's so bloody

---

[85] English journalist (b. 1944), BBC Political correspondent, 1981-2000.
[86] Peter Bottomley (b. 1944), Tory MP for Eltham, 1983-95; Parliamentary Under-Secretary of State for Northern Ireland, 1989-90, and his wife Virginia Bottomley (b. 1948), Tory MP for South West Surrey, 1984-2005; Minister of State for Health, 1989-91.
[87] Robert Adley (1935-93) Tory MP for Christchurch, 1983-93.

rigid. Heseltine is smarmy, no question, but one must admit that he does have your actual fluency.

Chaired the GayCon[88] debate. A lot of undesirables present, but at least it was a broad swathe of undesirables: from the tweed & halitosis types thro' to the Lord Alfred Douglas fan club & the leather-clad Clause 28 marchers, we had the lot. There was support for what I said, & a few tears when I told the story of Mr Stride & partner. One boy called Aaron from Carshalton stood up & said 'We're Conservatives. We believe in family values & self-reliance & stability. We believe in marriage & commitment. Just because I'd marry another man given the chance, how is that possibly corrupting anyone or anything?' It summed it all up perfectly. It's not about *intercourse*. Went & chatted to him afterwards with the instant coffee & signed his conference programme.

Friday, 12 October
I'm not imagining it: after the PM, I got the second loudest cheer when it came to assembling on the stage. Tho' I suppose that's not saying much. Maggie's microphone kept cutting out, so the tribute to Gow was annoyingly distorted, but the sentiments were right. The Monty Python gags were ill-advised in my view, but they got the laughs.[89] Apart from that, it was the usual spiel: 'I'm the only person who can do this job' was the main thrust. Ovations from the audience. Not so much from her colleagues. Howe had a face like a wet weekend… Belinda did the packing. Out fleetly after & just managed to catch the 16.58 back to Londres.

Saturday, 13 October
Went up to see Paul with a few bits of shopping. He was pacing gingerly, but was in good spirits. Then walked to Bar Italia for this interview. Curious chap, with a neckerchief. I only accepted because I thought A. A. Gill[90] was an intriguing name. Shouldn't have wasted my time. He was three-parts pissed when I arrived, & then he ordered grappas. Wrapped it up as swiftly as was polite… Found some sugar-free acid drops in Tesco & got them for

---

[88] Founded in 1975 as the Conservative Group for Homosexual Equality.
[89] Referring to the new Liberal Democrat symbol, a bird in flight, Mrs Thatcher utilised quotes from the 'Dead Parrot' sketch.
[90] Adrian Anthony Gill (1954-2016), British journalist, critic and author.

Lou. She said they were "Orrid', but that didn't stop her working her way through half a dozen during *Creatures Great & Small*.

Sunday, 14 October
Tom rang. Sounded awful, full of cold. I said 'You could do with sucking a Fisherman's Friend.' He said 'Chance'd be a fine thing…' Told him not to come in tomorrow. I don't want to catch his filthy diseases.

Monday, 15 October
Went to the House. A lot of exchange rate mechanism sniping, so I went to the canteen as it was cock-a-leekie, which they do *exceedingly* well. Popped back in. Bob Cryer[91] banging on about the Khmer Rouge, but then John Marshall[92] gave a good speech on AIDS & contaminated blood. Succinct & unsentimental, calling for more money for Macfarlane. I stood & offered my support. The disease is horrific enough without mistakes being made – balance sheets be buggered, it's the *morality* of the thing that counts.

Tuesday, 16 October
Had to laugh during PMQs… The Speaker called Sydney Bidwell,[93] twice. 'Not here!' was the cry from the Labour benches. A grumpy Weatherill went on a furious rant about attendance. 'Hear, hear!' was the slapped-wrist response from the benches. Forth shouted across the divide: 'And if you see Syd – *tell him!*…'

Dinner at Durrants with Stanley. He looked marvellous!! Told me all about filming that *Rab C. Nesbitt*. I'd assumed they'd been shivering away in Glasgow, but it was a weekend in Genoa, if you please. Alright for some – furthest I ever got was Llanberis.[94]

Thursday, 18 October
Mirth in the Foreign Office! To give annexed nations the illusion of lawful transition, Vstavlyat has created the Communist Union of New Territories of the State… so not only are Rumania & Bulgaria conquered, they're now in the C.U.N.T.S. – which, of course, tickled the lackeys pink. Bunch of

---

[91] (1934-94) Labour MP for Bradford South, 1983-94.
[92] (b. 1940) Tory MP for Hendon South, 1987-95.
[93] (1917-97) Labour MP for Ealing Southall, 1966-91.
[94] Whilst filming *Carry On Up the Khyber*.

Friday, 19 October
More gloom. The Liberals have taken Gow's seat & are rubbing it in. It's a disgrace – if they had any morals, the Opposition would've stepped aside. One can almost hear Heseltine's knife being sharpened… Dinner with Irving & Bowis.[95] It seems Charles does support the homosexual cause, but it's all hush-hush. If anything's to be done, *someone* is going to have to stick their head over the parapet. Alas, it won't be me.

Saturday, 20 October
As soon as I saw the American stamp, I *knew* it was a letter from Erich!![96] The same tiny scrawl as in days of old, just even less decipherable – but that's no wonder, the man must be pushing 80. Still, the legible bits are as affable & solacing as ever. Quite a fillip to think that I'm still in his thoughts. Spent all afternoon composing a reply.

Sunday, 21 October
Went in to Lou, but she was dozing. Left a note for Rita – invented a cold & asked not to be disturbed. Got papers & did crossword. Went for a walk. Purchased a poppy & signed for the old boy. Bumped into Rupert in the lobby. Bit awkward. Orlando has come down with something & is in the Middlesex where they're doing tests. 'They can't quite get to the bottom of it,' he said. Which, I expect, means they can.

'Phoned Rona & we talked about Gordon & laughed. Says she & the boys are doing alright. Oh, I do miss him.

Tuesday, 23 October
In the tearoom, the factions were split & whispering. Personally, I'm in two minds. I understand the PM's position on parliamentary sovereignty, I admire the cleverness & caution of Major's ecu compromise, but *fundamentally* I tend to adhere to the Delors plan – I think Britain's destiny *is*

---

[95] John Bowis (b. 1945), Tory MP for Battersea, 1987-95; sometime president of the Conservative Group for Homosexual Equality.
[96] Erich Heller (1911-90), Bohemian-born British essayist and author. Struck up a lasting friendship with KW in 1950 whilst Head of the German Department at University College, Swansea. Apparently desired a physical relationship with KW, but this was rebuffed.

with Europe & a single currency. With a bullish Kremlin flexing its muscles, it's foolish to presume that we can weather these storms alone. To compound the situation, Maggie's surrounded by yes men – they're all telling her that the majority support her view, but it's drivel. Someone should shoot her advisors.

Wednesday, 24 October
Heath back from Moscow, without Berners-Lee. They fed Ted some line about him sightseeing in Siberia & being unreachable. Our impotence was laid bare in that the civil servants advised Sir Edward to *threaten* cancellation of the Anglo-Soviet deal to bring British Home Stores to the streets of Leningrad. Utterly pathetic.

Thursday, 25 October
There's a lot to be said for *schadenfreude*. With the world collapsing around one, it's far easier to reflect positively on one's own situation. I may be a few pounds heavier than I'd wish, but nobody's trying to ram a hard ecu down *my* throat, so I must count my blessings… Mrs Thatcher stony-faced in the House. The Eyeties have called for a weekend summit in Rome to try & pin her down on future plans. They're boxing her in.

Friday, 26 October
I was in the third floor cloakroom when the power cut out & I was plunged into pitch blackness. Stumbled to the basins. The light flickered back on to reveal I'd peed all down the thigh. Spent five minutes under the blower, billowing *à la* Marilyn Monroe. Thank Christ no-one walked in; it looked as tho' I was having it away with the drier.

To Lime Grove for *Newsnight*. The place is a pigsty & reeks of stale tobacco smoke. Eventually got on, with Paxman[97] being needlessly rude & bullish. Of course he's playing the hard-hitting interviewer role, aiming to squeeze out uncomfortable admissions from cornered patsies, but he wasn't having me. I just smiled affably, which seemed to rile him even more.

Saturday, 27 October
'Phone interview for the *Express*. Same old pleb stuff. Trouble with otiose reporters is they presuppose that because I was an actor my heart can't fully

---

[97] Jeremy Paxman (b. 1950), English broadcaster, journalist, author and TV presenter; *Newsnight* host, 1989-2014.

engage in serious policy, & that I must be researching a part or in it for the *publicity*. It's a curious form of lazy journalism reserved for ex-performers: you never hear Ming Campbell[98] being asked to justify *his* place... 'that's all very well, but isn't the division bell just a poor substitute for the starter's gun?...'

Sunday, 28 October
Tom rang in the evening. He'd spoken to Hurd's assistant Adam (with whom Tom "plays badminton"). Bad news from Rome. The PM went in all guns blazing & the summit was a disaster. No agreements on anything – farm subsidy plans, GATT rounds, monetary union – she pooh-poohed the lot... Margaret Thatcher is a lioness, strong & noble – but fence her in & gang up on her, & there's no knowing how much damage she can do.

Monday, 29 October
Got in early for the Westminster Hall debate. Kicked off at 9.30. In the end we went with 'That this House has considered the reintroduction of capital punishment for specific, grievous offences', so we kept things ambiguous. I spoke marvellously – as did Fergus re. the Trafford attack – but I can tell it's doomed to end here. Parliament is fixated by Europe & nothing else will get a look in until the issue is resolved or there's an election.

Fed up, came back to the flat. Letter from Andrew!! He's doing a *Van der Valk*[99] but has two days off! Rang him at the Montcalm & we met at Biagi's at 6 o'c. Nearly collapsed when he said he's *fifty-one* – there's not a line on the face, & the bright blue eyes still pierce right through one. We talked about *Daffodils* & those carefree days. We didn't mention politics *once*, so it was a tremendous escape. Rushed back to tell Louie, but she couldn't care less. She was glued to some rubbish called *Keeping Up Appearances*, which was about as amusing & *aujourd'hui* as smallpox. Fled to the flat for the barclays. I played it all American & butch, quite fabulous. Thorough clean-up after & I stripped the bed.

'Phone went at 9.30. It was Belinda. 'The govt. chief whip would like to speak to you at 8 o'c. tomorrow morning,' so heaven knows what I've done now.

---

[98] Menzies Campbell (b. 1941), Liberal MP for North East Fife, 1987-2015; British 100m sprint record-holder, 1967-74.
[99] ITV crime drama set in Amsterdam (1972-92).

Tuesday, 30 October

They want me to second the loyal address!! He said 'You'll be following Younger,[100] so you can't go wrong.' It's a rare chance to talk to a full House, so I accepted.

Squeezed in to a raucous chamber. The 'No, no, no' thudded like three rounds of a cannon.[101] The whippersnappers hear-heared all around me, but I kept silent. It's sheer folly.

Thursday, 1 November

Shit's hit the fan – Howe's resigned. Saw Harris, his PPS, flying around the lobby, loving it. There's no question, it's bad news. The last member of the '79 cabinet *gone*, & the fourth minister to quit over Europe. Saw Portillo outside the library, pouting in deep thought. 'He's not going to challenge her, is he?' I said. 'Of course not,' snapped Miguel, 'it's far worse than that. He's highlighting that she's running out of friends. The only mercy is he's lost his voice so we've time to frame it properly.'

Friday, 2 November

Rupert Murdoch furious that BSB won't concede to the satellite merger. Tim Raison said his PPS had chatted to Lugholes Lill, the eavesdropping char of Downing Street, & *she* said there'd been shouting & hollering throughout his meeting at Number 10. Rumours he might even have his papers back *Ashdown* come the election… Lunched with Cecil. He says a change of Leader could be my chance. 'Butter up Tarzan & you could climb the ladder the conventional way…' I've no time for ladders or convention. In any case, I won't be disloyal… Saw Rupert as I was coming in. It is AIDS. Rupert has been tested & is in the clear, but he looks *shattered*. Couldn't quite muster up the right words, so just said 'I'm here if you need me,' rather lamely – & quite inaccurately.

Sunday, 4 November

Lou's got the skitters. Considered cancelling M., but Rita said she'd stay & keep her hydrated & comfortable, etc. I ought to have stopped in, but I need the

---

[100] George Younger (1931-2003), Tory MP for Ayr, 1964-91; Secretary of State for Defence, 1986-9.
[101] Having gone against her cabinet's position, rejecting *any* future UK membership of an economic union, Mrs Thatcher returned from the European Council summit in Rome to give a statement to the House. Her 'No, no, no' response to what had been proposed by Commission leaders was seen by some as angrily anti-EEC.

distraction. We drove to Chesham. Restaurant was cold, the food was lousy & M. wouldn't stop moaning about his toothache, so I wish I'd not bothered.

Louisa had recovered by the time I went in. She watched rubbish while I worked on the speech for Wednesday.

Monday, 5 November
We switched on ITN & saw the PM's speech at the climate conference. Not one of her best, but then we're all sick to death of the ozone layer. They showed more of that pint-sized Scandinavian oddball strutting around glumly, like a Khmer soldier with pigtails.[102] I blame the parents. There was more of it on *Wogan* with the little Macaulay chap – all very lovable in his suit & dicky bow, but it's got Bobby Driscoll[103] written all over it.

Wednesday, 7 November
State Opening. Filed thro' passing Skinner & the other republican idiots. Couldn't see a thing but listened to Her Maj deliver the chat. Pretty meagre stuff – we've less on our plate than a Somalian on the F-Plan – a paltry *fifteen* bills!! Came back & after Younger's sermon it was my turn.

Pasted in:

> Thank you, Mister Speaker; may I say what an honour it is for both myself and the people of Holborn & St Pancras to be asked to second the Loyal Address today. It's marvellous to think that having stood through one Queen's Speech already, I have the privilege of making you all sit through another, though admittedly one with fewer Crown Jewels on display. Might I thank the Honourable Member for Ayr for the words he just imparted; I've been on many a bill where the preceding act does the very opposite of 'warming up' a crowd, but that is an accusation that could never be levelled at the feet of my honourable friend. I have been told that those nominated to propose and second the humble address tend to be members from dissimilar parts of the country, one a hardened old veteran and the other a fresh-faced, eager new kid on the block: I should like to congratulate the selectors in maintaining this age-old tradition here today.
>
> However, Mister Speaker, in a break with convention, if you will forgive me, I don't intend to use my few minutes to extol the virtues of my

---

[102] Gretl Ernman (b. 1975), Norwegian environmental activist.
[103] (1937-68) American child actor. Died from heart failure caused by substance abuse following the decline of his career.

constituency and its residents; that would be an exercise in painting the lily, as everyone in this House is already well aware of their qualities. Instead I should like to sing the praises of a certain individual whose skill, determination, courage and elegance should be singled out for commendation at this time more than any other. I'm talking of someone raised above their father's shop in the nineteen-thirties; someone whose humble beginnings and strong Wesleyan upbringing stimulated within them a drive and unflappable resolve; someone whose style, poise and vocal reproduction have often been remarked upon; someone whose hair, like spun gold, has been their crowning glory through thick and thin; someone whose rise in the realm of politics has been astounding and unquestionably what our country has been calling out for; someone whose chic, tasteful sense of dress has roused many a column inch; and someone whose graceful feminine wiles have reduced the roughest of adversaries to putty in their hand... I am, of course, Mister Speaker, referring to myself, and I would like to take this opportunity to say what an honour it is for you to have me in your midst.

Turning to what we have heard today from Her Majesty, it is undeniable that there is something for everyone in this Queen's Speech. The change in vigour, economic strength, tenacity, resolution and spirit at the beginning of this decade compared to the last is nothing short of phenomenal, and the confidence with which we can move forward is both incontrovertible and exciting. The agonies of the Winter of Discontent are now so far in the rear-view mirror, in terms of the self-respect of the people and the opportunities they enjoy, that it is hard to believe that they ever occurred. It is essential, however, that we remind ourselves of just how bad things got, to insure that we never again allow our country to fall so far. After perusing the plans submitted in the Speech, I am happy to say that I warmly commend the Government's proposals.

Lots of laughs, and they all came crawling round afterwards. At 4 o'c. I said to Belinda 'O! hang this, d'you fancy a stroll?'... Can't be doing with the rank pecksniffery – emanating chiefly from Temple-Morris[104] & that crowd. Unthinking traitors. It's all very well being in the right camp on Europe, but there's no point in being *right* if we're in *opposition*, which is where Heseltine would take us... When we came back I leant on the statue of Lloyd George & chatted to Chris Moncrieff.[105] He said 'The trick is to

---

[104] Peter Temple-Morris (1938-2018), Tory MP for Leominster, 1974-2001.
[105] (1931-2019) Political editor of the Press Association, 1980-94.

subtly *cajole* the Prime Minister. This lot have all the subtlety of Timmy Mallett on acid.'

Thursday, 8 November
Went in with the milk & found Flo with a plaster cast!! She'd misjudged the latch on her sash window & it came crashing down on the wrist. I told her to go home but she wouldn't hear of it – 'I manage, I manage!'… James rang. Asked if I could get to the South Bank for 7 o'c. to do a new panel show[106] with Paul Merton. The ghastly Russell Davies[107] was booked but is stuck in Dresden airport: 'Apparently the Stasi aren't happy with his passport photo,' said James. 'Nor would I be if I had his colouring,' I thought. Paul had suggested me as a stand-in, so I got it approved by the Chief Whip & said yes… The show was dire. Reckons to be a be a witty review of the week's events. You'd find more wit in Dresden! It was me, Paul, Ian Hislop & Clive Anderson, & Angus Deayton chairing it. Yuppyish, cynical crap. Refused the drinks & fled when it was done. No wonder the BBC is dying on its arse.

Saturday, 10 November
Gyles rang. He said I'd done well on the panel show, but agreed it was pretty pleb. We discussed the situation in the House, but got sidetracked with pantisocracies & the notion of direct people power. 'Equality's for schmucks,' he said, & I fervently concurred.

Sunday, 11 November
Flicked thro' *Sunday Times* & read, to my horror, that Erich Heller died on Monday last. In his sleep at a place called Evanston. It really gave me a pang. Quite aside from the acquaintanceship, he is one of the writers to whom I've continually returned over the years – my copy of *Disinherited Mind*[108] is dog-eared & yellow, with passages underlined on nearly every page… Thought about it later & it made sense – the letter he sent the other week was, in effect, a farewell, as he must have known the days were numbered.

---

[106] *Have I Got News for You*, BBC TV (1990–).
[107] British journalist and radio broadcaster (b. 1946). Presenter of BBC Radio 4's *Brain of Britain*.
[108] *The Disinherited Mind: Essays in Modern German Literature and Thought* by Erich Heller, 1952.

Monday, 12 November

I feel all sorts of things. Excited, as we are living in dramatic times; exhausted, as the tension is tiring & the clashes fierce; & torn, as *so much* is in the balance – one wrong move and the whole edifice could tumble. The sensation is one of seasickness. You're flying high one minute – enmeshed in deep, variegated discussions with ministers of the Crown on Britain's place in the world, the future of the continent, the cloud of a warming Cold War – & then levelled the next, with a scrawled memo from Belinda shoved into the hand, nagging that one's urgent response is required apropos Mrs Whatshername's broken sewer pipe. It's a trap. A backbencher might *just* be able to get her nibs' plumbing fixed (albeit to the detriment of some other worthy cause), but only *ministers* get to pull the meaningful levers. I'm practically a spectator, only with a fancy ringside seat… And the light relief at home? A dotty old woman, a bandaged housekeeper & a desperate neighbour – nay, a *friend* – that I can't bear to look in the eye.

Tuesday, 13 November

Managed to get a seat in the House. Atmosphere electric. I didn't know Howe had it in him. Dignified & witty, yet catty & *scathing*. The cricket references, 'batting back' from Maggie's comments at the Lord Mayor's dinner, caused audible gasps from our side & rolling in the aisles from the opposition.[109] I don't think the call for 'others to consider their own response' was aimed solely at Heseltine, but I've no doubt that *he* will.

Saw Tarzanites in the lobby, guffawing with Andrew Neil.[110] So they're already erecting the gallows. It's treachery, that's what it is… Went for drinks with Portaloo & Whittingdale. Both ashen. Found myself trying to gee people up with my Heseltine impression, but no one was really in the mood. Came back to flat & found Flo cleaning up filth from the carpet. Lou couldn't get to the throne in time, again. She was asleep in the armchair. I ought to have helped, or at least shown willing, but I didn't.

---

[109] Mrs Thatcher's speech at the Lord Mayor's banquet on 11 November contained cricketing metaphors where she promised that hostile bowling would 'get hit all around the ground'. In the Commons the following afternoon, Howe famously claimed she had undermined his bargaining position in Europe so badly it was 'like sending your opening batsmen to the crease only for them to find, the moment the first balls are bowled, that their bats have been broken by the team captain'.

[110] Scottish journalist and broadcaster (b.1949), editor of *The Sunday Times*, 1983-94.

Wednesday, 14 November
There was something quite nauseating about the announcement.[111] Standing there on the doorstep, Mrs Heseltine gazing up adoringly at her hunk. The blond mop slightly tousled, the specs perched on the end of the nose, as though to convey resolve, determination & learnedness. All far too thought-out. The words were altruistic, but the image projected was one of bare, naked *ambition*. If the Party's prepared to overthrow the greatest peacetime leader of the century for a self-seeking Swansea spiv, then it deserves *everything* that's coming.

Thursday, 15 November
'Phoned in sick. Belinda could tell I was putting it on, but the 'We'll hold the fort' line she produced was convincing enough for anyone within earshot. Walked to the Rose Gardens with Paul. He made me laugh re. being in hospital. Sounded like cutting-room floor stuff from *Carry On Matron*: the chap in the next bed ordering a prostitute on the payphone to come in & administer the wank at visiting time… the chap opposite who thought he was made of Waterford crystal & refused to be touched… the lisping hunchback droning on about his *thcoliothith* (scoliosis)… Paul said 'I'd've got more peace at Rorke's Drift.'

Friday, 16 November
After prayers, Tebbit told me that she's decided to go to Paris for the Yugoslav EEC accession summit – so she'll be away for the vote!! It's madness. Even if she *has* the numbers – as Morrison[112] assures everyone she does – it reeks of complacency. Got a mouth ulcer coming, so Ethan popped out for some Bonjela for me. Made sure I got the change, as he's prone to 'forget'.

Saturday, 17 November
Peter Mario with Stanley. Had the risotto so as not to inflame the ulcer & chewed on the left. Told him that I think the PM is on brittle glass & that no-one's *doing* anything. 'Well do it yourself,' said Stanley. 'Give waverers a bit of the old flannel, if she means that much to you…' Pondered that on

---

[111] Michael Heseltine's announcement that he would challenge Mrs Thatcher for leadership of the Conservative Party.
[112] Peter Morrison (1944-95), Tory MP for City of Chester, 1974-91; PPS to the Prime Minister 1990-1; leader of Mrs Thatcher's leadership campaign team.

the walk home. She is full of flaws, as are most truly great men, but when one thinks back to '79 – in the ways that matter – we're *miles* better off. The youngsters get educated, the sick get treated & if all else fails, there's a basic safety net. That's as much socialism as any grown-up country requires. She has created a situation where people feel emboldened to open doors for themselves, rather than hope the Hampstead liberals will do it for them. The argument for doing away with her is that the policies will continue, but with a more electable figurehead. Bunkum. If we're on the way out, I say *she* should take us out, all guns blazing.

Sunday, 18 November
Telephoned Portillo. He's worried. Morrison says she's well over the line, but Miguel is doubtful. 'I spoke to her this morning. She refuses to get out & talk to them. She said "My eleven year record is my campaign."' I said 'I want to help.' Rang Tom & told him to come. Left Rita a note & walked to Miguel's flat. Went in the back way. It was Miguel, Howarth,[113] Whittingdale & the three Michaels. We sat with the curtains drawn, like the Gunpowder Plotters. Miguel had a list of all members & we went through it, marking them up with a tick, a cross or a don't know. I perused the final version & doled out ten undecideds each for of us to have a go at. It's probably all for nothing, but someone's got to try.

Miguel, Gerald & I remained & we watched this Dobbs thing, *House of Cards*.[114] If one didn't know better, one would think the BBC scheduler was a member of the Shadow cabinet. All very near the knuckle. We each nominated who we thought the Urquhart character was based on, but the reality is there's *no-one* in the government with a comparable mix of his wit, sophistication *or* organisational ability.

Monday, 19 November
Got in early & set to, apprehension bubbling up inside. Went through the list of ten & sent Ethan & some of Cecil's staff to do some digging. After lunch we are at this position:

---

[113] Gerald Howarth (b. 1947), Tory MP for Cannock and Burntwood, 1983-91.
[114] BBC political thriller (1990). Set after the end of Mrs Thatcher's tenure, the series centres on the rise to power of the devious and scheming Francis Urquhart (played by Ian Richardson), the fictitious Tory Chief Whip. Written by Michael Dobbs (b. 1948), Tory chief of staff, 1986-7.

Name	Seat	Heseltine/ Abstain	Pliable?	Inducement	Possible?
Denis Aniston	Fareham S	Heseltine	No	-	-
Oliver Martin	Devon SE	Abstain (?)	Yes	Intro. to Peter & Dudley	Yes
C. Thomas Alnwick	Maldon	Heseltine (?)	Yes	Lifetime comps to Nat. Theatre	No
John McDowell	Aberdeen E	Heseltine	No	-	-
Leslie Hollings	Moor View	Abstain	Yes	Dinner with Barbara Windsor	Yes
Edward Gorton	Wandsworth	Abstain	Yes	Guest on 'Just A Minute'	Yes
Antony D'Arcy-Yates	Pinner	Heseltine (?)	Yes	Get children's book published	Yes
Ellen Winter	Hitchin	Heseltine	No	-	-
J. Kenneth Evans	Cardiff E	Abstain (?)	Yes	Part in a Pinewood film	Yes
Baljit Singh	Ilford W	Abstain	No	-	-

Amazing how cheaply some value their votes. Spent the afternoon on the 'phones calling in favours. Put a trunk call in to Dudley who was breakfasting in Manhattan!! He said Peter wouldn't be happy, but if I bunged in bottle of Macallan Estate that'd grease the wheels. Rather depressing... Rang Gerry Thomas who was rather taken aback but complied in principle. He's doing a follow-up to *Second Victory*[115] in August, & said 'I dare say there'll be a non-speaking Nazi role that would suit...' Indeed... Barbara said 'It's a long time since I've been pimped out, so I suppose I should be flattered!'... Spoke to Liz at Dent & she begrudgingly agreed to have a look. Kept it very loose so promises can be dropped later... Ted Taylor[116] said that bookings for *Just A Minute* are being discussed, and that he'd put in a word... I won't deny it, it's rather exciting, this cloak & dagger stuff... We watched the PM arrive at Fontainebleau, shaking hands with starstruck Balkanians & frosty Community leaders. Cecil said 'It's bonkers. She should be *here*!'... Passed Alan Clark by the library. 'What are you up to?' he queried, warily. I gave

---

[115] *The Second Victory* (1987), WW2 drama film directed by Gerald Thomas.
[116] Edward Taylor (b. 1931), British dramatist and radio producer.

an abridged summary of the day's proceedings. 'Very admirable, old chap,' he smirked, every inch the jaded old-hand, 'but you've no need to worry. The Lady's safe, mark my words. Morrison's done the maths.'

Ethan brought in hot meat pies & crisps from the pub & we ate in the office on paper plates. Rang Flo to tell her I'd probably be very late. 'No worry,' she said, 'we watch *Telly Addicts*'... Tom straightened my tie like a proud spouse. 'Let's get 'em!' he exclaimed. All quite ludicrous... Went to the tearoom & made the offers. Couldn't find Hollings, but eventually Belinda tracked him down, slumped in Annie's Bar. One thing's for sure, Barbara has got a *treat* in store for her... Of course, members who are willing to accept bribes in a private ballot aren't necessarily to be trusted to vote the right way, but that's the risk one takes. Met with the coven as arranged at 10 o'c. Portillo stony faced and unsure. It seems none of the heavyweights are willing to discuss the matter, let alone change position. 'You had the easy job,' he said, 'dealing with the minions.' Charming. Anyway, I feel I've done my duty. It's in the lap of the gods now.

Tuesday, 20 November
Up at 6 o'c. after lousy night. Just had dry bread & grease with coffee at Louisa's. Knocked at Rupert's. He's thinner, but perky enough. 'I'm going in to see him tonight,' he said. 'Would you come? I know he'd love to see you.' He's clearly not been following events. Made excuses but sent best wishes.

Sat through Questions. MacGregor[117] answered for the PM. Understandably subdued, everyone's minds elsewhere... Saw the Tarzanites zipping round doing last-minute lobbying. Kenilworth[118] came up to me in the queue at luncheon. 'I don't suppose it's worth checking whether you can be tempted?' he chuckled, with that toothy grin. I looked him square in the eyes. 'I happen to be loyal to my Leader, you bald-headed country bumpkin.' He didn't hang around... Chatted to Michael Howard.[119] 'I don't understand it. I offered & offered to help, but they kept saying it's "all in

---

[117] John MacGregor (b. 1937), Tory MP for South Norfolk, 1974-2001; Secretary of State for Education and Science, 1990-1.

[118] Norrie Kenilworth (1935-93), Tory MP for Totnes, 1983-93. Staunch supporter of Michael Heseltine.

[119] (b. 1941) Tory MP for Folkestone and Hythe, 1983-2010; Secretary of State for Employment, 1990-1.

hand"... They've no idea how fed up people are.' Major & Hurd nowhere to be seen, which speaks volumes.

Subtly eyeballed my peons in the lobby. Politicians say a lot and make promises with tearful conviction, but they lie more than any other group of people, so I gave my best glares. Tom said 'How does it feel to be the heavy?' I'll not lie, it's exhilarating. But that's beside the point – needs must. Spent the afternoon writing letters. Went to vote.

Squeezed in to the Committee Room, shoved up next to Nick Soames, which was a novel experience. Caught Miguel's eye & he winked.

Candidate	Votes	Percentage
Margaret Thatcher	208	55.7
Michael Heseltine	152	40.7
Abstentions	13	3.5
Majority	56	15
Turnout	373	100

We've done it. But it was the minimum required – the absolute, bare *minimum* – a win by fifteen per cent. In a way, it makes the victory taste even sweeter – for tonight, at least. There will be questions as to why it was so close, but those are for another day... The faces in the room told quite a story – rhapsodic elation from the loyalists, devastated gloom from the traitors, & wincing lip-chewing from those whose fidelity had slipped. Hollings tiptoed up, sheepishly. 'In the end I abstained, I'm afraid. But I don't feel good about it... I'm glad she's over the line.' I gave him an old fashioned look. Still, Barbara's off the hook. Caught the late bus home & had toast with honey at Lou's on my own.

Wednesday, 21 November
Deserted corridors. Doubtless the defeated have scurried away to their constituencies to lick wounds. Scanned the headlines with Tom & Belinda over coffee. *The Mirror*, of all papers, mentions *me* as one of the saviours!! 'Someone must've talked,' said Tom. But who? And who in their right mind talks to *The Mirror*?... Sat through the second reading of the Disabled Living Allowance bill, but it was dry old stuff; in any case, the bum starts playing up if I sit on those bloody benches too long. Was on the telephone to Mrs

Sharpe, listening to her bellyaching about traffic noise on Hampstead Rd when Ingham came in! I shut the moaning woman up & welcomed him. 'The Prime Minister is returned from Paris & has asked to see you at Downing Street tomorrow morning. Does five past eight sound suitable?' For a split second I considered saying 'O! you are a dear, but I'll be washing my hair', just to be impish, but I smiled 'With pleasure.' I could feel Tom grinning from the other room. Heaven knows what it all means. Good news, surely? I'm summoned at a weedy 8.05 rather than a solid 8 o'c., however, so I shan't pack any sandwiches.

Thursday, 22 November
Saw the porter in the lobby. Old Mr Ratcliffe in Flat 3 finally expired over night, so that's another one gone. Will be interesting to see who takes it on, as it would be perfect for Flo if someone buys it to let.

Got the bus in. Very quiet streets. Unnervingly so. Reached the tall black gates of Downing Street at 7.57 & the constable let me through. Walked towards Number 10 with the sun streaming down through broken clouds. Without knocking, the great door opened & I was ushered in. The famous Cynthia[120] greeted me & said 'This way, Mr Williams, the Prime Minister is ready for you.' The place is grand with hints of chintziness, as one would expect of a Georgian house with such an occupant. Within 2 minutes it was 'You may go in now.'

Dressed in lapis, she was seated beside the open red box, pen in hand, the portrait of Winston behind her. She looked *breathtakingly* handsome. I saw for the first time what ordinary men see when confronted with her: Boadicea in an Aquascutum suit. No wonder they fall under the spell… After a purposefully long moment, she beheld me, smiled, stood up & approached. 'Ah Kenneth dear, come in, do…' After three seconds of smalltalk it was down to business. 'It has come to my attention that our success in the leadership election was, in some small part, assisted by your actions…' 'Why, that's very kind, Prime Minister – ' (I could tell from the *look* that my interruption wasn't appreciated so I shut the trap quick)… 'I think it's fair to say that your loyalty, & more particularly your determination to remind others of their own loyalties, was a quiet crusade, without

---

[120] Cynthia Crawford (b. 1937), Mrs Thatcher's personal assistant. Known as 'Crawfie' to the Thatchers, she helped run the household at Downing Street, and became the Prime Minister's confidante.

1990

which our task might've been an onerous one…' She went over to the window. I could tell it wasn't an easy thing for her to say. Even now, I can scarcely believe that she *was* saying it, to me, in private, in 10 Downing Street. 'Changes shall have to be made, of course. And I am minded to reward this dedication…' A half-pause followed, so I took a chance. 'There are two things, Prime Minister, which have been occupying my thoughts. Two areas of policy which would come under the heading of legacy rather than the day-to-day.' She looked away from the window & fixed my gaze. I had a rush of blood & the legs nearly went. But I felt Gordon in the room with me, steadying me. 'The first is classically conservative. The second, I consider to be progressively conservative, which I know you'll permit is no paradox. Firstly, I propose the reintroduction of the penalty of death for certain crimes, & secondly, the liberalisation of homosexual affairs, including the sweeping away of the local authority clause & to follow the Danish example with legislation guaranteeing legal rights to couples who share the same gender.' She replaced her specs & sat down. No reply was forthcoming, so to fill the void I carried on. 'In my experience, Prime Minister, the castigated are crying out for normality. Lambasting a tenth of our people pushes them to the fringes. They want to be families & they want to be free. I am a Wesleyan, brought up not to judge. I want our Party to be the standard-bearer for all our people's freedoms, not just most of them.' Elbows on the desk, she interlocked her fingers & skimmed thro' her papers. I concluded: 'This period gives us a golden opportunity to make bold changes while we can. To catch our opponents off guard, but mostly to bolster personal liberty. Those are my aims. I think both are policies worth pursuing, but I should be delighted for your guidance in focusing my attention one way or the other.' She flashed a surprised raise of the eyebrow, barely concealed, & said 'I had in mind the position of Under Secretary for the Arts. I should've thought that an area entirely more suitable.' She picked up the red pen again & started writing. 'I shall think on it. Good morning.' She pressed a button on the telephone. That was my cue to piss off.

Went back & told Tom & the team & Cecil. They sat, eyes agog. 'Well,' said Cecil, 'you've got balls, I'll give you that'… She was glorious at PMQs. Caesar returned from Gaul, with order papers being waved around as banners of victory. Labour did their best to pluck the 'by the skin of your teeth' string, but she returned the shots with the gusto of a Wimbledon championette. The Welsh windbag remained buoyant: I'm sure he thinks the result cements *him* as PM-in-waiting – but for today, it was the Iron Lady who shone like the star she is.

Friday, 23 November
Dinner with Stanley at Vecchia. Told him about my audience. When I related the feeling I'd had of Nodrog being in there with me he said 'He was. We are a portion of everyone we've ever loved. I've felt *you* by my side at crunch times in the past & I've sailed through.' Had to bite the inside of my cheeks in order not to weep. I don't know what I did to be blessed with such friends, but it must've been something *awfully* good.

Saturday, 24 November
I'd just parked Lou outside the gents' by the Boating Lake, & in the time it took me to wee & rinse, she'd managed to flag down a passing skinhead, cadge one of his fags & puff it down to the butt!! When I returned they were laughing & joking like old chums, Louisa hopelessly trying to cover her tracks. 'This young lad,' she said, 'he wanted to know the time…' And they both started laughing again. In the end I had to sign for him! Considered scolding her for the cigarette business, but at this late date there seems little point. In any case, she revelled in her naughtiness & was peppy – and relatively fluent – for the rest of the morning.

Sunday, 25 November
They've released this Gripper suspect. Not enough evidence to hold him any longer. Spoke to Roger at the Home Office. 'Put it this way,' he said, 'the bloke won't be able to have a dump without Chester House knowing about it.' So it seems they're not looking for anyone else. Having to let him go does look clumsy though – which will delight officials at Marsham Street; they've been looking for an excuse to get rid of the demonstrative chief up there for donkey's years.

Wednesday, 28 November
I'm cautiously optimistic. I haven't been promoted in the reshuffle or palmed off with some nothingy role, & this morning there is a note from Powell saying 'The PM will be in touch – All best, Charles'… So it's a sit & wait situation… At 2 o'c. accompanied Tim Raison to St Pancras station, as I'm the local MP. He's new in at Transport & is keen to flex the muscles. Plenty of limp, mistrustful handshakes with grubby British Rail workers

under the grim, creaking roof. Tim babbling on about grand proposals to make the station the English terminus for the Channel tunnel. I smiled along, but it's a senseless concept: Welcome to London, *messieurs*, please ignore the hookers & broken glass.

Thursday, 29 November
Rupert knocked at 9.20. & we drove to Missenden. Silence to begin with, but we thawed and, in the end, it was beneficial to be forced together in the motor to talk. Seems Orlando has weeks rather than months; he can't keep anything down. Tried to buoy the mood, but it's an uphill struggle when one's *en route* to a funeral… It was a curious event! Viking-style, adhering to your actual Norse rituals. The grave was filled with pencils & chocolates & Roald's favourite burgundy. Lovely reading of 'Do not go gentle'[121] at the finish, but that was the only part even *approaching* convention. The Anglicans have a lot to answer for, but one can't deny they've got incarcerations down to a tee. We stayed as long as was polite & then nipped to Mrs Jarvis's for coffee. The grandmother (who is 98) was there, all four foot of her. Relishing her sugared almonds she said, unequivocally, 'I love a good suck, don't you, Kenneth?'… Rupert nearly choked to death on his Viennese whirl.

Saturday, 1 December
We watched the breakthrough under the Channel. The reporter grandly declared that 'our 8,000 years as an island nation come to an end…' Not in the minds of the CIB[122] they don't. Graham Fagg, our fabulously drably named chief engineer, squeezed through the breach in the rock & exchanged flags with his Gallic counterpart. Rita said 'Imagine doing all that digging & all you find at the bottom is a Frog in grey overalls.'

Tuesday, 4 December
Went to Flemwell for the massage. 'You'll never guess who I had in 'ere last week,' he said proudly, that awful sibilance running right thro' me. 'Bert Finney himself! The greatest Poirot of them all, right?' 'Err, right,' I said, my face buried in the loo seat-shaped pillow. 'Right. And do you know, he's got the rhomboids of a Greek god… it was an honour to rub 'em.' So much for patient confidentiality. I spent the rest of the session worrying which

---

[121] 'Do not go gentle into that good night' (1947) by Welsh poet Dylan Thomas (1914-53).
[122] Campaign for an Independent Britain, a cross-party Eurosceptic campaign group formed in 1976.

intimate details of *my* physique would be poetically described to the next victim. Came out more tense than when I went in... Walked to HH. Spent an hour signing Christmas cards to various supporters & donors. I said to Camilla 'Isn't there a stamp that could speed up the process?' I could feel her rolling the eyes. 'Our friends prefer the personal touch,' she snapped, loftily. I rather enjoy winding her up.

To Hampstead in the evening with Mags & Bev[123] for *What the Butler Saw*. Bleak, but it was nice to flit backstage after to spread a few compliments & offer advice. Candlelit supper at Biagi. Mags is just back from doing *Peter Pan*[124] in California & said, 'Of course, once Robin[125] caught wind that I knew you, that was it... Matron this, bowels that. Asking all about you... I said "You must see for yourself", so you've got to promise to come to dinner when's he's in London.' For myself I'm not fussed, but knowing how much Lou loves *Mork & Mindy*, I had to give my word.

Wednesday, 5 December
Belinda off sick with women's problems, so Ethan deputised. He's a fetching boy, but the telephone manner leaves something to be desired. I'm all for regional accents, in moderation, but it sounded as though he was answering calls for the Cromer crab paste association.

Friday, 7 December
Confirmation that Gorbachev is dead. No one's comparing him to Albert Schweitzer,[126] but he *was* a glimmer of democratic hope for the east of the continent. The fact that Vstavlyat's thugs can snuff him out without even the veneer of legitimacy is deeply troubling... At 1 o'c. to the Women's Bright Hour lunch at Birkenhead Street church hall. They were knocking back the Asda manzanilla as though it were Malvern water. Managed to avoid the sherries but not the glutinous fare. I should think the old dears could do with a bit less Delia & a bit more Jesus... 'Oh *do* try the chestnut & apple stuffing, Mr Williams, it's simply divine...'

---

[123] Beverley Cross (1931-98), English playwright and screenwriter. Married Maggie Smith in 1975.

[124] *Hook* (1991), American adventure film, directed by Steven Spielberg; a screen sequel to J. M. Barrie's *Peter and Wendy*.

[125] Robin Williams (1951-2014), madcap American actor and comedian.

[126] (1875-1965) Franco-German theologian, humanitarian and philosopher; Nobel Peace Prize laureate, 1952.

Saturday, 8 December
We're snowed in!! Rita called to say the buses weren't running & she'd have to walk. I told her not to be ridiculous & to stay in & wrap up warm. We saw the TV news & it's terrible everywhere. The authorities generally get the blame when weather intervenes ('One flake of snow & this bloody country *grinds* to a halt,' &c., &c.), but it would be unsporting to chide the government for this… it's like a naff day in Spitsbergen.

Tuesday, 11 December
The 88 was crawling, so got off & trudged through the grey slush. The level of compensation for the AIDS hæmophiliacs has been set at £42 million, which is more generous than I was expecting… We watched the footage of President Kassis falling through the stage in Baghdad. Physically unhurt by all accounts, but his pride will be shot to pieces… as will the poor sod who built the dais, I shouldn't wonder.

Thursday, 13 December
After PMQs I went to Heath Hurst for a final surgery of the year. Tom having some bridge work done so I took Ethan. One of the punters, a Mr Saleem, lives at 18 Cromer House!! 'I lived a few doors along from you as a child!' I exclaimed, expecting some jovial 'Well I never!'-type repartee. Alas, my verve was met with the stoniest expression this side of Minsk. Mr Saleem was not in the mood for badinage, or even a touch of polite reminiscence: 'So, what about my toilet?' came the indifferent reply.

Monday, 17 December
Lift out of order *again*. Even with Flo on one arm & me on the other, it took fifteen minutes to get Lou down the stairs. I ought to enquire about the vacant ground floor flat, as that would be a permanent solution, but I can't face the upheaval… Went to C&A & found a nice cerulean cardie for Louie for £14.99. It won't matter that she's seen it; she'll have forgotten by Thursday. Then to Victoria Wine for Xmas presents for staff. M&S vouchers for Pat & Body Shop vouchers for Rita 'cos it's easier that way. Left Flo & Lou in the Baker's Oven & went to Tiffany to get bracelet for Flo & tie pin for Rupert. Pricey, but I think they both deserve a bit of sparkle.

Wednesday, 19 December
Dished out the booty & bade all parties the obligatory Yuletide good wishes. Lovely card from the Prime Minister on my desk. Picture of her on the front, of course. 'With enduring thanks, Margaret' – blue-black, in that vigorous, flowing hand.

Thursday, 20 December
Gave Lou the cardigan & smellies. She was a bit crotchety but perked up when Sandra & Cecil arrived. They played cards whilst Flo prepared the cake & I did the sandwiches. Stanley came at 11 o'c. & gave her a big kiss & we all sang Happy Birthday. By noon she was dozing off from all the excitement, so everything petered out. When I was doing her tablets she said 'Where's Charlie got to?' I ignored it, but it's a worrying development... With Stanley & Paul to the Queen's to see the three Redgraves in *Three Sisters*. Superb, especially the niece Jemma who was uncommonly good. We went back stage. Vanessa made a few comments about the government, but I didn't take on. Graham Crowden[127] said 'Your name was mentioned when they were struggling to cast Kulygin, you know.' 'How absurd,' I said. I was inwardly delighted.

Friday, 21 December
In the afternoon went with Rupert to visit the Orlando. Rather shocking. One could tell the nurse had put some Poudré Rachel on him, but it did little to mask the havoc the disease has caused. There's nothing of him. I'd be surprised if he sees out the year.

We saw Barbara in *Family Fortunes*. They were all done up in panto gear, going thro' the motions. Lovely to see Floella Benjamin![128] I scribbled a note wishing her a happy Christmas. She is a kind, sweet girl.

Tuesday, 25 December
Flo did the duck, I did the veg & Lou sat in front of Noel Edmonds scoffing Brazils. Had a rest after & then we wheeled Lou to the lake where we hurled bits of leftover pudding to the relatives of our main course.

---

[127] Scottish actor (1922-2010). Appeared with Stephanie Cole in the BBC sitcom *Waiting for God*, 1990-4.

[128] Trinidadian-British actress (b. 1949). Presenter of popular children's programmes including *Play School* and *Play Away*.

Monday, 31 December

Rang Pat, rang the electricity people & replied to fan letters which have been building up. Took until 4 o'c. to clear the backlog. Telephoned James to wish him a happy new year. Toyed with the idea of the Bottomleys' party, but thought better of it. Sat in with Louisa & played brag. Bed at 10.30.

1991

Tuesday, 1 January

Rupert rang at 7 o'c. Orlando died just after midnight. Took him to the Queen's Head which was mercifully quiet & ordered doubles. 'The feeling I can't cope with is the guilt,' he said. 'I didn't love him in the way he loved me, but I'm all he had. His parents threw him out when he was sixteen & the family cut him off...' It was the all too familiar story of old-fashioned *values* trumping what really matters. There are two painful truths within: on the one hand this is a release for Rupert – & on the other it's a confirmation that our absurd clinging to Victorian "morality" utterly *stinks*.

Thursday, 3 January

Tom arrived with the cab & we were at Gatwick by 10.15. Economy seats, but the 'plane was half-empty so it didn't matter. Arrived Luqa at 3.20. It's cool but bright. Taxi to the Grand Excelsior. We stayed here in '75, & I'll wager it's not seen a paintbrush in the intervening. Rooms OK. The porter, Joe, is a dead ringer for Marty Feldman, the eyes at odds with each other. He brought our complimentary tumblers of neat anisette & dutifully watched us sip them, as though he were doling out tranks in the infirmary. 'Is good, no?' he beamed. 'Delightful,' I said, grimacing. Soon as he'd gone we chucked the rest down the sink. 'Feel like I've been deepthroating Bertie Bassett,'[1] said Tom... Had a rest & freshened up. A shrivelled retainer was mauling some Chopin on an ancient Steinway in the bar, so we forewent the drinks & dined. I was tackling the red mullet when Tom said 'It's been a month. What are we going to do if she turns you down?' He's worried that

---

[1] The mascot of Bassett's Liquorice Allsorts, created in 1929 by Greenly's advertising agency.

I'll go loopy & *his* prospects will be damaged by association. I put him off with 'Never mind that, this is our holiday, we can worry about it when we get back.' Rotund couple on the next table, Ben & Jen from Loughton. 'We won the tickets on *Strike it Lucky*,'[2] they explained. 'He's a class act, that Barrymore... a real gent...'

Friday, 4 January
After breakfast we walked to the cathedral of St John where a fittingly Madonna-like creature called Claudette showed us round for 3 lira. It's very much Liberace's boudoir inside, every nook gilded with Baroque excess. 'One wonders what the Carpenter would've made of such extravagance,' I said. 'He would have loved it,' retorted Claudette, defensively... Lunched comfortably outdoors in the sunshine, then to the Upper Barrakka Gardens. Delightful, but Tom *constantly* reads aloud from this bloody Berlitz guide rather than just *looking* & in the end I snapped. He was morose for the remainder of the afternoon – but at least it was quiet.

Saturday, 5 January
Caught myself in the bathroom mirror & thought 'What on *earth* are you doing? A sad old man trolling about the Med with a member of *staff* to avoid despair...' Pathetic.

Sunday, 6 January
Coming from the great metrolops, one forgets that large parts of the civilised world still shut down entirely for the sabbath. The tedium was broken by luncheon, if not the tension: he's still sore with me for chastising him over the bloody guide book. Went for a walk & found the newsagent on Bakery Street open!! Purchased a packet of the nougat he's taken a shine to as a peace offering, as well as postcards & yesterday's *Today*. Headlines about the gales at home & 27 dead, which raised the spirits – we're lucky to be *au soleil*.

Monday, 7 January
Awoke potently, so engaged in rare morning tradiola... Taxi to Sliema & boarded the *Marija Kbira* on mercifully calm waters. Marsamxetto first, then bobbed in the open sea before cruising around the Grand Harbour. Thank heavens I took the overcoat!! At lunch we were buttonholed by a reeking

---

[2] ITV game show (1986-99), presented by comedian and entertainer Michael Barrymore (b. 1952).

hawker who went on & on about his experiences at Beaulieu during the war. It was only after the meal that Tom found his wallet gone!! We put two & two together, & realised it must've been nabbed when whiffy was reckoning to lace the boots. Walked to the police station, but they couldn't've been less interested if they'd tried. Back to the Excelsior to 'phone London to cancel cards, etc.

Tuesday, 8 January
If I never see a king prawn again it'll be too soon.

Wednesday, 9 January
After the war rooms at Fort Lascaris, Tom said, hurriedly, 'I'm going for a wander, see you back at HQ…' & was gone before I could reply. I was dressed for dinner when he returned, dishevelled with a lusty smirk. 'I don't wish to know,' I said. It's repellent behaviour & not what I expect from an assistant. I came up hastily after dinner & had *very much* the barclays.

Thursday, 10 January
We actually arrived back in London thirty minutes early. Went in to Louisa & gave her the Maltese cross brooch. 'Been away without me *again*, haven't you?' she said, which was rather fatiguing. We saw the News & the aftermath of this accident at Cannon Street.[3] Driver's blaming the brakes, but there's something fishy about the whole thing.

Friday, 11 January
Rupert knocked at 10.30 & we got the cab to the crematorium at Kensal Green. About twenty there, including *one* solitary relation. Apparently the mother wanted to come but hubby wouldn't allow it. It was all so small, so meagre. I barely knew the chap, but I *do* know his flamboyance & verve ought to have been celebrated – or, at the very least, acknowledged – & not swept under the carpet in such a feeble, abashed & dispiriting fashion. I was livid by the end & couldn't wait to leave.

Sunday, 13 January
M. came & drove me to the Paris for *Just a Minute*. Smashing audience!! Panel was myself, Paul, Wendy Richard & Su Pollard who, though useless

---

[3] A train failed to stop and hit the buffers. Two people died, 542 injured. An inquiry blamed the driver and ageing carriages.

at the game, was a riot! There aren't many female clowns who have the *confidence* to bare all & be laughed at regardless, but she's got it. Of course, she can only be taken in small doses. Mind you, that's what people say about *me*. Either way, I found her delightful… Sat with Lou & watched *Lovejoy*[4] & ate toast with strawberry jam. Turned in at 9.45.

Monday, 14 January
On the bus – Woman: 'It's been one heck a week! Our Carol's got appendicitis, & what with the weather, her Steve's stuck in Qatar.' Friend: 'Ooh, nasty. Have you tried him on Benylin?…'

Tuesday, 15 January
Spent the morning on the dictaphone replying to letters. Sombre mood thanks to the death of Donald Coleman,[5] triggering copious eulogies in the House. Then PMQs. The anti-European bile being spouted bordered on the neurotic. I fear she's so entrenched that coaxing's out of the question. Found myself nodding along to the Welsh windbag's responses! Oh, that ain't good… Ford rang to confirm this *After Dark*[6] thing on Saturday. The fee is £200, which will have to be waived.

Wednesday, 16 January
Heath Hurst, but nothing doing. Slunk off to Marlborough to help Flo with the decorating. She dropped hints about not being able to afford the rent, but I set her straight. My salary is stacking up & there's no point in it just sitting there. If this isn't a rainy day I don't know what is. She offered to go seven days, but I don't want her to tire of us, & she needs a bit of a life of her own. In any case, I haven't the heart to dismiss Rita… Flo served rissoles with mash & peas at 5.45. We saw *Coronation Street*. The script was diabolical! I don't know what kind of brain creates a character such as Reg Holdsworth,[7] but it ought to be studied *post mortem*.

---

[4] BBC comedy-drama series (1986-94), based on the exploits of a rakish antiques dealer played by Ian McShane (b. 1942).
[5] (1925-91) Labour MP for Neath, 1964-91.
[6] Late-night Channel 4 discussion programme (1987-91). Broadcast live and hosted by a variety of presenters, each episode featured a different topic (with subjects as diverse as the Mafia, pornography and alternative medicine), with a group of six guests – generally leading lights, celebrities and members of the public – invited to debate the issue at hand.
[7] Bumbling supermarket manager played by Ken Morley (b.1943).

Thursday, 17 January
Chief Whip came in. Big grin. 'Could I have a word, Ken?' Traipsed to the meeting room, joining Townend who was twanging an elastic band, irritatingly. 'After careful consideration, the PM is pleased to offer you a crucial role overseeing the Charities Commission…' He spoke as though I'd won a raffle. Townend sat there, lips pursed, eyebrows raised, implying I was a very lucky boy to be receiving such manna… 'I'm not remotely interested in that crap,' I said. Long pause. 'C-come again?' stuttered Renton. 'I shan't be accepting that. You can thank her & tell her "No"…' Stormed out leaving them slack jawed & bewildered… Came back & told Tom, who was waiting nervously outside the office.

In a way, I'm relieved. The uncertainty is gone, at least. They've shown their true colours & they've neither faith in me, nor gratitude for my efforts. So be it. All that remains to be seen is how much mayhem I can cause in what remains of this godforsaken parliament. I'm sick of the whole vile mess.

Friday, 18 January
They're to crown the new king of Norway on *Monday*. Can't imagine why there'd be such a rush. Impressive organisation, tho'… *We* couldn't arrange a jumble sale in three days, let alone a coronation.

Saturday, 19 January
Light supper before leaving Lou in front of Paul Daniels. Had the nap & the car came at 9.10. South Bank for the *After Dark* show 'Gays: Free at last?'. Coffee & smalltalk in the green room, then marched away to sign release form before a lawyer!! It was myself, Ray Gosling (bold activist), Jackie Forster (militant dyke), Mervyn Stockwood[8] (standing in for Jesus), Michael Shepherd (psychiatrist), Miriam Drake (gay conversion therapist) & "Martin" (dentally challenged dilly boy)… We didn't start till nigh-on midnight, the darkened studio done out like a dowager's parlour with maroon chesterfields & potted palms clustered round a coffee table. His Holiness nabbed the good seat, so I was lumbered between the rent boy & the awful Drake woman. Anthony Clare[9] chaired it & got the chat going…

---

[8] (1913-93) Bishop of Southwark, 1959-80. Despite KW's accusation of pontification, Stockwood was known for his liberal view of the morality of homosexual relationships – on at least one occasion as bishop he blessed a same-sex union.

[9] (1942-2007) Irish psychiatrist and radio presenter.

Quickly forgot it was being televised!! Started off well with jaunty debate before the droning shrink got into his stride. These intellectual types make me *sick*. Think they've got it licked from the comfort of their Harley Street *salons*. Badgering me endlessly with impertinent jibes & fanciful hypotheses. Then the rickety pulpiteer piped up, pontificating from her closet. It went on & on. Cinzano on tap, so I got rather tight & fell into the familiar traps. Ended up with the arm around the prozzie and, egged on by him, yawped 'O! shut your great mouth, you stupid fool!' at the Drake thing. Appalling, reely... Stuck to the guns apropos disagreement with govt. policy, but dropped more names than I ought. It finally came to a close with positions entrenched & my morale through the floor at a quarter past *two*... The lawyer bod took me aside after & said 'We might have a few problems with what came out, but we'll see how the dust settles...' Avoided the lone paparazzo at the door & fell into bed at 3 o'c.

Sunday, 20 January
Woken by telephone at *7.15* – Chief Whip. 'What the bloody hell was that all about?... How dare you break confidences?... Do you know what this could mean?'... I said 'I'm in the middle of my kippers' & hung up. One can't put up with *that* kind of drear, least of all at the crack of dawn... Then a girl from *The Express*, schmoozing, fishing for scandal. Rang James at home. 'I thought you were brilliant,' he said, 'but it might be best to cover our arses.' We concocted a bland, stock answer in case of press deluge... 'Phoned Tom. Predictably nervy. If I'm not sacked, he shall have to go. Plays things too safe, the poor sap. Well, if fifty years' boot-licking & a carriage clock at the end of it is the summit of his ambitions, that's his lookout.

M. arrived & drove us to the Paris. 'D'you think they'll remove the whip?' he asked. 'Fuck knows,' I said, & he laughed... Panel was myself, Clement, Derek & Les Dawson. Show went well. I don't think the average *Just a Minute* audience member is particularly *au fait* with late-night Channel 4, so Clement's taunts went largely over their heads. Les was *superb*... I knew he had the verbal dexterity, but the man's delivery & mock world-weariness is quite delicious. Met Tracy, the new wife, afterwards & the four of us retired to The Dell for supper. Gylrig *maître d'*. Blond. Very nice. 'You're rather young for a host, aren't you?' I asked. 'O! I was waiting tables in north Devon when I was *fourteen*!' he grinned. 'I needed the London challenge...'

'Well, it's better to reign in Dell than serve in Devon,[10] son' said Les, which was so wittily adroit I nearly fell off the chair. The man is a complete delight.

Monday, 21 January
Pathetic. They've not even the mettle to sack me!! The bare office was arranged in the style of *1984* (presumably with the objective of putting the willies up one), but in the finish it was a v. placid affair. 'We don't want such a non-event to attract more attention than it's due,' Townend muttered. Renton was even more mollifying – 'We understand your frustrations, Ken, but we're either a team or we're not.' Yellow dolts. God forbid they should actually *do* something. One of the many exasperating things about this place is that it's safer to sit & do fuck all – and the effort that goes in to doing fuck all is colossal… Typed note from the PM's PPS on my desk. 'After careful consideration, we have decided not to pursue either of the proposed policy concepts' etc., etc. Lunched with Clive Whitmore.[11] 'You've got to understand,' he said, 'she can't be beholden to anyone, at all. Your assistance in the vote will never be publicly acknowledged. And now you've snubbed the promotion, well… you're out in the cold.'

Tuesday, 22 January
Up at 7.30 & got papers. Comrade Honecker shoving me off the front pages. Decided I couldn't face a day of World War 3 babble, so went in to Lou & told Flo to get her ready. Lugged her to the lobby & hailed cab to Fenchurch St. Got the 9.58 & arrived at Southend at 10.53. Brass monkeys, but we pushed Louisa along the front & she messily ate chips. She kept calling Flo 'Alice'. Christ alone knows why… Of course, the place is a desolate dump, but it was good for all three of us to get some sea air in our lungs. There was a girl bound up in a sleeping bag outside the Kursaal, with a scruffy Bullmastiff tied to a bit of string. Put two pounds in her cup.

Wednesday, 23 January
After Trade (ha!) Questions I chatted with Tony Tichet-Sweeting. 'It's not the party I joined,' he said. 'Moral judgments, anti-foreigner. It's a sad state of affairs.' As an aside I half-jested that I regretted 'saving her job', but he took

---

[10] Satan, in John Milton's *Paradise Lost* (1667), declares "Better to reign in Hell than serve in Heaven" (1.263).

[11] Senior civil servant (b. 1935), Permanent Under-Secretary of State of the Home Office, 1988-91.

it at face value & clutched my arm – 'Don't blame yourself,' he whispered, 'and don't fret. This is 1901. Victoria's fading & Bertie's just waiting for the nod. Haven't you seen the spring in John Smith's[12] step? He's already picking out new curtains for No. 11 in his mind... and he's right to.'

Friday, 25 January
Lunch at Langan's with Francis Miller. Thought I was going in to discuss a poetry anthology, but he expeditiously pivoted to his idea of a tell-all exposé of the govt. to have ready-to-go when the axe falls. Snubbed the notion, leaving no room for doubt. I never was, nor never will be, false.[13]

Saturday, 26 January
Aside from the anal itching, & the occasional spot of lumbago, it's fair to say that I haven't felt as sprightly in years. Can't imagine why this should be. After all, if it weren't for this so-called *job* I'd be trolling up the P.O. to draw the pension. I know I ought to be grateful, but no numen answered my cries when I was in agony, so it follows that no credit should be bestowed for my salubrity. Except on Mr Chatham, of course.

Car came at 6 o'c. for *Des O'Connor Tonight*. The driver was the son of Len Essex who was with me in Rangoon!! Remarkable coincidence! 'He always talks fondly of his "pal Casey"[14] when you come up on the telly,' he said... Thorny smalltalk with David Bellamy[15] in the green room before going on. I told him 'I detest the countryside, you know,' and he said 'I doubt it thinks much of you either.' Des his usual chipper & creosoted self. Tried to shepherd it towards our cause, but he only wanted to know about the Prime Minister's wallpaper.

Sunday, 27 January
Came back from the Paris Studio & went in to Lou's for crumpets. As I was setting the table she looked up from her *Woman's Own*, studied me & said 'I know you, don't I?...' The heart plummeted like a lead weight right through my gut. Before I'd time to speak the confused glaze cleared & she

---

[12] (1938-94) Labour MP for Monklands East, 1983-94; Shadow Chancellor of the Exchequer, 1987-91; Chancellor of the Exchequer, 1991-4.

[13] Lord Stanley, Shakespeare's *Richard III* (Act IV, Scene 4): "Most mighty sovereign, You have no cause to hold my friendship doubtful. I never was nor never will be false."

[14] KW's nickname whilst in the forces; derived from his initials, i.e. K. C. Williams.

[15] (1933-2019) English botanist, TV presenter and environmental campaigner.

started on about some triviality & the moment had passed. But the briefness of the event doesn't negate its awfulness. I suppose I always knew things might come to this, but in that moment she didn't *know me*. I tried to hold myself together, but as soon as she'd finished eating I flew back to the flat & bawled. If that trice was a foretaste of things to come – of being truly alone – then I want no part of it.

Tuesday, 29 January
Even as Toff[16] lustily described the circumstances of the latest Manchester murder, I was thinking about Louisa. When I reflect on the laughs we used to have & the equal reliance we had on one another, it takes all I've got not to break down & weep. I'm now simply warehousing a shadow of a person, whose mind & magnetism have left the stage. I'm not even occupying the role of quiet martyr, patiently carrying out noble duties: I've subcontracted out the heavy lifting & dirty work to an alien drudge, too lily-livered to face my own obligations. It's a rotten, shameful mess & I wish I was dead.

Wednesday, 30 January
Drifted about for most of the afternoon in a daze. Tried to read some begging letters but couldn't concentrate. In the chamber it was the usual company of bores making endless, futile points of order concerning endless, vapid trifles. Talk about rearranging deckchairs on the *Titanic*… In desperation I 'phoned Rupert & we met at The Tent. I got stuck into Riesling & behaved atrociously. Pinched the waiter's backside & he wasn't best pleased, but Rupert managed to calm the waters. I don't know what I'm doing any more. If I were witnessing such behaviour in someone else I'd be completely appalled.

Thursday, 31 January
Chosen for a Question. Renton 'phoned the plant through to Belinda: 'Does the PM agree with me that the govt.'s economic policy is clearly working for all parts of our country?' I suppose it was an attempt to put me in my place… In the event I asked 'Does the PM agree with me that the anti-homosexual clause in the Local Govt. Bill nullifies her own mantra that our ambition ought to be to extend choice, extend the will to choose and the chance to choose?' I could feel the bristling vexation as I sat down, amidst

---

[16] Christopher Austin Parr (1931-98), Manx industrialist; joint Treasurer of the Conservative Party, 1984-91.

the usual 'Ooh, matron!' response from the other side & tutting from our own. It was batted away with the anticipated haughty apathy, but the point had been made... Saw Tom at the Norman Porch. 'How to lose friends and alienate people,' he said, reproachfully. He'll have to go.

Friday, 1 February
They're trying to make me feel bad. When Ogilvy was circulating the invites to Fowler's birthday do, I was pointedly *not* on the register... They think that's a punishment, whereas, given the choice, I'd sooner be on a Stasi hit list... Used the opportunity to get rid of Tom. He mustered all the right bromides ('It's been an honour', 'I've learnt a lot', & etc.), but in the event his loafered plates couldn't whisk him away fast enough. Ah well. One truly *can't* get the staff... Informally promoted Ethan, who was curiously elated. If the rumours are true that She's planning an October election, his duties will amount to little more than unplugging fax machines & turning out lights. Managed decline, I think is the expression.

Saturday, 2 February
Interesting letter from Tim at Stonewall, ostensibly lauding my antics at PMQs, but also floating the notion of a meeting (to be of my initiation) between a Stonewall representative (perhaps McKellen) and 'the person you think most apt to take up the reins in government if the post becomes vacant'... Dictated a careful reply, making it clear that my support is only indirect.

Sunday, 3 February
Shuddered my way to Peter Mario for this *Round the Horne* reunion lunch. Started off pleasantly, but Barry[17] got shirty after the mains – apparently I told the 'Covet thy neighbour's ass' story too loudly & people were looking. As if that mattered in the least... Betty[18] tried to mend the damage but it'd left a sour taste so got out as swiftly as I could. It was so dejecting to see how everyone has *aged*. Bifocals & beige hearing aids.

Just a Minute in the evening. Merton being grumpy. I've noticed it before – if Paul's in a downcast frame of mind, it colours the whole operation, & if he's buoyant the contrary is true. Curious how an

---

[17] Barry Took (1928-2002), English writer and comedian. Presented the BBC's *Points of View*, 1979-86.
[18] Betty Marsden (1919-98), English comedy actress; starred with KW in both *Beyond Our Ken* and *Round the Horne* on BBC radio, as well as *Carry On Regardless* and *Carry On Camping*.

atmosphere can be influenced so completely, especially by one as unprepossessing.

Monday, 4 February
Letter from Central TV – it seems they've exhausted the latex on my *Spitting Image* dummy & are to mould a replacement... and they ask whether I want the *old head* sent to me!! One must applaud the impudence I suppose. Sent a reply on HOC notepaper, thanking them profusely, & politely requesting they shove it where the sun don't shine.

Wednesday, 6 February
It's absolutely *freezing*. The overalled handymen are all over the building, scratching their heads & banging away at the Edwardian central heating with spanners... Chatted to MacGregor & he said I've made them a bit jumpy. 'They can't handle a loose cannon,' he said. 'You didn't hear this from me, but Harrison's[19] on his way out. Chemotherapy. Might be worth pushing your name forward if they decide to keep their enemies close...' He was referring to Harrison's place on the Select Committee (Foreign Affs.). It's true, it would be a chance to dunk ministers in hot water – legitimately & publicly – but it'd be an awful lot of extra work. Spoke to Roger & he echoed the sentiments: 'They'd probably be open to it, to bring you back into the fold.'

Friday, 8 February
Car at noon to the Brunswick Centre to open the new wing. I had to cut the ribbon & make the speech in the driving blizzard. A sparse band of overcoated onlookers shivered their way through the proceedings, the pathetic applause muffled by gloved hands. Then the tour of the dismal little shops with the standard wavy lines & soft lighting. Tried to be enthusiastic, but in point of fact it bored the arse off me.

Back to the flat at 4 o'c. Went in to Lou & sent Flo away so it could be just the two of us. She seemed alright, watching the TV, but after *Holiday '91* she turned to me and said 'What am I still doing here?' The look of lassitude & defeat in her eyes made me feel so utterly helpless that I didn't know what to do. Diverted her as best I could & then returned to the flat. I was sick in the lavatory.

---

[19] Christopher Harrison (1925-91), Tory MP for Kidderminster, 1983-91.

Saturday, 9 February
Thought of finishing it off last night, but this morning I went in & they were singing. There is a hazy sun, so I told Flo to get her layered up & we lugged everything down the stairs for a turn in the park. We saw Sam Sugar & he fussed over Louisa, who enjoyed petting his Dalmatian. We sat by the lake & Flo doled out the plastic cups & poured out the Thermos of Gold Blend. It was all lovely, & mercifully quiet, the Arctic blast clearly having committed avicide on a majestic scale.

In the afternoon called on Paul & we went up to Selfridges. My lovely friend Jonathan was there on the counter. I held up a pair of brown Oxfords & shouted "Ere, Jonathan, 'ark at these shit-coloured shoes!', much to the chagrin of his orotund manager.

Tuesday, 12 February
Sat in the Library. Daydreams of taking Louisa to the coast, renting a handsome, balconied room with views out to sea, ordering a bottle of Château Pape Clément & quaffing it together over the vial of benzodiazepine. Being found by the tiptoeing maid, dressed in our best, *Leamington*-like.[20] The concluded Fauré record still spinning on the gramophone, as the doctor is sent for, & the man from the local firm, discreetly solicited to tidy us away, decorously & without fuss… Snapped out of it when Wedgwood Benn[21] spluttered from his Queen Anne chair: 'The end for Sibelius – six letters,' & I said '*Finish*!' straitway.

Lovely debate in the chamber apropos the new fivepenny piece & its inadequacies.[22] Bidwell brought the 10 min. rule bill, claiming that *four hundred* constituents had written to him to complain about the coin's puniness. One has to admire the English public; with all that's going on, *this* is what gets them aerated. I stood in support & said 'There is a precedent from the predecimal period, Mister Speaker; I recall many occasions in my youth when my little joeys[23] would slip through my trousers… men were *desperate* to get their hands on some bigger thruppenny bits.'

---

[20] *Death in Leamington* by John Betjeman, 1932. KW and Maggie Smith recited this ballad before the poet himself on the *Parkinson* programme in 1973.
[21] Tony Benn (1925-2014), Labour MP for Chesterfield, 1984-2001; prominent and influential left-winger.
[22] The Royal Mint reduced the diameter of the 5p coin from 23.5mm to 18mm in June 1990.
[23] 'Joey', nickname of the silver threepence coin, weighing 1.4 grams; its nickel-brass successor weighed 6.8 grams.

Beyond Our Kenneth

Wednesday, 13 February
Went to the 1922. To see their faces, you'd think it was Göring showing up at a bar mitzvah. Most of them were as Thatcherite as all get-out when they were casting their votes, but now that MORI reckons they're for the chop, *I'm* the scapegoat. Well, *good*. They're useless farts anyway.

Saturday, 16 February
Some corporate wallah has evidently convinced the Beeb to blow its budget on oblique clips of a vast figure '2' being sloshed with blue paint. One thinks of a guzunder being emptied from an open window. Channel *identity*, they call it. If I were them I'd go incognito. 'This is BBC Two' declared the announcer, coldly, like an embittered widower introducing his brood to their new stepmother... Sickening to see our licence contributions frittered away thus. I suppose they think they're being *artistic*. Still, one mustn't grumble – after all, it *is* more entertaining than the actual programmes.

Monday, 18 February
Woke midway through a fabulous dream! It was my coronation at the Abbey, complete with adoring crowds & bunting for miles. I was in your actual ermine trim, cloth of gold robes, loving it, slowly advancing up the nave. Passed Lou (done up lovely), Charles, Pat, Stanley & Gordon, beaming from the balcony... A chilly Townend placed St Edward's crown on my head (presumably it was Mwangi's day off), then Rupert kissed it, knelt & said 'I do become your liege man of life & limb...' before everyone burst into peals of 'For he's a jolly good fellow', charging champagne flutes.

  Countersigned Braine's Early Day Motion. I've seen what heavy drinking can do to people & it's no picnic. After the Business Statement I stood to give my two penn'orth: needn't have been worried about the notes of levity, as in the event it didn't actually die the death. Hurried out of the chamber – thanks to Belinda's senna pods – to advance an early day motion of my very own.

Tuesday, 19 February
Sat with Belinda & tried to slim down the diary. Managed to limit events to a couple of school prize-givings & old folks' home visits. There's no point in schmoozing anyone at this point; there'd be nothing to gain... Walked over to the Treasury & fortuitously bumped into Major in the foyer. Timing was impeccable as his 11.30 had been cancelled & he had ten minutes for

me. I respect John. Rose from the bottom, so the well-mannered courtesy is genuine rather than a faux byproduct of breeding. Raised the Stonewall proposal with him. 'I'm not against the idea, in principle,' he said. 'My only misgiving would be the potential of frightening the horses... If it *is* to be October, we don't want to fall further than necessary by upsetting the core vote.' Came out more jaded than ever. The appetite for change is *dead* in this Party, & this obduracy will surely be fatal.

Wednesday, 20 February
I'm sick of this godforsaken job. Not only am I condemned to do the frilly stuff, but it's impossible to be both popular and prominent as well as thoughtful and good at policy-making. There is none more *impotent* than a backbencher in a moribund parliament... except perhaps Napoleon Bonaparte, if Lefebvre's book is to be believed. So much for the contemporary reports of his vigour. And so much for nominative determinism – he's got *pole*, *bona* and *part* in his name, but according to old Georges his drawers were as well-stocked as a Bejam's in Omsk.

Friday, 22 February
Arrived at Biagi's at 7 o'c. Rupert had booked the whole room, so we had oodles of space. Pat dealt with Lou, who was moaning throughout, but it meant I could tell Flo to let her hair down. She hit it off marvellously with Belinda!! After the mains Stanley gave a very touching speech & Rona sang *Now Sleeps the Crimson Petal*[24] with cassette accompaniment. She was better than Ferrier,[25] it was simply stupendous. I was so moved I could barely stammer a response, but I *just about* held true. Flo took Lou home at 9.15 & just as they left, Miguel arrived with Cecil, John Whittingdale & Tony T-S!!... Franco wheeled out the cake & everyone sang Happy Birthday as they poured out the Perrier-Jouët. I generally detest this kind of thing, but it couldn't've gone better. The only downside was catching oneself in the mirrored wall & seeing a *sixty-five* year old ruin staring back. I always said I never wanted to live this long, but I suppose it's done now. Felt wrong having sent Louie away, so fetched her back a slice of cake & read to her before turning in.

---

[24] Poem by Tennyson, set to music by Roger Quilter, 1904.
[25] Kathleen Ferrier (1912-53), English contralto.

Sunday, 24 February
Toff rang & told me about the party at Chevening. Sounds monstrously lavish. If the people actually knew what goes on there, or at Chequers, there'd be a revolution… Louisa dozed most of the day, which is becoming quite a talent of hers.

Thursday, 28 February
Swapped votes with Gatiss, so was free from 12.30. Lunched with Leadbitter.[26] He's getting it in the neck from the Welsh windbag for buying BT shares. He cut a bit of an ousted figure, so I thought I'd lick wounds with a fellow exile. Winsome chap, & surprisingly on the ball, for Hartlepool… Cab with Ethan to Denbury House at 2.30. They hadn't exactly hung out the flags, but the staff were pleasant enough. Just rushed off their feet. One old dear trolled up familiarly & said 'Izal's no good. They might as well wipe your arse with greaseproof… I'm 87, you know…' Loretta, the main carer, was playing piano in the lounge. I said 'D'you know any old numbers?' & she played *Everything Stops for Tea*, *I've Got Sixpence* and *The London I Love* & we all sang along, sat in our PVC bergères, nursing lukewarm beakers of Brooke Bond D. All the while I was imagining Lou in such a place. She wouldn't last five minutes. At the finish, Alison (the manageress) said 'Thank you, you've really perked them up.' I was about to come it with 'It's been a pleasure,' and so on, but she changed tack with 'If only I knew how we're going to see out the year…' & she went into a long – & I dare say justified – rant about the lack of funding. Of course, there's nothing I can do, but if getting it off her chest made her feel better, I was happy to bear the brunt.

Tuesday, 5 March
When Tony Blair[27] speaks in the chamber, people sit up and listen. He clearly loves the limelight & it's got more than a dash of the melodramatics about it, but the way he skewers government ministers is quite remarkable to behold. I could see him as a PM, just not a *Labour* PM, he's far too well turned out for that. Can't imagine why Kinnock has him washing the dishes. Threatened, I suppose.

---

[26] Ted Leadbitter (1919-96), Labour MP for Hartlepool, 1964-91.

[27] (b. 1953) Labour MP for Sedgefield, 1983-2005; Shadow Secretary of State for Employment, 1989-91; Home Secretary, 1991-4; Chancellor of the Exchequer, 1994-5.

Wednesday, 6 March
A strange phenomenon I've noticed is the curious capacity members of the public have for separating one's *persona* from one's *occupation*. A scruffy woman stopped me by Cromwell's statue & obstreperously groused about NHS waiting times, all irate & huffy, before turning on a sixpence & singing my praises about Rambling Syd! It was business followed by pleasure… Because they 'know' me in *two* guises – & quite discordant guises at that – they struggle to amalgamate an attitude. I wonder if Reagan felt the same when he first became Governor? On second thoughts, maybe I'd be wiser not to ask.

Friday, 8 March
Plenty of glum faces!! Losing Ribble Valley was to be expected, but in truth it was madness to shove Waddington up to the Lords at such a time. Dropping to *third place* in a safe seat is utter disaster. You've got to laugh at the ineptitude. I glid about the corridors noisily singing 'Valley, *Valley*, Old Ribble Valley' to the tune of Gracie Fields' *Sally*, much to the mystified animus of my august colleagues – except a hobbling Critchley[28] who failed to mask his smirk… Wyn Roberts[29] showed me the MORI in the *Telegraph*: Lab have a 31% lead. Lackaday! It stated that if there were an election today we'd have *no* seats north of the border & just *one* in Wales! *Nos da*, Vienna!!

Thursday, 14 March
Letter from Louis Tussaud's asking if I'd be open to having a waxwork done for the exhibition in Blackpool… First *Spitting Image*, now this. The country, it seems, is full of maniacs who want to recreate me in stucco & gunk… I think not. *One* inert, ceraceous dummy bearing my name is quite enough for this world.

Went in to Lou. Gave her the fags. I swore I wouldn't, but as soon as she lit up, so did her eyes. It's a failure, but if it gives her a bit of pleasure, I suppose that's something. Flo looked on disapprovingly, but hers is not to reason why… I made myself beans on toast & we watched the TV news.

---

[28] Julian Critchley (1930-2000), Tory MP for Aldershot, 1970-95. His 'hobbling' was a consequence of polio.

[29] (1930-2013) Tory MP for Conway, 1970-99; Minister of State for Wales, 1987-91.

Incessant blarney about the Birmingham Six,[30] so turned over to something called *Red Dwarf*,[31] which reckoned to be a comedy set in space. Gave that five minutes. Swill. Switched off & we played whist, but Lou kept angling the cards to the light & I could see them. 'For heaven's sake, hold your cards up, you silly cow,' I said, to which she took umbrage & refused to continue… I think I shall just run away to Blackpool and stand stock-still in Louis Tussaud's in place of a dummy. It'd have to be an improvement on *this* life, surely?

Friday, 15 March
Got in early for London members' meeting. Zikoma, the little cleaner, said 'You're on the tellybox tonight!', as tho' it were news of the second coming. Turns out they're showing *Make Mine Mink*[32] on satellite!! To think, lunatic saps are *paying* to have such rubbish beamed into their bed-sits via those ghastly dishes, welded to the brickwork like giant jerries. Yet she seemed tickled by the prospect… Meeting a waste of time, as usual. Endless prattling about that *revolting* Canary Wharf complex. They're all preoccupied with the "laser light display" that will herald its unveiling – never mind the fact that no sod has actually leased a unit yet… They glare at me with utter contempt. In the finish I'd had quite enough of Neubert[33] gawping so I said 'If you wish to stare, I shall be appearing on Sky television this evening, so you can ogle me all you want in the privacy of your own drawing room…'

Saturday, 16 March
Gave Louie her warm milk & joined Paul at the small Odeon for *Awakenings*.[34] Curiously fast-paced & contrived, but I thoroughly enjoyed it!! I rather relish the notion of waking from the coma, reassessing "life" for a while & then slipping back into catatonia. A marvellously comforting

---

[30] Six Irishmen whose convictions for the 1974 Birmingham pub bombings were quashed by the Court of Appeal.
[31] BBC science fiction sitcom (1988-99). One of its stars, Chris Barrie (b. 1960), provided the voice of the KW puppet on *Spitting Image*.
[32] British comedy farce film (1960), directed by Robert Asher. KW as the Hon. Freddie Warrington.
[33] Michael Neubert (1933-2014), Tory MP for Romford, 1974-95. Under-Secretary of State for the Armed Forces, 1988-90.
[34] American drama film (1990), directed by Penny Marshall, starring Robin Williams and Robert De Niro.

confirmation… no need for sorrow or a deathbed conversion – living really *was* as awful as one remembered. That's not what the picture was trying to convey, but that's what I took from it. Robin Williams is rather good. P'raps we're distant relations.

Tuesday, 19 March
The sense of distrust is palpable and repugnant. Parkinson is *out*, on the charge of briefing against the PM. *Cecil Parkinson* of all people!!! *Another* peer brought in to the Cabinet – somebody called Lord Goodhew of Woolhampton[35] – to replace him. It's no longer a Cabinet, it's a *court*… Spoke to Butterfingers[36] who said 'We're in witch-hunt territory. She trusts no-one… I love the woman to her very marrow, but Christ knows where it will end.' Why bother *now* to take revenge on those who didn't support her? Seems such a futile waste of energy. Baker's pulling his hair out. It'd be easier to organise an Arab-Israeli hoedown.

Tom Cox[37] cornered me in the lobby. He said 'I've never fathomed why you lumbered yourself with these born-to-rule pricks… You're one of us, deep down, plain as day…' They can't understand the concept of being born in the gutter & not wishing to stay there. They want us all to be the same, but each of us a deadbeat… Saying that, one does start to resemble a steward on the *Hindenburg*, only with an even bumpier landing in prospect.

Wednesday, 20 March
Lots of us crowded around the television watching the bombings in Sarajevo. Of course, it's a racial problem. These Serbs know full well they're better off in the Community – it's having to kowtow to the Moslems at home that irks them so. 'This is the trouble with Yugoslavia,' I said. 'A union only functions if the dominant group are *compos mentis*…' 'Amen to that!' said Salmond,[38] with a grin. But then he's probably got a poster of Milošević[39] on his bedroom wall.

---

[35] Victor Goodhew (1919-2006), Tory MP for St Albans, 1959-83.
[36] John Butterfill (1941-2021), Tory MP for Bournemouth West, 1983-2010.
[37] (1930-2018) Labour MP for Tooting, 1974-2005.
[38] Alex Salmond (1954-2024), SNP MP for Banff & Buchan, 1987-2010.
[39] Slobodan Miloševic (1941-2006), President of the Presidency of the Socialist Republic of Serbia, 1989-91.

Beyond Our Kenneth

Thursday, 21 March
Longing to get away, but the bloody division bell tolls again & again. I *loathe* Thursdays. If only one could 'phone the votes in. It's all based on the weekly whip in any case – they don't require a considered opinion, just a cadaver in the correct queue.

Nipped to Gordon's on Villiers St. with Miguel, John W. & David Bevan[40]... DB said 'It's the lesson of the War. We'd've been better off losing in the long run, at least we'd've been able to start from scratch.' 'If we lose 150 seats we *will* be starting from scratch,' said John, bitterly. These men have worked with her & sweated blood for her for a decade, & the unravelling of it is clearly a personal devastation. Miguel said 'Obviously, chaps, she's grooming me to take over. But I know that too close an association might be fatal.' He needs *her* supporters, but they alone won't be enough. I said 'The task is to make them conclude you're the only sane choice.' Miguel chuckled, wryly. 'Sane? We're talking about Tory MPs here.'

Sunday, 24 March
M. came & brought flowers for Lou. She was in a huff because I'd told her I was lunching out & that she wasn't coming. The daffs took the edge off, but she wasn't happy. Rupert joined us for the meal at Vecchia. We had a pleasant time. Rupert is putting on weight & when I told him so he was rather taken aback! 'Oh,' he said. 'I'd better leave the tiramisu, then...' He was quite hurt!! 'Don't be so thin-skinned!' I said. 'Well *apparently* that's the one thing I'm *not*,' he replied, crabbily.

Monday, 25 March
With Ethan & a few constituency hangers-on to Regent High School to open their new modern languages dept. Mainly scruffy tykes, but Daniel, the Head Boy was a delight! 'I'm thinking of going to Zaïre before university to dig wells & teach English.' He certainly has the charisma for it. And the brawn, from what I could see... Gave the speech. Chatted about learning German at school & rattled off a verse of *Nibelungenlied*,[41] much to their bemusement, but overall I think they were suited. They brought out copies of *Just Williams* and *Williams Carries On* for me to sign for their library. I said to the girl 'You needn't have gone to the expense, I would've brought

---

[40] (1928-96) Tory MP for Birmingham Yardley, 1979-91.
[41] Early 13th century epic poem written in Middle High German.

you copies from home.' She said 'O! don't worry, they were in the clearance sale at Dillons,' which was chasteningly tactless.

Wednesday, 27 March
Check-up with Chatham. Told him about the hard stools & he said to lay off meat, three days out of seven. I said 'That's totally against government policy, you know.' He laughed. 'With the greatest respect to your position,' he said, 'government policy can take a long walk off a short pier.' Other than that, he seemed pleased with the bum.

Had to go to this poxy 'Crossrail' meeting, 'cos apparently the plans have it dissecting the constituency. I couldn't give a toss – I'll be long dead before a single shovel is lifted in anger. Sat & surreptitiously did the crossword.

Thursday, 28 March
Never been so happy to get out of a place. Thank heavens for these drawn-out holidays. Went to Foyles & bought Rimbaud's *Illuminations*[42] in paperback on Tichet-Sweeting's recommendation. He's mad about the French poets. I shall persevere, but thus far I think it's impenetrable trash. What *is* interesting is the biographical preface. He was certainly a scamp, the lad, and a dish to boot. The description of his time in London with Verlaine is awfully vivid... certainly got me going!

With Goldsmiths Oliver in the evening. Palladium for the preview of *Joseph* & his multicoloured bloody coat. O's boyfriend is playing Issachar. Did nothing for me, of course, but the night was saved by Tim Rice!! 'Is that my lovely Ken?' he shouted across the bar. He embraced me & we chatted about old times. Realised I was neglecting Oliver, so I brought him in on the chat. Tim clearly took him for my Rimbaud, until I explained. 'What are you doing next Friday?' he asked. 'Nothing, as far as I'm aware.' 'I'm dining with Tony Perkins[43] & some friends at Simpson's... please say you'll come.' I zestfully accepted... The boyfriend arrived & I did the dutiful 'You were marvellous' schtick before getting away.

---

[42] 1886 suite of prose poems by the French poet Arthur Rimbaud (1854-91), who engaged in a violent romantic relationship with fellow poet Paul Verlaine (1844-96) in the 1870s.
[43] Anthony Perkins (1932-92), American actor, most famous for the role of Norman Bates in the Hitchcock film *Psycho*.

Friday, 29 March
M. arrived & we took a run out to Ashby-de-la-Zouch. A friend of his has taken over as choirmaster at St Helen's, so we went to meet him & listen to the rehearsals. Went to the Bull's Head for a hotpot after. Lovely original Jacobean interiors – unfortunately the lamb tasted a tad Jacobean too. Talked about Lou & got a bit choked… M. asked if everything was in order, paperwork-wise. He's always been practical. A bit too practical perhaps. But, as a rule, I admire the eschewing of sentiment.

Sunday, 31 March
Went in & she was shouting & hollering at Rita who was close to tears. 'She keeps touching me! I don't want tarts swarming around touching me…' R. was trying to get the beef & tomato down her when Lou snatched the bowl & flung it across the carpet. Rita sponged it whilst I tried to calm things down. Eventually averted her attention with the Easter egg (even though it was carob), but it's all so entirely dispiriting – and *tiresome*: I'm sick to the back teeth with all this… Cab to B.H. for *Sunday Politics*. Joan Lestor[44] was the Labour guest, so I was fine. The format is too tight tho', cos the presenter – who looked about fourteen – didn't leave enough time for considered answers before butting in with his supplementaries. *Three times* he did the 'wind it up' motion to get me to shut my trap, so in the finish I resorted to single-word replies. Waste of time, apart from chatting to Gorden Kaye[45] in reception.

Tuesday, 2 April
Saw Paul humping a huge crate across the landing. 'Who are you burying?' I asked. 'My bleedin' self if I'm not careful,' he said, perspiring. It was books from his dealer friend in Hay who's ceased trading. Said he'd go through it all & let me know if there's anything I'd fancy… Walked to Woolies to get pick 'n' mix. Belinda's got me mad for these foam bananas!! We're sucking them all day long. Repellent, really. As I scooped them into the paper bag, one winsome fellow citizen snorted & said 'Up yours, you Tory shithouse…' Smartish woman, about seventy, in an eau-de-Nil pully… Came back & Paul had left a note with four books by my door. Three poetry volumes

---

[44] (1931-98) Labour MP for Eccles, 1987-98.
[45] English actor (1941-2017), best known for playing the womanising café owner René Artois in *'Allo 'Allo!*.

(including a Faber 1st ed. of *High Windows*[46]) and a paperback of the script of *The Third Man* dedicated 'To Millicent' & signed by Orson!! 'Phoned P. my thanks & suggested Biagi's tomorrow.

Wednesday, 3 April
Paul came into the restaurant & said 'Well, you'll have to give me back that softback... Sue Lawley just said Graham Greene's kicked the bucket... it'll be worth a fortune now.'

Friday, 5 April
Up at 7 o'c. & did letters. One funny note from a Mr Allan Glossop, enclosing a magazine cutting on the latest 'research' into King William II's homosexuality. He underlines "...this chronicle suggests that Rufus was merely *sterile*, in a roundabout way..." – 'A bit like Milton Keynes,' writes Mr Glossop... Another from a constituent called Moira Potter-Ashe, bemoaning these United Colours of Benetton billboards: 'I don't pay the Community Charge to wake up to umbilical cords outside my kitchen window. I don't pay the Community Charge to commute to work past colossal placentas. As a matter of fact, I don't pay the Community Charge *at all*...'

Cab to Simpson's at 8 o'c. Met the guests, including Anthony Perkins, over pink gins. Curious fellow. Thousand-yard stare. No wonder he goes in for all these macabre parts. Tried to engage him on Ruth Rendell (he's over here filming an adaptation[47]), but it was like getting blood from a stone. Tim lovely, as always, but Heaven knows what he's got in common with old Psycho. I'd *assumed* he was family – nearly choked on my roulade when he mentioned a wife & children. Wildean, I suppose, but without the charm.

Saturday, 6 April
Found the teeth gritty from all these banana sweets, so chucked the remainder in the bin & had a nap. Wrote these lines on waking:

> They call them Golden Years
> When things are winding down
> Where recreation rules and requiescence comes to town

---

[46] By Philip Larkin, 1974.
[47] *A Demon in My View* (1991), directed by Petra Haffter.

They call them Autumn Years
The glint in harvest's crown
As languidly the tree of life swaps verdant leaves for brown

They call them Sunset Years
A spell of great renown
Free rein to make the lazy choice and ditch the doer's frown

They call them Twilight Years
And use the proper noun
With peace and relaxation, idle pleasures all around

They're fucking liars.   KCW 6.4.91

Sunday, 7 April
We drove to Bernie Winters[48] for the lunch. Sitting outside in the warm sun, eating tinned salmon quarters with the crusts cut off, was wondrous. Biggins was there, in a pink & turquoise jumper. Bernie held court superbly, tho' he looked ever so thin. Siggi was quiet. As we drove away, M. said 'If you ask me, I don't think he's long for this world.'

Tuesday, 9 April
District Line to see Johnny Johnson. Just north of Earl's Ct the train came to a sudden halt – we sat & sat for ages. The carriage got talking & when it became clear we were in for the long haul, a swarthy chap at the end of the car said 'Oh, bugger this!' & got out his guitar & began strumming. Then an Asian woman with one of those red dots on the forehead started singing something in Indian, & others clapped along. Swept up in the gaiety, a moustachio'd gallant in a mustard waistcoat got to his feet & recited *Ozymandias*,[49] which was extraordinarily well done, despite the cleft lip. Eventually I was clocked & in the finish I was hand-in-hand with an off-duty Hare Krishna, belting out the Grace Darling song.[50] Subterranean

---

[48] English comedian, actor and musician (1930-91). Half of a double act with his brother, Mike, followed by solo performances with the aid of his St Bernard dog, Schnorbitz.
[49] Sonnet written by Percy Bysshe Shelley, 1818.
[50] *And She Pulled Away*, folk song written by Felix McGlennon (1891); also known as *The Shipwrecked Crew*.

Opportunity Knocks[51]… The train lurched into action again, mostly emptied at Earl's Ct, & it was as though none of it had happened – the grim, anonymous faces of London Transport oozily returned, as plain as a pea-souper creeping up from the River.

Wednesday, 10 April
I quite clearly wrote 'Squash, Butter, Nuts' on the list for Flo… What I'm meant to do with a butternut squash is anyone's guess. It seems she & Lou now refer to Robinson's orange barley water as 'juicy drink', which I suppose is to be expected when a foreigner & a 90 year old are in cahoots.

Thursday, 11 April
Woke with a splitting headache that really throbbed in the temples. Walked to Boot's to get the co-codamol cos it's cheaper there. The woman on the till had extremely yellow teeth – almost ochre, like shards of toffee jutting from the gums. Quite unsuitable for a chemist's – well, quite unsuitable for *anywhere*. Came back. Had to wait *ages* for the stuff to kick in.

Headlines are all about the arrest of the Gripper.[52] The accused has confessed to all twelve. They showed a photo on the TV news. Surprisingly easy on the eye. Clips of neighbours saying he was 'quiet', the last person you'd expect to be doing such things, blah blah… So, I suppose it'll be luxury lodgings at Broadmoor with satellite TV, *à la carte* menus and a restart course in graphic design. Or perhaps a book deal? *Gripping Yarns – A Strangler's Struggle*.

Friday, 12 April
Went to get papers. Nattered to Bill about the *Moby Prince*.[53] He said 'If you ask me they could've done with a foghorn at Leghorn…' I laughed, but the fishwife next to me piped up with 'What a disgusting thing to say… People have *drowned*, you know?…' Bill squinched & said 'She clearly ain't had *her* Weetabix!' as she stormed off.

---

[51] BBC/ITV talent show. Hosted by Hughie Green (1956-78), Bob Monkhouse (1987-9) and Les Dawson (1990).
[52] Roger Spivey (b. 1955). Eventually convicted of fourteen murders at the Old Bailey in February 1992.
[53] The ferry MV *Moby Prince* collided with an oil tanker in the harbour at Leghorn (Livorno), resulting in 140 deaths.

Saturday, 13 April
After the surgery took Ethan to Biagi for lunch; Sir Hugh joined us at 12.35, looking bedraggled & ghastly… He was rather taken with the Orvieto, & launched into a long, would-be shocking story about a 'fling' he had with the late Lord Boyd.[54] All totally fanciful. 'He & Chips[55] were all over me like white on rice, my dears…' Oh, these poufs do go on sometimes. I was *mad* to invite him… Then Foyle's where Ethan wanted a half year diary – of course I recommended the Letts, but he preferred the Collins layout.

Sat with Lou in the evening. She scarcely said a word, just gawped at *Perry Mason*.[56] She isn't smoking, even tho' I've allowed it, which I think is a worrying sign. I said 'Do you want help getting in bed or will you be alright?' She looked at me, puzzled. 'Bed? I ain't going to no bed, thank you. I don't need a bedtime, I'm not a kid…' Returned to the flat and read Auden. Listened at her door at 10 o'c. & she'd clearly turned in.

Monday, 15 April
Dreaded going in today. Woken by the alarm, which I detest. *Longed* to turn over & go back to sleep… Got the 88. Lots of chatter about a swathe of new privatisation announcements – British Rail… even the Health Service. Spoke to Ivan L about it. 'The train stuff will pass, but hospitals? It won't get through,' he said. 'She's just bombarding us so that when Miguel proposes more restrained measures, folk'll be used to the idea.' I'm not convinced… Came back from lunch & Belinda was standing by the photocopier, clutching a potted yucca. Gang of decorators within, slopping peach emulsion up the walls as if they hadn't a minute to live. Friendly enough chaps, but now the corridor reeks of paint & has the look of a gynaecology ward… In the finish the fumes were causing headaches, so at 5.15 I said 'The Red Lion's open!' & I took Belinda, Ethan & Neville for drinkettes.

Thursday, 18 April
Everyone standing about in clusters, thumbing through the NHS white paper in disbelief. It amounts to a wholesale sell-off to private concerns, &

---

[54] Alan Lennox-Boyd, 1st Viscount Boyd of Merton (1904-83), Tory MP for Mid Bedfordshire, 1931-60.
[55] Sir Henry Channon (1897-1958), Tory MP for Southend West, 1935-58. Lord Boyd's brother-in-law. Like KW, a prodigious diarist.
[56] American courtroom drama, 1957-66.

the recommendation of an American-style insurance system. *Personally* I can see the merits, but the plebs won't... Saw Portaloo. Furious. She might be grooming him for leadership, but there's no point to that if there's nothing left to lead... At 4 o'c. we heard that Brocklehurst[57] & Millward[58] were crossing the floor (to Labour & the Liberals respectively). Lobby *full* of noisy hacks, all clamouring & begging for comment. I smiled at them & refused to say anything. Came home to Louisa & we watched Russ Abbot and devoured a box of soft centres.

Friday, 19 April
'Phone ringing off the hook, faxes streaming out of the machine. Chiefly abuse. Dictated the stock reply to Belinda: 'Mr Williams will listen to the Government proposals on changes to Health Service funding, and will closely consider the views of professionals and his constituents if and when any such motions are debated in the House of Commons.' It's tricky because, although I can see it's electoral suicide, I don't care tuppence for the medical fraternity – and *patients*, even less so... Rang Kenny Connor. Told him he was a fool to accept the MBE, & he suggested lunch. Bit his arm off. Met at Wiltons at 1.20. O! we had a *superb* time. I do miss being with actors. It's only when it's contrasted with the company I've been keeping latterly that one realises how much one has lost. Kenny showed me the letter he'd received apropos the MBE, then acted out the event, playing all the parts. I don't know if his Lord Chamberlain voice was accurate – it was a blend of Vincent Price & Dinsdale Landen[59] – but it had me in stitches... So odd to see Ken with a head of white hair. Not that I can talk. We were the living rendition of Statler and Waldorf,[60] sitting there kvetching pugnaciously.

Saturday, 20 April
We saw the protest marches on the television. If the English do have a religion, it's the National Health – the doctors its bishops, the nurses its nuns,

---

[57] Phillip Brocklehurst (1947-2020), MP for Wood Green (as a Tory, 1983-91; as a Labour member, 1991-5).

[58] Stanley Millward (b. 1939), MP for Westminster North (as a Tory, 1983-91; as a Liberal Democrat, 1991).

[59] English actor (1932-2003); frequent performer in Shakespeare productions at Stratford and Regent's Park Open Air Theatre.

[60] Characters from the sketch comedy series *The Muppet Show* (1976-81) – a pair of cantankerous old men, who heckle the rest of the cast from their balcony seats.

& the earwigging parishioners listening out for dissension & blasphemy at every turn… Left Rita to give Lou the flan. Tube to Pimlico & met Jeff & Jean-Jacques at the Tate at noon. We were admiring Millais' *Ophelia* when a repulsive Mick in a brown trilby chimed in with 'I was surprised to see you fellers so taken with dis one, so I was, what with 'em having the Blakes on show… all dat male flesh, I'da taught dat'd be more your ting, lads…' The halitosis nearly knocked one sideways. Laughed it off & went to have a quiet word with the gallery attendant, who discreetly disposed of it. The *filth* one has to put up with in the name of cultural equality. Ugh.

Sunday, 21 April
On bathing I suddenly felt very sexy, & played out a scene where I was preparing for the arrival of Loïc, poet & stablehand – he having finally escaped from Aincourt,[61] telegramming ahead that he was *en route* & for me to be ready… Must've jabbered away to myself for half an hour before ending quite audaciously… Got papers. Pages and pages on the violence overnight. Rang Toff who said 'She's lost all reason… and she's turned nasty. She might've been a lot of things before, but she was never spiteful…' She's at Chequers today, seeing cabinet members one at a time to 'test their allegiance'. I ask you… Effectively, we're in Jonestown, waiting for someone to pass round the drinks.[62]

Tuesday, 23 April
Buses not running thanks to the T&G[63] solidarity strike. They all talk as tho' British Rail were some marvellous, peerless service that's being wrenched away from them, whereas in truth I should think *Calcuttans* travel in more comfort, and more reliably… They're jumping on the anti health reforms bandwagon, of course, which is a sensible tactic I suppose… In any case, I *walked* in. Spent most of the morning doing the cryptic in the library. 'Hard at it?' said Bernie Braine, jocosely. Trouble is, I don't know what I'm meant to be doing. Helping the government? Battling *against* it? Aiding constituents?… All three sound a pain in the arse.

---

[61] WW2 internment camp in the Seine-et-Oise department, used to detain members of the French Communist Party.
[62] Reference to the mass suicide at the Peoples Temple Agricultural Project (better known as 'Jonestown' after its cult leader, Jim Jones), Guyana, in 1978. 909 people died from cyanide poisoning, after ingesting a soft drink laced with the drug.
[63] Transport and General Workers' Union.

1991

Wednesday, 24 April
Was just about to speak in the special meeting on Welsh road signs when a secretary tapped me on the shoulder & whispered 'You're wanted at Number 10...' Rushed out, thinking I was for Traitors' Gate, when Powell seized me and said 'Would you come & meet the Governor of Crete? It seems he's rather a fan'... Whisked over there, taken in the back way & then introduced to Mr Papachristodoulopoulos in the Green Room. Huge hairy thing, like Demis Roussos[64] stuffed into a Burtons suit... He grinned widely at me & yawped a bit in Greek. Gripping the hand, he rabbited on & on about listening to *Round the Horne* when he was up at Oxford, & how he'd laughed so hard at *Khyber* that he broke his seat at the Heraklion Empire... Eventually I got a word in, & told him about visiting the mosaics at Toplou Monastery all those years ago, & the old monk & the lice in the beard, etc. He laughed effusively & went off pleased as punch. Coming out, Lamont said 'Sterling work, Kenneth... I think that's swung things Thomas Cook's way...' Glad to be of service, I'm sure.

Friday, 26 April
At 3.30 the beige 'phone on the shelf in the corridor – the one which never rings – rang. I picked it up & a woman said 'Is that the eel shop at Dalston?' 'Yes, that's right, speaking,' I said. 'Oh good, well the thing is, you see, I had one pie, double mash and liquor at your place yesterday, about two o'c., and I know that's £2.10, so I give the girl a fiver and took the change, but I didn't look at it, see, and when I've gone and checked me purse this morning there's three pound coins in there, and I ain't done any other shopping 'cos me grandson's not coming till Monday to take me up the big Asda, so I can only think your girl's given me too much back and I didn't want you to fret in case your books didn't tally...' Once I'd thanked her for calling & calmed any fears that she was some sort of pastry felon, I sat for twenty minutes with her, learning about her son's managerial job at Carpet World in Norwich, her daughter's ingrowing toenail and her fondness for Acker Bilk.[65] Eventually Townend wanted me, so I signed off with 'Not to worry, Joyce, but I must fly – these spuds won't mash themselves...'

---

[64] Portly Greek singer-songwriter (1946-2015).
[65] English clarinettist and vocalist (1929-2014).

Sunday, 28 April
M. came with more bloody daffs for Lou. She filled him in on all the latest goings on in Summer Bay until I managed to prize him away for our stroll. I don't know how he does it, but M. has the gift of being able to gee one up, with only the wispiest threads on which to tug for inspiration. I look at him sometimes & think I ought to have pushed for something more. But at the final analysis I think I've always been best flitting from pillar to post – short holidays here & there, then back to home port to recuperate. Anything more could lead to a muddying of the waters, which would never do. In any case, M. has an inexplicable penchant for women, the fool.

Wednesday, 1 May
Can't bear to look at any more Dangerous Dogs photos – endless images of maimed & mutilated tots. I was a teller after the debate, which consisted of the usual bleeding heart brigade making excuses. Rose to support Baker. I said 'The normal course of action in this country is to punish the owner of the unlicensed weapon and then to destroy the offending article, or melt it down for repurposing. Before Members pile out to enjoy the canteen's offerings of Wienerschnitzel and steaks tartare, Mister Speaker, I trust we can agree that, whilst all of God's creatures have feelings, those feelings are trumped on every occasion by the right of a human child not to have its face ripped off by a pit bull terrier?' A few hear-hears. I stood in the lobby trying to look official & announced the results v. grandly.

Waterhouse stopped by to discuss the idea of parachuting me to a safer seat next time round. 'Barney Hayhoe[66] is standing down in Brentford & they're open to your name being added to the list.' I told him straight: 'I shall never abandon my belovèd constituents.' He ran through the latest polling data for London, which was the clearest allegory for 'better book your slot with Pickfords' that e'er I've heard.

Friday, 3 May
Car with Ethan to St Clements to dispense the prizes. Lots of rather unpleasant, precocious oiks showing off their ballet routines & crimes against watercolour. Can't blame *them* for being yuppy offspring, but it doesn't make things easy. The occasion was saved by Thomas Price, a shy little boy who struggled but eventually read aloud his marvellous story,

---

[66] (1925-2013) Tory MP for Brentford & Isleworth, 1974-91.

Gavin the Grump. I was so beguiled that I went off-course & gave him the improvised special prize of my personal fountain pen (brass Parker – no loss as I've never really cared for it) & a crisp £20 note. The boy was overwhelmed & the snooty ones turned a delicious shade of green.

Saturday, 4 May
Rained stair-rods all morning. Went in to Lou who was going on and on about Mabel Trigger. 'Where's that taxi got to?' she kept saying. In the end she snapped out of it & I invited Paul down for Scrabble. Lou played *freezing* across a triple word for 113 points, entirely on her own! My jaw nearly hit the floor!!

Tuesday, 7 May
Belinda passed me an envelope with a smile on her face – a letter from a *bona fide* happy camper. Mrs Ross of Emerald Street, praising my mediation 'twixt the Met & the local residents regarding the clogging of the road with panda cars. Showed it to Jack A. who said 'Strike me pink, a satisfied customer! You should have her pickled in aspic…'

Thursday, 9 May
It came out during elevenses that she's blocked the big Sky deal – allegedly due to anti-government headlines in *The Sun*. Upshot being that ITV gets the rights to this premier soccer whatsit… Never seen her so vulnerable in the House. Kinnock couldn't believe his luck. Not only does it have the appearance of unjust meddling in free enterprise, but it suggests *punishment* of (what the Welsh windbag had the drollery to call) 'our free press'. To make matters worse, she's clearly got a touch of 'flu & trying to mask it, so she looked & sounded frail, false & dreadful. O! it was mortifying to behold.

Friday, 10 May
Lunched with James Ford at Wheeler's. He's ditched the wig and the result is a *vast* improvement. Apparently Lawson's son has been in touch to see if I'd be interested in contributing to *The Spectator*, on an ad hoc basis. It's certainly a flattering proposal.

Toff's party in the evening at Dolphin Square. The punch slid down easily, which was fatal. At one point I had my arm round the Greek Cypriot postmaster's neck, shouting 'I bet you've got a colossal cock!' He laughed along with the others, but the eyes very much said 'Get your filthy faggot hands off me.' Rather sobering. Cecil called me a cab. Felt wretched for the behaviour, so I got out the syringe & had the purging enema.

Saturday, 11 May
Of all the masseurs I've been to, I rank Philip the best. He chats during the treatment, rather than filling the silence with cassettes of farting whales or Chinese harpists.

Sunday, 12 May
I didn't see Rita leave, by then I was dozing in the armchair. When I woke, Lou was sat embroidering a flower on her hankie by lamplight, looking serene, absorbed & quite beautiful. 'Are you alright?' I said. She looked across & smiled, v. much the cat with the cream. Back to her stitching, she said, quite quietly, 'I'll never forget what you do for me. Thank you for staying with me.' It's the sort of thing that would normally choke me up solid. But it felt unawkward & right to say 'It's because I love you. More than anything.' Still, I was glad when the tangent came & she cut the emotive tension with 'Does that mean I can have a Mars bar then?…'

Thursday, 16 May
We saw the report on the Queen's visit to America. Even the fairy dust of monarchy can't frustrate Dukakis's talent for putting his foot in things. Apart from the podium being too tall for Her Majesty (so that her face was entirely obscured by microphones), he kept referring to her as 'Your Honour'. It was like watching an am-dram version of *L.A. Law*.

Friday, 17 May
I'd just finished the piece for ITN on College Green, arguing with Tony Banks[67] about GLC legacy, when we heard a far-off thudding noise. "Ello 'ello… that didn't sound good,' said Tony. The cameramen sprinted off up the road & we followed around to St Stephens, but the Police were already stopping people going in as crowds flooded out. Went to Members' Entrance but same story there. Hung around at New Palace Yard waiting for a face I knew to come out & reveal all. Jim Spicer[68] scrambled across. 'It's

---
[67] (1942-2006) Labour MP for Newham North West, 1983-2005.
[68] Sir James Spicer (1925-2015), Tory MP for West Dorset, 1974-95.

a mess, Ken... I didn't see the chap, but Tapsell[69] said he ran into the chamber ranting and raving and blew himself up, right in front of the Mace'... Eventually my people were accounted for. Belinda said that she'd overheard a constable saying there was just one fatality (the perpetrator), but multiple injuries otherwise.

Ingham came over & asked myself & a few others to do the media rounds, briefing us that: PM not present, all Tories & Palace staff unharmed, one female Labour member seriously injured, two male SDP members slightly so – no information on the offender at all, except that he's brown bread... Found a bench & sent Ethan to Marks's to get us some sandwiches.

Didn't get home until 5 o'c.!! Went in to Lou & it was all over every channel. I switched it off & we enjoyed a remarkably good steak pie with new potatoes & green beans. Flo ate with us. Rupert knocked to see if everything was alright. 'Come in, dear,' said Louie, 'we're about to play rummy.'

Saturday, 18 May
There was a strong sense of *déjà-vu* in listening to her speech – a lot of it rehashed from Brighton, tho' admittedly with an added sharpness. The official line is that enquiries are still ongoing, but Michael Howard rang & said that clues point to him being Russian... they found tombac in some mangled bridgework, which implies Soviet dentistry.

Super afternoon with Bill Maynard!![70] He was bright pink, just back from Manila having filmed a thing about dull Welsh bachelors in search of asiatic wives.[71] He said their hotel had been crawling with local wantons, who latched on to the company in the evenings in hope of free drink & trade. Sounds abhorrent. Bill said he'd had his suspicions from the outset, but that Charlie Drake[72] had taken a shine to one particularly uninhibited native. An hour of revelry elapsed before he clutched something that oughtn't to have been there & *leapt*... Madam came running after him, crying 'What the matter?' & in front of a packed bar he bawled 'Call me old-fashioned, sweetheart, but I tend to prefer birds *without* a great walloping pair of Brian Horrocks...' The joys of being 'on location'.

---

[69] Sir Peter Tapsell (1930-2018), Tory MP for East Lindsey, 1983-95.
[70] English comedian and actor (1928-2018), appeared with KW in five *Carry On* films.
[71] *Filipina Dreamgirls*, written by Andrew Davies for the BBC's *Screen One* series.
[72] English actor, comedian and singer (1925-2006).

Beyond Our Kenneth

Wednesday, 22 May
Townend came. 'Kenneth, the place is yours if you want it.' I accepted. Officially it's the Joint Committee on Palace of Westminster Security Standards. Cecil came to congratulate me & tell of some of the rancour the appointment has caused. 'Boyson said "That's all we need, the Khasi of Khalabar[73] queering the pitch"...' I'm just flattered that the loathsome cunt has followed my career so assiduously.

Thursday, 23 May
It's a pain traipsing across to the Conference Centre for debates, but one thing is beyond question – the calf-covered cushions on the seats are much kinder on one's posterior than the Commons benches. That is, however, the only comfort. Her authority is dwindling by the day, in a way I hadn't thought possible. Everyone looks shell-shocked: she turns to her own benches for succour, but those who once would've crawled over hot coals to offer a platitude just keep shtum & feebly glance away. You can see it writ large in the now-constant smirk on Kinnock's face, one word: *bingo*.

Sunday, 26 May
I am ashamed that I've not lived up to Platonic axiomata, touching carnal relations. By this age I ought to have long since extruded those base animal urges & escaped from the frantic, savage master. But every so often, with the raw heat of a flaming appendix, the uncivilised impulses of some primitive organ burst forth to cause havoc. It is *unclean, unwholesome* and *un-English*.

Monday, 27 May
Such a wonderful feeling to get out of London!! Rupert was naughty in having stumped up for First Class tickets & I lambasted him, but was quietly delighted once we boarded the 'plane. The Errol Flynn-esque steward kept bringing brandies. He asked if I wanted to go up to the cockpit, & foolishly I accepted. Instead of a disciplined 'Keep up the good work, lads,' it was 'Ooh, captain, can I have an 'old of your *joystick*' and other repugnant filth that they half laughed off… Arrived Barcelona at 2.45. It's 80°, which is a marvellously civilised temperature. Train to Sitges & cab to hotel. The place is spotless, thank God. We have connecting rooms, it's quite scandalous…

---

[73] KW's role in *Carry On Up the Khyber*.

1991

It's lovely to hear the Catalonian accents. Shame about the cawing of the bloody *gulls*.

Tuesday, 28 May
Glad I brought the Shredded Wheat with me. I know it smacks of the uncouth Briton abroad, but I shall *never* be convinced of the merits of cheese & melon for breakfast… I sat by the pool & read *Wild Swans*,[74] but couldn't get on with it. Every so often I looked up at him, swimming or stretching or snoozing on his lounger. I wonder what he's thinking. I give no encouragement. Quite the opposite, on occasion. And yet I feel so deeply thankful, knowing he's there. It's so different to how it was with any of the others… He's maniacally clean to boot, so I can't even wean myself off on that score.

Wednesday, 29 May
We did the Cau Ferrat & then the Museu Romàntic before meeting up with Roland & Lionel from the hotel for drinks at Balmins. Lots of time admiring the view. Shameful, reely. Lunch at Mare Nostrum before Maricel palace… Back to Balmins. Rupert & I looked on from the terrace as R&L went on to the sands. Of course it's revolting, but witnessing such a procession of flesh is like watching an episode of *Wildlife on One* – pink flamingoes smugly strutting on the beach, disdainfully looking down their beaks at each other's gently grilling hamptons.

Thursday, 30 May
We went into town to watch the Corpus Christi procession. It's your parade of vast *papier-mâché* puppets done up as mediæval Jack & Vera Duckworths, proudly brandished by the musclier locals, as the frailer boys blow on their *dulzainas*. They all seemed suited, but after an hour it was a relief to get away from the racket… Had a rest, then drinks at the Voramar. Jordi & Iker joined us. Rupert suggested inviting them back to the room. I said 'You can do as you please,' which was enough for him to back down. We returned to the hotel & I had a cup of tea & gave him the wank, but it was all rather mechanical & cheerless.

Friday, 31 May
O! the truth is, it doesn't work. The entire thing is just a hopeless, sordid fantasy. I'm sick and tired of the whole rotten mess.

---

[74] *Wild Swans: Three Daughters of China*, non-fiction novel by Jung Chang (1991).

Sunday, 2 June
Some woman on the 'plane had a "panic attack" as we taxied to the runway & the decision was made to abort!! so back to the gate we went. They bundled it off, but we were 98 minutes late leaving the tarmac. These people really should have the decency to go by boat.

Monday, 3 June
When I came down there was a new bunch carting their stuff in, making an awful mess. I sailed past, but got 'G'day! I'm Jacko, that's Janelle – fabbo to meet you, mate!'... Brisbane's loss is evidently our gain. Louie will be delighted, she'll think she's landed in Summer Bay.

First sitting of select committee. Room 4A, which is the nicest. Buckley[75] in the chair, hopelessly out of his depth. The poor clerks kept having to discreetly intervene. First up was Hurd outlining the latest facts. The Kremlin is remaining tight-lipped about this Miroshnichenko[76] (if that is, indeed, his real name), but with the iron grip they have on all goings-on, it's impossible to conclude anything other than Moscow sponsorship. He travelled to London on a tourist visa issued by the consulate in Leningrad.

In the internal post was a letter offering me an MBE in the Birthday Honours!! Awarded in recognition of services to *film*!!! Who'd've thought that *Carry On Dick* had been such a hit with the gongs panel?! It was delightful to loudly & dramatically dictate a letter to Belinda, telling them to get stuffed.[77]

Monday, 10 June
After the surgery, Hardy called me into the meeting room. Dame Olive[78] & Lurch were there, looking stern. 'What ho, my darlings!' I said. Hardy shuffled uncomfortably & babbled, but eventually got to the point. 'We wish to know your intentions concerning the coming election...' I think they were *genuinely* worried that I might want to stand again. 'My intentions?' I asked. 'Well, to get as far away as possible from dreary, priggish dolts such

---

[75] Dr Joseph Buckley (1929-96), Tory MP for Forest of Dean, 1966-96.
[76] Andrei Miroshnichenko (1967-91), Byelorussian member of the KGB's 'Alpha Group' (black operations). Native of Minsk.
[77] The letter (delivered with a signed photograph) closed with 'Very sincerely yours, Kenneth C. Williams, TTFN PTO RSVP'.
[78] Olivia Salinger (b. 1924), Deputy Chair of Holborn & St Pancras Conservative Association, 1978-95.

as yourselves, I should imagine…' I smiled, & after a long pause Olive lit a fag, and that was that… Skipped down the road in the sunshine singing *Born Free* in my best Matt Munro baritone. Hopped on the 24 back to Parliament, & in the afternoon I ignored the double-line whip & voted against the health reforms. The government won, but only by 8.

Thursday, 13 June
Nice letter from Horace Cutler.[79] He says that myself & Soames are the only ones with the elegance & skill to *communicate* policy to the public in a coherent & enthusiastic way. I agree entirely. Apart from the Soames bit.

Committee in afternoon. Questioning the Serjeant-at-Arms, complete with his sword & Regency stay-ups. It was like cross-examining an extra from *Poldark*. I'm all for tradition, but as a last line of defence it's *lamentable* – and dangerous. After, in the anteroom, I heard one blimpish-looking twit saying to his companion (about *moi*) 'Huh! Looks a bit different without his make-up, doesn't he?!'… You'd have thought I was Quentin Crisp or somebody. I pointed him out to Waller[80] who said 'O, it's the new chap from *The People*. Bad egg.'

Monday, 17 June
That bloody Australian thing was again in the lobby when I came down, inflating the tyres on its byke. 'How you going, you old poof?!' it bellowed, loud enough to chime the lampshades. I ignored it & paraded past, but it said 'Ah, don't take it that way!'… I said 'I'll take it how I want, you simple-minded, backward colonial.' I felt awful, teetering on the edge of a tautology in that manner, but I soldiered on: 'I'm off to Westminster. In the meantime, why don't you clear away this muck? This is a vestibule, not a private garage.' I don't know… it *almost* makes one yearn for the return of the dreaded Lurgy!!

I found Tichet-Sweeting in the Library. He asked what was wrong & I expressed my fatigue with this kind of knockabout bigotry. He suggested a conflab with Topher Jones:[81] 'It's a bit late for us, but Topher is highly thought-of by Kinnock – he might have a strategy in mind.' At 3 o'c. Belinda

---

[79] (1912-97) Conservative Leader of the Greater London Council, 1977-81.
[80] Gary Waller (1945-2017), Tory MP for Keighley, 1983-95.
[81] Christopher Jones (b. 1962), Labour MP for South East Essex, 1983-2015; Shadow Secretary of State for the Environment, 1989-91; Secretary of State for National Heritage, 1991-5.

handed me a note from Tony: 'Have suggested to T.J. – Fauve landscapes at Royal Academy, Saturday noon, followed by lunch at Bentley's.'

Friday, 21 June
We watched *Fast Friends*, the new 'vehicle' for Les Dawson. I could've wept for the poor man, reduced to such torturous drivel. I don't know which was more depressing, this or John McCarthy's hostage video. Yes I do: *Fast Friends* is the more tragic… at least McCarthy can say he was chained to a Lebanese radiator against his will – whereas Les presumably *signed up* for this dross.

Saturday, 22 June
Strode down Portland Place & Regent Street in glorious sunshine. Met Tony & Topher at 11.56… Exhibition itself was rather pleb, what with all the garish Matisses & Derains. Topher was loving it, though, in the way a Midlands polytechnic alumnus would. 'I could've sworn that was a Braque,' he gasped, 'but the frame says Friesz.' 'O! it'll be a Friesz-frame then,' I said, but he wasn't listening… Luncheon at Bentley's. Rotten table by the gents. Topher implied that Hattersley's manifesto is purposely *restrained* on major matters, shot through with histrionic announcements on secondary issues (electoral reform, Europe, etc.)… He hinted the 'progressive, modern bits' would be social policies to prove they "care", in addition to them being fiscally sound. Topher said 'I've spoken to Neil & he was keen to listen.' Tony said 'Well, he can afford to listen with the kind of poll leads he's had,' but Topher shook his head & said 'No, it's more than that. There are times when you just have to be brave enough to do the right thing, even when it's going to be awkward & difficult.' I mentioned Tim from Stonewall & he said they were already acquainted. 'Kenneth, trust me. Getting rid of 28 will be just the start. We've quelled the Militant tendency, it's time to quell the knuckle-dragging attitudes of the man on the street too'… I walked home reflecting on how wonderful it must be to be young & hopeful. At Duchess Street a man in a white van called out 'Hallo Ken, you old fruit!'

Sunday, 23 June
M. came & joined us for lunch. For all Rita's scatterbrained cloddishness, the girl can certainly rustle up a fine meal, with the minimum of fuss. Lou, of course, managed to find plenty to complain about (gravy too thin, meat too fatty, parsnips undercooked), but by the end she'd left nothing on her plate but the pattern.

Wednesday, 26 June
I thought we were finished with irritating & intrusive bleeps when the portable 'phone fad went by the wayside – but these memo pad gizmos, or whatever they're bloody called, are a damn sight worse... They've all got them, dangling from their belts like Webley revolvers. Let's hope it leads to *appalling* tinnitus in their old age.

Chatted to Mawhinney.[82] Apparently the PM was very buoyed by the *Sunday Times* poll, but Brian said 'She got the same bounce after Brighton. Bombs always bring a bounce.' 'Bouncing bombs,' I jested, limply... The *naïveté* is quite fascinating, the way they fervently believe the situation is salvageable. They wouldn't have been out of place at Balaclava some of them, save for their polyblend suits... The electorate being afraid of the opposition only gets you so far. Voters were scared of Labour in '87, especially in economic terms. They're still unsure now (well, who wouldn't be?), but not enough to stick with the devil they know. It's crystal clear to me now that victory in the leadership election was pyrrhic. I should've left well alone. I saw ingratitude & got sentimental, when I ought to have stood aside & watched a wounded hind expire with dignity.

Friday, 28 June
It's funny how Lou & I have always enjoyed *Coronation Street* and yet neither of us has ever taken to *EastEnders*. I suppose it's because, being Londoners, we *know* how far the latter strays from reality, whereas it's easy to imagine that Weatherfield endures in isolation, gently retaining its "ay up, cock" cheeriness. I said to Louisa, 'I must write to Amanda Barrie,[83] I've not seen her since *An Audience With*,' but Louie said 'What about that pilot you done?'... I dismissed this as delusion, but looking at the '87 diary now, I see she was right!! Some rubbish called *Drop That Name*. I'd completely forgotten!! She might not remember what happened yesterday, but when it comes to recalling my appointments from four years ago, she's positively elephantine.

---

[82] Brian Mawhinney (1940-2019), Tory MP for Peterborough, 1979-95; Minister of State for Northern Ireland, 1990-1.
[83] English actress (b. 1935), played Alma Sedgwick in *Coronation Street*, 1981-2001; starred with KW in *Carry On Cleo* in the title role.

Saturday, 29 June
More & more I hear people say "haitch" when they mean *aitch*. I went to Ottakar's to get the new Michael Crichton, but the girl in front of me kept asking the assistant for *Kipps* by 'haitch-gee Wells'. She repeated it three or four times until I could stand it no longer. Dumped the book on the counter & walked to Hatchards. They're that bit more dear of course, but at least one can browse in a lettered air.

Thursday, 4 July
There was actual *applause* in the House for Mildred Gordon[84] on her return to work. They stood up & clapped as if it were the Oscars. It's despicable. I mean, we're all delighted she wasn't blown to bits, but the round in the chamber went on & on, and was quite undignified. Weatherill hesitated, clearly reluctant to halt the mawkishness unpopularly, so it just persisted. I remained seated & cross-armed… The poor cow looked thoroughly embarrassed by the whole thing, & rightly so.

Friday, 5 July
I'm going to have to do something about this elbow, it's driving me up the bloody wall. Usually with an ache or pain one begins to learn its traits & remember to *not do* something if it's going to spark agony… Alas, for whatever reason, I keep *not* remembering to stop myself from rotating the left elbow. Every sodding time, a thousand volts shooting up the humerus. I moaned about it to Adley & he said 'Have you been overexerting your left arm?' 'Not inordinately,' I replied, 'but then one is a confirmed bachelor.'

I was sitting in the committee room pretending to listen to Imbert's[85] evidence when I suddenly thought: none of my political friends (well – let's call them *associates*) have met Louisa. Granted, my *real* chums know her thanks to introductions made outside of the home – opportunities for which are now restricted – but still, it's rather telling… I thought of Charlie's maxim about not making friends with anyone I'd be ashamed to bring back to No. 57 to meet him & Lou. In truth, I'd be ashamed if the *dustman* knew I was acquainted with half these people.

---

[84] (1923-2016) Labour MP for Bow & Poplar, 1987-99. Her book *An Ordinary Friday Morning* (1992) was a personal account of the suicide bombing at the House of Commons.
[85] Peter Imbert (1933-2017), Commissioner of Police of the Metropolis, 1987-93.

Tuesday, 9 July
Up at 7.10. Shredded Wheat, then went to Dr ffoulkes. He examined the arm & puts it down to tendonitis. When he said 'Paracetamol should do the trick,' I kicked up a fuss & he grudgingly prescribed the codeine. The sole benefit of forking out for Harley St. care is that the quacks are more apt to relent when one's hankering for opiates... Castle Road at 12 o'c. for the tube station reopening. A number of locals came up to thank *me* personally. I tried to divert their praise towards more deserving parties from London Transport, but they wouldn't have it... In the end it was a hoot, as the other members of the ribbon-cutting contingent were Princess Michael & dear Alan Coren.[86] I'm not ashamed to say it: I *rejoice* in railway fanatics & trainspotters – they're far more interested in engine numbers & track gauges than the invited bigwigs, so one is left mercifully alone whilst they take photos of signalboxes. On the dais I read out some of Betjeman's short story[87] & Alan gave a very funny speech on the wonders of bureaucracy, touching on the recent quarrel over whether to rename the place *South Kentish Town* or *Kentish Town South*... HRH unveiled the plaque, we all got a badge, then it was back in the car & home in time for a pilchard salad with Lou.

Thursday, 11 July
Another unexpectedly positive poll.[88] The change in mood is palpable: whistling in the corridors as opposed to whispering – from loyalists in marginals, at least... She was accordingly magnificent in the House, swatting away digs & traps with consummate ease, indeed with *pleasure*. It's the first time I've felt her in control of the place for ages.

Escaped early. Paul & I got Lou downstairs & we pushed her to the park where we sat & had ice lollies in the afternoon sunshine. We read out the jokes on our lolly sticks. Mine was 'What did the sink say to the toilet?' & quick as a flash Lou said 'You're full of shit,' which had Paul choking on his Mivvi. The correct answer was 'You look flushed'... By the time we were back at Marlborough it was 5 o'c. & Paul said 'I'm peckish. Shall I fetch us

---

[86] English humourist, writer and satirist (1938-2007). Former editor of *Punch* magazine.
[87] *South Kentish Town* (1951). Based on a true incident when a gentleman accidentally alighted from a train at South Kentish Town shortly after its permanent closure.
[88] *Today* published a poll showing the Conservatives ahead of Labour for the first time since August 1988: Con 39, Lab 38, LibDem 17, Oth 6.

some fish & chips?' – So he popped round to Spiro's whilst Lou & I got out plates and buttered some Nimble. Lou told Gran's story of Mrs Houth & the bloomers & the mouldy boots in the piano[89]... Paul's heard it a hundred times before, but he was in fits with Louie doing all the voices. Then I sang *The Lady's in Love with You* as she had him up doing a kind of geriatric jive till we were all bent double & in tears.

Watched *Elizabeth R*[90] on BBC2 and it was the final act where the declining Gloriana dazzles at the last. 'Before it goes out, the candle always flares...' I thought of our own leading lady – & of the weakling milksop that stands in the wings, destined to accede.

Saturday, 13 July
Saw Flo off at 9.15. There can't be many employers who lug their housemaid's trunk to a cab so she can jet off to the jungle for a week. The woman's in the air more than a sprout picker's arse... Pat arrived at midday, which allowed me to run round to Vecchia for lunch with Nick Lewis. Stefano gave us the alcove table, which was a considerate touch. We had a pleasant time, and nattered about this & that – theatre, poetry, men – & I tried to allay some of his silly worries. The company was such a change from the dusty nonentities I'm generally stuck with at table nowadays.

Barry & Giovanni came at 3 o'c. with flowers for Louisa. They're just back from the brother's place in Viareggio & were both brown as berries. We had a pleasant time; Pat made sure glasses were brimming. Lou wanted games, but I said 'No dear, we're talking,' which caused the sulk until I gave in. So eventually it was semi-sloshed *I Packed My Bag*... She coped with the initial round of Apples, Brandy, Castanets & a Dustbuster – but by the second loop it was 'I packed my bag & in it I put Apples... Bran flakes, Catalogues... Oh, I don't bloody know. Sod this, pour me some more *sovereign blonk*...'

Monday, 15 July
All the bunting out for the G7[91]... It's alright for some – the inner circle and the *cognoscenti* get suited & booted for a booze-up at Lancaster House, while the rest of us have to stay behind dictating letters to the Association of

---

[89] 'Green boots' – a favourite chat show anecdote concerning a Mrs Houth, an incontinent neighbour of KW's paternal grandmother, who kept a pair of mildewed boots inside a piano.
[90] Dramatisation of the life of Queen Elizabeth I (1971), starring Glenda Jackson.
[91] The seventeenth Group of Seven summit, held at Lancaster House, 15-17 July.

British Prosthetists on behalf of Mrs Bansari Akter's faulty glass eye. I said to Belinda, 'Have you got any irons in the fire for when I'm gone?' – assuming that she mightn't've yet considered the prospect. 'Oh, good gracious!' she said, smiling. 'Plenty, thanks.' It was the smirk of a Sir Humphrey:[92] the civil servants & staff never have to worry – it's a job for life.

Pat cooked sausages for tea. Then Lou wanted *Takeover Bid*, so we had to sit through that. Pat was in hysterics at its sheer *crumminess*. 'Mum! How can you watch this tripe?' Lou scowled & said 'It ain't tripe, it's Brucie. I won't hear a word against Brucie...'

Tuesday, 16 July
Woken by a very strange dream. I was helping Charlie dig the yard at Marchmont Street & Joy Kaufmann was sitting on the low wall, stroking Bob. Annette Kerr[93] up in the window – I was waving but she didn't wave back. Charlie kept saying 'It was always going to come to this...' Couldn't get off again, so I was up & about by 6 o'c.

Wednesday, 17 July
That pustule-peppered shortarse from *The Sun* sidled up to me as I was going in. 'Hallo, Ken... Are you pals with Mellor?[94] Word's going round that he's been a bit of a lad... Got any dirt on anyone? What about Jeffrey, is he up to his old tricks?...' Thankfully, just as we got to New Palace Yard I saw David Lightbown[95] – all three-hundredweight of him – coming the other way, so I pounced. 'David! This gentleman from the press requires information on some of our colleagues – perhaps you could elucidate on my behalf?'... In a cowardly flash I was back at school, howling for Reefy to bash a bully for me... Got upstairs & the new intern chap was waiting eagerly by the vending machines. Poor little sod... talk about rotten timing!! It must be like sprinting for a ferry & *just* making it up the gangplank in time to hear the tannoy blare out 'Welcome aboard the *Herald of Free Enterprise*...'

---

[92] Sir Humphrey Appleby, the fictional Permanent Secretary for the Department of Administrative Affairs in the BBC sitcoms *Yes Minister* (1980-4) and *Yes, Prime Minister* (1986-8). Played by Nigel Hawthorne.

[93] Scottish-born actress (1920-2013), friend of KW since appearing together in rep at Newquay in 1949. She turned down his proposal of marriage in 1961.

[94] David Mellor (b. 1949), Tory MP for Putney, 1979-95; Minister for the Arts, 1990-1.

[95] (1932-95) Tory MP for South East Staffordshire, 1983-95; Vice-Chamberlain of the Household, 1990-1.

Beyond Our Kenneth

Thursday, 18 July
After Lou had gone to bed, sat up with Pat & talked. She couldn't stop laughing when I mentioned the late 'Mrs' Peabody with the five o'c. shadow, and the time Charlie nicked the drayman's earlobe with the Kropp razor & said 'Stone the crows, I've dabbed some Stork on it, what *more* d'you want?...'

Friday, 19 July
'Phone rang at 7 o'c. & it was Raison. 'Better get in pronto,' he said. Hailed a cab. Pandemonium on arrival. Press & cameramen swarming around the main entrance, clambering over each other. *Just* managed to slip inside unscathed. None of the rank-and-file knew a thing, so of course the gossip started. 'She's going,' said Critchley, confidently. Eventually we saw on TV each member of the cabinet breezing into No 10 one by one. Howard came back & the mood changed at once – it's not a resignation... she's going to see the Queen!!... At 12.57 we gathered in the committee room to watch it on the screen. Election Day is to be 5th September. *My sentence is finally at an end...* Went up to the office, but the corridor was emptier than Moreschi's[96] drawers. Came & sat in the library. Robert Walpole[97] joined me & we attempted last week's Mephisto.

Torrence came in & half-jogged over. 'Mr Williams, sir, there's an officer in the lobby who wants to talk to you.' In actual fact there were two. Both plainclothed. We went into the Pugin Room as it was free.

They drove me back in a blue car. Pat was sitting on the settee, snivelling into a tissue, next to a woman policeman. The ambulance had already been & gone. The detective showed me how it must've happened & whereabouts on the credenza she'd hit her head. Blood & what not on the carpet. Two or three times, Pat sputtered about only having left her for a few minutes. The police girl put the kettle on... Paul came & I asked him to ring friends to let them know. M. arrived at 4.10 & dealt with the remaining officials. Everyone speaking in the past tense. Did, was, were... I came & sat in the flat. At 6.30 Rupert knocked & said he's taking the weekend off & that we'll 'deal with everything together.'

Walked to Great Portland Street and went to the end of the platform. Stood there for ages, watching the pattern of the arriving trains. Got cold

---

[96] Alessandro Moreschi (1858-1922), Italian *castrato* singer.
[97] 10th Baron Walpole (1938-2021), hereditary crossbench peer.

feet. A little girl in a cornflower dress was crying cos she'd tripped & grazed the knee. The mother knelt down & staunched her sobbing with a hanky… I am obliged to feel the grief. I'm duty-bound to live thro' the pain, else it's just another self-deception. So I must perforce remain… I don't know why, but I can't cry. I sat in the bedroom and tried & tried, but nothing came.

Sunday, 21 July
'Phone kept ringing but I didn't answer. Rupert knocked at noon, to check that I've been eating. I said I didn't fancy it, but he practically *marched* me upstairs & served sandwiches. I said I didn't care about anything any more, & that I just want to go… Smartened myself up a bit & he drove us to Heathrow. Flo knew as soon as she saw my face. She was very English about it, ironically – melancholy but stoic. Took her for something to eat at Ringer's.

Received 4.8.91 & pasted in:

> 21/7 – 11.30 p.m.
> Hi Ken,
>
> You implied this afternoon that you've neglected your diary these past days. I can see how low you are, so I didn't want to query it while you were upset – But if it is the case, I think it's something you might eventually regret. I'll raise the subject again when things are more settled and decide whether or not to give you these notes. If I have passed them on to you, then this is a rough list of events from Saturday onwards:
>
> Sat. 20/7 – Police came. There will be a post mortem on Monday. Louie's weekend carer came, you sent her home. I called your sister a cab and she left at 1.30 p.m. You went home to make phone calls. I saw Mr Dunthorpe downstairs and he said a reporter had been sniffing about, but he told him you were out.
>
> Sun. 21/7 – I invited you up for some lunch. At 3.00 p.m. we drove to the airport to collect Louie's carer. I waited in the car while you told her the news. We drove back to Osnaburgh Street, arriving at 4.50 p.m. We went for supper at the pub.
>
> I know it's not Chaucer, but perhaps it'll be a useful aide-memoire.
>
> Love,
>   Rupert

Beyond Our Kenneth

Monday, 22 July

Received 4.8.91 & pasted in:

> Hi Ken,
>   Daily events, cont'd.
>
> Mon. 22/7 — I drove us to Camley Street. Autopsy confirms cause of death as an acute subdural haematoma due to blunt force of accidental fall. Coroner determines no inquest required. 4.30 p.m. – Drove us to Eversholt Street registry office.
>
> Tues. 23/7 — After work I picked you up and we went to Leverton's to make arrangements. Cremation on Weds. 31st July at East Finchley… 7 p.m. with Paul Richardson for supper at Vecchia Milano.
>
> Weds. 24/7 — I came home to take you to lunch but you'd just banged your elbow on the door jamb and you told me to go away.
>
> Thurs. 25/7 — Day off. We walked to Marchmont Street and Cromer Street. You told me all about your childhood. Went to Boot pub – they agreed to do a spread for thirty people and you paid them. Then to Leverton's – you delivered the dress to them.
>
> Fri. 26/7 — I gave you the sympathy card from the tenants' association. You handed it back to me and said "They can shove it up their arses". I've kept it in case you change your mind.
>
> Love,
>   Rupert

Wednesday, 24 July

Letter from CCO. Sympathy and gratitude, of course – but confirmation that my resignation has been accepted. So that is an end to it.

Went down to Flo to talk things thro'. I've said that I shall retain her at the current rate until 31 August to give her enough time to find something else. She was politely resistant, but in the end accepted the terms. She asked to go into No. 7 to clean, but I forbade it. I'm not having *anyone* in there… Rang James Ford. He went on and on about this crackpot in America that's been found with trade chopped up in the bath & pickled in the pantry.[98] I reminded him that there's actually been a corpse *chez-moi* this week, which

---

[98] Jeffrey Dahmer (1960-94), American serial killer.

thankfully shut him up... Came out of the loo & bashed the arm on the doorframe. What with that & the rosacea, I'm beginning to resemble a battered wife.

Saturday, 27 July

Received 4.8.91 & pasted here:

> Hi Ken,
>   Daily events continued:
>
> Sat. 27/7 — We met Paul and went to the Sainsbury Wing at the Nat. Gallery. You said it calls to mind a Tuscan NCP car park. I bought ice-creams and we sat on a bench in Trafalgar Square. A scruffy man with a D.A. haircut came over and asked for your autograph. He said "I thought you were top drawer in that Grace Brothers programme."
>
> Sun. 28/7 — Michael arrived at 12.30 p.m. - you invited me to lunch, but I had to go to Missenden.
>
> Mon. 29/7 — I came to knock after my shift, but you were loudly arguing on the phone, so I thought better of it. Came back at 7.00 p.m. but you were out.
>
> Tues. 30/7 — We drove to Houses of P'ment to collect your things. I parked in Canon Row and we had drinks with your staff in St Stephen's pub. I got parking ticket and kicked the lamppost. You laughed.
>
> Weds. 31/7 — Cars at 11.30 a.m. You and your sister in front and myself, Michael, Paul and Stanley behind. Service 12.15 p.m. Back to pub afterwards.
>
> Love,
>   Rupert

Wednesday, 31 July
It's the *waiting* bit that I can't cope with. And it's tiring, sitting in the dark, watching the second hand carve its way silently round the clock face. Went & sat in her flat, to absorb the spirit whiles it lingers... It's curious how the irritating parts of a person's character fade so completely when they're out of the way – the banal prattling, the infuriating slowness, the maddening deafness, the insensitivity, the incomprehension... all quite gone. It's designed that way, both to comfort and to taunt. I have known loneliness & despair, and the panic of sheer desperation. But thro' all that *she was there*,

Beyond Our Kenneth

my other self, attentive to nothing but me, nothing but *we*. I kept her, but she kept me, even in dotage. I know we were blessed with uncommon closeness. And cursed with it too... She was chief cheerleader, chief ego-*masseuse*, chief friend, chief concern, chief responsibility. That type of love isn't chosen, it's bestowed by wayward Nature & becomes as essential & vital & automatic as the need for food or air. I reaped its rewards in better days & I see I must now pay the price.

M. brought Pat at 10.45. Didn't say much, but M. tried to keep things cheerful. Stanley came, very upset. Cars arrived at 11.27 and we went down... Standing room only at the crem. Mercifully cool inside. Nearly broke down straight away when I saw Mags & Bev as I was sure they'd be in America... The officiant handled it lovely, very understated. I got through *How Great Thou Art* alright, and Stanley's eulogy because it was funny. But when the man said 'as we bid farewell to our friend Louisa', it hit me: a great, boiling wave of heartache & the floodgates opened at last. I wept, open-mouthed & uncontrollably into the handkerchief, stifling it as best I could. Joan Dunbar[99] impertinently placed a hand on my shoulder. I hastily brushed it off – but it *did* have the effect of snapping me out of the blubbery... We retreated to The Boot. Couldn't face the gloom-talk & the constant questions about how I'm coping, so I had gin with the orange & told Harry O. to play & we sang her favourite songs.

'How are you coping?' they say. It's nothing but empty smalltalk. *I'm not coping.* How would *they* cope if they'd had their heart torn out? Pat tried to break the ice, but I'm not ready to forgive, not yet, not for a long time to come.

Saturday, 3 August
At 2 o'c. I walked to the Rose Gardens. Wandered under the pergolas & sat on her preferred bench by the Huntress fountain. I talked to her for a bit, but mainly just sat quietly in the sunshine. Not a single cloud in the sky, & just the faintest of cooling breezes. The late blooms are aburst with aching, plummy colour, stood at determined attention like loyal, sweltered guardsmen. I scattered the ashes there, facing the Diana statue. It is a handsome spot.

---

[99] KW's cousin.

Sunday, 4 August
I was about to pop into Lou's to thaw out a chop, but Rupert rang & asked me to lunch at L'Escargot. When we got there he said 'Don't look at the prices, it's my treat.' During the *crèmes brûlées*, David Langton's son Simon came & introduced himself. He's a television director. 'I was sorry to miss Gordon's funeral,' he said, 'he was a sweet man.' I asked to be remembered to his father… When we were back in the car, R. handed me some letters – he'd got the wrong end of the stick & thought I'd given up the diary!! He's been deputising whilst I was in mourning, the soppy sod. The whole thing is too, too madly adorable.

Tuesday, 6 August
Barbara 'phoned to thank me for the birthday letter & Madeira snapshots. She sounded down. Marital cracks by the sound of things. I said 'Oh, let's just run away somewhere!' and she laughed, 'I wish we could, darlin', I really do…' Ten minutes later, she rang back: 'Sod it, we're only young once. Just book somewhere & we'll go.'

Tuesday, 13 August
We could see the 'plane from the window at the gate. I asked the severe-looking woman from *Jugoslavenski Aerotransport* how old the aircraft was. 'Is good, is strong' was all I got. Thank heavens I'd shoved up a diazepam… We arrived at Split at 12.45 & then caught the Hvar ferry. Felt as if we were on the pirate ship at Margate. I clung to the banquette as Barbara staggered across with the coffee sloshing its way out of the cups, her tits rolling in unison with the swell. I said 'Your cami looks like it's hosting a fight between the Mitchell brothers.' She said 'Whoever they are, they needn't brawl, there's plenty to go round…'

After the dreaded Dubrovnik, anyone would have misgivings about Yugoslavia, but – thus far – Hvar seems to have a more easy-going appeal. Hotel is unexpectedly spotless, which is a miracle. While Barbara unpacked I went to the *Konzum* to try & break down the totally impractical one-thousand dinar notes we'd been lumbered with at Gatwick. The gargantuan palone eyed me suspiciously through the grate & examined the money forensically – I suppose as any wary checkout girl would inspect a fifty back home. After lots of exasperated bellyaching in Serbo-Croat, I *eventually* left with my wad of change.

Most of the tourists are West German, which is such a relief. We were left entirely alone at dinner, sitting in the open square, knocking back the local plonk & getting slowly, wonderfully, pissed.

Wednesday, 14 August
B. had neglected to check in with the dishy husband last night, so the air was blue when she eventually 'phoned before breakfast. 'Miserable sod. I've said it before, Kenny, & I'll say it again – all men are *cunts*.' She clocked the startled waiter who was pouring the coffee & said 'Oh, I didn't mean you, dear. I meant *English* men. You're an angel. Come to think of it, if you're at a loose end later, I'm in room sixty-eight!' He smiled & blushed. 'And I'm in *sixty-nine*,' I said, 'so you mind you choose *wisely*...'

Thursday, 15 August
I wonder if Croatian islanders get fed up with the unremitting sunny days & sea air, and if they *long* to get away from it all? Perhaps these hardy little people dream of a capitalist week in a Feltham B&B to recharge the batteries? The wafting scent of the Chinese take-it-away, the thrum of the Heathrow flightpath, the elegance of the urban fox boring through a bin liner...

Friday, 16 August
One comes halfway across Europe – to a communist state – to escape the bloody election, & there at breakfast is every English paper, hot off the presses, fanned-out for perusal, as if we were sat in Wapping. I told them, no more of that... Günther & Jutta gave us a lift to the beach at Pokonji Dol. It's an idyllic horseshoe-shaped bay, & the water is crystal clear. Barbara wanted me to put the cream on her back, but I refused. She asked Günther, and he did it, much to Jutta's glaring disapproval... Lunch at the *konoba*. Fatal. They started pouring the slivovitz & we were still there at 7 o'c., Barbara with the sarong tied round her head & me arm-in-arm with Hvar's answer to Bella Emberg,[100] dancing a Balkan hokey-cokey to the strains of a one-stringed banjo. A boy called Petar drove us back to the hotel, where we demanded chips. It is *disgusting* behaviour, and I must make a point of apologising to the concierge.

Sunday, 18 August
Heavy rain all day. It's refreshing, but limits activity. Resorted to charades with the Müllers and the Dutch chaps. 'You're good at this, Ken!' laughed Piet. 'It's the *Give Us A Clue* training, sweetheart,' I said, 'I've dedicated my life to it.' Of course that went skyward. I'm not complaining. Anonymity is priceless. But sometimes it's tiresome when one *isn't* recognised.

---

[100] Stout English actress (1937-2018), best known for performances in *The Russ Abbot Show*.

Monday, 19 August
I curse myself. My want of humility getting its inevitable comeuppance with the arrival this afternoon of Karen & Gary from Harlow. All over us like eczema. Their fawning left Günther & Jutta quite baffled!! The holiday is now totally ruined & the thought of home tomorrow is simply *divino*.

Wednesday, 21 August
Annette said to me once that I begin to loathe friends if I spend too much time with them. It's always been a truism in my case. The only exceptions that have ever proved the rule are Mags & Barbara. These girls aren't merely fun & ebullient: they share an ineffable ability to make me rather keen on *myself* when in their company. Not by massaging the ego, or by playing the part of yes men… whatever they've got, it rubs off & infects one, for a time. It is a gift more valuable than any other I can imagine.

Friday, 23 August
Perhaps I'm foolish to accept this invitation, but simply being here is too painful. Yugoslavia lessened the pangs, so perhaps the Highlands will do the same. Went to Army & Navy for a thin waterproof.

Wednesday, 28 August
The sleeper pulled into Inverness station at 8.42 after eleven hours of absolute *death*. Sleeper?! That's a joke. Had more peace at Kalyan[101]… Adelaide was there to meet me. She's not at all how I'd imagined; much more rustic than both her penmanship & writing style portend, and far prettier than you'd think for someone so catty. Ensconced myself aboard the dent-ridden Land Rover & we embarked on the half-hour drive to the cottage at Inverfarigaig. It is a fantastically desolate & beautiful spot, right alongside the loch. I've never felt further away from civilisation – even in Nuneaton. The room is small, clean, cool & spartan. It could not be better… The children, Douglas & Marie, arrived home from school at 3.30. They are confident, articulate & unselfish and I'm already hooked. Douglas said 'Ah tellt Miss McClean yous wur comin' tae bade wi' us, bit she didnae believe me.' The husband, Joe (a glassblower, if you please), came at 5 o'c. & immediately thrust a wee dram into my hand & engaged me in a fascinatingly enjoyable & varied

---

[101] City near Bombay; KW arrived at a transit camp there as the war was ending in Europe, May 1945.

conversation. Adelaide served a huge spread of tempting delicacies & it was simply delicious. Fell into bed at 9.30… *This* is what Judith Chalmers means by 'getting away from it all'.

Thursday, 29 August
After breakfast we walked the dogs alongside the loch to Foyers. Whilst all the monster talk is idiotic, there *is* something spooky about the place. It's the blackness of the water. Luckily most of the gawping tourists are crammed into the hotels & hostelries on the other side at Drumnadrochit, so we're well away from all the plastic trash.

I offered to help Adelaide prepare the meal, but she said 'Don't be daft. We both know that's the last thing you want to do. Read your book & I'll call you when it's time for gin…' She's a rum 'un… I played hide & seek with the little ones. Young Marie giggled helplessly when I found her in the airing cupboard. They call me Uncle Ken. To feel so at ease & assuredly welcomed in such unconventional circumstances makes no sense. But then hardly anything *good* ever does.

Friday, 30 August
Joe drove me to Fort Augustus & showed me the studio. His stuff's a notch above tourist ware; indeed some of the pieces are rather delicate, especially the thin vases. I told him I didn't think much of the Nessie models. 'Aye,' he said, 'they're shite, but the Japs can't get enough'… Pub lunch at the Lock Inn, then the boat ride up the loch. That was mainly Japanese too. The stereotype holds water – they photograph *everything*. One peppy article insisted on having me in all his snaps, despite not knowing me from Akihito. It was certainly invigorating to be on the loch, but I wish we'd gone *before* the Cullen skink – belly like a cement mixer by the time we came ashore.

Sunday, 1 September
Drizzle all day. Rather keen to return to London now. After lunch I suddenly felt very bored with all this walking about & breathing fresh air. While Adelaide did the washing-up, we hunkered down & the children coaxed us into their *Guess Who?* game.

Tuesday, 3 September
Told them I was dreading the train. Adelaide suggested flying. That seemed frightfully excessive, until she said 'They've forecast eighty degrees. That'll

mean ninety in the carriage.' Telephoned Dan-Air & there's an Inverness-Heathrow service tomorrow at 9.50 for £43... It's not the train itself that daunts me. It's the thought of travelling home & not having Louisa there to return *to*. The sooner the journey's over the better, so I've mentally chalked it up as a necessary extravagance.

Thursday, 5 September
Posted a note to Adelaide, thanking her for my holiday. On reflection, going there at all was an *extraordinarily* brave move. I would never have acted so recklessly years ago, relying so riskily on the kindness of strangers. Perhaps I just got lucky.

Friday, 6 September
Up at 7 o'c. & did letters. Wet the carpets & shampooed them, as they'll dry in no time in this heat. Had mackerel fillets & brown bread. Curiosity got the better of me, so I went into Lou's and watched the lunchtime news. Labour have a majority of 17.[102] She is going to see the Queen this afternoon & Kinnock will go shortly afterwards. In my seat the Labour chap[103] got 67 per cent of the vote. 'Phone rang twice but I didn't answer.

    Knocked for Flo & we walked all the way to the Tower & back in the hot sun. I told her that I want her to stay, at the same rate as before. She is to cook, clean & do the laundry, and any other errands. The weekends are her own. She was taken aback, but agreed... Rang Stanley. He said it was a very sensible thing to do. He has a cold, tho', so I didn't linger as I wasn't in the mood to hear his moaning through a veil of snot.

Monday, 9 September
After the News we saw this Spanish soap thing[104] which has replaced *Wogan*. It's a long while since I've read my Book of Revelation, but if this crap isn't mentioned, there ought to be an inquiry. The only saving grace is that the sound recording is so shoddy one can barely hear the asinine twaddle the poor cast are being forced to deliver.

---

[102] Actually 21 – final result: Labour 336 seats, Conservatives 271, Liberal Democrats 20, Others 24.
[103] Keir Starmer (b. 1962), Labour MP for Holborn & St Pancras, 1991-.
[104] The ill-fated *Eldorado*, created by Tony Holland, set in the fictional town of Los Barcos.

Thursday, 19 September
Walked to James. He showed me the fax from *The Spectator*. I'd imagined they were after a *warts 'n all* political disclosure, but not a bit of it… They want a 'funny diary of 1991' to shove in the Christmas issue. 'In effect, it's a thousand quid just to type out your real diary.' I said 'They specified *funny*. I doubt my journal will be much help.'

Saturday, 21 September
A boy called Jenő has written from Hungary. It's dated April 13th & arrived this morning!! The English is as broken as a jilted swain's heart, but it's the thought that counts. 'You very big up Budapest,' he relates. Apparently the *Carry On*s and *It Ain't Half Hot Mum* are the only Western things Hungarians are allowed to see. Poor sods. Still, it's nice to know that Wisdom[105] doesn't have a *monopoly* of fans amongst the Magyars. No, I'm wrong – it's the *Albanians* that adore Norman… Nonetheless, I wrote a reply – tho' I'll probably be in an urn on Pat's mantelshelf by the time he receives it.

Thursday, 26 September
Flo did steak pie, new potatoes & string beans & we had it on our laps in front of the TV. On the News they announced that Portillo has won the leadership contest. Got it in the first round. Heseltine will be apoplectic, which is rather satisfying. I penned a brief congratulatory note to Miguel… M. rang & mentioned Lou's flat. I know it can't be a museum, and I wouldn't want it to be. Scribbled these lines whilst listening to the *Sicilienne*…

> A home that's lost its resident
> Becomes a voided shrine
> Does one forget the precedent
> As truth and grief align?
>
> The head of course says *sell*
> While the heart just waffles hooey
> But strangers there to dwell
> In the place of darling Louie?

---

[105] Sir Norman Wisdom (1915-2010), genial English actor, comedian and musician. His fame was notable in communist Albania, as his films were the only Western releases permitted by dictator Enver Hoxha.

I do not want an altar
It's time that I moved on
As hope begins to falter
Should I withal be gone?

How much pain can God allow?
What the sod do I do now?

Friday, 27 September
Final payslip in post. It made up my mind… I shall *retain* Louie's flat, for the time being. Flo & I shall eat there & watch television. I shall entertain in there if needs be. I told Paul. He said 'It'll give you time to decide what you want to keep & what you can let go.'

Saturday, 28 September
I walked to the baths. Stopped by the steamed-up windows & watched Rupert giving a lesson. He's a sight to behold in his little blue trunks & no mistake. He looked so masterful, with all the youngsters gazing up in wonder at his demonstrations with the polystyrene float. Got the half-hard as I stood there!! Realised it wasn't the ideal place to be discovered, peering in at a load of kids whilst *demi-solide*, so I pressed on to Dolcis to get insoles.

Tuesday, 1 October
Saw Rupert. He said 'It's my birthday today.' I said 'I know. I didn't get you anything.'

Sunday, 6 October
Arrived at Kettners for lunch with Lionel Blair, Nigel Finch[106] & Jimmy Jewel. From the cloakroom I clocked Jimmy noisily *sneezing* into a hanky, & that was that. The repulsive sternutation rang out thro' the room, so I turned round & came straight back home.

Monday, 7 October
Wrote apologies to Lionel. Heaven knows why… *I* wasn't the one polluting the atmosphere with droplets of plague, but such are our lunatic conventions.

---

[106] English director and filmmaker (1949-95), whose work influenced the growth of British gay cinema.

Wednesday, 16 October
At 4 o'c. went for a stroll, for something to do. It's got rather chilly, but being windless, it's the perfect walking weather, with the pearly sun dying in the vanilla sky. On Clifford Street a woman with her arm in a cast was struggling to shut her boot, so I offered assistance. It was as tho' she was witnessing the second coming… 'Oh my goodness! I can't believe it! Are you…? It is *you*, isn't it?…' I was expecting the usual 'I loved you in *Carry On up yer Whatsit*, I pissed myself rigid,' or 'Oh, *go on*, say "stop messin' about"…', but – throwing me completely – she said 'I came to *Saint Joan* at the Albery – must've been 1954. Simply mesmeric. The best Dauphin I ever saw; I've never forgotten it…' Half the world seems to have seen that production.

Sunday, 20 October
M. came at noon & gave me lunch at Joe Allen. First time we've been since Louisa. We talked about Rupert… M. said 'Of course, you're freer now than you've ever been before, if you *did* want to get involved.' It's so typical. One finally tracks down the person, finds the time, possesses the funds, builds the courage – but a single look in the glass reveals it's twenty, *thirty* years too late, & not only has one *missed* the bus, but the bus has long since been decommissioned, gutted and scrapped.

 Spent the afternoon starting this *Spectator* diary nonsense. I'd been putting it off, but it's actually rather a hoot, recreating the year as one might have lived it. I've substituted Lou for Tom on the Maltese trip – I don't think the new member for Charnwood would appreciate tales about him slipping away to make free with dusky striplings in the backstreets of Valletta.

Wednesday, 23 October
Letter from Michael Anderson! Says he & Enzo are fed up with Australia and they plan to return in the new year. Certainly don't blame him. There's only so many barbecues an erudite man can endure.

Thursday, 24 October
Shouted at Flo about the radio. I'm having no more of it, at least while I'm in the flat. If I hear that *Everything I Do*[107] racket *once* more, I'll crack…

---

[107] *(Everything I Do) I Do It for You* by Canadian singer-songwriter Bryan Adams. It spent sixteen weeks at Number 1 in the UK singles chart (7 July – 27 October 1991).

Wherever one goes – lift, car, supermarket, waiting room – the same fucking tune blares out. It's Orwellian.

Friday, 25 October
The constipation continues. BM at 7.30 insufficient & very painful. Went to Harts to get prunes, and Boots for the Lactulose. Bus to chiropodist. To the Renoir at 1.15 with Paul for the Jarman film, *Edward II*. Seedy, distasteful dross. It manages to besmirch not only the King, but Marlowe's text *and* homosexual activists too, which is quite a feat in ninety minutes. It strains to make points & draw modern parallels at every turn, but one is left feeling unsatisfied and unclean – like visiting a knocking shop on a Wednesday afternoon. Paul said 'Hmm. Don't think I'll bother with *Edward III*.'

De Quincey's at 8 o'c. for dinner with Susan Sylvester. All these years & she hasn't changed a bit. I don't just mean in demeanour, but to look at! It's extraordinary… She remembered the party at Marchmont Street where the carpet caught fire, and saving the Scotch vagrant from choking by smacking him with a rolled-up *My Weekly*. We ordered *chartreuses* & she said 'So then, when are you coming back to the theatre? You've had your fling, isn't it time to come home?' It's astounding. I told her I'm very much retired, with no intention of doing *anything*, apart from sitting quietly & dying as painlessly as possible. 'Silly sod,' she said.

Sunday, 27 October
After lunch M. drove me to Docklands and we looked at the monstrosities they've shoved up at Canary Wharf. Far worse in person than they appear on television. It takes a certain level of ineptitude & poor taste to spend six hundred million pounds making something look so cheap & ugly. Don't know why I'm surprised – after all, I've spent time with the cretins who approved it… That proud, bustling area, that humming centre of imperial trade, reduced to a soulless, corporate wasteland… 'Course, we detractors will be labelled 'philistine', but sooner *that* – and defend the architectural glories of Hawksmoor, Cubitt & Wren – than mutely acquiesce to such ghastly rubbish.

Tuesday, 29 October
After Flo's interpretation of bubble & squeak we saw that *Every Second Counts*. She shrieked 'Oh! Look!' as it started & nigh on gave me a coronary. Turns out that the middle pair on the programme were her first employers

in service over here!! Judging by the running commentary ('Stupid cow', 'fat cow', 'old shit', &c.), life under Ian & Pam wasn't an altogether joyful experience. Her ire was placated somewhat when they finished the game in last place & left with nothing. In the end, the victorious couple won a holiday to Florida. Some victory! You couldn't *pay* me to go there.

Will have to ring Adrian Chatham about the constipation. I'll need a Channel Tunnel boring machine if this goes on much longer.

Tuesday, 5 November
As I passed Greenwell Street I saw three scruffy boys & a little girl tending to their rudimentary mannequin by the kerb. 'Penny for the Guy, mister?' yelped the eldest, who had a cigarette behind his ear. 'Sorry, kids, I've no change,' I said. 'That's all right,' said the cheeky mite, 'we take *folding money*...'

Wednesday, 6 November
Headlines are all about Maxwell[108] going overboard. Papers say how *lucky* it is that the bosun needed some air, witnessed the splash & 'managed to drag him up on deck' – Kenneth Horne came to mind. Lucky? Well, perhaps... All sounds a bit queer to me.

Thursday, 7 November
Had the Weetabix with prunes in an attempt to get things moving. It doesn't feel the same as the old trouble of restriction, but stool *consistency* is affected. Each movement is like trying to birth Ayers Rock. 'Phoned Chatham and got appt. for 4.45... Wrote to George Borwick in South Africa & Paul in Sydney and went to post. Heavens opened while I was waiting for the idiot girl to stop talking. 'Hallo darling', 'Morning sweetheart' & other rubbish in a similar vein until I wanted to scream. Such familiarity is *detestable*. Got drenched on the way back to the flat.

Flo grilled the fish & served it at 12 o'c. Then we saw the News. They showed Tom at PMQs: 'As a former leading light of the Labour movement, up to his neck and sinking fast, surely the Prime Minister can sympathise

---

[108] Robert Maxwell (1923-2002), Czechoslovak-born British media proprietor; Labour MP for Buckingham, 1964-70. Having been rescued from a fall from his yacht, it was discovered he had used hundreds of millions of pounds from his companies' pension funds to shore up the shares of the Mirror Group to save his companies from bankruptcy. He stood trial in 1992.

with Mr Maxwell?' Lots of faux outrage. Boothroyd[109] actually dismissed him!! I cannot get used to seeing Kinnock, flanked by Hattersley & Litany, sitting on the government benches… grinning away, they look as if they've won a competition, or Jim'd fixed it for them. Freetening.

Walked to Chatham. After the pleasantries I dropped the strides & assumed the position. He donned the curious torch headgear, looking for all the world as tho' he were ready to join the NUM & go down t'pit. He did the examination. 'I can't feel anything out of the ordinary. Let's try the Macrogol, and if there's no improvement in a week then we'll have a deeper look.' My bum is, without question, the most cursed in Christendom.

Sunday, 10 November
Streets quite busy thanks to Remembrance idiocy, so we parked up & walked to Joe Allen where M. gave Peter Cadley & me lunch. I had the salmon & veg, but no starches. I fear I may have been slightly too descriptive when detailing the ins & not-so-outs of the condition, as Peter quietly cancelled his brownie cake.

Got home and the BM was smooth, generous & pain-free. Rather dark in colour, but one can't have it all. Spent the afternoon getting on with the writing for *Spectator*. Getting a bit sick of it, frankly. Rang Rita & she came round for crumpets & tea at 5 o'c. She says she's working for a Mrs Featherstone in Redhill Street. 'I only have to do the meals and wipe round with the Liquid Gumption & she's happy.'

Wednesday, 13 November
Portaloo 'phoned!! I said 'Surely you've more pressing matters to attend to?', but he laughed & said 'Nonsense. One must always put one's friends first… in any case, nothing *I* say or do here will matter a jot until we've moved *her* upstairs (meaning shoving Mrs T to the Other Place[110]), so I'm treading water a bit.' He explained morale was surprisingly good, as Labour's majority is small, and Pillock can't ride roughshod with wild ideas. He asked how I'm getting on & invited me to a party at Central Office next Friday, but I fibbed & said I was otherwise engaged. I couldn't face it… it'd be comparable to attending a forces reunion not four months after getting

---

[109] Betty Boothroyd (1929-2023), Labour MP for West Bromwich West, 1974-2000; Speaker of the Commons, 1991-2000.
[110] The House of Lords.

demobbed. Nauseating chatter with people I (for the most part) couldn't stomach in the first place.

Tuesday, 19 November
Halved the Macrogol 'cos, if anything, this morning's motion was *too* loose; I had to run for the throne. Sick of prunes, so I'm back to just the Special K – Rupert put me on to it & I'm rather taken. It's filling but light, you see… Flo came in to do the bed & collect the laundry. She keeps needling me about switching to a continental quilt, but I don't want anything to do with them. Of course, it's laziness on her part that provokes such boldness. Be that as it may, if I don't firm up soon it'll be an *incontinental* quilt I'll be wanting. Told her not to raise the matter again. The fact is, I'm not comfortable with her being in the flat at all. It didn't matter as much before, but she's more than just the hired help now.

Walked to Doughty Street. Met Lawson[111] the younger. Spitting image of his father really, especially round the chin, with the pleasing mix of black Jewish hair & the inability to find a suit that fits. He's only 30-odd, but the rise in readership speaks for itself. We chatted amiably, and he praised the stuff I'd submitted via James, with only a few notes & suggestions. I asked if he'd considered following the old man into politics. He laughed. 'I've got more clout sitting behind this desk than I would sitting in the House… in any case, it's not healthy to do the same job as your dad.' Well, I heartily agree with that!! I'm to send in the final edit by close of business on the 6th.

Went up to Rupert & we watched the late news. We saw Terry Waite[112] bounding down the aeroplane steps in the pouring rain. He almost tumbled headlong into the tarmac, but a steward rescued him. They kept saying how tired he must be, how he'll be *longing* to get home as soon as possible to spend time with loved ones… In the event, the speech he gave in the open hangar needed heavy editing by ITN, as it went on and on and on.

---

[111] Dominic Lawson (b. 1956), editor of *The Spectator* magazine, 1990-5. Brother of TV chef Nigella.
[112] English humanitarian and author (b. 1939). Whilst negotiating the release of hostages in Lebanon as an envoy for the Church of England, he was himself kidnapped and held in captivity for nearly five years.

Saturday, 23 November
Got papers from Adonis. Heard the 'phone go as I was on the landing & just caught it in time. 'Hello Ken, it's Nick Hytner.[113] I need an enormous favour…' They're doing Bennett's *Madness of George III* at the Lyttelton – Cyril Shaps[114] has fractured his leg & they open on Thursday. He asked if I'd deputise for Shaps in the bit part role of Dr Pepys until he's recovered. 'Alan tells me you're rather keen to get back to work,' he said. I was *livido*. It's absolutely shameful behaviour, the barefaced cheek of it. I slammed down the receiver.

Cab to the National for the costume fitting. Tight around the nadgers, but otherwise quite fetching. It really is a puny little part, no more than a handful of lines. Rather amusing ones though. Pepys is the doctor captivated by the King's *motions*, much to the irritation of the other quacks. Pretty camp stuff… Nigel Hawthorne is a delight, & made a little speech. *Molto imbarazzante!* He said 'Whilst we despair over our friend Cyril's rotten luck, providence has smiled on our company most glowingly, by sending us Kenneth Williams – and a more capable pair of hands it is impossible to imagine.' They all laid it on thick. But it is a pleasant group… After they'd showed me the blocking, Alan came to the dressing room, looking chuffed with himself. 'I'm doing this to save a production from disaster,' I said, 'my conscience wouldn't allow it to flop. But you are an opprobrious, fibbing shit. It's an outrage.' He laughed & said 'I hope you spoke to Mrs Thatcher in that tone.'

Rang James to tell him. Wrote to Stanley & Michael Anderson. Had supper of poached eggs & toast, and Rupert came down to run thro' the lines with me, tho' there are so very few he needn't have bothered. I groused on & on to Rupert about how much of an inconvenience it all is. It's disgraceful. Oh, I also wrote to Maggie to tell her, and to Andrew Ray and Peter Nichols.[115]

---

[113] Sir Nicholas Hytner (b. 1956), English theatre and film director; Associate Director of the National Theatre, 1990-7.
[114] English actor (1923-2003), went on to play Dr Pepys in the 1994 film version, *The Madness of King George*.
[115] English playwright (1927-2019), author of *A Day in the Death of Joe Egg* and *Privates on Parade*. A CSE comrade of KW.

Beyond Our Kenneth

Sunday, 24 November
Rang M. to cancel lunch. Walked to Regent's Park, as the Bakerloo will save a fortune in taxis. Straight to it on arrival. Most of my stuff is opposite Jeremy Child. 'Of course,' he said, 'you'll want to put your own twist on things, but Cyril was doing it *this* way…' I told him I couldn't give a rat's how Cyril was doing it. The impertinence, from a fellow actor, is jaw dropping. I told Harold Innocent[116] & he placated things by saying 'Oh, don't dwell on it, darling, I'm sure he was just offering up shortcuts in case you felt overwhelmed.' It is a generous analysis & I decided to adopt it… It has to be said, Nigel is very good. He spins dual plates all over the show – not just mad-sane ones, but public-private, cerebral-corporal, cæsar-farmer, even English-German. He keeps them turning so energetically that the minute he's strapped to the torture chair, even the staunchest republican couldn't help but be moved… Line run then technical run. During my bits I heard the laughs from the gods & Nick beamed at me afterwards.

Monday, 25 November
After the dress I sat on the terrace with Nigel & Trevor, and Julian Wadham, as it's *remarkably* clement. We had sandwiches sent over. Nigel is a bag of nerves!! Trevor feeds him sedatives as tho' they were breath mints. Not surprising, I suppose; it's the part of a lifetime & he knows it… Meredith rather overdid it with the make-up, what with the white powder & beauty spot, but as soon as Nick saw me he doubled up like a deckchair & shouted 'Yes!… Oh, yes!!', which settled any argument.

First preview. Not a bad crowd, for press types. Nigel triumphant; he really was quite superb. I went down very well, there's no point being coy. Alan came to the dressing room & squeezed my shoulder.

Got home at 11.30, quite ravenous. Looked in the fridge to find Flo had left a slice of quiche under clingfilm with a bit of lettuce & beetroot.

Tuesday, 26 November
No papers at tube so went to Cleveland Street. Once one gets past all the Freddie Mercury[117] stuff, the notices for us are marvellous!! Nigel takes most

---

[116] English actor (1933-93), worked regularly for the National Theatre and the Royal Shakespeare Company.
[117] British singer-songwriter (1946-91); he had died on 24 November from AIDS-related bronchial pneumonia.

of the acclamation, quite rightly, but I am mentioned in all of them. Maurice Tenby of *Today* writes 'Seeing and hearing Kenneth Williams work his larynx around the soggy scatological parlance of stool-obsessed Sir Lucas Pepys, rather than some lifeless Downing Street communiqué, is as welcome and comforting as a warm bath after two years of cold showers…' Much more of that & I'll be working my larynx 'round Maurice Tenby!

Went with Paul to the Monmouth for a coffee & eclair. We nattered about Maxwell & concurred that he's buggered. 'I'd have him work off the debt, rather than do time,' said Paul; 'Thirty years scrubbing public toilets sounds about right.' 'Or six months in *Eldorado*,' I said.

I'm riding the proverbial bike with this play. The self-discipline returns, the *technique* clicks into place, the unspoken contract between actor & audience is restored. It's incredible. Even though I'm nothing but a place-filler in borrowed togs, I feel like a paroled lag – finished with unfamiliar chores & the fatigue of frustration, back in the land of the living and, as Voltaire endorsed, cultivating my own bit of garden. My vocation, I suppose. It raises the morale no end.

Thursday, 28 November
Arrived at the theatre to find a bottle of champagne & a card in the dressing room, compliments of Cyril Shaps. It is a mightily kind gesture. No stamps, so 'phoned through a telemessage in reply… Everyone strangely jittery as the half approached!! Not me. I just went around telling dirty jokes to the wardrobe girls. James Villiers had a lovely limerick that he bellowed loudly during the warm-up:

> There's a tavern in Cavan that's staffed
> By a barmaid who's ace at her craft:
>   She serves out the liquors,
>   Then whips off her knickers,
> 'Cos you can't beat a nice cooling draft.

It allayed the nerves, & everyone joined in with their own rhymes until the atmosphere was quite changed & charged with excitement… When we were doing the 'purge' exchange, Harold did a Cissie & Ada-style bosom lift, & I very nearly lost the thread… I had to bite the inside of the cheeks *hard* in order to avoid the corpse. Years ago I'd've been furious at such unprofessionalism, especially on an opening night, but not now.

Saturday, 30 November
Bell went at 7.18. 'What do you want?' I said. 'Delivery, mate. Interflora.' I pressed the buzzer & told him to come up. Slipped off the pyjamas and greeted him at the door with the cock out & everything. Not a flinch!! 'Sorry it's early,' he said, 'I'm trying to get a shift on so I'm at Upton Park in time for kick-off...' It must be all these nasty magazines and late night Channel 4... the young are *unshockable*... The flowers were from Stanley. He's in Glasgow doing *Cinderella*. Kept the card & gave the chrysanths to Flo.

Sunday, 1 December
On the way to the station I passed Tesco's & found it open! On a Sunday!! I said to the girl 'It's scandalous really, but handy.' Got a box of All Gold for Richenda[118] 'cos she was utterly splendid yesterday... Show went well. Audience good. Markedly different to last night: much more attentive to dialogue rather than simply riding the waves of sentiment. Harold responded well to the more serious tone... we came across as pathetic & ambitious rather than knockabout & silly.

Thursday, 5 December
Paul knocked & we went to Oxford Street. The mild weather jars oddly with the tinsel & the giant Santas hanging from the lampposts like bloated Mussolinis. Feels as tho' we're gearing up for a colonial Christmas – turkey on the beach & all that. Went to Debenhams where I got a lovely wallet for godson Robert[119] & some leather gloves for Rupert. Outside M&S we ran into Julian Lloyd Webber, just back from playing in West Berlin. 'Things are tense,' he said. 'Three days I was there, and in that time *ten* people got shot crossing over...'[120] All the while we stood chatting he was messily devouring a Danish pastry. 'That looks tasty,' said Paul, 'where did you get it?', and Julian swung around & patted his arsecheek. I inferred this was a revamp of the 'wouldn't *you* like to know!' nose tap... but apparently it just means 'Asda'.

Monday, 9 December
As soon as the curtain went up it was clear we had a *talker* in the stalls: some oaf intent on providing a noisy running commentary to the proceedings.

---

[118] Richenda Carey (b. 1948), English actress; widow of actor Nigel Stock.

[119] Robert Chidell (b. 1975), KW's godson. Great nephew of the actor John Vere, the man who, KW said, 'taught me all I know about comedy'.

[120] Deaths of East German escapees increased from three in 1989 to 47 in 1991.

'Ooh look, it's Nigel!'… 'She's going to stab him!'… 'He's got the right 'ump now!'… it went on & on. Eventually the audience's tutting progressed to groans of indignation, which forced management to pluck him out.

Julian drove me home. I said 'That face you pull when he says "Married, Mr Pitt?" is sheer perfection. They mightn't catch it in the circle, but *I* can see it.' He went all shy! 'Gosh! Thanks ever so,' he said… Went in to Lou's & had the cream of mushroom. Wide awake so sat & watched *Tonight at the Comedy Store*. One has to feel for these alternative comedians. Now that Labour have got in, they don't know what to do with themselves. In fact, they begin to reminisce & repeat old material – which is precisely what they accused their predecessors of doing. As for the cutting-edge, *avant-garde*, boundary-pushers among them… well, I heard most of their filthy jokes in Singapore in '47.

Tuesday, 10 December
The catchphrases from last night's chatty loon have stuck. Whenever he enters the room we have peals of 'Ooh look, it's Nigel!'

Thursday, 12 December
Posted a card & the wallet to Robert for his birthday. Sixteen – it doesn't seem ten minutes since his christening. Walked thro' the park *en route* to the station. Already pitch black at 5.30. Acutely aware of footsteps behind me, so quickened the pace, heart rate soaring. Then, to add to the horror, the ghoulish voice: 'Don't tempt me… It's meant to be…' Finally reached the safety of York Bridge & stood under the streetlight to watch the would-be assailant pass… It was a sodding yuppy on his porta-phone thing: 'Yes, that's the one – get a bottle of Bolly off to him with my compliments would you, Yvonne?…' *Oeuf sur le visage.*

Show went OK. Bit slow, I thought, but I'm not in it enough to do much about that. Ken Branagh came backstage afterwards – much to the excitement of the youngsters. They acclaim him as the New Olivier, hanging on every word. He's spruce, I'll give him that… He pulled me aside & said 'What are you up to in February? I'm doing a spot of Chekhov with Johnny G, and we're looking for a Nikita. It's only a short. I think you'd enjoy it.' I was rather stumped! He said 'If I send a script, could you let me know by Christmas?' and I agreed. Harold smirked at me & winked.

Thursday, 19 December
Osteria Lariana at 12.30 for lunch with Simon Riley. He's writing the *authorised* book on the suicide bombing in Parliament. 'Call me Si,' he said. I didn't. Brought the diary along & read out the relevant passages, not that I was anywhere near when it happened. 'No matter,' he said, 'anything you've got just adds that little bit of *glamour*…'

Friday, 20 December
Up at 8 o'c. Did letters & went to post. Got papers from Bill & only *then* did I realise the date. Pang of shame. Went into her flat & talked to her. I was chatting away about *Madness* and larking about in the wings with Harold when I stopped mid-sentence… I saw, quite abruptly, right through the whole *façade*, through the deceptions of grief. I finally got the message, in bold & underlined. I was talking to the wrong person.

Pat arrived at 12.20 & I served the cottage pie. 'I suppose I ought to apologise,' I muttered. I know I should've said it better, but I find it so hard to muster more with her, even when the heart is willing. 'Am I forgiven then?' she said, timidly. 'There's nothing to forgive, you silly mare. Eat your trifle'… We spent an hour looking thro' the tortoiseshell photo album & laughing about old times. I poured us each a brandy & Pat gave a toast. I invited her to the matinée on Sunday & she accepted. 'I've got to go, Ken,' she said, 'a two-hour dinner break is pushing it, even for me.'

Saturday, 21 December
Nipped to Menzie's to get *Spectator*. They haven't edited down my stuff at all & it has to be said, it looks very smart. Secured ten copies, as I want to send it to chums abroad.

M. came at 12 o'c. & we drove to the Tent. I told him it'd just be me & Flo for Xmas. He said 'I'm surprised you're still having her do for you, when you've managed all this time.' I said 'Yes, well, it gives her something to do.' The truth is, of course, that I'm now accustomed to it: there once was a pride in doing it meself, but I've longsince swallowed that… Jeremy Beadle was there, and came over while we were waiting for coffee. He burbled on about this programme he's done where the public send in videotapes of domestic accidents they've captured on film. Sounds deplorable. 'Alas,' I said, 'I haven't got a TV set… but it sounds marvellous!'

Came back & read the shooting script of *Swan Song*. I was rather moved by it, which I wasn't expecting at all. Of course, *I* should be playing

Svetlovidov rather than the dresser part, but I can't see Gielgud submitting to a swop. 'Phoned Branagh at home to accept the invitation. He was out, so I left a message with the wife.[121] She said 'I remember you coming to the house when my father was directing you.'[122] Penny didn't drop at first – it had completely passed me by that KB was wed to Eric's daughter. I'd rather put *him* from my mind.

Wednesday, 25 December
Flo knocked & said 'Dinner at one, is alright?'... Just a small turkey crown, which was plenty for the two of us. I opened the Moulin-à-Vent & Flo served the pâté at 1.07. The entire meal was sumptuous, she simply surpassed herself. We talked about last Christmas, & Louie, and Flo's family back home... I've tried to explain in my own mind the *contentment* of sitting at a dead woman's dining table, eating shop-bought plum pudding in the company of a pockmarked factotum. On paper, as I write, I can *see* that it comes across as the ultimate failure, or at least an extreme case of making do. O! there's no point scrutinising. All I know is that when I gave her the perfume & she gave me the hankies, it seemed like the most natural thing in the world.

Rupert rang at 8 o'c. to thank me for the gloves. He's in Missenden & fed up. I listened for a bit, but cut him short because BBC2 were showing *The Clemency of Titus*,[123] & it was so good I didn't want to miss it.

Friday, 27 December
Richenda said 'It seems such a waste, getting you in for a cameo... What next? Michel Roux wheeling round the tea trolley?' She is a sweet girl. And in ordinary circumstances she'd be quite correct. But I'm happy as a sandboy – coming in for the chat, mincing on stage, & doing the crossword with Celestine. It's quite enough... At the stage door there was a boy from

---

[121] Emma Thompson (b. 1959), multiple award-wining actress and screenwriter; one of only twelve performers to have received nominations in two different Oscar categories in the same year.
[122] Eric Thompson (1929-82) had directed KW in *My Fat Friend* at the Globe Theatre in 1972; the association was a stormy one, and the rehearsal period was hampered by a persistent conflict between the two men.
[123] *La clemenza di Tito*, a 1791 opera by Mozart. BBC2's version, mounted at Glyndebourne, was directed by Nicholas Hytner and starred Philip Langridge as Tito Vespasian, Emperor of Rome.

Londonderry who wanted a picture with me. 'As soon as I heard you was doing this I saved up to come over, so I did.' Fine ecaf. Said he was staying at a boarding house in Spitalfields. Gave him £10 and instructed him to upgrade.

Tuesday, 31 December
Hard to believe that this volume has reached its end. The year seems to have flown by on restless wings... just *considering* the upheavals that have occurred along the way is withering. The three principal events – Louie dying, leaving Parliament & my return to the theatre – whilst not *unimaginable* twelve months ago, were certainly not imminent concerns. Yet I sit here today, in the unseasonable mildness of 1991's denouement, in an unseasonably mild mood: the winter of my life, whilst not without its hardships & its sorrows, is peculiarly benign. It is thanks to the total acceptance of Fate... the 'phone may ring with joyous news or bad. It's all one to me now.

1992

Friday, 3 January
A dark, drizzly day. Very me. After lunch I had the barclays *again*. It's the third day in a row that I've been overcome in such a fashion. Did the preamble where I was the injured Tommy, invalided out & under the strict ministration of a burly taskmaster. Audacious, what with the curtains being open... As I was leaving for the theatre, Rupert was coming in!! Seeing him after there's been a gap invariably stirs the ardour: that mad rush of yen, bashfulness & inferiority charging thro' the veins. So, of course, all this wanking makes perfect sense – and straight away the cloak of eroticism drops to reveal squalid impurity.

Sunday, 5 January
In make-up I read out the *Sunday Times* article about this Baylis[1] character & his windup wireless for Africa. 'I've just done the jingles for Capital FM,' interrupted Janet. 'Don't worry, dear,' said Iain, 'I doubt they can receive that in Bulawayo.' Alan got quite irate – 'It's *food* they want, not bloody gadgets. There's nothing appetising about radios.' 'Oh, I dunno,' chaffed Harold, 'they make first-rate crackling.' 'Oi!' said Joe, 'stop winding him up...' The ambience is one of constant, rolling, Weimarian jollity. It's not healthy, it's ill-disciplined and one can begin to *sense* the impending fall.

---

[1] Trevor Baylis (1937-2018), English inventor of the wind-up radio. He developed the device in response to the need for information about HIV and AIDS to be communicated to the African population.

Tuesday, 7 January
It seems ITV showed *Carry On Behind* on Sunday, so inevitably one receives a tidal wave of letters in its wake. In the post office a foreign woman in a yashmak butted in whilst I was buying the stamps: 'You was so funny on the telly. Where do you get your ideas from?' I said 'O! Nietzsche is the main influence, dear, as you can imagine… and – of course – Jane Asher.' Even with the veil in the way I could see she was wholly nonplussed.

After the show, Nick came & said 'Couple of notes, Ken, is that alright?' He was eminently tactful & discreet. As expected, he feels it's getting a bit stale and puerile. 'I quite realise,' he said (in muted tones), 'that it's because you haven't got enough to do. I'm only saying this to *you*, as the others all take their level from your performance…' It was the most amiable slap on the wrist I've ever had.

Friday, 10 January
Michael A. came backstage!! 'We only arrived Wednesday evening, but I just *had* to come & see you…' He went off to congratulate Nigel, & Enzo said to me 'We stayed away too long. There's a difference between recharging your batteries & sunbathing your life away.' No afternoon show on Sunday so I asked them to lunch.

Sunday, 12 January
M. came at 11.15 wearing a terrible taupe ulsterette. I told him he looked like a dreadful old flasher. 'Oh,' he said, 'I thought it was rather smart.' I could see he was put out, so I changed the subject… Arrived Poule au Pot at noon. Such pretension, I *loathe* the place. Michael & Enzo were there already; Barry & Giovanni came at 12.03. For someone declaring such a keenness to return to England, Michael did go on a bit about the poxy Gold Coast. Eventually Barry cut in with 'Well, if you start to miss it, there's always *Neighbours*… Did you *see* Derek Nimmo on the beach?! Made *All Gas & Gaiters* look like *Peer Gynt*…' The Château Talbot flowed liberally. As we were leaving Michael said 'I'll give you a ring in the week, alright? Just for a chat.' We're a pair of reluctant born-agains, wary of a return to pastures old, but inwardly giddy about it too… Still feeling the *vin de table* when M. dropped me at the National. Wonderful Richenda clocked the flushed cheeks & fetched me a coffee. 'Here you are, young man,' she said, 'just how you like it – hot, black and Colombian.' 'I'm saying *nothing*,' mumbled Harold.

Wednesday, 15 January
Kemp came into the dressing room & said that Shaps is on the mend & aims to return w/c Sunday 2 Feb. That'll suit me fine, as it's better to get out while it's still enjoyable, and when one might still be missed… Taxis to Villiers'[2] *pied-à-terre* in Pimlico after the show, with Julian, Harold, Alan, Celestine & Brian. James had only just handed round the brandies when Harold started wheezing. I was chatting to Tina, but she broke off & dived across the room – he'd gone purple & was clearly having trouble catching the breath. The noise was appalling, quite otherworldly. He was still struggling after a minute or two, so James 'phoned for the ambulance. The sweat was pouring off him; I was convinced it was curtains – but by the time the paramedics arrived, he'd rallied. Alan & Brian managed to get him over to the balcony & got some fresh air into him. The chaps took the blood pressure & it was thro' the roof, so they carted him off to Chelsea & Westminster with Tina in tow. We finished our drinks, but the mood was rather dampened, so I left at about 12.30.

Thursday, 16 January
I could actually *see* my breath in the bedroom when I woke. Had to have the two-bar fire on in the bathroom. It's at times such as this I think O! sod it – just *leave*, sell up & go to Tenerife, read books in the sunshine, write poetry & die sublimely… 'Phone rang at 10 o'c. & it was Tina. 'He's O.K.,' she said. 'The doctor had a good look and says he's very overweight & out of shape.' I had to laugh. 'It's that kind of expertise one only gets on the NHS,' I said. They've told him to take it easy for a week. It's alright tho', as Matthew knows the part & can deputise.

Friday, 17 January
Did letters & went to Marks's with Flo. Showed her the things to get as I can't abide the rubbish she brings back from Gateway… I'm all for thrift, & I know there's a recession on, but the pathetic chops we endured yesterday just made you want to weep.

Lunch at Lariana with Michael. He doesn't want to return to ICM, but is making a list of a few select clients that he could represent independently. I told him that Ford had handled the bits & pieces of *literary* stuff well enough in the interim, but with *Madness* and the Gingold thing coming up, it would

---

[2] James Villiers (1933–98), English character actor; great-grandson of the 4th Earl of Clarendon.

be preferable to have his guiding hand once more on the tiller. He said he'd contact the Spotlight & get records amended & so on.

About to leave for the theatre when Flo came in, tears rolling down the cheeks. The sister had just rung to say that their mother's at death's door & has been howling for Flo, so I had all that. Of course, she wants to go. It couldn't have come at a more inconvenient time, but I said 'Certainly you must go.' I tried to show concern, but it was a thin veil. Inwardly I was furious. O! I don't know. Maybe it's an opportunity to part ways. After all, if keeping one's dead mother's live-in carer on the payroll isn't an extravagance, I don't know what is.

Show wasn't good. Matthew ballsed up the lines & I was distracted, so it all went south. Managed to escape without having to sign autographs.

Saturday, 18 January
In the second post was a letter from a drag performer called Arsula Undress (real name Russell Morton) asking me to the opening of some club in Soho as *invité d'honneur*. I sent a copy of the book with a note of thanks – 'Alas, dear Arsula, I am yet bedridden with the gout – just punishment for a life-long dependance on pear drops, gin & guardsmen – so an appearance in person is out of the question. One in spirit, however, is guaranteed...'

Monday, 20 January
Dunthorpe helped Flo with the case. Put her in a cab at 8.30. I ought to have gone with her to the airport, but I've allowed myself to become too involved already. It's best kept at arm's length... Walked to Guild House[3] in the slush. The dippy girl didn't recognise me. After typing half of *War & Peace* into the computer she said 'So, it's Ken Williams – 501 Fairview Avenue, Ottawa?' Thought to myself 'If it's obscurity one wants, a stint on the back benches will do it.' Thankfully her superior saw me & leapt to the rescue – 'Alright Cherry, I'll deal with this...' Rejoining the union is more of a symbolic act than a necessity, especially as it's no longer a closed shop. I signed the form as one would a wedding certificate in a registry office – a formal commitment, but not an occasion worth dressing up for.

---

[3] Home of Equity, on Upper St Martin's Lane, WC2.

Tuesday, 21 January
Woke with dreadful headache. No paracetamol!! Went into Lou's & all I could find was half a packet of Fennings powders with the Timothy Whites[4] label still on – 1/7 or 8p. Decided not to risk it… Couldn't face cooking, so rang Paul & we lunched at the Snackateria next to Halfords. It's pleb, but people tend to keep away, and the leek & potato is very good… Paul said he knew Harold from when they did *Ruddigore*[5] at Sadler's Wells! So we bought satsumas & jumped on the 73 to pay a visit… He's fine, apart from being bored. Bijou gaff. Paintings of nude adolescents all round the walls. 'That's a Tuke,'[6] he said proudly, pointing at a picture of three bare-arsed youths sitting on a rock. 'Is it a copy?' asked Paul. 'You cheeky bitch!' snapped Harold. 'We don't use the *c*-word in this house, dear…'

Wednesday, 22 January
The mutation in style & quality from night to night is quite fantastic. Without thinking, I went on and did the whole thing in broad Edinburgh. Child was patently unimpressed, but it drew the laughs – and a pronounced cheer when I came on for the call. Afterwards, Tina said 'Brace up, Jean Brodie – we're going to Cribb's for last orders.' Got cab back to Marlborough instead. Intended to knock at Rupert's due to *no contact* whatsoever for more than a fortnight, but thought better of it. Went into Lou's & had roes on toast. After the late news it was *Confessions of a Driving Instructor*.[7] Egad, what unimaginable dross! Even in the darkest days of the *Carry On*s, we never lowered ourselves to such mind-boggling depths. One asks 'How did the nation which gave the world *Whisky Galore* and *The Ladykillers* slash its standards so dismally?', but quite quickly one pauses & replies 'Oh quite easily…'

Thursday, 23 January
Telephone rang at *four a.m.* It was Flo. She'd done the maths wrong & thought it was 8 o'c. in London. She apologised for getting me out of bed. At any rate, the mother is dead, but it won't be a long drawn out affair as they

---

[4] British chain of dispensing chemist shops, acquired by Boots in 1968.
[5] 1887 comic opera by Gilbert & Sullivan.
[6] Henry Scott Tuke (1858-1929), English artist, best known for his paintings of nude boys and young men.
[7] 1976 British sex-farce film, directed by Norman Cohen.

have to bury 'em in short order due to the heat. I tried to tell her not to rush back – after all, it's not as tho' she's really been *missed* – but it was a dreadful line which got ever more fuzzy, so in the finish I just gave up.

Monday, 27 January
At 11.30 walked to Broadcasting House for *Moral Maze*. Buerk in the chair, & the panel was me, the Bishop of Ely, Janet Daley & that Starkey.[8] Topic was about obligations to relatives, so I'd a lot to say. Oh! it was lovely to be in a studio, quarrelling with sage & serious people. Tearing arguments to shreds with aplomb and flair – I attest, there's nothing finer. At the end, the producer said I had been the best, and he was quite right.

Tuesday, 28 January
Can't decide what to do about this flat business. The options, after selling up, would be (a) a *house* in London, in as quiet a district as possible, yet within walking distance of civilisation; (b) a seaside *cottage*, in as non-touristy an area as is affordable; or (c) an *apartment* abroad, adjacent to an Anglophone community, but not overwhelmed by it… The townhouse is the safe option – but would I be lumbered with the status quo, just with more hoovering? Wrote to Druce to ask for latest property listings.

Stanley telephoned, home from the panto. 'I'm *drained*,' he said. 'That last fortnight is the killer: all the lucid folk have been & gone by Twelfth Night, so you're left playing to coach parties of the *wayward*…' Asked him to the last performance, but he & Moira are off to Cyprus on Friday, so he's coming tomorrow instead.

Friday, 31 January
Went to see James Ford at Wells Street. Told him of the rearrangements. 'Oh. I see,' he said, frowning. 'Did I do something wrong?' I had to conciliate like mad, 'No, of course not, you've been marvellous… but Michael is an old friend… I do owe it to him…' It was like letting down a tenacious suitor… Cab to Ian Wray, where we ran through figures. He said if flats went for 110, there'd be a property fund of about 285 thousand, if we closed the HICA account. That might *just* be sufficient to get something decent on the fringes

---

[8] Michael Buerk (b. 1946), BBC journalist and newsreader; Stephen Sykes (1939-2014), Bishop of Ely, 1990-2000; Janet Daley (b. 1944), American-born conservative journalist, columnist for *The Times*, 1990-6; David Starkey (b. 1945), historian.

of Bloomsbury, especially if the recession continues… Quickly home to change, then to BH for *Word of Mouth* with Frank Delaney.[9] I had to talk about my favourite *broadcastable* rude words. Settled on 'nadgers' as my first choice. I'd wanted 'berk', but as it's a clipping of *Berkeley Hunt*, it was turned down… In the midst of the silliness, one wonders if the Kenneth Williamses of Kampuchea or Upper Volta or Belorussia troll up to *their* local studios to chew the cud o'er such matters for the listening public? I s'pose they've other things to worry about, alackaday.

Saturday, 1 February
The stuff people send!! Packet of "poems" from a Letitia Brewer (Mrs) in the post. Says she is 'delighted we share a passion for the glorious Auden' & that she'd be pleased to share some of her own work with me, hoping I'll 'know the *right* hands in which to place them' – one is called *Oblongs*:

> Out it comes
> Beige – or so you'd think !
> I yearn for it and yawn for it
> (Am I right to do so ?)
> Lie back and think of Thisland and Thatland
> and all the wondrous oblongs.

Wrote 'Not at this address' on the envelope & shoved them back in the box.

Flowers & chocs in the dressing room. The performance was splendid… they know I love it pacy, so they all upped the *rhythm*, and it went down a treat. Lovely cheer during the curtain call! Afterwards we came on stage & Nigel adorned me with the prop Imperial State Crown for cast photos and Nick gave a little speech. Alan presented me with a miniature silver-plated po with 'For Kenneth · *Madness of George III* · Lyttelton Theatre 1991-92' engraved on the side. It is a wonderfully stylish & generous gesture. I came home & wept for the loveliness of it all.

Monday, 3 February
Haven't been eating much & the fasting has certainly worked – 9 stone *seven*, which is excellent. Had to dig out the charcoal corduroys as the slacks are

---

[9] Irish novelist, journalist and broadcaster (1942-2017).

too loose!! Went to Café Hélène as a reward & asked for a toasted cheese. 'We only do the *croque-monsieur*,' said the fat girl, 'gruyère and Jambon de Paris.' The attitude stank almost as much as the breath. 'No, I want a toasted cheddar sandwich.' It scowled with plain despite & said 'Well, you're bang out of luck, then.' The dregs one encounters nowadays fair fuddles the mind. Went to Baker's Oven instead. Stopped at Burton & got trousers – grey, 32".

Tuesday, 4 February
Flo back. Couldn't bring myself to do it. Had crumpets & cocoa alone and went to bed at 9.45.

Thursday, 6 February
M. came at noon & I gave him lunch at the refurbished Biagi. It's ghastly. One's left in no doubt of the circumspect mood of the country; every hint of delicacy has been junked in favour of utilitarian plainness. I mean, really – I can get *that* at home. It reminded me of a Sally Army canteen... Assurance from M. that decadence hasn't died altogether though – lovely story about a couple of ancient dowagers in the queue at Waitrose: 'I had Phipps take me to the food hall at Marks & Spencer on Friday.' 'Really? What's it like?' 'Oh, my dear – the lighting is *brutal*.'

Friday, 7 February
Loads of mail about the play. Jonathan Rowan-Lyons writes regarding the new headshots, and I am to go to Bermondsey on Tuesday to be photographed. Got papers from Adonis & saw Rupert as he was coming out. 'You've been avoiding me,' I said. He gave some excuse about not wanting to encroach. O it doesn't matter, I don't care. Told him to come for dinner with me & Paul this evening.

Tipping it down, but waded to Terrazza for 7 o'c. to meet Paul and Rupert. Posited this vague idea of Flo doing the cleaning for all three of us. Lukewarm response, but said they'd think on it. Lovely *zuppa inglese* to finish, but then they've always been the cat's whiskers when it comes to your actual continental puddings.

Monday, 10 February
Walked to Hampstead & gave Rona the Courvoisier as I'm not keen. She had the television on & we watched the white smoke billow from the Sistine chimney and the '*Habemus papam*' stuff. Peruvian, the new chap. More than

a dash of the Pinochets[10] about him. He's chosen for himself the moniker 'Pope Innocent', so he clearly has quite the sense of humour... Rona on good form. She gave me one of Gording's neckties.

Tuesday, 11 February
The blitheness of my current mood would once have been of grave concern – a Christian sense of guilt would've long since kicked in, engendering activity & toil. Something or other's made me see the light!! I left the breakfast things unwashed on Lou's draining board without the teensiest trace of remorse.

Tube to Bermondsey for this session at 11 o'c. Jonathan was professional, fast & winsome, so it was no trouble. I only felt sorry for the lamb, that he didn't have something more attractive at which to point his big lens.

Wednesday, 12 February
I've been using House of Commons headed paper to write to chums, as it tickles me, but I ran out this morning. 'Phoned Ethan – who now works for some poor sod called Stephen Milligan[11] – and he said he thinks there was one remaining lot of stationery & he'll send it on if he can find it... Right nostril was streaming all afternoon, clear mucus. Last thing I need now is a cold, so I squeezed Jif Lemon into boiling water & breathed in best I could, towel draped over me.

Monday, 17 February
Car to Acton for rehearsals.[12] Met by Gerry the runner & taken to a large room in what appears to be an abandoned sanatorium. Cracked plastic commodes line the corridor walls & dusty copies of *The People's Friend* are stacked all about... Gielgud was already there, Methuselaic, navigating a bowl of Alpen. 'Dear boy,' he said, gravelly, 'I knew this day would come...'

Vernal swagger aside, Branagh is good. Doesn't shy from gaiety – there's even a touch of campery – but focus doesn't wander. He *knows* the text & isn't afraid to debate it; I'd not expected such reciprocity, or preparedness.

---

[10] Augusto Pinochet (1915-2006), President of Chile, 1974-90. Detained in London in 1998 under an international arrest warrant in connection with numerous human rights violations.
[11] (1948-94) Tory MP for Eastleigh, 1991-4. Died accidentally from autoerotic asphyxiation.
[12] For *Swan Song*, short film of Anton Chekhov's 1887 play; adapted by Hugh Cruttwell, directed by Kenneth Branagh. Starring John Gielgud as the ageing actor Svetlovidov and KW as the prop-master Nikita.

If only one could say the same for Johnny G. All *over* the place. 'What was it again?...' 'Where am I standing?...' 'Oh, I am *tired*...' One tries to convey all in a glance to Ken (*i.e.* "Switch us over; *I'll* do it better!!"), but the boy is far too accommodating & sentimental about his nibs' past glories for that. By 1 o'c. we'd got the shape of it, tho' I suspect it's gone in one ear & out the other. Pappy, catered sarnies were wheeled in on tin trays. The old dear made a *beeline*... It was like watching a moth-eaten whippet gorge on Chappie. Quite undignified. Still, it might be an idea to keep a jar of beef paste handy from now on, as he was slightly more *engaged* having filled his face.

Tuesday, 18 February
O! I'm so *useless* with props. I can tell that this gas lamp & I aren't going to get on. If Celia says 'Hold it round the neck' once more, I'll be holding *her* round the neck... They've got me in a tatty workshirt and at one point Cruttwell said 'I'm not convinced about the duds, Kenny. We're a blade of straw away from "*'Ello, me dearios*"...' I've been told to neither shave nor visit the barber, so heaven knows what state I'll be in by the end... Sir John a tad more present today. Got a lot done. As an aside, Ken revealed it was *Harold* that recommended me for this!! Richard Briers had been earmarked, but when Harold mentioned my name KB said 'D'you think he'd be keen?' – It's the altruism of such an act that I find so overwhelming. When we were dismissed I got the driver to drop me at Eagle's & I asked if they had anything in the style of a Tuke (with a price-tag *not* in the style of a Tuke). He had a lovely Harold Knight preparatory charcoal sketch of a boy for £475. It's a madly O.T.T. gift, but I know it'll be appreciated. Wrote a card & asked them to deliver it, which was a refined flourish to boot.

Wednesday, 19 February
It's a curious thing, preparing for a film in the manner one would a play. KB keeps saying 'Smaller' or 'Less, please' to rein in the theatrical instincts. You feel you're *fighting* against the Chekhovian will, but they all seem suited. John just trying to keep up. I was rather good. Final day in World of Commodes, thank goodness.

Flo dilemma finally resolved. Charring & shopping for me, plus any impromptu extras. It means she can do her two days' volunteering at Our Lady of the Assumption with her little goitred chum, and one day at the hospice.

Thursday, 20 February
Typically, the fancy heating system they've just spent an arm & a leg installing at the Criterion is up the spout, so conditions are *arctic*. Gerry proffered the tinfoil blanket, but I declined. 'I don't suit the refugee look, darling.' No such qualms from JG. He sits there enveloped, like a spent marathon runner – or an oven-ready duck... I concede, however, that I underestimated him. All that groundwork *somehow* seeped in. In the event it was rather slick! The laughs were there, but I never felt I needed them as a crutch to get thro'. Against all odds, I believe we actually squeezed a constructive amount of *truth* from each other... It's as if someone's changed his batteries. At lunch he talked exhaustively about understudying Coward in *Vortex* in '25, and the perfectness of Marlon Brando's arse.

Saturday, 22 February
Sat by one of the portable heaters and did the word ladder with Harriet, the clapper loader, whilst they set up... Reflected, as I watched them, on this peculiar experience – playing the foil for a beknighted myth of the theatre, in a short film that no sod will ever see, skippered by an adept & voguish dish, *all* to reverberate the dolorous musings of a *fin-de-siècle* Slav. One wonders what old Mr Miles[13] would've said... 'I still think lithography is right for your future, Williams...'

Somehow managed to escape unnoticed. Full tilt to Nick for a trim and spruce, then to Rules at 8 o'c. where M., Rupert & Paul were waiting... M. ordered Pol Roger '88 & they all sang 'Happy Birthday to you'. Got quite pissed & ended up on the next table telling a couple of startled newlyweds that the secret to a successful marriage is spending as little time together as possible, and they both smiled obligingly.

Sunday, 23 February
The sun finally made an appearance, so when Rupert came we walked to Speakers' Corner to listen to the rants. Religious lunacy predominant, of course, but one fellow was very good on Maastricht & European unification. A sudorific little woman in a moss-green pinafore dress was having none of it. 'I don't want no Wops here!', 'You can't trust the Greeks,' & more in that

---

[13] KW's boss at the drawing office of George Philip & Son Ltd. in Acton in 1948; evidently Mr Miles attempted to dissuade KW from his planned change of career, that of draughtsman to actor.

monotonous vein. Eventually the chap had had enough of the interruption & when she squawked 'What've *I* got in common with a German?', he said 'Well, there's your moustache for starters, sweetheart,' and everybody cheered.

Monday, 24 February
Ken Branagh telephoned & thanked me for doing *Swan Song*. He said 'I'm going to the opera on Friday with Jacobi & Blessed, would you like to come along?' and I said yes.

Friday, 28 February
As I reached the corner of Conway Street & Warren Street, a beige Cortina ploughed straight into the side of a Radio Rentals van at full force. A woman coming out of Evans's screamed & dropped her bottle of Lucozade... The carman leapt out & was hopping mad & ready for fisticuffs, but when he saw the state of the driver he went white as a sheet and ran into the shop. We bystanders stood tight; a lad in dungarees peered through the windscreen as he crossed the road toward us – 'Nah,' he muttered, 'he's a goner.' Police and ambulance were there in three minutes, but it was plain on their faces that nothing could be done. A woman with no teeth asked me to sign her copy of *Bella*. Hardly an appropriate moment. 'Not now, dear,' I said, & it hobbled away.

Dressed as dapperly as I could manage & met Ken, Brian & Derek at the Opera House. We were in a box, if you please, for *Tales of Hoffmann*.[14] Interminable. Giulietta was sharp, the Bellinis were flat, and my bum was numb. I'd've much sooner just sat in a pub with these absorbing men – we four have far more interesting things to say than anything Offenbach can muster.

Saturday, 29 February
Awoke to a note under the door: '6.15 A.M. – Gone to Missenden. Grandma passed away in night, will call later. R'... Rang M. & he said he'd take me. Arrived Cambridge at 2 o'c. & met the society president, Miss Balding. Turns out she's a direct descendant of Cromwell! I said 'It must be unnerving, trying to study with your ancestor's skull buried in the wall.' 'It *is* a bit spooky!' she affirmed, 'And mildly ironic, as my unofficial title is Head Girl'... It was a very relaxed affair, with Clare asking questions & soliciting more from the ample congregation. A few anti-Thatcher attacks, of course,

---

[14] *Les contes d'Hoffmann*, an *opéra fantastique* by German-born French composer Jacques Offenbach (1819-80).

but mostly good-humoured chat. One boy asked 'How do you think your life would've been different if you'd attended university?' Nearly caught me out, but I managed to fudge an answer about the war intervening & how *that* was my schooling. Drinks afterwards in the union bar. One dreary don gabbled on endlessly about the Russian threat until I interjected, 'May I compliment your wife's knockers? For a woman of her age, I mean – they're simply delectable. Were they dear?' That stumped him. When we came away, M. said 'How you haven't copped a fourpenny one, I'll never know.' Home by six. Rupert 'phoned at 8.15. They think it was a stroke. It's bad luck, really, as the old girl would've turned a hundred in May.

Monday, 2 March
Letter from Peter Rogers asking me to play Don Juan Diego in *Carry On Columbus*. Give me strength… He says Jim Dale has signed & will perform the title role!! He must be fed up with doing twice nightly on Broadway. That, or they've offered *megabucks*… I could burst into tears for poor Peter: on the cusp of eighty & still peddling this insipid junk. One wonders how much humiliation the man can sustain. I rang Ken, Joan, Bernie & Barbara, and we all agreed to *decline*. Enduring the last one cleared all outstanding debts – we can turn this down without any semblance of guilt.

Tuesday, 3 March
Got paper from Cleveland Street. Turns out the man who got killed in the Cortina was a part-time harlequin with Piccolo Mori's circus… 'On the back seat of the car, police found Mr Applegate's sixteen inch long clown shoes alongside a novelty water-squirting carnation, thought to be a family heirloom…'

Thursday, 5 March
The three smallest toes on the right foot have become desensitised. It'll be the loafers. I don't know what possessed me. Tried rubbing the foot to stimulate the nerves, & then bathing with Epsom salt, but it's had no effect.

Car to TV Centre for this sitcom thing.[15] What a cordial bunch!! Belinda sweet & welcoming and Gary Olsen terribly funny: quite manic, but exuding such warmth. And the youngsters – oodles of talent & acumen. The casting director should be lauded for assembling such a coterie. The script is

---

[15] *2point4 Children*, BBC sitcom (1991-9) by Andrew Marshall, starring Belinda Lang and Gary Olsen; KW as Mr Podd.

bromidic, and my bit thin, but they fleshed it out handsomely. The director, Richard, handed me an advance copy of Alan Clark's diaries as I was leaving. 'Here,' he said, 'have a read of that. See if it tallies with yours…'

Friday, 6 March
Ahead of the News, Kinnock came on for the address.[16] They'd done their utmost to tidy him up, but the man could make a Huntsman tweed look like a plumber's overall. He banged on about the Soviet threat, with all the gravitas of Zebedee, & then they played the all-new nuclear attack alarm sound. Put me in mind of *Rhapsody in Blue*. Perhaps that's the idea, to lull citizens into a jazzy mood so that missiles can rain down unheeded.

Saturday, 7 March
Cecil Franks 'phoned!! He said 'Rumblings are getting louder.' There's talk of Euro unification *and* currency votes before summer, perhaps even referenda. It's madness. That sort of thing could split the country. 'Surely they won't ask the *people* to decide?' I said. 'You'd think not!' he laughed, 'But rumour has it that Kinnockio's in favour. After all, if it goes tits up, they can blame the public.'

Sunday, 8 March
As we were having the coffee, June Whitfield & Tim walked in! She came & gave me a kiss. I said '*You're* not doing this *Carry On*, are you?' & she coyly said 'I'm afraid I am. But I only said yes because I thought all of you would be in it… Frankie & I are to play Ferdinand & Isabella.' The poor woman.

Went up for drinks at Rupert's at 6 o'c. Told him my life was essentially meaningless, as I don't have the ability to share. 'But you *do* share your life,' he said. 'What about Louie, and all your friends?' He was deliberately misunderstanding me. I said 'I'm a lost cause. Even for *you*, I'm unable to go for broke. It's all too late.' He paused & said 'The problem with you is that you won't allow yourself to love yourself. You'll never let anyone in until you've crossed that bridge.' Told him I shan't be coming to the funeral, & that I'd prefer it if we didn't see each other for a while. Came in to Lou's & watched *May to December*.[17]

---

[16] In a simulcast on every British television and radio channel, the Prime Minister explained the government's plans in relation to threats of aggression from the USSR. The six-tone nuclear alarm, codenamed Unity, was 'composed' by Andrew Lloyd-Webber.

[17] BBC sitcom about a widowed solicitor and his younger lover (1989-94), by Paul Mendelson, starring Anton Rodgers.

Tuesday, 10 March
'Carry On Without Us!' on page 7 of *Today*. Someone at Pinewood trying to irk us into submission, I'll wager. A whole page based on Kenny Connor's prudent quote that he'd prefer to be remembered as a star of the films than a bit-player. I wrote a peacekeeping letter to Peter wishing him & Gerald luck with the film, thanking them for adventures past, but reasserting that – for my part – those days are *done*.

Walked to St Anne's Court where Michael is set up. Gillian is on the desk! He's poached her from Conway's!! She's a blonde now, & about twenty pounds lighter… Michael v. buoyant. 'Perhaps we should all go off and be MPs for a year if this is the result,' he said. I am to meet Simon Langton on Monday, and then some other chap on Tuesday to discuss *Poirot*. Oh, & apparently Peter Hall[18] has requested a word; Michael thinks he might want me as his Malvolio… It'll all come to nothing, of course, and I'm not fussed either way. But it beats doing *Through the Keyhole*, or sitting through a committee meeting. The three toes on the right foot are still numb. Would that they'd come back to life.

Wednesday, 11 March
Louie's iron has finally given out! I purchased it at *Marshall & Snelgrove*,[19] so it doesn't owe us much. Chose a replacement from the catalogue & sent Flo out to fetch it. Within the hour she was back, empty-handed. Turns out the silly ass had gone to Index instead of Argos. If you want something done, *et cetera*.

Walked through the park for Dilys Laye's birthday party at Oslo Court. O, what a lift to see some of those faces!! Anita Harris, Victor Maddern, Pat Coombs – a cavalcade of geniality. Marsden leant across the sole Véronique with 'So, the prodigal son's returned, then?' I laughed & said 'Ah, it's only transitory, Betty: I'm up for Chief Rabbi next week.' Put away quite a lot of Chateau Beauregard, but Gertan & Gwendolyn[20] drove me home so it was alright.

---

[18] Acclaimed English theatre director (1930-2017), founder of the Royal Shakespeare Company and Director of the National Theatre (1973-88).
[19] Oxford Street department store, closed in 1972.
[20] Gertan Klauber (1932-2008), Czechoslovak-born character actor and his wife, actress Gwendolyn Watts (1937-2000).

Friday, 13 March
Invitations galore! Speaking engagements, mostly. Albany Trust, London Gay Movement, Humanist Association... Rang James & asked him to accept on my behalf. He was delighted just to be involved. I told him to reject the *Hysteria* concert,[21] however, as I think I'd be out of my depth with that crowd. He said 'It's not only your Ben Eltons and Ruby Waxes... Clement Freud did it last time.' I said 'You're not making the case you think you're making.'

Sunday, 15 March
M. drove us to the Paris Theatre for *Just a Minute*. Parsons in a wheelchair after shattering the shin disembarking from the Aylesbury train. It was me, Merton, Freud and Maureen Lipman. Masterly waffling from Paul, who got through the entire 60 seconds on "Who is buried under Platform 10 at Waterloo Station?" without faltering... he plucked the names Dag Hammarskjöld, Lillian Gish & Jelly Roll Morton[22] straight out of the air, quite brilliantly... Ironside was hemmed in at the end, surrounded by gluey consolations. I just walked out. Maureen berated me on the stairs for not doing the film. 'I was depending on you being there... *Why* did I say "yes" to it? I must be losing the plot...'

Monday, 16 March
What a day to get the pruritus ani! Typical. Washed everything twice & daubed with the hydrocortisone. Put some on a cotton wool pad and left it up there.

Tube to Putney to meet Simon Langton & Sue Birtwistle. There's an adaptation of *Pride & Prejudice* in the works. Auntie is stalling and ITV is ready to pounce.[23] 'I think you could pull off a superb Mr Bennet,' said Simon. Madam expressly less keen. I asked if they'd decided on a Mrs Bennet. '*Nothing* is decided yet,' she said, flatly. I was conscious throughout of my constant wriggling thanks to the bum, & in the end it just petered out. Waste of time... If he was so eager to have me, he might've worked on her a bit before having me schlep all that way.

---

[21] *Hysteria 4*, the fourth in a series of comedy benefits for the Terrence Higgins Trust, produced by Stephen Fry.
[22] Dag Hammarskjöld (1905-61), U.N. Secretary-General, 1953-61; Lillian Gish (1893-1993), American silent film actress; Jelly Roll Morton (1890-1941), American jazz pianist and bandleader.
[23] The six-episode drama was eventually produced by the BBC in 1995, with Benjamin Whitrow as Mr Bennet.

Tuesday, 17 March
Set out early & walked to Waterloo to buy tickets for tomorrow. Returned via Floral Street to meet this Fleming.[24] Dour sort of fellow, clearly half cut at half past ten in the morning, and the office *rancid*. He offered me three parts, and I'm to choose the one I find the most appealing. On the face of it, the Austrian doctor in *Death on the Nile* would be a lark – especially with Elaine Stritch having been pencilled – but I doubt the abdomen could cope with 3 weeks on an Egyptian barge. *Lord Edgware Dies* would be safer, especially as he kicks the bucket before the first ad break.

Wednesday, 18 March
Shepperton for British Gas. Lots of floating round a drawing room set, twisting radiator knobs. I had to glare into the camera, click the fingers & say 'Don't you just *love* being in control?'… He had me do it ten or eleven times. 'Could you say it as if you're really *hesitant*?', 'Could you put the emphasis on the *you*?' Finicky little poof. Clearly thought he was directing *Ben-Hur*.

Thursday, 19 March
Irena Sedlecká[25] came to take photographs for this bust – a *commission*, no less. Mousy little woman with a bright red nose. She was meticulous yet swift. I slid out the portrait from behind the wardrobe & said 'This is a Noakes'. 'Yes,' she replied, 'Pretty frame…' Thereupon she showed me the polaroids – I looked elderly, lank & miserable. 'It is a beautiful face, isn't it?' I said. A protracted pause. 'It's memorable,' came the hollow Silesian retort. I laughed.

The television was dominated by the York separation.[26] Fergie's Texan, it turns out, has more to offer than a Prince of the Realm… Poor Queen. It's plain bad luck to be lumbered with such ludicrous offspring.

Tuesday, 24 March
Ford rang. Asked if I'd go to TV Centre on Saturday to make a film for children about how radio programmes are made. I said yes, but made it clear

---

[24] Desmond Fleming (b. 1949), director of episodes of various ITV dramas including *Agatha Christie's Poirot* (1989-2013).
[25] Czechoslovakian sculptress (1928-2020), Fellow of the Royal British Society of Sculptors. Other commissioned head sculptures by Sedlecká include those of Laurence Olivier, Bobby Charlton, Richard Briers and Paul Eddington.
[26] The Duke and Duchess of York announced their separation after the latter's friendship with Texas multimillionaire Steve Wyatt gained press attention.

that things of this sort should now go through Michael, otherwise it gets messy.

Went next door to Regency House for the meeting. Saxby chaired it, after a fashion. The predictable dubiety from the fretters. 'On the telly Kate Adie[27] says shelters don't work...' 'I read you're safer staying put, as long as you hang tinfoil in the windows...' Skinflints. The *pots* of cash most of 'em have got, but they'd willingly melt into the carpet before loosening the pursestrings. Eventually we voted to get a quote for enlarging the basements.

Friday, 27 March
Howling winds all day, rattling the windows & stirring up a baleful gloom. Street empty. The hum of traffic isn't much of a companion, but take it away & one starts to feel even more detached than usual... Trapped indoors, so titivated the notes for the Gay Movement speech. It's the familiar tightrope – namely the blend of candour, vigour & humour, and the squirrelling of vulgar gags in the back pocket in case of emergency.

Found the lino in the lift was filthy, so got the Flash & went over it. It's still not perfect, but it's better than it was. Saw the Antipodean pair come in. I'm no Columbo, but if that's not a black eye then I'm a Dutchman. Expect he's been knocking her about.

Saturday, 28 March
I know it's easy to say it after the event, but I smelt something fishy from the start... First off was the girl who collected me from reception with the extravagant hiccoughs: I *knew* I'd seen her before – in the lift I kept looking, but it just wouldn't come to me. Then there was Rosemarie Ford[28] avoiding eye contact & the "producer" with sweaty palms; it all seemed a tad *off*. By the time we were in the studio with this man in a big pink costume,[29] I was certain it was a fix, but couldn't put the finger on it. When the electrics exploded & this arsehole character fell thro' the set, all doubt was gone, but I played along. The eventual appearance of Noel Edmonds as the man in the suit was somewhat of an anticlimax, but I think I pulled faces befitting the

---

[27] English journalist (b. 1948), Chief News Correspondent for BBC News, 1989-2003; celebrated for reporting from war zones and trouble spots.
[28] English dancer, singer and TV personality (b. 1962), Bruce Forsyth's 'Girl Friday' on *The Generation Game*, 1990-4.
[29] The infamous Mr Blobby.

occasion. Turns out the girl in the lift used to sit two machines along from Ivy Tilsley at Baldwin's Casuals.

Telephoned Ford. Told him he is a total shit for placing me in such a situation, and that our association is over… I gave the 'Gotcha' statuette to Flo, who was over the moon.

Sunday, 29 March
I glanced over the '86 diary. Blimey O'Riley! Talk about bleak!! *That* was the year my position wholly changed from companion to carer… and what with my own ailments… it's a wonder I got through it. Reminded of a droll encounter with Joan Rivers, so I dusted off an aerogramme & wrote her a long letter before turning in.

Monday, 30 March
Old Mr. Zubarev was holding open the door when I went down. Police had been called by the little round woman from No. 19, after screams were heard coming from the Australians' place. He's been carted off & she's gone to a shelter for battered wives. Heaven knows who we'll get next. That flat has always attracted the batty.

M. drove us to Le Bon Goût on Dean Street as Joe Allen's have put up the prices. It was teeming, mostly with bohemian types nursing flagons of Chablis & half a lettuce leaf. We sat at the marble bar like a couple of bookends waiting to be served. After a quarter of an hour we gave up & went to Lariana instead.

Arrived at the American Church at 7 o'c. Felt as if we were at the annual conference of Lewis Leathers, a fœtor of cowhide & Brut hanging in the air. The chairman introduced me to a sea of neatly groomed moustaches & mannerly applause. I launched into an historical resumé of prominent poofs. They were receptive, but *boy* – talk about fixated!! Their condition takes priority over every other aspect of their identity… they can't entertain the fact that their behaviour is repulsive to many people who don't want to think about it. Questions at the end, & one butch sort asked if my portrayal of Sandy *reinforced* a stereotype of limpwristedness. Bristling, I grandly replied 'My interpretation was in the great English tradition of caricature, and there's plenty of evidence that those characters were adored by the public, neutralising any "anti" feeling…' I ought to have assumed my seat then. But I went on… 'What's more, gentlemen, talking of caricature, it can't be ignored that all of you *pose* as masculine – but, without exception, you are dressed in cultish fashion. How caricaturistic can one be? To dress in the fashions of the type one would wish to go to bed with couldn't be *more* subjective.' A hundred shocked faces. They genuinely hadn't considered that they are a *type*. On a hushed high, I concluded: 'Go home, dears. Arrange the flowers.' I'll not be asked back, but it was what they needed to hear. On the way out to the car, M. said 'You're a braver man than me... Some of 'em looked about ready to lynch you...'

Tuesday, 31 March
As we walked to the Post Office, Paul & I took it in turns to shout aloud all the slang words for the male organ we could think of. Plenty of startled looks from passers-by. We summoned 28... his favourite was *tallywhacker* & mine was *fun-truncheon*.

In the afternoon I walked to the Guinea to meet Peter Hall where he offered me the part of Malvolio in his production of *Twelfth Night* and I accepted.

Friday, 3 April
Car to Trident for the *Timewatch* voiceover. Met the producer, Roy, who was well disposed towards me. 'I had to fight for you, but they came round eventually.' I'm seldom the *unanimous* choice... The script is all about Richard Lionheart being a homosexual, and purported new evidence to support that claim. Seemed pretty specious to me. I must've read out the word 'sodomite' forty times. The temptation to throw in the occasional 'Ooh, mar dear!' was acute, but I resisted.

Saturday, 4 April
To St. John's Wood with Goldsmiths Oliver at 11 o'c. His new beau is a "conceptual" painter, with a piece on show at the Saatchi... Never seen such a load of rubbish in all my born days. *Young British Artists*, they call it. Young Piss Artists, more like. They stood around in soiled denims, the long hair chaotic & greasy, knocking back gallons of champagne and spouting pretentious drivel. Awestruck twerps gawped in wonder at the dead shark suspended in a tank of Sarson's.[30] I think it's vacuous trash. After half an hour I told Oliver I'd had enough & left... Met with a *monsoon* coming out

---

[30] *The Physical Impossibility of Death in the Mind of Someone Living* (1991) by Damien Hirst, a tiger shark preserved in formaldehyde and displayed in a glass case.

of the tube! Tykes from the second floor flat hung out the window chi-iking blissfully as they watched me, soaked & struggling with the key.

Tuesday, 7 April
Glanced at the appointment book, assuming it'd be clear, but saw with horror that I've got to go to Wandsworth for this tedious "celebrity" quiz.[31] It's the final vestige of the Ford affiliation, but I'm loath to cancel, even tho' I'll hate every second.

Astonished to find that not only was Gyles doing it, but Lionel Blair *and* Matthew Kelly as well!! along with others I've met, which was a great relief. They showed us a civilian episode, so as to establish the format, & then it was straight into the studio. We were behind our flashing lecterns in an arc around Bill Stewart, who fired preposterous questions at us. Mine concerned rugby union and New Kids on the Block, so I was in the soup from the off. 'It's a conspiracy!' I shouted, & it got the laughs, but I did feel a mite irked. Gyles & Rory McGrath[32] made no bones about wanting to win. I recognise the competitive streak, but as this lark was *manifestly* not my province, I joined the other dunces in sending it up. The main benefit of failure, of course, is getting bumped off early & consequently one sits in the green room drinking coffee & chatting while the swots continue with the game. Jim Bowen[33] told me about a woman contestant on *Bullseye*, who had that syndrome where foul language is bellowed involuntarily & without warning. Every time a dart hit the board, the head would fly back & she'd scream 'Bollocks!' at 90 decibels, which rather distorted the filming. As Jim said, 'Folk don't want bollocks of a Sunday teatime'… Eventually it was over, Brandreth victorious. The producer mentioned that a portion of our waived fees is promised to a bird sanctuary in Ebbw Vale, to which I remonstrated most sharply.

Wednesday, 8 April
I was lazy & jumped on the bus and, of course, paid the price. A loquacious misfit boarded at All Souls & immediately spotted me. It sidled right up,

---

[31] *Celebrity Fifteen to One*.
[32] English comedian and writer (b. 1956), regular panellist on the BBC1 sports quiz *They Think It's All Over*, 1995-2006.
[33] English stand-up comedian (1937-2018), one of the original line-up of ITV's *The Comedians* (1971-93), and presenter of the darts game show *Bullseye*, 1981-95.

reeking of chip fat, and vented phlegmy nonsense at me until I could stand it no longer. Fled at Piccadilly & walked the rest of the way. Lunch at Le Ruisseau with Anderson. Overpriced muck. Michael had a stinking cold and the sneezing was endless. I should've stopped at home and had a fucking ham sandwich.

Saturday, 11 April
They showed the grainy video of Vstavlyat's weapons testing. With the sound off, one would presume it was documentary footage of '50s Nevada. There was an interview with Charlton Heston,[34] who looks certain to get the Republican nomination. The Yanks will love him because they know him, he's still a looker, he appears tough and because he *isn't* Dukakis. But if he's the answer, someone's asking the wrong questions.

Thursday, 16 April
Michael has managed to get me out of the *Noel's House Party* bind. Said he'd sue the arse off them if they dared to broadcast a second of it, as it hadn't been approved. In point of fact it *had*, by the Ford fool, but it sounds as tho' we've got away with it.

When I was undressing I saw that the cobblers are drooping lower & lower. They'll need their own hammock at this rate. And the skin on the shins is so pale it's almost *blue*. I imagine the orderly, indifferently sponging me down in the morgue, pausing at the shanks to reflect 'That colour would look nice in our box room…'

Sunday, 19 April
Parsons still milking this sodding leg. 'We soldier on,' he said, lapping up the sympathy. The guest was Stephen Fry. He's filming with Branagh up at Wrotham Park and said 'Ken often regales us with tidbits from life on set with you & Sir John.' I looked blank & said 'He must have a fertile imagination. I just recall being freezing cold & bored shitless.' I fear I was irritable throughout the show.

---

[34] American Oscar-winning actor and politician (1923-2008), star of many classic Hollywood movies including the epics *El Cid* and *The Greatest Story Ever Told*; latterly President of the United States, 1993-7.

Monday, 20 April
I had an unusually long soak, using the Radox, but inevitably one emerges sagging like a Basset hound. The 'phone went and it was Goldstone.[35] 'Kenneth, I've just had a call to say that Frankie Howerd is dead.' Apparently the heart gave out yesterday morning. 'Of course, we're all devastated this end,' he said flimsily, 'but he was due to start shooting at Pinewood on Friday... I know it's horribly short notice, and I *know* you made your feelings clear to Peter, but – would you reconsider?' Starting to think I'm only called upon when cripples & corpses require a backup. Said I'd ponder it & let him know by lunchtime... Telephoned Michael to discuss. He suggested agreeing, with the proviso that I'd do *three* days only, *they* would cover transport, with the remuneration of fifteen thousand. 'They can only say no,' he laughed. I left him to deal with it... He rang back at 2 o'c. to tell me they'd acquiesced!! Couldn't get thro' to Bresslaw, so I gave Joan Sims a bell to own up to my breaking of the pact. She was wailing about Frankie so I had to listen to that... On the News, after all the Howerd stuff, they announced that Benny Hill has pegged it too! Doubtless the offer to replace *him* will be winging its way.

Wednesday, 22 April
Went to St Anne's Court & read the script of the *Carry On*. 'I've seen his testimonials...' It's customarily dreadful, but there's a lovely bunch of people involved, so I shall treat it as a three-day stroll up memory lane. Besides, I'll be wearing a crown, which has been an abiding aspiration.

Thursday, 23 April
Wardrobe girl on the line from Pinewood. 'Could you let us know your measurements? The feeling is we'll have to take Mr Howerd's tunic in a few inches to fit you.' Indeed. I should think so too. Went down to Flo & she put the tape round me. I was surprised to see her blush at the sight of me stripped to the waist... you'd think a naked torso would be meat & drink to a Filipina.

Friday, 24 April
There was a small but perceptible flurry when I came on set, which swelled to a clunky meet & greet type affair. Curiouser, the vanguard was made up

---

[35] John Goldstone (b. 1943), English film producer; credits include *The Rocky Horror Picture Show* (1975) and the Monty Python films.

of the *alternative* comics that have been cast – Rik Mayall[36] said 'Now we *know* we're in the right place!'... Perhaps it's not the domain in which one would've wished to be vital, but beggars can't be choosers. The Clary boy[37] was very practical in getting me out of the ruckus. He took my arm & whispered 'Thank God you're here! We've been lined up like boys & girls at a school disco – veterans on one side, newcomers on the other & never the twain shall meet.' June & I went in for the fitting. It's a gorgeous velvet robe with faux stoat, purple cap under the diadem & jewels everywhere. If nothing else, the stills will look nice... Jim Dale came into the dressing room. O he's aged! But still vigorous & madly attractive. We did the throne room scene. The tone *around* the set is one of excited merriment, yet the minute the cameras roll, the air is sucked out and it's death. If anything, we're not parodying the story of Columbus – we're parodying the filming of a *Carry On* film. Gerald rather standoffish with me, I thought, but he was the only one: the alternative types couldn't've been nicer, which I hadn't expected.

Monday, 27 April
They were ages setting up, so I swanned around chatting. Cribbins & I did the 'Ooh, Doctor' sketch (with Jim his son & the Philadelphia girl[38] doing the blowing-off noises) for the group. I think Alexei[39] pulled something; he was *crimson* with relish... Bedroom scene with the nightcap and candle. Had to do ten takes as the lighting kept going wrong. Various suits from the production company creeping about, rubbing chins, butting in with 'Are we *sure* about that shot, Gerald?' and other disquieting interjections... Chatted to Julian in the dressing room. Of course, they'll bill him as my successor, but he is far freer than I could ever wish to be, and revels in his queueness. I regaled him with stories about Sir Hugh's promiscuities. He fell about at my

---

[36] English alternative comedian (1958-2014), famous for his anarchic appearances in sitcom hits such as *The Young Ones*, *Bottom*, *Blackadder* and *The New Statesman*. Appeared as the Sultan of Turkey in *Carry On Columbus*.

[37] Julian Clary (b. 1959), English comedian and novelist, known for his outrageous and flamboyant costumes and make-up.

[38] Sara Crowe (b. 1966), Scottish actress; began her career as a ditzy blonde in commercials for Philadelphia cream cheese.

[39] Alexei Sayle (b. 1952), English actor and comedian, a leading figure in the alternative comedy movement; known for his angry, cynical persona, a clamorous style of delivery and a political awareness in his act.

Lamont impression!! which was a victory, as it's not easy to garner laughs when Norman is the subject matter.

With Paul to see *My Own Private Idaho*.[40] Essentially *Henry the Fifth* on Benzedrine. Headache-making. On the walk home, we fell into step with a man with a parrot on each shoulder. Excrement all down the jumper. 'This is Joey and Chloe. We're just out for the evening constitutional… It's Chloe's birthday on Wednesday… The big four-oh, she won't mind me telling you…'

Tuesday, 28 April
Met Harrison Ford at lunch. He said 'I saw you in *King George*. You were real funny,' in the timbre a doctor might adopt when diagnosing something terminal… We did the gold & slaves scene, then the promotional shots, then I was released. Spoke to Jack Douglas while I waited for the driver to appear. 'It's an insult to the original films,' he snarled. He forgets that he said the same thing after the last two. Julian was very sweet & waved me off with a hanky, as tho' we were on the quayside at Harwich.

Thursday, 30 April
Letter from Mags in Belgium, which she describes as 'very much the *Belgium* of countries.' Says she's doing *The Secret Garden* in August & the Polish directress wants *me* for the gardener part. 'I said I'd ask you, but that she shouldn't hold her breath…'

Friday, 1 May
Walked with Paul to Selfridges where he wanted tablecloths. We bumped into the Blewitts!![41] Two sticks apiece now, but unfathomably still upright. 'Stocking up on goodies, ladies?' asked Paul. 'That's right, dear,' said the scraggier one, 'We're having relations this evening.' 'Ooh, that'll be *lovely*,' I said, nudging Paul.

Saturday, 2 May
Did letters and got papers. There's a nagging sense of disjointedness – or at least an upset hissing in the background. It's always there & I know what it is. It's *him*. It's pathetic to be derailed thus, brooding vainly as a lovelorn boy, but it won't be shaken. I tried the crossword but I just sat & wept,

---

[40] 1991 American adventure drama film, directed by Gus Van Sant, starring River Phoenix and Keanu Reeves. A gay cult classic, very loosely based on Shakespeare history plays.

[41] Elderly spinster sisters who occupied a first-floor flat at Marlborough House.

glaring out the window. With God and Louisa gone, the chasm is no longer negligible. I had thought the spate of work would suitably fill the void, but it hasn't. Perhaps it *is* the Almighty, telling me He told me so.

I telephoned Mark.[42] He listened to my garbled fears. Eventually he said 'I think that ultimately you believe that *reality* is trustworthy and worth sticking by. You may not know what the point of all this is, but trusting that there is a point is enough to sustain you.' He read Sonnet 19[43] to me.

Sunday, 3 May
M. came at 10 o'c. and drove us to Romsey for Frost's[44] party. We pulled into a filling station behind a vanload of rugby players. The one at the pump spotted me & cried 'Well bugger me! It's Kenny Williams!' & they all cheered. I played up to it shamelessly ('Ooh, what a lovely big nozzle you've got!'), before signing Little Chef napkins for them.

Arrived Michelmersh at 12.30. Ludicrously ostentatious & immoderate, precisely what one would expect from Sir David. 'Belovèd boy!' he blurted, pink gins on a salver appearing on cue... An eclectic crowd of worthies. M. fell on his feet, as the choirmaster of Chichester was there, along with one of Prince Charles's equerries, evidently an old sparring partner... The Merchant-Ivory boys[45] accosted me, just as I was negotiating an asparagus tartlet. 'We'll be filming the Ishiguro novel soon,' the American one disclosed, 'all over the south-west. Your name has come up...' They bestowed the news like kindly benefactors, presumably expecting me to gush. 'How thoughtful,' I said rigidly, 'you must telephone my agent.' Naturally, I was thrilled, but I wasn't having *them* knowing that... Oliver Reed was sitting in a deckchair alone in the corner, eating a whole bacon quiche with his hands. I got lumbered with the Catholic bishop of Arundel, banging on about some 'moral' point or other. I told him about the brawny rugby lads & their *bulging* arm muscles. That soon shut him up... Saw Mellor from afar, but managed to give it the swerve & prized M. away from his chums. We were indoors by 5.30.

---

[42] Mark Oakley (b. 1968), Church of England priest and writer; engaged in sporadic conversations with KW on the topics of religion and poetry.

[43] Holy Sonnet XIX, by English poet John Donne (c.1572-1631).

[44] Sir David Frost (1939-2013), English television host, journalist, comedian and writer.

[45] Ismail Merchant (1936-2005), Indian film producer; James Ivory (b. 1928), American film director and screenwriter.

Wednesday, 6 May

Flo has altered all my trousers to a 32, and she's done a splendid job – dare I say, *better* than Tony Philips. All the money I could've saved, doesn't bear thinking about. As a reward I rang Hamish to see if he had any tickets going cheap. 'I've got a pair for *Moby Dick* you can have gratis – but I hope you've got a strong constitution.' I took them, but also heeded the warning & told Flo to invite her deformed friend to go with her in my stead. I spent the evening composing a verse.

> If I should pause to think of him -
> If I should dare to seek -
> Imagining him here to stay,
>
> And drifting, ever infinite,
> Upon a silver creek
> Along the shore of better days,
>
> I'd see the sunken galley there
> In soft abounding mist;
> I'd hear the taunting voices yet,
>
> The gleaming water, by the sun
> Of ever-evening kiss'd…
> And find my eager eyes were wet.
>
> Regrets. KCW.

Thursday, 7 May

9.22 to Manchester Piccadilly. Met Gordon Burns[46] in First Class & talked about his programme. I told him of my experiences on the assault course at Carlisle & he said 'Well, I'll happily send you an application form for the next series if you're keen.' I pointed out he'd been spotted by a pigeon & he blew up furiously: 'Bloody things!' Incommensurate, I thought. I was itching to say 'It's the Crapped-on Factor,' but I held it in… Cab to New Broadcasting House for *That's Showbusiness*. It was me & Carolgees with Gloria,[47] and the other team was Everett, Kathy Tayler & a fruit in skirts

---

[46] Northern Irish journalist and broadcaster (b. 1942), presenter of ITV's mental and physical game show *The Krypton Factor*.
[47] Bob Carolgees (b. 1948), English comedy entertainer, and Gloria Hunniford (b. 1940), Northern Irish television and radio presenter.

called Lily Savage.[48] They had quite a job in governing Kenny & the drag act, who were at each other like cats. It came close to overshadowing the proceedings, but I saved blushes by getting up & singing *Hawkin' Me Greens* and that diffused the malignity. Afterwards, the queen introduced himself as Paul & he said 'We've spoke before, on the 'phone, when you were trying to get home help for your mother…' Turns out he used to work at Camden Council!! He said 'The only thing that stopped me channelling Guy Fawkes and sticking a bomb under Parliament was the thought of you sitting in there…' He's actually rather a sweetheart & I was quite taken with him.

Friday, 8 May
I had a tin of soup at 5.45 & washed the things. I'll never be able to explain it, but as I replaced the plastic on the hob, I *knew* he would knock. The three raps came & I opened the door. It's as tho' the moment had been built towards, that we'd been leading up to it. He came in, pushed the door to (not shut) and – without a word – embraced me, his huge arms tightly clasped around. He held me there for a lingering beat, kissed my cheek and left. It was simply perfect & one of the most romantic moments of my life. I went and finished the drying-up.

Sunday, 10 May
We were reduced to watching Thora Hird on *Praise Be!*… If Henry VIII had foreseen this, he'd have stuck with Aragon & left the Church well alone.

Monday, 11 May
Leather Lane for *Twelfth Night* rehearsals. Martin Jarvis[49] leapt from his chair & shouted with joy 'Kenny's here! Kenny's here!' and everybody cheered. It's dumbfounding that my entry should elicit such fanfare. Perhaps they know something I don't. Martin was equally brilliant in deftly introducing the people I'd not met – 'Of course you know Silas, our Valentine,' & so on. Funny to see the Philadelphia girl again so soon. In the interim she's *married* Jim Dale's boy, so they've not let the grass grow… Right away Peter had us seated in a circle & I thought 'Oh Christ, it's going to be endless sitting about *theorising*,' but not a bit of it: we went straight into run-throughs, pausing only for queries. Landen a bit shaky on lines, but everyone else is

---

[48] Stage persona of English comedian and drag artist Paul O'Grady (1955-2023).
[49] English actor (b. 1941), particularly noted for his mellifluous vocal tone.

off-book, as it should be. Such a relief to see that the homework has been *done*. David Ryall's Feste is already robust & well-formed & is likely to be the stand-out.

Tuesday, 12 May
I felt unnatural doing it whilst seated, so I instinctively got up & moved into the middle. PH gave a slight nod & so some of the others joined. Ciaran & Peter moved in a couple of flats and taped an outline to the floor, so gradually we had a space to work with. There's a beautiful assumption from on high that people understand what they're saying, and – staggeringly – for the most part, they seem to.

Rupert called for me at 7 o'c. & we hailed a cab to Durrant's. He toasted 'To us… whatever that *is*.' I said 'It can't have a title, because it won't stay the same. I'm not like the rest & I won't change my ways, not now.' He looked into the flickering candle & said 'I don't care about any of that. I'm well aware that you'll be avuncular on Monday, affectionate on Wednesday and a surly wanker on Friday. But so long as I know you're there…' I felt the hairs on the neck go up. 'Then you're a fool,' I replied, ''cos I'm leaving all my money to the cats' home.' I diverted the topic elsewhere, but we'd both made our points. He looked so perfect in the candlelight – so horribly, mockingly perfect. Every smile is a dagger, affirming that I should've been bolder at 33, because at 66 it's simply not the same. Like an out-of-date chocolate bar – the flavour's still there, albeit weakened… but instead of sweet satisfaction, it's liable to give you bellyache. I thought of Erich in those remote days, recommending that I find an older man that could look after me – I've done it arse backwards, as usual.

Thursday, 14 May
They were bogged down in technicalities & exhaustive deliberation, so I sat at the back with the boy Benson[50] and we told stories. I *thought* we were comporting ourselves with the utmost discretion, until PH hurled his script to the floor & roared 'Will Kenneth Williams *please* stop yacking about "wide-open orifices"? We can hear every word!…'

---

[50] David Benson (b. 1962), English actor. Aged 13, he won a story-writing competition for the *Jackanory* programme, which was eventually performed by KW. In 1996, his one-man show *Think No Evil of Us: My Life with Kenneth Williams* won the *Scotsman*'s Fringe First award at the Edinburgh Festival.

Beyond Our Kenneth

Saturday, 16 May
Flo 'phoned at 8.45 – 'Come in here, now!' she squealed. Shot down there & was greeted by a scene from *Sink the Bismarck*: the ancient twin-tub industrially spewing out grey water, the carpet sodden and the foaming torrent creeping towards the door. I managed to switch it off & found the stopcock, but the mess is *biblical*. Didn't know what else to do, so rang the plumber, but all he could say was 'Yeah, your machine's knackered.' Thank you, Niels Bohr... The bell went, but it was more anti-EEC doorsteppers. 'Never mind Europe,' I said, 'we've got a sopping Axminster in here.'

Wednesday, 20 May
Martin is my favourite. He never lets the ball drop, and he puts *effort* into Aguecheek's dimwittedness, rather than just shamming idiocy. Benson is good too; he makes the most of the 2nd Officer. When we came back from lunch, PH had us playing hide-and-seek & when people were found they were given a prize from a velvet bag. I won an aniseed Black Jack and a blue pencil sharpener. It's all too barmy for words. Sara had a go at me for calling her Phil (short for Philadelphia cheese). Phil it shall remain.

Walked to Devonshire Close where the girl from Druce's was waiting to show me the mews house. It is beyond idyllic, compact and *quiet*. It's on for 350, but it's been hanging around since March & apparently the owners are quite keen to go. I said I'd think about it. It *is* lovely. 1770, and solid as a rock.

Thursday, 21 May
Up at 7 o'c. & went to vote *yes* on both counts. Walked to rehearsals & we worked until noon. Landen mouthing off about the referenda & the 'bloody sausage-suckers,' &c. Very demoralising... PH called lunch, but took me aside. 'You know what I want from you, don't you?' he said, zealously. 'I want Princess Angelica, I want the Dauphin, I want James Bailey.[51] I want you and your father in the hairdressers' shop. I want every scrap of puritanical, fun-spoiling, jealous, snobbish pomposity that's ever clung to your ribs... because we're not playing here. If you give me the Kenneth Williams act I'll be down on you like a ton of bricks...' The cleverness of it (aside from the well-informed grasp of one's life & career) is its unexpectedness. I'm

---

[51] Characters played by KW during his lifetime – Princess Angelica (from Thackeray's *The Rose and the Ring*) at Manchester Street School in 1935, the Dauphin (from Shaw's *Saint Joan*) in 1954, and James Bailey (in *Carry On Sergeant*) in 1958.

annoyed at myself for not spotting it a mile off. The games and sweets were a device to soften us up, & now we're getting thwacked between the eyes. It's unorthodox, but the thrill of the attack was almost *sexual*, & now all I wish to do is please this wonderful man. Oh how easily one can be manipulated! Like a child I've been converted with a short, sharp shock & off I run to joyfully follow orders.

Friday, 22 May
Went to get papers from Bill and we discussed the results. Curious that the affirmative for the currency won by a larger margin than for the Union[52]... but I suppose people found the idea of relinquishing the pound slightly less of a wrench than the idea of a load of *forriners* coming & going as they please. Have to say, I'm delighted – old Vlad will be furious, which is at once satisfying & worrying... Landen predictably curmudgeonly, with talk of "traitors" & similar tripe. I said 'Oh do shut up you stupid old fool,' though in point of fact, I think he's younger than me. Rehearsed all afternoon. Peter stood at the lectern, beating out the meter of the text. He's determined that the younger actors don't pull apart the verses & the *rhythm*, as they seem wont to do, but that they speak it as the bard intended.

Sunday, 24 May
M. came & drove us to Barry & Giovanni. The meal consisted of toast with a load of chopped tomatoes & a few forlorn herbs shoved on top. 'I just thought we'd have something light,' said Barry. Well, he wasn't kidding... Giovanni perturbed about Europe. 'The last-a thing we want is all them a-comin' in.' I mean, it's a bit rich; he's practically fresh off the boat himself. Eventually they got out the projector screen & showed us stuff from their trip to Toronto, but I could only take so much & gave M. the signal. When we came out I said 'My stomach thinks my throat's been cut,' so we went to Manze's.

Tuesday, 26 May
PH has clearly told them to ignore me, so that *I* feel ostracised as much as the character. It's a corny trick, but effective. Diane brought fairy cakes, and didn't offer me one. *Très bolde!* One starts to feel an outcast &, consequently, I was rather good. It's a dangerous game, as he harps on about the concord

---

[52] For adopting the Euromark currency: Yes 57%, No 43%; for joining the Union of European Nations: Yes 51%, No 49%.

& harmony of a company being paramount, but I expect he's determined that bringing down an august personality like mine is worth the risk for the general good of the play. Cakes looked rotten in any case.

Wednesday, 27 May
I said to Martin 'The trouble with these youngsters is that they've no *economy* with the text… *I* get it out as quickly as I can.' He said 'Well you mind it doesn't get caught in anything.'

Friday, 29 May
That awful Garnett crept up. 'Just a tiny point, Ken… you're saying "My lady bade me" (as in *had me*), whereas I think "My lady bade me" (as in *made me*) is more elegant…' *This*, from someone that not three days ago was banging on about the "nucular" threat we face. I informed him of modern reflexes of Old English words, and how vowels changed in the first person singular of the past tense, and that this informed pronunciation in the Middle Ages so *biddan* & *bæd* became *bid* & *bad*, and that the vagaries of spelling didn't affect this at all, and that if he accosts me with any more inane, erroneous twaddle in future, I shall pull him up on *his* shortcomings in front of the entire cast in order to demean & crush, only this time with legitimate examples. He's the weakest link of this lot by a country mile, & I won't put up with such temerity. "More elegant"!! That's a joke! The man makes *Steptoe* look genteel. Martin tried to smooth things over, but it's a grudge I am resolved to hold on to.

Saturday, 30 May
Took M. & Rupert to the mews house. Both had some valid ideas about what could be done with the yard area. 'It's the sort of place you've often talked of,' said M., which made up my mind. Caroline said she'd personally sold the back flat, No. 20, at Marlborough (Mrs Pratt's place) in March, which went in 72 hours & realised 112,250. She advised listing 7 & 8 for 125 apiece. Even with only 8 years left on the lease, she said they'll be 'snapped up'… Rupert drove me to Wray, who advised offering 315, with an expectation they'll accept 330-ish. It'll mean selling the Universal Energy shares & closing HICA, but that's no real torment.

Came home & deliberated. It's mad upheaval, but the fact is if I don't do it now I never will. And I'm rather keen. It's white, peaceful, manageable & charming. Bit like me.

1992

Monday, 1 June
Caroline telephoned to tell me that the offer of £332,000 for No. 1 Devonshire Close has been accepted. For surely there is an end; and thine expectation shall not be cut off.

Thursday, 4 June
Photographer came to take pictures of the flats. He must've been thirty, but was wearing one of those caps with a big peak that children wear. 'I see you've already started clearing out,' he said. I've not touched a thing... Rehearsed until 7. Rushed back & Flo made me an omelette. Car came at 8.35 & took me to the Conference Centre for *Question Time*. It was myself, Robin Cook, Teddy Taylor, Charles Kennedy, Uffe something (Danish foreign minister) & some dizzy creature from CND.[53] Surprised to hear Sissons doing tongue twisters in the wings. I said to Charles, 'She must think she's on at the Palladium...' Quite a number of old duffers in the audience, lamenting the loss of our "millennium of sovereignty". I challenged one frenzied blimp directly, and said 'I expect you'd sooner die in agony, clutching a Union Jack to your chest, than work in concert with your fellow man to expunge tyranny?' In the end, of course, our side left the anti lot in the dust. Afterwards, the Uffe number said 'My cousin stayed at your house when he was working in bacon.' I laughed it off, assuming it was Viking humour, but I came back to look it up & he is right!! 24.2.52 – Søren Welling... I put him up overnight at 57, much to Charlie & Lou's disgruntlement. Extraordinary coincidence!

Monday, 8 June
The designer came in to show us the costumes and to do the parade. I'm taken with my austere blacks – severe & rigid – and the contrast with the garden stuff is colossal: The tights are outrageous lemon, with a dozen bows tacked on. I asked O'Brien 'Is the ruff mine too?' & Ryall piped up with 'Here we go! Kenny's after another bit of rough.' 'How *dare* you?!' I said, 'I'm chaste as ice, I am...' 'Of course you are,' he simpered, 'I suppose the chap that's been dropping you off is a nephew.'

---

[53] Robin Cook (1946-2005), Labour MP for Livingston, 1983-2005 and Defence Secretary, 1991-9; Teddy Taylor (1937-2017), Tory MP for Southend East, 1980-2005, staunch Eurosceptic; Charles Kennedy (1959-2015), Liberal Democrat MP for Ross, Cromarty & Skye, 1983-2015; Uffe Ellemann-Jensen (1941-2022), Danish Minister of Foreign Affairs, 1982-93; Janet Bloomfield (1953-2007), National Vice-Chair of the Campaign for Nuclear Disarmament, 1991-3.

Tuesday, 9 June
When I got back Flo told me there'd been three viewings. She said 'Two Indian men were here for half hour, knocking on everything & taking numbers,' by which she meant measurements. Caroline called & they want a return visit on Thursday, and have asked me to be present.

Saw the News. Maxwell trial stuff. The pressure is plainly getting to him; he looks drawn & desperate. Lost a lot of weight, tho'. Wore the latex glove for the wank & was pleased with the result. I shall have to stock up.

Wednesday, 10 June
To dinner at Peter & Thelma Nichols'. Quilley[54] told us about the Dowager Countess of Mesborough on her visit to the physician: 'May I enquire, ma'am, as to whether you've ever had chlamydia?' 'Good gracious, no! I detest *all* shellfish'... After the meal, Brian Glover[55] stumbled over the sheepskin & spilt his Viognier right across it. 'Don't worry!' parped Wendy, shooting across the room, 'I'll save it!' & before anyone could stop her, she flung her glass of Shiraz on top. In a pissed stupor she'd got the old wives' tale arse-about-face, and the result is an altogether buggered rug. I glanced at Thelma. If looks could kill.

Thursday, 11 June
Rushed back from Leather Lane to meet this pair. Messrs. Chakrabarti, brothers from Patna, via Enfield. I was expecting questions about life in the block – noise levels, what the neighbours are like, & so on – but all I got was 'Could you sign a picture for our auntie?' I said 'If you offer the asking price, I'll take her for tiffin.' They laughed gingerly.

Last run-through before moving to the theatre. PH suggested we try it at double the speed which, naturally, got my vote. The indulgent youngsters can't help themselves, putting the brakes on during their bits, but everyone agreed that the accelerated rendition was thrilling to play. Two hours with an interval, that's all people want... Went to fetch my brolly from the dressing room & walked in on Cardy sitting on the lav with the door wide open, parking his lunch. 'Don't mind me,' he said, totally unperturbed.

---

[54] Denis Quilley (1927-2003), English actor and singer.
[55] English character actor (1934-97), notable for his gruff yet likeable roles. Had previously been a professional wrestler.

Friday, 12 June
The Chakrabartis have only gone & bid the full amount!! Caroline says there are other people who want to view this weekend, which could lead to higher offers, but I told her I just wanted it done. She said she'd make the arrangements & start the ball rolling… I just pray it all goes smoothly. Rupert came down with a bottle & we cautiously toasted the venture.

Tuesday, 16 June
First day at the Playhouse. One of the boys painting the set came to me & said 'My sincere condolences. I'm sure it's very hard.' I stared quizzically & he said 'Your mate Frankie… it must be a crushing blow.' He rubbed my arm familiarly and said 'It'll be alright, give it time.' He crumpled his lips to a sober smile & walked off.

Wednesday, 17 June
Diane said 'I know we've all been played like fiddles on this, with the silly game of ignoring you & what not, but I just want to tell you how brilliant I think you are. I can't wait for people to see you in action.' I was stunned. The entire set-up of this production has been to treat each other offstage in the same manner we do on, so one doesn't *see* Diane or Martin or Silas, but Maria, Sir Andrew & Valentine… This one heartfelt comment jarred so markedly with the prevailing pattern that it rang out in my thoughts for the rest of the day.

Friday, 19 June
Couldn't do much in the morning due to Diane's mysterious absence. Benson told me, confidentially, that it was due to the agonies of a suddenly inflamed vulva. When she did eventually appear, there was a definite limp – though the official line is that it's a bruised thigh thanks to overdoing the yoga… Returned to find Flo had been busy. Nearly everything in Lou's flat crated neatly & categorised. She handed me a yellowed polythene bag, containing Teddy!! I couldn't believe it. Quite a pang to think that Lou had kept him all these years, at the back of the wardrobe. Rang Pat to see if she wanted to go thro' anything, but she just said 'Nah, chuck it.' I sent Flo down to Oxfam with the shoes & clothes. I just want to get *out* now: the sight of her place empty is thoroughly depressing.

Saturday, 20 June
On washing, found a rash all up the cock & across the crotch. Retribution for scoffing at madam's ailing quim, I shouldn't wonder. Took me ages to realise that it must be the gloves. Penny-pinching will be the culprit, settling for the cheap ones in lieu of the Marigold. I slathered the region with Savlon. I use so much of the stuff I ought to get it delivered with the milk.

Rehearsed in the afternoon. It is *aching* for an audience; everyone (with the possible exception of Landen) is on the edge of treading water now.

Monday, 22 June
They brought in the musicians for the first time. Helen Keller must've had a hand in the arranging. We were better off with the cassette… PH apoplectic during the run. He shouted at Landen from the gods: 'For crying out loud! Upstage! You're meant to be *upstage*. Wake up, for Christ's sake.' It's last-minute nerves, but it's the first time the composure has cracked. Cesario's ginger beard is out, to everyone's relief. The poor girl looks like Willie Rushton[56] with it on… That painter condoled me *again*: 'How are you bearing up?…' I told him to sod off.

Wednesday, 24 June
More form-filling. Bus to the bank, then Ian Wray for photocopying. Passport, land registry, leases, gas certificates, it just goes on and on. Then to Druce. 'As soon as I get the green light from their end, I'll be in touch & we can get you your keys.'

Huge bunch of peonies from Mags in the dressing room. She must've forgotten I can't stand them. A beautiful note from Miguel, and – bizarrely – a carton of Kendal mint cake courtesy of Joss Ackland ('for energy')… PH wandered about, talking gently to everyone individually, as is his wont. He placed his hand on my shoulder & said 'It's all been for this.' A chilly, arcane comment, yet oddly rousing.

There's no point beating about the bush. It was a triumph. It was as though we were performing a *new* play. The laughs were raucous & authentic: far from the pompous titterings of the "cultivated" one would typically expect. Ryall was good, Martin was good, and so was I.

---

[56] Bearded English actor, cartoonist and comedian (1937-96), co-founder of *Private Eye*.

1992

Thursday, 25 June
Tony Sher[57] came into the dressing room! 'Well, that's it then,' he said, 'they can call off the search; we've finally found the definitive Malv.' He was exuberant in his praise. And rather tactile in it too… PH practically ignored me, until as we were leaving, he said 'I don't want to hear a mouse fart during the dungeon scene, got it?' I murmured to Benson, 'These inspirational edicts are getting a bit fucking cryptic for me.' Loads of fans & hangers-on at the stage door, and I breezed past them airily.

Sunday, 28 June
Got papers from Adonis, who was shirtless, the braces hanging on bare shoulders. Smashing. Purchased a copy of each & heaved them home. There's the anticipated toadyism, but that's because PH can do no wrong. One or two good notices for me. *Mirror* less impressed, but it's a bit rich of them to criticise *anything*, if you ask me. O! at the final analysis it's all nonsense. Except for *Observer* and *Telegraph*. And *Independent*, surprisingly – their man does communicate *some* passion, as opposed to the customary derisive crap.

Pasted in:

The Independent

"…But the element destined to sell tickets is surely the appearance of Kenneth Williams as Malvolio. The name jumps off the poster, filling one instantly with rapture and trepidation — the casting makes perfect sense in theory, yet as the curtain goes up (Ooh, matron), the ineludible fear is that we're destined to be treated to a live-action adaptation of Carry on Henry… We need not have feared. The tales of Williams' star turns on the London stage in the early sixties have been oft-repeated (to the extent that their validity comes into question), but this remarkable interpretation of the Bard's pompous, vain retainer expels any such doubt. Whilst the infamous cross-gartering scene is handled with foreseeable comic aplomb, it is Williams' treatment of the quieter, more reflective episodes that are the most enthralling. The audience is left perplexed: why has this actor spent three decades in the cinematic (and, latterly, the political) gutter, when seemingly effortless displays like this are part of his toolkit?…"

---

[57] Anthony Sher (1949-2021), South African-born British actor, best known for his work at the RSC.

The Sunday Telegraph

"…It's no exaggeration to declare that Malvolio is the role Kenneth Williams has been waiting forty years to perform. In hindsight, the overwhelming thought is 'Of course! The part was practically written for him!', and you're left feeling as foolish as, presumably, do casting directors citywide. This is not the vulgar, camp jaunt that might be expected – it is a cleverly framed examination of arrogance, that eventually tips over the edge, from exasperating farce into despairing ignominy…"

The Observer

"…From top to bottom, these familiar characters are handled with the clarity required whenever Twelfth Night is taken on, but the success story here is the reliance on the text and the company's assumption that the audience don't require spoon-feeding. Instead of coddling, the actors busy themselves in their own realities. This admittedly results in fewer outbursts of chortling at the confusing silliness of the plot, but the pay-off is more bitten bottom lips of empathy for these individuals. This is exemplified by Kenneth Williams, as the authoritarian steward Malvolio, who arguably delivers, to our great relief, the most complete and satisfying performance of his stage career…"

Monday, 29 June
'Oh look, it's Fleet Street Fred!' said Landen. The man is an arsehole.

Thursday, 2 July
Move to Devonshire Close. Flo & I put the boxes in the lift & Rupert brought round the car. He put the back seats down so there was room, even for the armchair on the third trip. 'Lou's sofa is never going to fit,' he said. I've half a mind to leave it in No. 7 & buy a new suite. The thing's caked in old lady detritus in any case… At 2 o'c. Paul came down & we gathered in Louisa's bare flat. I gave each of them a souvenir: the gold & ruby brooch to Flo, the Staffordshire milkmaid to Paul, the blue paperweight to Rupert. We walked round to Devonshire where M. was waiting. I gave him the Whitefriars vase & Flo handed round beakers of Asti. Getting this all done & dusted in a month must be some kind of record… Walked to Sound, Inc. at 3.30 for the Lockets lozenge voiceover. Three lines, half an hour, nine hundred pounds. It's lunacy. Came back to find Flo struggling with the cooker. I could smell the gas – she'd been trying to light the hob with matches. Could've blown up the street. I opened the windows, left it for five minutes, then showed her how to work it… Playhouse at 6.45. Silas in & out with the squits. I sent the

DSM to the chemist at Charing X to get Loperamide. Forced a few down the boy & he *just* about got through.

First night in the new bedroom. Stiflingly hot so I couldn't get off. Came downstairs & sat in the kitchen. Got out the cuttings & reread them. Such things should probably be meaningless this late in the day, but so seldom have I been taken seriously in this life, one just likes to double check that they really did write those things.

Saturday, 4 July
We put up the bedroom curtains. At 10 o'c. the Habitat lorry arrived with the settee & it is OK. Doesn't really matter as I shan't be sitting on it. Plugged in the TV. Still unsure about keeping it. Jiggled the aerial & watched the News. The unrest in Kiev being subdued with predictable ferocity. They showed old Vlad inspecting a collective farm, shaking hands with terrified, grinning wretches, the groaning tables laden with shining veg, quite clearly made of wood. One wonders if the Kremlin truly believes that this kind of rubbish fools anyone… Show went well, apart from just after yellow tights, when instead of 'And laid mine honour too unchary on't,' Philadelphia said, with cut-glass diction, 'And laid my honour to *an 'airy cunt…*' Miles's jaw hit the floor, Phil went scarlet & the crowd gasped. Somehow they struggled to the end, but Phil raced off, mortified.

Sunday, 5 July
We went to the Regal. The food was alright, but the awful couple on the next table kept interrupting. I said 'I've come for a quiet meal with my friend, we don't want to be bothered.' The bloke, who was grossly overweight & clammy, said 'Yes, I'd heard that you were an ass in real life.' I paid their bill on the way out.

Monday, 6 July
It will take time to get used to the size of the rooms, especially the bedroom. I'm hardly rattling around, but a life of compact quarters isn't easily shaken off. Rupert came after work to paint the kitchen. 'You're adamant on having white in here as well?' he said.

I *warned* Blanche that the elastic in the left stocking was going, but she hasn't mended it. As a result, it kept slipping down & I was forced to frequently yank it up. In the event it got the laughs as an extra bit of business, but it was more by luck than judgement. The most celebrated garment in the

Shakespearean canon, and she's more interested in nipping out for rollups & rabbiting on about the time she dressed Gina Lollobrigida. Cow-cunted bitch.

Friday, 10 July
Delightful letter from a man in Scarborough, who relates a story of Thomas Posthumous Hoby, a godly MP of that town, that might've been the inspiration for Malvolio. I confess, it was new to me – & compelling – but I still prefer the Wm Knollys[58] theory… As we haven't been provided for, I hauled one of Louie's electric fans to the theatre so that we don't all drop dead of heat exhaustion in the dressing room. Diane said 'You didn't think that *we* might be hot too?' The gall of the woman is stunning. O! the tedium of clones!

Saturday, 11 July
On returning from getting papers, I met the couple from No. 2. 'Sorry it's taken this long,' said the man, 'we only got back from Barbados last night.' Smartish pair, fifty-odd – Jasper and Estelle (give me strength!)… He's high up in Tie Rack & she designs wallpaper. 'Just wait till the boys hear about this!' she said, 'You couldn't go five seconds in our house without an Evil Edna[59] impression when they were little…'

Tube to Richmond to meet James, Ismail & Celestia.[60] We discussed the part – that of the old, fading butler – & I read some scenes. They didn't give much away, but were perfectly civil.

Sunday, 12 July
Only half full for the first show. I don't blame 'em, the place is like an oven. Sod's law, reely, as it was our finest rendition yet; they were so keen to get it done & remove the clobber that we *raced* thro' it. I praised Ryall: 'You're marvellous when you do it briskly.' He crossed his eyes – 'Have you been talking to my missus?'… Came back to find a New Home card on the mat from Jasper and Stella. Please God! don't let them be clingers… Deposited it in my *new* stainless steel pedal bin.

---

[58] William Knollys (1544-1632), nobleman at the court of Elizabeth I; derided as 'Party Beard' because his facial hair was white at the roots, yellow mid-way and black at its ends. Purported to be Shakespeare's muse for the Malvolio character.
[59] One of the characters voiced by KW in the animated series *Willo the Wisp*, 1981.
[60] Celestia Fox (b. 1947), casting director.

Tuesday, 14 July
Michael Anderson rang. Merchant-Ivory have proposed that I should play Old Mr Stevens in their film. M.A. also offered me *The Late Late Show* in Dublin, which I declined, & a new *Round the Horne* script which Took has written, to be recorded for the BBC's 70th anniversary, which I accepted. Michael said he's got an inflamed gallbladder & they might have to operate.

Wednesday, 15 July
Flo brought the shopping round. Says she's doing the cleaning for the new lot in Flat 18, who evidently pay her better than I ever did. She told me the Indian chaps have been coming in & out to decorate Lou's place. They probably won't bother with mine; it's the archetypal blank canvas… Will have to do something about the loo seat, I can't get on with it. It's a queer shape, and my arse slides uncomfortably into it. In any case, wooden fitments on a lav have always struck me as somewhat unhygienic.

Anthony Hopkins[61] came backstage after & was abundant with the tributes. 'I hear you're going to be my father in November,' he said, with sceptical eyes. 'Perhaps,' I said… It's a disgrace, them bandying my name about before I've even accepted.

Thursday, 16 July
Bad house tonight, not a peep out of them. It was appreciable because the company have become accustomed to laughs at specific points (always fatal) & the distinct *lack* of them this evening put everyone disastrously off their stride. 'Miserable twats,' said Cardy, 'they should've stopped in & watched *The Cook Report*.' In the interval, PH came in & said 'Keep the faith, boys and girls – they're loving it… just placidly,' but we all saw through that.

Rupert collected me. We sat quietly, basking in his air conditioning, until I said 'You were right, of course. The kernel of it all is that, fundamentally, I don't like myself very much. Not underneath. And I am afraid of love. But I am aware of it, which is a start.' He changed gear and touched my knee… It was a candid comment I'd ordinarily preserve for the diary, but – for some reason – I have faith in him. He came back & left about one o'c.

---

[61] Acclaimed Welsh actor and director (b. 1937); from the Margam district of Port Talbot, the same suburb as KW's great-grandfather.

Friday, 17 July
Called in at 2 o'c. to talk to this dreadful LWT lot. The girl clearly hadn't seen the show & was brainlessly parroting the questions some researcher had jotted down. She ended with 'What do you say to the gossip about you being certain to win an Olivier award?' I swelled majestically & said 'I've no interest in trinkets, dear.'

Blanche rigged up her portable set & we watched the piece on the Frank Bough programme.[62] They cut most of my stuff – including the accolades bit – in favour of footage of Ryall larking about with his padding.

Sunday, 19 July
Pat arrived at 9.30. Gave her the tour. All she could say was 'Don't think much of the cornices,' and 'How much did this set you back then?' Evidently concerned her inheritance has been whittled away. I fibbed gaily – 'O! practically every penny I have!'... M. came at ten with the flowers & we walked to Rose Gardens. Pat soon restless & moaning about her feet. There was a groundsman with a binbag, leisurely picking up litter with grabber, fag hanging out the mouth, singing loudly. I went straight up & told him 'My mother's scattered here. Have some respect for the Dead.'

Two shows, both fair. Phil on her monthlies, so she was rather muted.

Monday, 20 July
Got the paper. Lots of stuff about the boycott. It certainly leaves Barcelona up the swanny... with Dukakis, Kohl *and* Mitterrand forbidding athletes to travel, it'll be a championship of dosed-up Russkies, bulging Potsdamer *fräulein* & skeletal blackamoors. Copperknob is dithering 'cos we'll be staging the thing in '96, but I dare say our withdrawal is imminent... Dozed off after lunch!! Only woken by Flo coming to clean. Told her off for not diluting the Domestos – I'm all for thoroughness, but she slops it around with profligate abandon. 'Don't be fucking Scrooge!' she said, which made me laugh, so she got away with it in the end.

Notes after the show. I escaped unscathed, but Silas got an earful over his perceived mumbling. I've an idea he's sickening for something... Drinks in the bar afterwards & I was goosed by Lorraine Chase![63] 'Oh Ken!' she said,

---

[62] *Six O'Clock Live*, presented by broadcaster Frank Bough (1933-2020).
[63] English actress and model (b. 1951); famous for her strong Cockney accent. Appeared with KW in *The Undertaking*.

'you weren't 'alf funny. And *knockout* in the prison bit… I cried me eyes out.' She was in a scarlet & gold silk number, & looked divine.

Thursday, 23 July
Thinking about it, all this time I've been seeking a replacement for God. I itch for the days when I felt Him there, but they're gone, & all subsequent alternatives have been temporary and, by their nature, faithless. It is surely folly to submit one's soul to earthly pursuits, and wallowing in *ideas* only leads to nihilism… The answer, perhaps, is to make a God of another; to deify a trusted one. Maybe that's why real people, intuitively, get married.

Friday, 24 July
8.14 to Norwich for this wretched gameshow.[64] There's always been a bleak shabbiness to regional television, but the guileless attempts at sophistication dotted around Anglia TV are positively *endearing*… The swan-folded flannel in the dressing room, the "beef borginyong" in the canteen, the complimentary tin of Altoids… sheer tat, but so well-meant… The programme itself was desperate. I was paired with a woebegone biddy with all the charisma of a cat turd, who plain refused to engage. The other 'star' was Chegwin, so there was nothing doing there either. That said, the fellow hosting the thing, Jeff, was v. kind to me & kept it going quite well.

Exhausted by the time I got home. It's foolish to think that at this age I can tear across the country & back, *and* do a show in the evening to boot.

Sunday, 26 July
Paul came & we walked to the coffee bar on the Serpentine. It's sticky, and the breeze off the lake was v. agreeable. He told me that the quote for augmenting the basement at the block is 38 thousand, which was voted down by the residents, so they've decided to take their chances with the A-bombs… On the way back we found a family of Italians, plainly lost, noisily studying a map. Eventually established that they were after an address in Brixton! Took them to Marble Arch, put them on a Number 2 & asked the conductor to tell them when to get off.

Wednesday, 29 July
Funny letter from Joan Rivers!! The poor woman has been reduced to peddling cheap jewellery on satellite TV, but she's very droll about it. 'Thank

---

[64] *Jumble* for ITV, presented by actor and comedian Jeff Stevenson (b. 1961).

God for fat housewives from Wyoming who can't tell the difference between diamonds and paste,' she writes, 'and thank Him again for their husbands' credit cards...' She's got the daytime show of course, and she *implores* me to come to New York and be on it (with Julie Andrews, no less) & stay at the St. Regis on Fifth Avenue... I think not, but it's sweet to be asked.

The show went excellently. Everyone acquired the right rhythm from the off & the audience was entirely engaged throughout. Took Martin & the Davids for supper at Giorgio's. Alison Steadman was there with her cast from the Cottesloe. She invited us over & we sat drinking Amaretto with Cognac until half past one! Postlethwaite did a vulgar trick where he took a lit cigar stub into the mouth & puffed smoke out of his ears. 'I always knew you had a decent Hamlet in you, Pete,' said Martin.

Saturday, 1 August
Letter from the chief curator at the Portrait Gallery. Someone called Rhidian Jones has bequeathed the Bratby painting of me & they wish to display it!! 'Mr Jones purchased the canvas at a boutique in Lytham St Annes in February for £10 and submitted it to our trustees...' *Boutique* – at that price?! Jumble sale, more like. Bratby dropped dead last week, so this canny Cymro is doubtless cashing in opportunely. I replied with 'I've no objection to the picture joining your collection, though might I request you hang me next to someone uncomely, or perhaps a war criminal? I couldn't bear to be sandwiched between two beauties; I'd far sooner court comparison with a monster.'[65]

Sunday, 2 August
M. collected me at 12.15 for lunch at Coq au Vin at Gyles's invitation. It was quite a gathering! There was a very indiscreet barrister ('My dears, I actually met Myra Hindley, and she was nice as *ninepence*...'), a footman to the dowager Queen of Jordan, the chief engraver of the Mint, and Ned Sherrin.[66] All that breadth of experience, yet most of the chat revolved around Maxwell. Eventually I'd had enough & said 'Let's talk about something else, I'm sick of that fat shit.' Gyles daintily changed the subject... He defended his teddy bear museum after a mean-spirited rise-take from Rumpole. I told

---

[65] The painting of KW by John Bratby (1928-92) was never hung in the gallery, and is now lost.

[66] English broadcaster, author and stage director (1931-2007).

G. that we'd found Teddy when clearing Lou's flat, & he breathlessly asked if I'd donate him to the exhibition! 'O! you don't want him,' I contended, 'nobody wants to see my tatty bear behind glass…' 'Nobody wants to see your tatty bare behind *full stop*,' said Ned, and they fell about.

Monday, 3 August
Went to Samuels to order goblets to be engraved for the company. When I got to the theatre I heard Benson doing an impression of me for Blanche & Hannah. I went in & he clammed up sharp. I picked up the jerkin and left. When they called the half he came into the dressing room to apologise. 'Please, think no evil of us,' he said, 'it was done in admiration.' I pretended to be miffed, but it's impossible to be angry with the boy. After all, I've been similarly caught taking people off many a time, so I'm in no position to grumble – what's more, his impersonation was unsettlingly good.

Tuesday, 4 August
Overslept!! Scarcely had time for a lick & a promise before the car arrived. To B.H. for *Thought for the Day*. They waved me through at the desk & I was in the booth at 7.46. Realised as I sat down that I'd forgotten the specs! Had to hold the thing at arm's length. Humphreys[67] said after that it was fine, but I fear I dithered a bit… Ciaran gave me a numbing gel for the perianal ache. He swears by it. It says for oral use only but, as C. said, 'Gums or bums, it's sensitive flesh. You've got to look after your entrances.'

Performance felt clunky, but it went down well. If there is an ideal degree of ribaldry, we've found it. From the wings one sees the starchy drears wince, but the groundlings are spellbound… After the bows they played the national anthem for the Queen Mother & Princess Elizabeth's b'day. We stood there like idiots, some of the audience got up (mostly to unstick their undies from their arses), whilst others hesitantly filed out. *Shambolique*.

Wednesday, 5 August
An eight-week run is quite sufficient for this play. Long enough to leave a mark, but not to outstay its welcome. In any event, Rupert's booked 7 nights in Rhodes from the 20th, so I shall be gone.

---

[67] John Humphrys (b. 1943), Welsh broadcaster; presenter of BBC Radio 4's *Today* programme, 1987-2019.

Friday, 7 August
Threw away Ciaran's ointment. It has the desired effect pharmacologically, but it sloshes around in the crack. Too *viscous*. One squelches walking across the room. Went to Boots & asked the man if there's an equivalent that permeates, and he recommended Lanacane. It's designed to soothe itching, but he said it contains comparable ingredients… Walked to Broadcasting House to talk to Humphrey Carpenter.[68] O it was a boon to chat to such a fetching and responsive man. None of the trite fatuity I was set for: it was questions about poetry, aesthetics – even maternal love!! I was fluent, unabashed & engaging. At the end he asked 'Is the real Kenneth Williams becoming a happy man?' The use of *becoming* was jarringly perceptive. The programme is called *Night Waves*, so it'll only be heard by truckers & security guards, but I enjoyed meself nonetheless… Strolled back lazily, a lovely zephyr cutting through the heavy heat. I was loudly singing *O for a Thousand Tongues to Sing* when I saw an old boy in a thick black coat sleeping up against the feeder pillar on Portland Place. Went to Ravi at the newsstand & got two tins of lemonade & put them on the pavement by him… Ryall's sciatica has flared, so it was an understudy job, but it went alright. Diane said 'My Auntie Mary is coming back after the show; she's been on & on at me about meeting you.' 'I'd be delighted,' I said, but in the event I bolted as swiftly as I could & got the bus. There's only so many good deeds one can brook in a single day.

Saturday, 8 August
When I came out, Stella was there, watering the hanging baskets. 'I can't get my lobelias to thrive,' she said. There's no answer to that… Got paper from Adonis. Ravi is closer, but without A.'s *advantages*… Long article about this sex nonsense – bolshie sophists with nothing better to do, maintaining there is in fact just *one* gender, and that current pronouns are outmoded & offensive. Brief mention of a debate in the chamber, and Syd Chapman[69] referring to himself as Sydney Personperson!! I had to laugh at the proposed alternatives: *e, em, eir, eirs, emself*… it would seem the nit that coined them was born within hearing of Bow Bells.

Cold shoulder from Di for dodging the old dear last night. I don't mind. In fact it added spice to scenes which have been drifting of late, so it couldn't have worked out better.

---

[68] English biographer, writer, and radio broadcaster (1946-2005).
[69] Sydney Chapman (1935-2014), Tory MP for Chipping Barnet, 1979-2005.

Monday, 10 August
Paul 'phoned to say that the new tenant in No. 8 had been round with a parcel for me that'd been delivered in error. He came at 10 o'c. & dropped it off... It's a maquette of the sculpture by Sedlecká. She's captured something of me, I must admit. Writes that the full-sized work is completed & the client is pleased – tho' she doesn't say who the client *is*. All v. enigmatic. Odd to think of my severed bonce, cluttering up some nance's sideboard in Mayfair. I wrapped it back in the package and addressed it to Goldsmiths Oliver, with a note saying 'You once told me you enjoy receiving head, so cop this...'

Friday, 14 August
Saw the lunchtime news. This uprising in Sofia has *already* been put down. They're saying 800 dead. They showed Charlton Heston being macho, irritatingly repeating the 'Not on *my* watch' slogan. Saw Paul for coffee at Alpino's. That tawny piece from the fruitmonger's joined us. 'Dukakis is bloody hopeless,' he griped, 'but where's the sense in electing Chuck?' Paul shrugged & said 'They see him & they think of *El Cid*.' 'Well, *I* think of El Sid James,' said the grocer, thrilled to pieces with himself. The point stands, tho': when in doubt, voters will plump for a face they *know*, as I'm only too aware.

Of course, I understand why I'm so good in this play, and why they're raving about it... A conventional artist has to act up the part, to revel in the quirks & peculiarities. But, as those things are inherent in me, Hall has encouraged a quelling of archness & artifice, and the result is pure, authentic, controlled brilliance. A film star would flippantly call it 'doing nothing' – but it is, in actual fact, the management of emotion & fierce command of the text. And I've got that in *spades*.

Tuesday, 18 August
Returned from Vecchia to find Flo in tears, the black velour jacket a limp, saturated mass on the kitchen floor. I'd asked her to get it cleaned, but the silly tart put it in the machine. I was incensed, but said 'Don't brood, it can't be helped now.' It's *baffling*. She's a dab hand at most household tasks, but give her an unfamiliar fabric & she's all at sea.

Cards & other clutter from people who'd forgotten to send anything on opening night. After it was over we gathered on stage & had the drinks. I handed out the goblets & Peter Hall gave a succinct oration. The others were going on to the Connaught, but I made excuses. Rupert met me at the corner of Craven Street & we went for a late supper at Place Cuire. He said 'You look drained. I think the end has come just in time.' He's right, I'm done in. The legs ache, the feet have had it, I'm *ablaze* with the acne... but to sit there, in the corner, in the wake of a job well done, in the company of a patient, beautiful, spotless & confident man – well, I'm not worthy of a bit of it.

Thursday, 20 August
Arrived Diagoras at 3.45. Went to the Hertz desk, then spent half an hour trying to find the car in 40 degree heat. The mirrors are held on with tape & there's a dirty great hole in the floor on the passenger side. I had asphalt hurtling between my legs all the way to Rhodes... Incongruous, to arrive at such an hotel in such a wagon: this place, the Nikolis, is ritziness *embodied*. Fourteenth century stone, but all mod cons & chiched up to the eyeballs. Tassos, the bellboy, showed us up to the third floor. 'You in the Queen's Suite,' he said. 'They must've known I was coming,' I quipped, but to no avail. Accordingly huge room. Ornate four-poster & a bidet. Even the other *guests* are swish: Tassos says the Marquess of Lindsay[70] is next door but one... Thickset nance couple from Godalming in the bar, Greg & Rowan. Apart from them & his lordship it appears to be all foreigners, which is a great blessing.

It was gone twelve when he tapped the door. I let him in and we sat on the bed, me in the pyjamas & him in pants. Without a word he wrapped his arms around me & rested his head on the pillow. He smelt clean & scrubbed – a heady mix of leathery sweet carbolic & fresh skin – redolent of those safe Sunday bath nights of my boyhood. I laid there in the silence, counting the embroidered doves on the tester. I could've happily died at that moment. I've never felt so secure nor genuinely cherished... it was like the comfort of God. Eventually he tied the belt round my wrists, yanked down the jarmers & lightly tanned my backside with the carpet slippers – but by then I was desperate for a pee. He went back to his room.

Friday, 21 August
There's heat, and then there's *this*... It saps the energy and addles the brain to the extent that all one does is seek out shade & respite. We went to the Grand Master's palace & the Street of the Knights. There was a group from Ilfracombe on a guided tour. I had to pose for photographs with them by the sign of the 'Inn of the Tongue of England'. They were intent on seizing me,

---

[70] Tarquin Otterbourne Gordon (b. 1965), 9th Marquess of Lindsay.

but Rupert stepped in with 'Sorry, ladies & gents, we'd love to stay, but Mr Williams is on the island to film *Wish You Were Here*, and we're on a very tight schedule…'

Saturday, 22 August
Rupert wanted to go to Mandraki & see where the Colossus once stood. I questioned the sense of going to look at something that's no longer there, but he was resolute. Godalming Greg joined him. Rowan and I stayed at the Nikolis under the big ceiling fan in the bar, drinking ouzo martinis & playing Pass the Pigs. It's absolutely *baking*.

Sunday, 23 August
It stands to reason that *climate* has such an effect on national characteristics, or the attitude of a people. It's a miracle these Greeks get anything done at all. But then again, they worked out long ago what matters & what doesn't.

Monday, 24 August
I was scarcely decent when the chambermaid burst in unannounced. Ten seconds earlier & she'd've caught me akimbo, thumbing in the Lanacane… We clambered aboard Death On Wheels & drove to Lindos for the Acropolis. There was a slender boy sitting on a wall selling tourist pamphlets. Rupert said 'Will you show us around for a thousand drachmas?' He shot up like Soyuz One… Christos, it was called. Greece's answer to a Pontins bluecoat: 'You want to see the stone relief? Well, that's a relief…' 'This is Ottoman, but please don't sit on it…' 'The remains of the Doric Temple. Alas, poor Doric…' A polished act, amusing to begin with, but rather trying before long… Perused the various eateries. All much of a muchness, until we found *Taverna Areola*, which tickled us enough to take the plunge. A few intoxicated expats beckoned us in – 'Tits Tavern' they call it. Rupert went native with the vine leaves; I played safe with moussaka, washed down with retsina… Should've let it subside before tackling the journey back. On arrival at Nikolis I had to *run* upstairs. The assault on the bathroom was beyond words – I hope their plumbing's up to it.

Tuesday, 25 August
We got chatting to Lord Lindsay. Undeniably *so*, despite the fiancée talk & whiff of Aramis. He asked us to lunch at Mandraki marina & we accepted… After a stroll round the port we arrived for this meal. I hadn't twigged it'd be

Beyond Our Kenneth

on water!! Lindsay introduced us to the mayor, Mr Kokkinos, who sweatily kissed us on both cheeks, and then we were shoved on the yacht & flung out to sea. I've never tackled taramasalata in a tornado, and now I shan't need to try: we clung on for dear life as the half-naked deckhands slid about with plates of octopus & stuffed pittas. His Grace lounged feyly, every inch the Bosie[71] to the hairy mayor's Oscar. Felt like death by the time we docked, the stomach swirling... Came back to Nikolis for a rest. Mrs Mop has pointedly left extra loo rolls in the lavatory, the cheeky mare.

Wednesday, 26 August
Drove to Monolithos. The trek up to the castle nearly killed me, which must've been evident – a girl at the top asked Rupert 'You like a photo with your father?...' Went in to the chapel, which was cool & tranquil. A monk in a stovepipe hat sat down & gave us a potted history, but he soon got on to the 'all donations welcome' bit, so we made excuses & began the descent... I've had my fill of craggy ruins. It's too much like looking in a mirror.

Thursday, 27 August
The Godalmings came it with 'We mustn't forget to exchange numbers', but we managed to circumvent. Flight was fair. At Gatwick the girl in passport control said 'Silver hair really suits you,' and a woman at the bag carousel said 'You look lovely with a tan,' so the ego was somewhat restored... Got in at 7 o'c. Flo was sitting there, feet up on the coffee table, watching *Top of the Pops* & eating crisps. You give people an inch. I went mad... I rang M. He said 'Did you have a pleasant time, the *pair* of you?', rather obviously. I downplayed it. I've no need to, but I can't be doing with insinuations & remarks. In any case, I didn't get this far by crossing wires when it comes to friends. The further apart the strands are kept, the smaller the chance of shorting the circuits.

Sunday, 30 August
We saw *Press Your Luck* on ITV... Question: 'Which city is known as the Big Easy?' Answer: 'Umm – Colchester?'

Wednesday, 2 September
The tragedy of being successful & lauded at this age is that one is aware of its inconsequence. Anderson rang to say that the Theatrical Management

---

[71] Nickname for Lord Alfred Douglas (1870-1945), the lover of Oscar Wilde.

Assoc. wish to give me an award. Told him to turn it down. In the old days I declined such trophies owing to high-minded principle… Today I refused as it'd just be another ornament for Flo to dust.

As I was getting ready for bed I heard the pair at 49 rowing again. I turned out the light & cracked the window, but I only caught snippets: 'It's *always* the same when you're on the Pernod…', 'You know *exactly* how it looked…', 'Oh! be a *man*, Dominic…'

Friday, 4 September
Letter from Alasdair Macmillan asking if I'd be interested in doing *Another Audience With…*, but I don't think I've got the material. In any case, I think the format has run its course, judging by the Jackie Mason offering.

Went with Rupert to see *Sister Act*.[72] The only remotely amusing bit was seeing Mags done up as the Mother Superior – she looked like a bottle of Quink… Came back to the house and had bread & jam. Got out the spare key, but I've decided not to give it to him. He deserves a reward of some sort, but not that. Some things ought to remain unpenetrated, this sanctuary among them.

Saturday, 5 September
Walked to Gloucester Crescent for tea with George Melly.[73] He only had that revolting camomile stuff, which I rebuffed. Straitway he said 'Oh dear… It'll have to be rum then.'

Monday, 7 September
To Broadcasting House for the *Round the Horne* rehearsal. We're doing it in the Radio Theatre, which they've tarted up with comfy seating & carpeted walls. I'd assumed it would be a rehashing of old stuff, but Took has written a brand new script. It is me, Betty, Paddick & Pertwee. Barry is standing in for Kenneth Horne. Before we started he said 'I know I won't measure up to the great man, but I'll do my best.' In actual fact, it works very well – an imitation of KH would be crass, whereas Barry brings a temperate appeal of his own… For me there's Gruntfuttock, Jule & Sand, Fallowfield and a Rumpo, to the tune of *The Farmer's Boy*:

---

[72] 1992 American musical crime comedy film, directed by Emile Ardolino, starring Whoopi Goldberg and Maggie Smith as Reverend Mother.
[73] English jazz and blues singer and critic (1926-2007).

Beyond Our Kenneth

The moon was fat behind yon mills,
A'garn the pucking moor,
Fettered and game, a swain there came
Up to a tadger's door.
'Can you say me if any there be
That could pray me employ,
To flug and go, or splaff and blow,
And be a gargler's joy?'

'My pludger is bent, and yet I be left
With some jizzups, thick and tall;
But what is more my thrombling twig
Is the broadest of them all.
Though little, I'll blodge as hard as a Vike,
If you'll give me employ,
To flug and go, or splaff and blow,
And be a gargler's joy.'

We went thro' it twice, but Iannucci,[74] the boy directing it, said 'That's enough, we want to keep it fresh.'

Tuesday, 8 September
Went to get papers. Sam & Helene were there & we discussed this Soviet flu business. I avowed 'I'm sure we won't get it here,' but Helene said 'I hope we do. I've got a stone to lose for my sister's wedding…'

At 12.30 walked to BH for the recording. It's a queer sensation, appearing before an audience that one *knows* will be rolling in the aisles regardless, owing to sentiment alone. Before the prelude, Betty whispered 'We're on to a winner here,' & she was right. Overwhelming goodwill swept across the stage and carried us through… That said, I did think that the ovations at the end were overgenerous. It went on & on. I turned to get off, but there was the skulking figure of Aspel with his red book, & the awful penny dropped. A camera crew appeared from nowhere & was rammed in the face. Somehow dredged up a few flimsy *bon mots*, but in truth I was fuming… Pat was there, backstage, all smiles. That didn't last long. Blazing row with her in the corridor, harked by all and sundry. Eventually the producer, Malcolm, came to mediate & win me round.

---

[74] Armando Iannucci (b. 1963), Scottish satirist, writer and director.

1992

Car to Teddington. Swift cheese sandwich in a glorified cupboard, with a researcher telling me how *wonderful* Pat had been. My tan suit was laid out in a dressing room which reeked of wet dog. A girl dabbed on some powder, dragged a comb thro' the hair, then it was straight on between the sliding doors. Pat was sitting in the chair ordinarily reserved for spouses, next to Joan Dunbar, the Colyers, Aunt Phyllis, and a few of that lot. Behind them was M., T&C, Paul & Rupert. Huge cheer from the stalls!! They can't've known it was to be *me* they'd be seeing (lest the 'surprise' be ruined), but they gave the impression of felicity. Sat down & saw Anderson, Codron,[75] Sheila, Nanette, Andrew, Richard Pearson & Lorraine Chase crammed on the benches opposite, with Janet Brown, Tyler Butterworth,[76] Gyles, Rona & others shoved up the back. Burning sense of unease right from the off, with so many worlds colliding. I'm a fussy eater when it comes to chums: I prefer things separate on the plate & not touching. Aspel introduced the *Round the Horne* troupe right away, & they were unveiled like prizes on *Sale of the Century*. We had to embrace each other, despite having spent all afternoon together. Thence began the eulogy: 'So, parties assembled, I can say Kenneth Charles Williams, this *is* your life; you were born *etc.*, *etc.*' They showed photos on the screen – the baby portrait, the one with Charlie & Lou at Southend, and Princess Angelica. Then a voice thro' the speakers which completely stumped me. It was Wreyford Palmer!! Heaven knows where they dug him up! He looked *dreadful*, shaking like blancmange, doddering on with his National Health stick. Not a hair on his head. He babbled vaguely about 'Our Game' & other playground tales from Manchester St… Then a video of Val on mapmaking at Stanfords, before Stanley, Rae & Peter Nichols came & told army stories. I was up & down like a yoyo. O! but Stanley was so handsome in his suit. Pat kept clutching my arm in hysterics, building up the part… Annette Kerr walked out, looking as courtly & gentle as when I first laid eyes on her. She told the Mumbles lemon meringue story, which went down well. Freddie Treves[77] appeared! Such a tonic to see him, sprightly & alert. He talked with fondness about Newquay and Birmingham Rep… More pictures (*St. Joan* &

---

[75] Michael Codron (b. 1930), English theatre producer; played a large part in KW's early career, casting him in many of his successful stage roles.
[76] English actor (b. 1959), son of Janet Brown and KW's *Carry On* co-star Peter Butterworth (1915-79).
[77] Frederick Treves (1925-2012), English character actor; great-nephew of Sir Frederick Treves, the surgeon who rescued Joseph Merrick, the 'Elephant Man'.

Beyond Our Kenneth

Shaffer plays), then Bill Kerr[78] on film from Australia with stuff about Hancock – but the video went wrong, playing without sound, so they had to pause & redo it, which blunted the immediacy of it somewhat. Aspel rattled on as the lineup across the way gazed at me, the accused in the dock... Then it was the *Carry On* bunch, *en masse*: Kenny C, Barbara, Joanie, Bernie, Cribbins, Phillips, Jack & Liz Fraser. Peter & Gerald came forward & P. did the chat. 'We're a family, and with 27 appearances, you're the preeminent member of that family, treasured & indispensable...' Bit much, reely... Parsons, Freud & Nimmo next thro' the gates, then dear Jeremy Swan & Nick Spargo[79] apropos children's programmes. Cecil Franks & Tony T-S trudged on to tepid applause. Cecil declared my time in Parliament as 'brief but crucial' – I heard Codron laugh. Then footage of Miguel, sat in his panelled office, with further adulation. And to round it off, Mags was revealed, in lemon yellow, clutching a letter I'd sent to her at the Old Vic in 1960. I'd quoted Sonnet 104, & holding my hand she read it back to me – '...*For fear of which, hear this, thou age unbred; Ere you were born was beauty's summer dead.*' She kissed me on the cheek & Michael handed me the book. Then we had to slowly walk towards the footlights as a company, like something out of *Les Mis*, my apostles surrounding me, grinning.

Drinks after in the restaurant block. Everyone stood in clustered factions, loath to mingle... The producer said 'There's not much we can cut from that. Might have to ask ITV if we can run to 45. It's lucky Peter Cook was under the weather, else we would've needed the full hour.' I said 'Surely the bit with old Wreyford can go?' 'On the contrary!' he shrieked, 'it's the childhood bits the punters love most'... Joan Dunbar held my elbow and lamented 'If only your mum had been here to see it – you've really *made* it now...' That was as much as I could stomach so I told Rupert to bring the car round... Got in at 9.30. Had a tin of soup. Rang Flo & asked her why she hadn't been there. 'Your sister tell me it was friends only.' She was clearly hurt. Oh! I should've stuck to my guns & said *no*.

Monday, 14 September
To Holland Park for *Lord Edgware Dies*. We're in Debenham House with its Italianate exterior and arts & crafts adornments. There are worse places to

---

[78] British-Australian actor, comedian, and vaudevillian (1922-2014); he had a regular role as an Australian lodger in the radio version of *Hancock's Half Hour*.
[79] Nicholas Spargo (1921-97), creator of *Willo the Wisp*.

work, I s'pose. Except I'm done up in white tie, penguinesque, with the collar digging in. I appealed to Fleming, the director, 'I feel like my head's on the block in this,' but all he said, indifferently, was 'Well, we've all our crosses to bear. Better get on.' Heaven knows where they find these people... Loverly to be with David Suchet. He told me it was Ustinov himself that recommended him to Eastman for the Poirot part... David's been on the opposite path to me, *vis-à-vis* God. 'I had an epiphany in a hotel room five or six years ago,' he said, 'and that was that. I got baptised a fortnight later.' He's rather a fan of St Paul, but we were called on to the set before he could expand.

Went to Tesco's for some cakes. First time I've actually seen price labels in pounds *and* euromarks. Quite momentous in its own way. Walked round to Flo's & had tea with her there. We saw the News. Seems the Turks have caught this Russian bug and are dropping like flies. Might teach them to use a drop of Parazone in future.

Tuesday, 15 September
This girl, Helen McCrory,[80] is very good. She was debating a touch of blocking with the director & I shouted 'I say, *someone's* bold for her first time.' Hands on hips she said, *à la* me, 'Well, we can't have you being the only *bold* one round 'ere, ducky, can we?...' Merriment from the crew, thwarted by Fleming with 'Right, enough of that, let's push on.' O! he's a miserable sod... It's trivial stuff, plodding about faux-aristocratically with a cantankerous arseholean streak. Bread & butter to me, but fabulously enjoyable... Hugh said 'The missus tells me your episode's on tonight.' 'Come again?' I said... It turns out he's married to Belinda Lang! I'd no idea. Rupert came round & we watched the *2point4 Children* thing. Nothing to write home about, of course, but I did *look* rather lovely. Pert, vivacious, bleached, boisterous, Bloomsbury blond & etc.

Wednesday, 16 September
London Studios for the final bits. It's no expense spared, I'll give them that. The First A/D said, when I was finished, 'And that's a wrap for Mr Williams, everyone'... There was a small round, quickly followed by the miseryguts, muttering drably 'Right, time and tide, let's get on.' Heaven knows where the man needs to be, but he's determined to get there. I shook him warmly by the hand & said 'Oh! my darling, would that I could plant an English kiss upon your cheeks!' & breezed out.

---

[80] English actress (1968-2021); *Lord Edgware Dies* was her first professional TV job.

Went to the old Jew on Carburton Street to collect the Tissot. He has mended the second hand which was sticking. He said 'We saw you on the telly last night. You always brighten the screen, and our hearts along with it... That'll be eight-fifty please.' Too touched to conjure a reply, so I hastily handed over ten pounds & left.

Went to Flo's & had meal at 6 o'c. We sat & watched *Eldorado* and she polished off an entire box of chocolates without offering me *one*, the selfish cow. When I remonstrated she said 'It Black Magic Wednesday, I don't change it for nobody.' Told her 5.30 for dinner tomorrow as I'm going out in the evening.

Thursday, 17 September
Sometimes I wander round the house & marvel at it. I think of the men who built it, the architect in his silks & finery, the gangers roaring orders at sweaty masons, the unshod urchins, hands raw and calloused before their time, hurtling about the dusty site. They'd be proud of me, leaving their workmanship uncamouflaged by tat. Stella came round bearing flapjacks and said 'Gosh... you certainly do favour the *minimalist* look,' which was very pleasing.

Walked to Sound, Inc. for the Parker pens voiceover. The boy running it, Robert, is only 22, & told me his alopecia is pervasive. I reflexively said 'I *am* sorry,' but he laughed. 'Don't be! Think of all the dosh I save on Carmen rollers.'

With Rupert to the Vaudeville for *Someone To Watch Over Me*.[81] Adequately handled – but oh! it dragged... This littering of chasmal pauses does nothing but bore onlookers to death. If they'd stuck to the lines we could've been out & in the pub by 9. When the bows finally came, I felt I'd done six years in a dungeon myself... R. peckish afterwards, so we stopped at Kentucky Chicken. It's about as refined as feeding time at the zoo – patrons are invited to graze from a cardboard bucket. I left him to it & walked home.

Saturday, 19 September
Mountain of letters. One postmarked Uttoxeter, from a woman who claims to have been contacted by Louie 'from the other side'. Asks if I'll submit to

---

[81] Actually *Someone Who'll Watch Over Me* by Frank McGuinness, a play focusing on the ordeals of three Beirut hostages.

a *connection session*, for a modest fee… Leaflet enclosed, her huge porcine face over the words 'Kimberley Parish, a Medium in East Staffs' (and an Extra Large in Dorothy Perkins). I replied with a signed photograph, telling her to stop being so silly & to take up aerobics or country dancing.

Wednesday, 23 September
They showed the signing ceremony from Maastricht.[82] Kinnock *tries* to rein in the Cambrian instinct for drama & showmanship, but it's hopeless. A leaders' gathering requires solemnity, a dignified stringency of statesmanship in earnest… yet old Nelly can't resist instigating the joining of hands, the raising of arms in triumph, as if it were a curtain call at the Adelphi. Kaufman[83] looked terribly uncomfortable, I had to laugh. Seems odd to think now that I sat across from these people in the House.

Thursday, 24 September
Got the new telephone at Rumbelows, then to Ivor for envelopes. He said 'We buried my brother on Monday. I had to take the wreath off the coffin & toss it over my shoulder into the crowd, like a bride's posy, to pick who'll be next to peg out. Len made me promise… He was a card… Oh! I will miss him…'

Friday, 25 September
Walked to Museum Street to meet Jane Jenkins.[84] I read for this Governor part in the Bond film, but don't think I made much of an impression. Heigh ho. Went to Marks's for socks.

Sunday, 27 September
Hawley Crescent for *Breakfast with Frost*. I was looking forward to seeing David, but on arrival they told me he's come down with something contagious, so I spoke to Moira[85] instead. That was no hardship; hers is one of the few mellifluous news voices we have left. Dame Jill[86] was on with me, ranting about how the government has gone 'soft on homos' – I reminded

---

[82] The Maastricht Treaty (1992), the foundation treaty of the Union of European Nations.
[83] Gerald Kaufman (1930-2017), Labour MP for Manchester Gorton, 1983-2017; Foreign Secretary, 1991-5.
[84] American casting director (b. 1943); credits include *Ghost*, *Home Alone* and *Jurassic Park*.
[85] Moira Stuart (b. 1949), the first female newsreader of Caribbean heritage to appear on British national television.
[86] Jill Knight (1923-2022), Tory MP for Birmingham Edgbaston, 1966-91; helped introduce the 'Section 28' amendment.

her that deviation is part of the human condition, & as the electorate have released her to enjoy her retirement, she should endeavour to do so *quietly*. Afterwards Moira said 'You enjoyed that, I can tell.' She was right. I'm enjoying lots of things at the moment… Lunch with M. at the Dell. That butch article Sandro was tickling the baby grand in the corner… he clocked me & interrupted his jazz with the Minute Waltz. The other diners applauded us all the way to the table. Quite luvvly.

When I got home I saw I'd received my first message on the answer machine!! It was O'Grady! 'Ken, I'm in a kiosk in Vauxhall & there's someone waiting & it's pissing it down, but I had to ring to say well done for layin' into that nasty cow on the telly this morning, you were fucking fabulous…'

Monday, 28 September
Got the bus to visit T&C. Sat upstairs in front of two spiffy young business types.

'…I suppose you've seen the new sort in personnel?'
'Phwoar, just a bit. Tasty little thing.'
'Well, no word of a lie, Steve Dyson asked her out for dinner and she said "Can we make it tea instead? I only get half an hour for me dinner" – she thought he meant lunch!'
'No!… That's hilarious!'
'I think he said she's from Doncaster. Or Dorchester… one of the two.'
'That's *classic*.'

I wanted to throw up & join the Socialist Workers right there & then.

Wednesday, 30 September
9.03 from Euston. Nobody waiting, so got a taxi to Pebble Mill for *The Archers*. Met by Keri, the producer, and an old girl served me tea & Battenberg… It's only a small scene, with Syd Rumpo passing thro' Ambridge on his way to a folk festival. In the rehearsal, I did the line 'If I don't reach Lower Dripping afore nightfall, I'm liable to 'ave me *dividends* severed!' & it took them a full five minutes to stop laughing. They're easily pleased in the provinces, bless 'em. Norman Painting[87] said 'Will you join me for lunch, Ken? They do a super fettuccini in the cafeteria here.' Couldn't

---

[87] English actor (1924-2009); played the role of Phil Archer from 1950 until his death, a world record for character longevity.

summon an excuse quick enough, so I was condemned to it... The pasta was served with bread & margarine, cut into triangles.

Friday, 2 October
There's no escaping the fact that this house is just too big for me. I've pretended it's a matter of acclimatising, but that's humbug. It's the fundamental precept; a single man shouldn't live alone in a house. A bachelor should have *rooms*, anything more is excess & indulgence. Still, the thing is done now.

Car to Leicester Square for the premiere. I had to be photographed with Jim Dale. The cameraman said 'It'd be nice if you were holding something nautical.' I said 'Someone fetch this man a fishcake,' & Jim said 'Failing that, get Lotte Hass.'[88] In the end they made us pose with a plastic life ring... That Monica from *Newsroom South East* said 'Aren't audiences a bit too sophisticated for films like this nowadays?' I thought 'If only!!', but just repeated the guff about Chaucer & vulgarity being essential. The picture itself is appalling, but it *just* about squeaks by on the coattails of nostalgia & novelty – though I doubt that will fool Barry Norman... I said to Cribbins 'D'you think we got away with it?' & he said 'Well I don't know about you, but I shall be changing my name to Philippa & going to live in the woods.'

Saturday, 3 October
Gerald 'phoned to thank me for attending. He asked if there's any book I'd like. He said 'I hear the new Robert Harris is good,' but I can't stand those alternative histories. Told him to play it safe & get the latest Ackroyd. He came at noon. 'Barbara wanted to send you chocolates, but I thought peaches were best, in your condition...' Gerry *always* does this, making out I'm at death's door.

Rupert arrived at 5 o'c. to cook his 'stir-fried' veg. It was pleasant enough, for what it was, but one is left waiting, in vain, for an encore – namely, a dirty great slab of meat.

Sunday, 4 October
M. is in Luxembourg, so I rang Nick Courtney[89] & we met at the Guinea for lunch. Said he's had to postpone visiting friends in Egypt thanks to the travel ban, but he's off to Camber Sands in the morning for *Doctor Who*, so it's the

---

[88] Austrian diver and underwater photographer (1928-2015).
[89] Nicholas Courtney (1929-2011), Egyptian-born British actor, known for his regular role of the Brigadier in *Doctor Who*.

next best thing. They brought the puddings and Nick found an enormous black hair in the custard, must've been ten inches long. He wasn't remotely fazed, but I was having none of it. I said to the waitress 'It's disgusting, we're paying good money to dine at this establishment & this is the thanks we get… Look at it, would *you* eat that?? Get the manager over here this instant…' Nick said 'For God's sake, Ken, it's only a hair, give the girl a break.' It's giving people a break that leads to these filthy epidemics. The chap brought a new bowl of roly-poly & two Fernet-Brancas on the house.

Monday, 5 October
The plasterer came to do the bedroom wall. 'Well bugger me!' he said, 'I see the name on the docket & I thought "Nah, it can't be" but it *is* you! I can't believe it!' and that went on for a while. When I brought the tea he was up the ladder & said 'Course, I thought about the acting game myself – well, with *this* boat I'd be mad not to, wouldn't I? – but it's all them words you have to learn, I'd never get 'em to stick…' I said 'Oh, that'd be the least of your problems! What about all the smitten nancies, swarming round trying to grab at your personal portions?' He laughed. 'Nah, I don't mind that. Comes with the territory, dunnit? I mean they're only human…' One has to admire the chutzpah, 'cos he must be 18 stone, with more than a passing resemblance to Violet Carson.[90]

Wednesday, 7 October
Read in the paper that Denholm Elliott[91] has passed away in Ibiza. I worked with him on the *Baskervilles* fiasco & liked him. They're blaming the Russian flu, but that strikes me as diplomatic, after what Sinden told me of his habits… It got me thinking about Peter. I really ought to get in touch. Richard says that this Malay woman has managed to calm him down & staunch the flow of booze. Perhaps I shall write a letter… The *Express* says the *Carry On* has already been pulled from Cannon cinemas due to abysmal ticket sales!

Thursday, 8 October
Marion from the baths rang to say that Rupert had hit his head & is at St Thomas's. I 'phoned the reception & eventually got thro' to the Nurse who

---

[90] English actress, singer and pianist (1898-1983), popular as the no-nonsense battle-axe Ena Sharples in *Coronation Street*.
[91] English actor (1922-92); he was diagnosed with HIV in 1987, and died of AIDS-related tuberculosis.

said he's fine, just a badly bruised cheek. Some beastly boy had pushed him & he'd slipped and hit the face on the edge of the pool... Went shopping & did everything with a Morningside accent. It was obviously superb, as the chap in Menzies said 'Cheerio, Jock' as I left.

At 5 o'c. went round to Marlborough. He's alright, in spite of the clownish cast. It's the pride that's knocked more than anything else. I said 'Yes, well you'd better hurry up & recover. I've no time for disfigured invalids.' He went over the story again, about being shoved into the drink by the youth, but I said 'I've heard all this, I don't need it repeated.'

Friday, 9 October
Michael Anderson telephoned. 'Would you consider being a giant head on Channel 4, talking about computer games?[92] You've got first refusal, else they're going with Patrick Moore.' I said 'I've neither the energy nor the inclination to decipher that crapola,' & replaced the receiver.

Sunday, 11 October
After lunch with M., I got out all the diaries from years ending in a '2'. Fascinating to educe that each one records a landmark, of sorts... In '42 I started working life at Stanford's; '52 saw the first TV & film work; '62 brought an end to Charlie; in '72 I moved to Marlborough House; I did *An Audience With* in '82, and this year *This Is Your Life*. Thereupon, I shall aim for a baronetcy in 2002, and canonisation in 2012.

Monday, 12 October
Letter from Cecil Franks saying that I get a mention in Mrs T's autobiography!! He says 'No word of a lie, the only one who comes out of it better than you is Denis.' It's a 900-page tome, so Murdoch must've had her *chained* to a typewriter to get it out so quickly.

Nice afternoon, so I strolled through the park & up Fitzjohn's Avenue to Perrin's Walk. Peter came to the door in a string vest & sou'wester. 'I've got a leak in the boudoir, but I suppose you'd better come in.' It's a little Regency place, tucked away like Devonshire, except he has all his relics lying about. He said 'I'm fat now because I'm eating rather than drinking. Here, have a fondant fancy. Take a pink one, 'cos I don't care for them.' Said he regretted not

---

[92] *GamesMaster*, Channel 4, 1992-8. The monocled amateur astronomer Sir Patrick Moore (1923-2012) took the job.

getting in touch when Lou died. 'If you want the truth, I was disappointed when you went in with the Tories. I've no right to be annoyed, but I was.' I told him it was a favour that got out of hand. I said 'Work was drying up & it was something to while away the hours… I knew within a week I wasn't cut out for it.' He spoke fondly of Lin, the wife. Three years married, but they don't live together. I told him about Flo & reflected on the parallels in our lives. I stayed an hour, during which time he smoked a dozen John Player Superkings… Glad I went, but I shan't go again.

Got to Flo's & she served the hake at 5.40. We saw the TV News, with Heston tearing the President to pieces in the debate. The sound kept cutting out when Zorba was speaking & when the moderator announced 'I'm sorry everyone, we're having mike problems,' Chuck said 'Are you referring to the microphones or Mr Dukakis?…' Cue peals of laughter & at once one knew it was game, set & match.

Friday, 16 October
Note to Wolfenden to alter the will, so that provision is made for Flo; I don't want her left in the lurch… Had to listen to *Room 101* at noon, as Michael says they want me to be a guest. I am to select ten things I have an aversion to – people, places, television programmes, songs, etc. – in the hope of having them banished forever. It's *Desert Island Discs* for sneering misanthropes, and I shall look forward to appearing.

Monday, 19 October
Up early. Forced down dry toast & coffee… 7.33 from Euston to B'ham. The immense driver was waiting for me on the platform. 'Are you really that tall?' I asked. 'Six-eight in my socks, bab,' he said. I skittered in his wake to the car. Awful traffic, but got to the studios in time for *Good Morning with Anne & Nick*. The set is done up like a through-lounge, *achingly* bourgeois & Laura Ashley. I was meant to be discussing stomach ulcers (and to champion Mr Chatham's methods), but we were waylaid by reports of the Russian bug being detected in Ipswich. I didn't mind a bit, 'cos they brought on the dishy Doctor Porter & he shared my settee. It was worth the journey just for that… Mutton casserole for lunch, with Ruth & Judi.[93] Ruth said 'My gran was a Williams, Ken, from Swansea.' I wanted to say 'A *Williams*… in *Wales*? Have

---

[93] Ruth Madoc (1943-2022), Welsh actress, best known for her portrayal of Gladys Pugh in *Hi-de-Hi!*; Judi Spiers (b. 1953), English radio and TV presenter.

you rung the papers?', but I said 'Fancy. My father's lot were from Port Talbot, but they're long dead,' which put the nutcrackers on that... Into make-up again at 2 o'c. for Christmas *Telly Addicts*. There I met Michael Ball, Danny Baker & Geoffrey Hughes,[94] who plonked himself in the chair & said 'I don't need much, girls. If you're out of miracles, a bit of Crème Puff will do...' Edmonds came into the dressing room & apologised for the ill-feeling over the "Gotcha" business. He said 'I've seen the rushes and it's really great stuff... it doesn't show you in a bad light at all, quite the contrary.' I agreed to think it over... Started the game at 4 o'c. The other team was Rosemarie Ford, the pair from *Birds of a Feather*, & Michelle somebody from *EastEnders*. It was death!! I sat there without the faintest idea what was going on, so of course I overdid it. I know I was dreadful... but I've been around long enough for that seemingly not to matter: they respond *despite* the awfulness, which is at once heartwarming and plumb depressing. When it was all over Danny said 'Sod the train; I'll give you a lift back to the Smoke.' We talked without lull all the way home! I became quite uninhibited. He knows all the old turns & the related yarns tickled him rouge. He's read both my books!! There's the Left-wing disposition, of course, & he was pointedly *caustic* about 'your bloody mate Maggie', but it wasn't personal. He said 'Yentob's[95] been talking to me about a late-night chat show... would you come on & be a guest?' & I said 'Of course I will.'

Tuesday, 20 October
Stanley rang. 'Get your glad rags on, I'm taking you out for dinner.' Il Pentolone on Ganton Street at 7.30. What a find! Secluded & cosy. He said 'We came here for Biggins' birthday party. If you don't have the Pasta alla Norma, then you've only yourself to blame.' We talked of the virus. Stanley's convinced it's biological warfare, but I said I doubted the Ivans are capable of that. He admitted he's desperate to retire, but finances won't allow it. 'Scots are meant to be frugal,' I said, 'what have you been spending it on?' Giuseppe (the owner) trolled up, clutching his Instamatic. 'I want to make-a pictures of all the impotent people what 'ave come in 'ere,' he said. 'Well,' muttered Stanley, 'we certainly fit the bill.'

---

[94] Michael Ball (b. 1962), West End singer and actor; Danny Baker (b. 1957), comedy writer, journalist and DJ; Geoffrey Hughes (1944-2012), Merseyside actor, noted for roles in *Coronation Street, Keeping Up Appearances* and *The Royle Family*.
[95] Alan Yentob (b. 1947), TV executive and presenter; Controller of BBC1, 1992-6.

Thursday, 22 October
Typed a long reply to Barbara & Tony in Hull, but the '*n*' key has now totally gone west – every missive comes out in desperate need of Alan Turing… Flo came to vacuum, & then we watched the news with cheese rolls. After more Ipswich drear, they showed the designs for the new banknotes… in place of the Queen's head they've stuck a dirty great dove over a continental map. Pigeon fanciers will be beside themselves, but there's something dismaying about the whole thing.

At 2 o'c. walked to Museum Street for the *Remains* table read. Nice to meet everyone (especially Superman,[96] who was *eminently* charming & quite beautiful), but these things are generally a waste of time, especially for a film such as this where half the story is conveyed through dewy-eyed stares.

Friday, 23 October
The stupid fool left *eight* pints of silver top. It'll be kids tampering with the dial, but now the kitchen is little more than a Unigate depot… Spitting, so got a cab to BH. Never been up to the Radio 5 studios before. All fur coat & no drawers – state of the art equipment transmitting rubbish & repeats. Met Nick Hancock in the pristine gallery. He's skittish, but quick-witted & likeable. He dispensed with prefacing and said 'I'm cocky, but not enough to give *you* direction, I'm not that stupid!…' We had a pleasant conversation. My choices for oblivion were the *Nine O'Clock News* title music, *A Man For All Seasons*, jelly under soap, *The Isle of Capri*, poor hygiene, *West Side Story*, "teamwork", the sound engineer on *Eldorado*, Beethoven's Opus 48/4, and His Holiness the Pope… He agreed with the whole list, with the exception of Beethoven: 'We have to be fair and concede that it's not a bad tune, for a deaf bloke.' The producer wanted to take us for drinks afterwards, but he has one brown eye & one blue, and I can't be doing with that.

Saturday, 24 October
Letter from Andrew Davies,[97] asking if I'd play *myself* in the follow-up to *House of Cards*.[98] I think not… I was only pretending to be a politician in the

---

[96] Christopher Reeve (1952-2004), American actor; played the 'Man of Steel' in four *Superman* movies, 1978-87.
[97] Welsh screenwriter (b. 1936); notable adaptations include BBC productions of *Middlemarch* and *Bleak House*.
[98] *To Play the King* (1993), directed by Paul Seed; the role mooted for KW, Lord Quillington, was eventually played by Frederick Treves.

first place; I don't think I'd get away with it a second time… Rupert turned up at the door with bagels. I said 'How dare you come here unannounced?' It's too bad of him. For all I know he'd spent the morning being coughed over by some careless Suffolker, who's to say? I shut the door in his face. Rang Flo to tell her No Meals next week, as I shall be fasting. Went upstairs for the tradiola. Used the gloves & took my time.

Monday, 26 October
Holloway Road at 10 o'c. for the *Remains* fitting. I only have two costumes; the butler getup & the pyjamas. They seemed satisfied. On the way back I relented & purchased an electronic typewriter. I avoid the Japanese brands ordinarily, but this Panasonic was reasonably priced, chiefly because the boy at Currys let me have the display model with a further discount. 'An idiot could work it,' he said candidly, 'you just plug it in & you're away.' Dragged it home and had a practice, after disinfecting the keys. It'll take some getting used to. There is an ultrasonic buzz when it's switched on – one can *feel* its presence in the room. Still, it's a bit of company.

Tuesday, 27 October
Woke early, jolted by a dream. I was standing in the shop, cutting hair next to young Graham (Gordon's boy), but here he was *my* son, and I said 'Don't throw it all away like I did…' Couldn't shake the image all morning. I think of what I might've been as a father – overloving the child like mad in order to spite Charlie, indulging his passions, encouraging his curiosity. If I'd been typical, I imagine I'd've made a decent fist of it, and it may have brought some meaning to all this. I looked around the drawing room from the armchair & mused that 'Soon this'll all be in black bags, silently waiting to be claimed by the dustmen.' Not a discomforting thought.

Had one slice of toast for tea. Saw the News. Thirty English dead now, 28 in Suffolk and two in Essex. When I was putting away the ink rubber I found a crumpled note from Louie in the sideboard. It had got stuck behind the drawer. 'Come in when you're ready, son. I have made cheese straws.' Of course, I cried.

Friday, 30 October
Car at 6 o'c. for Pinewood. That Mad Alice did my make-up!! 'Oh, 'ere we go,' she said, 'look what the cat's dragged in...' John Landis[99] came & took me thro' to the hangar-like stage & introduced me to Cubby.[100] He was wedged into a canvas chair next to the fan heater, sucking on a panatela. It's slightly barmy, hearing oneself say 'How d'you do, Mr Broccoli?' as tho' one were back on *Jackanory*. He smiled & said 'You're here to make sure we don't take ourselves too serious.' Charmed, I'm sure.

Absurd to think that all this goes on, whilst fifty yards away we made *Carry On Spying* for tuppence ha'penny – if something's not up to scratch here, they throw a cheque at it. I was with Brown & Llewelyn[101] in the office set. Landis took me aside & said 'I know this guy (Governor of Hong Kong) is hopeless, but I want him to be likeable, OK? Not too annoying... Inept, but in a fun way, that's what I want.' He seemed satisfied with the tone I set. I've not much to do, but it's interesting to see how the Americans work. Hard & humourlessly is my conclusion. They're flagging a bit (after all, they've been shooting for seven months), so I recited a few vile variants of *There once was a man from Nantucket* to buoy the mood. Alas, the response was somewhat muted.

Monday, 2 November
The canteen staff are now compelled to wear face masks when dishing up the vittles.[102] The aim is to imply sterility, but in practice there's a sense of having lasagna flung at one by the cast of *Jimmy's*[103]... I ate with Dalton, Whoopi Goldberg (his inamorata), & Cubby's daughter Tina. W.G. said 'I was talking about you just yesterday!' It seems Mags has agreed to do a sequel to that ghastly Nun rubbish. 'How about coming over to Frisco to play one of the pastors?' I laughed & said 'It's a darling thought, Whoopi – but I'm strict

---

[99] American filmmaker (b. 1950), director of films such as *The Blues Brothers* and *An American Werewolf in London*.
[100] Albert R. Broccoli (1909-96), American-born producer of eighteen James Bond films, 1962-95.
[101] Robert Brown (1921-2003), English actor, "M" in five Bond films, 1983-92; Desmond Llewelyn (1914-99), Welsh actor, "Q" in eighteen Bond films, 1963-99.
[102] The government ruling on compulsory face masks for food preparation personnel came into force on 31 October.
[103] ITV documentary series (1987-96), focused on the staff and patients of St James's University Hospital, Leeds.

Wesleyan, you see, & I don't travel far 'cos of the bum...' I said to Tina 'They're not really calling the film "Bond 17", are they?' She said 'No, that's the working title. We're pretty set on *Property of a Lady*.' Typical! My first shot at something butch & it has a schmaltzier name than a Barbara Cartland knockoff... They started grousing about Chuck & the election, but fortunately Tim & I were called away to the set.

Tuesday, 3 November
In stead of saying 'But the place will be crawling with MSS' (Chinese secret service), I said 'crawling with M&S'... They cut & I apologised: 'I do beg your pardon – it's the name of an English department store, you see, and I'm a *slave* to their knitwear...' Landis shouted 'Yeah, we don't need your life story, honey. Let's go again.' Afterwards he came up & said 'I'm sorry, there was no need to snap. Only we're a week behind & United are all over my ass.'

Wednesday, 4 November
Went to Philip for the massage. The technique he employed on the lumbar – a strenuous dough-kneading motion – radiated warming waves right up the spinal column, and had the most curious effect on the loins... when I turned over it was iron-solid & bouncing to the heartbeat. He didn't bat an eyelid. 'Don't worry about that,' he said. Worry about it?! At this age I was proud as punch.

Came back and studied the shooting script of *Remains of the Day*. Watched the News. Heston is in, with a landslide.[104] At the end of the muddled speech he said 'And to our enemies, know this: playtime is over. Your worst nightmare just got elected.' Everyone in the hall cheered, maniacally.

Thursday, 5 November
Rupert came to the house & cooked a frittata. I made him scrub his hands twice with the germicidal. He says they've upped the chlorine levels at the pool, and people are complaining that the water is stinging their eyes... He has booked us five nights in the Algarve from the 26th, to recuperate after the filming.

Friday, 6 November
Went to Silksound for the Nestle's voiceover. The girl perfunctorily rubbed a wet wipe over the microphone 'to be on the safe side'. I had to say 'Aero.

---

[104] The Republicans won 512 electoral college votes, the Democrats 26.

Ooh! lovely bubbly!...' Four words, and the week in Albufeira is paid for. Then to the Dickens Coffee House in Covent Garden with this Robert Ross[105] who wanted anecdotes for a book he's writing. Ebullient fellow; courteous & bonny. And positively *encyclopædic* apropos comedy history. He knows more than me!! They're a curious breed, these young chaps with their wide-eyed obsessions. I did the usual test & held his hand all the way from Wellington Street to Charing Cross tube, & he didn't flinch once... Home to a message on the machine from M.A. 'I've had Peter Shaffer on. He's written a play with you, Maggie & Eileen Atkins[106] in mind. Could you come to the office on Monday to look it over?' Gadzooks!! I'm more in demand than Dettol!

Monday, 9 November
Walked round to St Anne's Court. Gillian looked like death warmed up, so I kept my distance & went right through to Michael. Read the manuscript from Shaffer. It's called *Triple Entente*. What starts as a maladroit love triangle between a thinly veiled Denis Thatcher, Raisa Gorbacheva & Nancy Reagan culminates in a clandestine *coup d'état*. Everything takes place in reception rooms, whilst the grand poobah spouses are busied with state affairs. It is wittily done & I should very much like to be in it.

Had tea at Flordeliza's. The problem with being a dinner guest, instead of the *employer*, is having to uncomplainingly accept what one is given. I told her 'Nothing too spicy' – but the stuff I was served could've stripped lacquer. I managed a few conciliatory morsels, but within minutes I could feel the pylorus raging. Went home for preemptive Milk of Mag.

Wednesday, 11 November
Car came at 6.30 & we arrived in Chippenham at 8.43. I'm in the Angel Hotel, which has been commandeered by the production; all cast & crew are here, save for the big fish who have rented apartments for the duration. It's bloody freezing & the sash window in my room wouldn't shut properly. I sent the runner to complain, but he's a frightful Mary Ann & achieved nothing, so I had to go down myself... At lunch I met Pigott-Smith & James

---

[105] English writer (b. 1970), author of reference works on British comedy, including *The Carry On Companion*, 1996.
[106] Prolific English actress and screenwriter (b. 1934); marched with KW, Vanessa Redgrave and others from the profession in 1976, protesting the arrest of actors in apartheid South Africa.

Fox,[107] and afterwards they drove us to Badminton House to get our bearings. Ivory came to me & said 'Hi.' He's a man of few words. Emma Thompson said 'Oh, it's marvellous direction; he just told me "don't sigh, *ever*" – which is all you need, really.' Well, it's better than her father could muster, and that's a *fact*. Still, it's all quite convivial. We watched a scene & there's no rehearsal, they just get on with it, which is super. Thence to the make-up portacabin where they fiddled about with the hair & decided on the slap etc. There's a boy, William, who looks after us. 'Whatever you need, let me know,' he said, 'Tea, coffee, soup, hot choc, your wish is my command.' I said 'Ooh, you're giving me ideas,' & he winked cheekily.

Dinner at the hotel with Lonsdale[108] who couldn't be duller if his life depended on it.

Thursday, 12 November
We did the scene where I go arse over tit with the silver tray on to the patio. They strapped foam to the knees & elbows, and brought in a mat painted to resemble the flags. A Bostonian called Hank, sporting a sleeveless denim jacket, came & instructed me on how to fall. 'Don't sweat it,' he said, champing on his Wrigley's, 'You're 130lbs & padded, you'll practically float down…' I got away with three takes, and everyone applauded. 'Buster Keaton *lives*!!' shouted Emma… Whilst they laid the dolly track we sat in the blue drawing room & drank coffee. Christopher is so stupefyingly attractive it's beyond ridiculous. Of course, I panic in such company and start to show off: I dropped the strides to reveal the sagging thermals & shouted 'Yo-ho! the bum, it's hanging down in pleats!…' Emma howled, but the repulsion was writ large across Superman's face, which sent my mood to the gutter for the rest of the day.

Friday, 13 November
In spite of their efforts, the legs are black & blue. The runner redeemed himself by fetching some arnica cream from Boots, and I caked it on. At breakfast they informed us that the continuity girl had spent the night coughing her lungs up & has been taken away. A puissant tang of disinfectant pervades the hotel

---

[107] Tim Pigott-Smith (1946-2017), BAFTA-winning actor for *The Jewel in the Crown*, 1985; James Fox (b. 1939), BAFTA-winning actor for *The Servant*, 1963 – a member of the Fox acting dynasty.
[108] Michael Lonsdale (1931-2020), French actor; played the villain Hugo Drax in the 1979 Bond film *Moonraker*.

– they all moan, but I find it a vital comfort. From the sparse trolley I selected a miniature box of cornflakes. Heartbreakingly unappetising, but sterile.

We filmed the bit where Tony shows the old man to his room. Struggling with the stairs required little acting, as I was in genuine agony... I do admire Tony. He is disciplined and rapt, certainly, but there's a lightness of touch – after all, we're making a picture, not curing the contagion. All talk aside, it's larking about in fancy dress, only more finespun & refined than perhaps one is used to.

Back at the ranch I was stuck with Lonsdale & Pigott-Smith. Before the meal I asked to see the kitchen staff, on the pretence of thanking them for their efforts, but it was really to scrutinise the working practices. They were all gloved, but I stuck to jacket potato (flesh only) & tinned tunafish. One can't be too careful... I escaped from the old duffers & had a nightcap with Mr Ishiguro & Lorna. He said 'I saw the rushes today. You've silenced a few naysayers, sir.'

Sunday, 15 November
The Duke of Beaufort appeared, to ensure we're not wrecking his house. I said 'It's delightful to see you again.' '*Again?*' he replied, which put me in my place[109]... Easy day for me, as I was in bed throughout. The only trying bit was retaining stillness whilst dead, thanks to a persistent bluebottle that took a shine to my nose. Norman eventually despatched it with a shatterproof ruler.

Dined with Savident & Wickham.[110] Jeffry said 'I've come to think that it takes an American to properly film a British story... This lot know what they're doing. Did you see *Howards' Way*? Dynamite.' Of course, he meant *Howards End*.

I went & sat in the bedroom with the light off. The days and nights here bear no relation to each other. Nighttime loneliness is acuter when the day has been excessively peopled, so much so that I find myself relying on Louie. I thought I'd put all that behind me, but it appears to be an essential last resort. I talk to her, & strain to hear the reply. I'm reminded of *Pinfold* – 'I don't exist, but I do love you'.[111]

---

[109] See entry for 11 June 1990.
[110] John Savident (1938-2024), Guernsey-born actor, played Fred Elliott in *Coronation Street*, 1994-2006; Jeffry Wickham (1933-2014), English actor, President of Equity, 1992-4.
[111] 'Margaret' in *The Ordeal of Gilbert Pinfold* (1957) by Evelyn Waugh.

Monday, 16 November
They put me in an apron for the Brasso scene. A faded chitty in the hem read 'Mr Hudson, Series 5'... they'd actually given me Gordon's smock! Bright said 'Yes, lots of this stuff was used on *Upstairs*; it's all the right period.' I felt secretly proud wearing it, & peculiarly close to my friend.

I can't face three days hanging around until the location change, so I asked Luciana if I could go home. She leapt into action. Within half an hour a car was there, ready & waiting. William caught me and said 'Slinking off, are we?'... The driver was one of the 'What d'you make of all these Pakistanis?' set, so I feigned exhaustion & closed my eyes. Got back to Devonshire Close at 6.40. Flo had neatly arranged piles of fan letters on the table. It seems my *This Is Your Life* was shown last week. Rupert came to make the dinner whilst I set about replying. Over salmon flan he told me about a buxom signora at the pool whose bikini strap got caught in the filter, forcing her to shed it & bound starkers past the diving boards. 'Her wet tits slapped together,' he recounted vividly, 'applauding her all the way to the changing room.' The baths close on Wednesday until further notice because of the virus.

Tuesday, 17 November
Met Paul outside Joe Allen's. We waited ages to be seated, as they've had to reduce the number of tables & space them out to comply with regulations. I told him my news & he said, with a proud countenance, 'You're blooming. It's about time you enjoyed yourself and fed the soul a bit. It's such a boost to see you like this.' On the way back we chatted to a road sweeper on Montague Street. He was taking down the tarts' adverts from the telephone boxes. 'We pin 'em up down the depot,' he said. 'They make a cracking *muriel*...' Heartening to hear that the spirit of Hilda Ogden lives on.

Wednesday, 18 November
It's strange to consider that I should feel so satisfied when the world is crumbling to bits. Time was, I'd be as mentally engulfed by a national crisis as the next man, particularly in financially perilous days. But this public hysteria seems entirely remote to me. What's more, their rackety discontent is something of an ugly comfort. I suppose it's a mean symptom of irreligion, endorsable to myself only by virtue of having already served my time, and a brutal judgment that now others must serve theirs.

Flordeliza showed up to clean, wearing her face mask!! She *is* oriental, & consequently more accustomed to heeding authority, but they remain a vitiating barrier... I sat at the desk, watching as she lissomely ran the duster up the radiator columns, robotic yet elegant in her motions. I wondered what she might be thinking as she set about her task, if anything. I was going to say something profound, touching on our association & the snugness of our routine, but she cut me dead with the supremely mundane 'This is shit, I prefer Mr Sheen'... I asked her to iron the shirts & do the packing. She did it, tho' it was sulkily done.

Thursday, 19 November
Got to Dawlish in time for lunch. No fretful mood here: the nippy salt air rolls in off the Channel, puffing cobwebs & apprehension clean away. The digs are more salubrious than the last place, prudent & unfussy... I sat with John Calley[112] & Hugh Grant (who is a *honey*) and they served us the catch of the day, brill with fennel. I like Hugh. Not only for the prettiness, but he's a real sourpuss, which is so comely in the good-looking. An agitated Glen interrupted the suet sponge. 'Schedule change, folks,' he sighed dourly, 'Peter's had to race back to Yorkshire, so we're up a gum tree.' 'An ee bah gum tree,' said John & I laughed. Well, it was pretty good for an American. Glen unimpressed. 'It's not funny, his wife's been hit by a Volvo'... The change meant that they decided to do the staircase stuff *today*. I hadn't even time to unpack before it was on to the minibus to Powderham. I was busting by the time we arrived, but couldn't face the Tardis.[113] The Earl is in Bermuda, so William slipped me upstairs to one of the guest bathrooms. Gold taps, *u.s.w.*[114] The most upmarket piss of my life... All sounds in the great hall echo for days, so there was an army of crew stood around the stairs holding foam boards to dampen things down. It went alright until little Sairita, roped in from catering, came over queer & flaked out. I watched the polystyrene panels fall like dominoes, until the last bashed into the priceless Tompion grandfather clock, cracking the glass. Mrs Denbigh, the house manager, was in floods of tears, fearing for her job. They took her outside to calm down. Emma clutched my arm & said 'There goes the no-claims bonus.'

---

[112] American film producer (1930-2011); credits include *Catch-22*, *Postcards from the Edge* and *The Da Vinci Code*.
[113] Portable toilet.
[114] German, *und so weiter* = 'and so on'.

Friday, 20 November
I was predominantly in the background, serving coffee. The right arm was soon aching, but Terry came to the rescue by pointing out that no liquid was visible in the shot, so they emptied the pot & I mimed... There's a nurse that hangs around now, rather boot-faced & broad in the beam. Her approach is heralded by a niff of TCP, & if you don't move sharpish she's ramming a thermometer in your ear.

A revived Sairita came with refreshments and informed us of the conflagration.[115] We gathered by the portable TV in wardrobe & watched the firemen struggling to keep the blaze under control. The Queen & Prince Philip have been rushed to hospital with smoke inhalation, but Jennie Bond[116] – looking windswept & grave – reported that both are conscious... The dining room scene went well. Tyrwhitt, Lord Courtenay's butler, was on hand to show me the ropes. He said 'Twist it slightly toward your body to catch the last few drips & send them back down the neck.' 'Story of your life, dear,' said Halliday,[117] & everyone fell about. I loathe such vile crudity.

The hotel manageress told us that one of the reception staff has fallen ill, so I dined in my room. Saw *News at Ten*, live from the castle. A few orange flames continue to lick the night sky, but for the most part it's out. It seems that burning above HM's apartments caused damage below, and they couldn't get the door open. She & Philip were trapped for ten minutes, choked by the fumes, before rescuers axed their way in. Hundreds of priceless artworks in ashes... I was in bed when Paula knocked!! It was gone twelve! She was on the scrounge for Optrex as she had a lash caught. As it happens I had some in the brown washbag, but once it's lent it's polluted, so I sent her away empty-handed.

Saturday, 21 November
Mrs Denbigh is watching everyone like a hawk. What with that & Fat Hips Houlihan doing the rounds, there's a *Cell Block H*[118] feel to the proceedings... Various outdoor bits to do. Drear, but I chatted to Fox about his stint with

---

[115] The Windsor Castle disaster; faulty lighting equipment in a room above the Queen's apartments was later established as the cause of the fire. The final death toll was four, and the total cost of repairs, which took place from 1993-8, was £52.8m.
[116] English journalist and TV presenter (b. 1950), the BBC's royal correspondent, 1989-2003.
[117] Peter Halliday (1924-2012), Welsh actor.
[118] *Prisoner: Cell Block H* (1979-86), cult Australian soap opera set in a tough women's prison.

the evangelicals. We've only use of the house till Tuesday, so it all has to be crammed in. His Lordship returns tomorrow, but I will be gone!! I'm not required again until the Dyrham Park stuff on Jan. 2nd. I bid my adieus, but most were too busy to notice.

Sunday, 22 November
They cancelled *House of Eliott*,[119] just so we could see Miss Bond standing outside the Edward 7th hospital, telling us in a myriad of ways that she hadn't the faintest idea what was occurring inside.

I made myself sardines on toast. Pat 'phoned to say she's come down with the virus! Interesting letter from a lady in Truro who swears that strips of tinfoil attached to the gutters helps to deter birds. She says 'they get dazzled and cannot cope…'

Monday, 23 November
Went to post & got stamps. 'You really ought to be wearing your mask, dear,' said the woman with the drawn-on eyebrows. Told her to mind her business. I'm not hanging a clammy incubator round my nostrils, I'll take my chances with the fresh air. Went to bank to order escudos, but returned to a message from R. to say that Portugal's been put on the red list, so the holiday's off!! Hang this bloody plague!

Wednesday, 25 November
Someone called Otis from *QT* magazine telephoned asking for an interview. 'We're doing a feature on gay celebs' houses & I'd like to come and photograph *the real you* at home…' When I dismissed the idea, he changed tack with 'We'd also like to know if your lifeguard friend is a live-in partner or something more casual.' I said 'I have lived alone my entire adult life, and I shall put your impertinence down to tiredness,' & I hung up.

Walked to Duck Lane for the Tandy voiceover. Usual crap. Came back & R. 'phoned but I said I didn't want to see him. Saw the news & the Queen is still in hospital!!

Friday, 27 November
Contract in the post from Ted & Ian for *Just a Minute*. They want to take the programme around the country when the panic subsides, so that 'a wider

---

[119] BBC drama series (1991-4), centring on the lives of two sisters who establish a *haute couture* fashion house in 1920s London; created by Jean Marsh and Eileen Atkins.

1992

range of audiences get to experience the show…' That's all very well, but it won't be *them* stuck in some grotty doss-house in Aberdeen… I had two bananas for lunch. Hardly *haute cuisine*, but riskless. Watched Channel 4 News, 'cos I think it delves a bit deeper. They had Vstavlyat sat at an enormous desk in the Kremlin. He rubbished claims that the BND's[120] footage shows Soviet scientists concocting the virus, denouncing it as western propaganda… but then he would, wouldn't he? He was wearing an awful custard-coloured woolly & no tie, and I saw him, I saw my banana skins on the napkin & the hail stones tapping at the window and I suddenly felt so suicidally depressed it was quite overwhelming. Tears raced down the cheeks, & I couldn't even raise the energy to staunch them.

Saturday, 28 November
Went to get papers. Sam Sugar was exercising the whelps & we discussed this Queen business. Sam thinks it's worse than they're letting on. He said 'Can't you find out from one of your political compadres?' I told him that I ain't got any… It does seem grotesque that a *lack* of news about Her Majesty warrants more column inches than the startling fact that 650 of her subjects have gone to their glory since Monday.

Monday, 30 November
I was admiring the streakless clarity achieved on the fanlight by the new man when, before my eyes, a gull deposited a prodigious alabaster turd right across it. I ought to've seen it as an omen & gone straight back to bed. Before 9 o'c., I'd received a letter from Shaffer to tell me the play's off till *August* 'cos Maggie's signed up to do Lady Bracknell for Hytner, a 'phone call from St Mary's to say Pat's been admitted & can I bring her in some nighties, and to top it all the incessant banging from 49 began thanks to their sodding loft conversion… Walked to Pat's to collect things. It's like an Aladdin's cave of crap. Small wonder she's succumbed, living in such filth. Went to drop off the bag at the hospital, but they wouldn't let me in as I refused the mask. A Bangladeshi porter called Vidyut took pity on me & said he'd take the stuff up to the ward if I signed for him. Just as well, really, as one isn't permitted to truly *visit* the afflicted (they're taped off in isolation), & I wouldn't want to be lumbered anyway… Had to wait outside Marks's, as they're only allowing thirty people in at a time. I stood quivering on the pavement with

---

[120] The *Bundesnachrichtendienst*, West Germany's Federal Intelligence Service.

other would-be shoppers. O! it's draconian, and completely futile. Half-arsed measures will bear no fruit whatsoever; they should either close *everything* or let nature take its course. All this faff just emanates an *illusion* of safety, nothing more.

Tuesday, 1 December
At 10.15 the telephone rang. A girl called Phoebe from Research Services. 'We're conducting a brief survey to evaluate public opinion on the government's handling of the H1N1/92 Soviet Influenza outbreak. Would you be willing to take part?' 'Thirstily, my dear,' I said, 'in fact, I've been *praying* you'd call.' 'Err… right. Thank you… So, on a scale of one to ten, with one being "not at all" & ten being "very much so", do you feel you have been provided with sufficient information by the authorities concerning the spread of the H1N1/92 Soviet Influenza virus & ways in which you might protect yourself & your family from it?' 'Oh Phoebe! that's such a *well-proportioned* question, & divinely asked, if I might say so. Has anyone ever told you you've an exquisite speaking voice? It awakens memories of Sandra Dickinson[121] in her prime, I don't mind telling you. Quite lovely. I'm imagining you as a pulchritudinous strawberry blonde, resplendent with peach eyeshadow & an aubergine twinset, am I close?' 'Umm… I just need a number between one and ten, sir.'

It's ever so quiet here. I think I've had enough. The drawing room has become a waiting room.

Wednesday, 2 December
Flo came with the shopping. I didn't let her in. She left the bags on the step & I sent her away. She'd been to the small Londis (as one isn't forced to queue outside), so it was slim pickings, just some tinned stuff & a few small veg. Had the Lean Cuisine, which was surprisingly good. The packet said to microwave-heat it, but I did satisfactorily at regulo 4… At 3 o'c. they interrupted *Starsky & Hutch* to confirm HM's diagnosis. Jennie Bond (whose ubiquity is beginning to nark) speculated that it was probably contracted *at the hospital*, after admittance. Rang Sylvia to cancel chiropody appts. until further notice. No point in needlessly putting meself in harm's way.

---

[121] Anglo-American actress (b. 1948), famed for her 'dumb blonde' characters with high-pitched voices.

Thursday, 3 December
Note from Ken Branagh to say that *Swan Song* is to be nominated for an Oscar!![122] and that I'm welcome to join him in California for the ceremony, virus permitting! It's nothing short of potty. A spot of flowery lingo in period weeds & the Americans turn to jelly. The whole stupid thing's a junket anyway, a fancy fashion parade with lashings of smoked salmon... There was a break in the rain at 4 o'c. so I went to Doug to get throat sweets for this tickle. Audrey was serving. 'The old man's got gut rot,' she said gaily, 'can't keep nothing in.' I asked if they'd a powder in stock that might cure him. 'Christ no,' she laughed, 'this stuff's nine-parts plaster dust.' With purveyors like *that* on the staff, it's no wonder Doug's got the runs.

Friday, 4 December
Up at 8.10 after a dreadful night. Didn't bother with paper. That sibilant nurse from St Mary's telephoned to tell me that Pat is much recovered. 'Oh, right,' I said. 'She's one of the lucky ones, you know' came the pert reply, as tho' I ought to have dropped to my knees & wept with gratitude. I coughed on the 'phone & she hissed 'Someone should see to that, have you been tested?' Told her to stick to her knitting.

Rupert came after work. They've reopened the baths, but only ten in at a time, so he's bored to tears. He said 'I know it's probably just a cold, but will you go & get it looked at? For me?' Told him I'd think about it. Truth is, I'd sooner not know.

Watched Neil Kinnock at 9 o'c. Best I've heard him, with an apt sense of decorum & precision. We are called on to stay at home if we have *any* of the Five Symptoms and are *ordered* to wear face coverings in indoor public places, on pain of prosecution. He was brief about the Queen, but it don't sound good. The only helpful news is that I won't have to go to the Conservative Assoc. Xmas Party, as the ghastly thing's been called off.

Saturday, 5 December
The sensation lies somewhere between gargling staples and fellating a cactus, & all the while the nose drips like the parish pump. I managed to get dressed, but the exhaustion was *immense*, so I just had hot water with lemon & read

---

[122] In the Live Action Short Film category; the eventual winner was the French film *Omnibus* by Sam Karmann.

Beyond Our Kenneth

the Motion book on Larkin.[123] It's thorough, but there's the inevitable Wagnerian reality, in that great art somehow springs from the most flawed or drab of personages. Interesting that he instructed the secretary to burn the diaries. Presumably they detail events so disgusting that the ignominy would've eventually transferred to the poetry, and that would never do.

 Couldn't manage any food. At 3 o'c. I got through to Dr Shanmugaratnam & described the symptoms. He hedged his bets, but said 'They are typical signs, although the fact you're up & about is good.' I am to keep hidden & hydrated, like a block of Oasis foam.

Sunday, 6 December
Pat called to say she'd been discharged. I couldn't *bear* the thought of her bestowing endless advice as a "survivor", so I kept quiet about my own worries & rang off. I feel weak as a kitten, but prepared. I have decided to put all the strength that remains into writing Five Letters, one each to M., Stanley, Mags, Paul and Rupert. It'll have to be on the Hirohito, because I get P+N if I hold the pen for too long.

Monday, 7 December
Got thro' to M.'s secretary. She said 'He's in a meeting, but they're meant to be finished at noon, shall I get him to 'phone you back?' I said 'No, it's alright, dear, I'll hang on with you.' She laughed, thinking I was joking, but I went on with 'He's a darling man, your boss. He's my best friend in all the world. Is he a good employer?' It stumped her momentarily, but then, earnestly with a smiling voice she said 'He's very patient, kind, and I know he really cares about me.' I was moved by her perception & said 'How delightful. Aren't we the lucky ones?' I told her I'd ring again later, but I had some tea with lemon & typed my Letter to him.

 Constant coughing saps the energy. The pain is lessened, but to simply get up & switch the kettle on requires Herculæan efforts. Of course, I'm not blind to the irony. I've shunned visitors, I've sluiced the mitts in scalding bleach & I've sought out foods no mortal can've touched… yet I'm still up the creek. At 6.30 Flo stopped by. I argued for a while, but gave in eventually. She is going to stay.

---

[123] *Philip Larkin: A Writer's Life*, winner of the 1993 Whitbread Award for Biography.

Tuesday, 8 December
She practically force-fed me the porridge. Getting three spoonfuls down was a major operation. I said 'Get away from me, you sadistic cow,' but she just swore at me in Tagalog & persevered. She brought up the post & there is a letter from the Society of West End Theatre. I have been nominated for a Laurence Olivier award! I hope I win. I shall get the will amended to state my desire that any prizes won posthumously must be collected on my behalf by Bishop Muzorewa,[124] or not at all. I wrote a letter to Paul.

At the final analysis, it is a fitting time to go, verily *mediæval* to be pathetically swept away in a pestilence along with the countless hordes. Praps we'll be dumped, with haphazard haste, into bulging pits on dockland waste ground, dispassionately encased in clay & promptly forgotten. Lou heated up a tin of chicken soup, but I couldn't eat it.

Wednesday, 9 December
I hear the heartbeat, as jagged, spluttering & raspy as an unravelling spool on a run-down Singer. Flo brought the plastic po, but I didn't produce much worth mentioning. The cough is less prominent, but I've no energy whatsoever. One can feel the systems shutting down – elbowed pitmen clocking off & switching out the lights. I've enough layers on me to rig out soft furnishings at Gamages, but I'm still frozen to the bone. I got her to bring the telephone & plug it into the socket by the bed. I rang Mark at Oxford. He is to be made deacon in June! He was very patient & read Holy Sonnet 19 to me, twice. Then the Brontë. I wept & he comforted me. He is a sweet boy.

> No coward soul is mine
> No trembler in the world's storm-troubled sphere
> I see Heaven's glories shine
> And Faith shines equal arming me from Fear

Flo gave me water & paracetamol at 8 o'c. & told me that the Queen died during *Going for Gold*.[125]

---

[124] Abel Muzorewa (1925-2010), served as the first and only Prime Minister of Zimbabwe Rhodesia, 1979-80.
[125] BBC daytime quiz show (1987-96), hosted by Henry Kelly. Queen Elizabeth II actually died at 6 o'clock that morning.

Thursday, 10 December
There was a Christmas card in the second post from Baroness Thatcher. I'm sure I heard Gordon outside the window, but I couldn't get up to see. Of course, it can't have been him anyway. I ate half a tangerine.

Sunday, 13 December
She brought me the *Sunday Times*, all three hundredweight of it. Big picture of the King & Queen on the front. Diana coiffured to within an inch of her life. Edward II & Isabella mk. 2, I shouldn't wonder. He long since despensed with this younger model, & she's doubtless already been rogered by a Mortimer or two.[126]

M. came. He tried to hide the shock, ineffectually. He said 'This is the first time I've been in your bedroom.' 'You haven't missed much, dear,' I said, '*Eastbourne* has more bustle than my quarters.' He sat by the door & we talked until the rain stopped. He was whispering to Flo by the door for quite some time before leaving, but I couldn't catch any of it.

Monday, 14 December
It took an age & all of Flo's might, but I got downstairs. She went to Boots and got the liquid food for invalids. It's swallowable, but revolting. It purported to be Irish stew & carrots. I had a sniff & said 'I'm not having that muck,' but she as good as thrust it down me. Michael Anderson telephoned. That Curtis[127] wants me to play some old iron in a film he's making. 'I'm drowning in phlegm,' I wheezed, 'tell me about it next week.' He said 'Yes, you do sound a bit under the weather.'

At 6.30 Rupert called round, but I told her to send him away. I'm not having him see me like this. I watched him thro' the nets, looking put out. I haven't the energy to care.

With all the endless royal stuff jamming the airwaves, now is the time. I daren't miss the opportunity.

---

[126] A play on words on KW's part. Isabella of France, wife of King Edward II, overthrew her husband with the help of her lover *Roger Mortimer*, Earl of March, in 1327; the king's (possibly sexual) relationships with his favourites, including *Hugh Despenser*, helped lead to his downfall – KW makes parallels between these characters, the contemporary royal couple, Mrs Parker Bowles, and others.

[127] Richard Curtis (b. 1956), New Zealand-born British screenwriter, producer and director. The proposal to KW was for him to play the role of Gareth in the film *Four Weddings and a Funeral*; in the event, this part was performed by Simon Callow.

Another pile of ribs and berylled flesh
Is wheeled across the ichor-spattered floor
A skivvy just arrived from Bangladesh
Comes trudging in to flannel off the gore
Absurd to think this foul Meccano set
Could once enkindle laughter and debate
Small wonder that we make ourselves forget
Our destiny is to disintegrate
He wafts away the fœtor and the flies
The relics weighed and slung into a bag
Zipped up and labelled sure to minimise
The truth in case it makes the living gag
The worms commence their squelching olid feast
The rest addressed by eulogist and priest

Tuesday, 15 December
Got her to fetch me the address book. Wasn't sure C.'s number would still work, but it did!! He was very discreet & understanding. Said he knew a chap with Mandrax[128] capsules, but that he wouldn't be around until Thursday. I have to be in control in case things get worse. Not having an escape plan is foolhardy.

That liquid stew came out looking precisely the same as when it went in. It's fascinating to note that the bum has behaved itself marvellously throughout all this. A silver lining.

She brought the laundry up to the bedroom to fold. She put a tea towel on her head & sang broken renditions of *Pack Up Your Troubles* and *I'm a Lady Policeman* that Louisa had taught her & I laughed. Then she sat by the bed. Had forty winks, after which I wrote to Mags by hand.

Wednesday, 16 December
Vivid dreams of Joe in Morocco and, curiously, Michael Hitchman[129] & myself – starkers in a rowing boat – pulling our oars & singing *As Long as He Needs Me*. At 9 o'c. Dr Shanmugaratnam 'phoned. I said I was much the same. Which is a lie, of course. It was hopeless trying to get me up, so she

---

[128] A combination sedative containing methaqualone and diphenhydramine.
[129] English actor and poet (1913-60). Close friend of KW throughout the 1950s; the pair would often engage in long philosophical conversations.

produced a clock radio from her flat & I listened to Radio 3. They played the Fauré quintet (No. 2)!! Naturally, I cried all the way through it. The tears of a sinking, shrivelled old man.

At 6.30 Stanley called! All pantomimes have been cancelled, so he's twiddling his thumbs. I told him I have a dreadful cold, but he was more interested in complaining about his feet. 'Ye could fry bacon on ma bunions,' he said.

I managed some sliced pear & it went down alright, so perhaps I'm on the mend. I hope to God I am, as I want to be in control of everything.

Thursday, 17 December
As one lies here in the stillness, thoughts inevitably turn to the culprit & theories on *who* planted the fatal seed? One yo-yos between fury & gratitude. Hope it was someone nice-looking with fine dentition. *Hateful* to think I'm going thro' all this due to some bucktoothed ogre.

Got down the stairs almost unaided, and settled in the armchair with two blankets swaddled round me. C. rang at 11 o'c. & we agreed a price. After a bit I said I fancied some pineapple juice, so I told her to go to Ravi's. Whilst she was gone, he dropped round with the packet. They're only little things. Pale pink. *Hergestellt in Westdeutschland.*

Had tomato soup from a beaker. Saw the King on the lunchtime news, grumbling about his *annus horribilis*, tho' scarcely able to conceal his delight that the top job has fallen his way so prematurely... Dozed off. When I woke, she was watching an old war film with Don Ameche,[130] and working her way through a tin of Roses. I watched her sub rosa – no, sub *Roses*! – as she nimbly untwirled the crackly foils & rolled the chocolates round & round the mouth in ecstasy. She's so very brave, throwing herself into the lion's den like this. I'm rather proud of her. It was the first time I can remember feeling *warm* in ages, wrapped up snug in my Georgian drawing room, observing my makeshift Louisa, who I *know* will cope well in the moment, and will act with delicacy & aptness.

Friday, 18 December
The sun is shining & I feel slightly better. Well, less dreadful. It'll be someone up there tempting me to stay, but I'm not seduced. There is a letter from Vancouver which says 'If ever I'm down, I turn to you – your movies, your

---

[130] American actor, comedian and vaudevillian (1908-93).

records, your books. You have a gift for spreading delight, which is the most special gift of all.' One has heard this gushing *veneration* since the earliest days, from giggling classmates egging one on, to the lunging idiots clustered at the stage door with their chewed biros & notepads. I've invariably dismissed it as sycophancy, flattery & mindless truckling – and I was right to. Yet an awful lot of that repudiation is down to the upbringing ('Don't get too big for your boots', 'You oughtn't think too much of yourself', etc.)... and, above all, a sincere mistrust of the sentiment, as I've *never* shared it. Seems unfair, on reflection, having the capacity to raise a smile in others but not in oneself. But perhaps it's necessary.

Sunday, 20 December
Sat in the yard with a hot water bottle. The fresh air was delicious. A huge black crow circled and then landed on the wall, tilting his head at me. Others will come, 'cos they know. She boiled me an egg & I said 'You've been a marvellous nurse. I've made sure you'll be alright, when the time comes,' but she was bleaching soiled smalls & only half-listening.

 I telephoned him & said I felt well enough for a turn in the park, to visit Louie on her birthday. Met him outside Marlborough at 2 o'c. What a vision!! in his brown leather coat & the maroon scarf I purchased in Scotland. Sod the Mandrax, *he* is the real tonic. I slipped my arm through his & we strolled to the Rose Garden. We sat on the bench by Lou & he offered salted cashews to the bolder of two squirrels. 'When this is all over I'll take you to Elba,' he said, 'You'll enjoy all the Napoleon things & they do a cake with figs that's to die for...' We meandered back thro' the chilly streets. He squeezed my hand & I watched him walk away.

 I'm thrown. I'd geared myself up to go, having been gifted the catalyst of a convenient plague. But now the creamy sunlight bathes London in a golden glow that makes one want to weep for the loveliness of it all. The irony is that this body, that has so often let me down, is fighting off its would-be conqueror with aplomb, and what remains is a svelter, superior frame. A glorious 9 stone 2. After the nap she prepared spaghetti on toast & we had it on our laps in front of *The Generation Game*. "Life is the name of the game..." All the while I was thinking of the pink tablets in the bedside table, and of sitting on that bench arm-in-arm... The 'phone went & it was Conor from Merchant Ivory saying I'm to travel to Dyrham Park on New Year's Day rather than the 2nd, & that they'll send a car. She came back from switching on my blanket &

said 'That was a happy evening.' As a treat I said she could use my lavatory, just this once, instead of traipsing round to Paddington Street. I don't like it, but she's earned the privilege, and it's bitter out.

Thursday, 31 December

Pasted in:

31/12/92 — 10.30 p.m.

Hi Ken,

    The day went to plan, all in all. It's been quite the task, organizing everything, what with Christmas and the world falling apart around us. A real eye-opener for me, I can tell you. Above anything else, I just hope it was how you wanted it to be. It's late now, and I'm in the living room, unwinding with a very large Glenfiddich and Felix Mendelssohn.

    The facts aren't crystal clear yet, but we're getting there. As of this evening, the lady that asked for your autograph, Mrs. Prentice, remains in intensive care, so we've only got the one eyewitness account to go on, a window cleaner. As bystanders go, he's not ideal — he told the Police he'd been Victor Borge in a previous life, which is all very well, except for the minor detail that Victor Borge is still alive.

    Flo says you went out at about 11.30 on the Monday morning. The downpour started just before midday, and old Vic says he saw you sheltering next to this woman under the ledge beneath the Caryatids at St. Pancras. I haven't seen all the evidence, but the investigators' theory seems credible. The statues aren't made of single slabs of stone, but are constructed in blocks — they think water was able to accumulate in the gaps between the sections, freezing and expanding over a long period, loosening the mortar and opening up cracks. You just happened to be signing 'Best wishes to Hazel' below the figure on the far left when it decided to give way. 'Bad timing' the chief rozzer called it. The insolence!

    They're saying it was very quick, if not instant. I've seen the segment itself, so I'm prepared to believe them. More than that, I need to believe them. The tabloids, who've been having a field day as you can imagine, report that it was a pair of concrete tits that hit you, but in reality it was the midriff of a Greek goddess. At the weekend I went to the church and saw the four figures, now surrounded by scaffolding and plastic sheeting. I spoke to the vicar, who was very good. The subject of blame came up, but he tried to dissuade me from going down that road. I suppose if ecclesiastical masonry falls down, it's the definition of an Act of God, but I expect the inquest will sort that out.

1992

    M has been wonderful. He took charge, and on the Wednesday he called myself, your sister, your agent, Stanley and Paul round to the house. Flo prepared a spread and we made some decisions. M was very good at talking Pat around to his way of thinking. You know how she can be.

    In the end <u>restraint</u> was our watchword, and I think it was as minimal and modest as you would've wished. It was the same man that presided over Louie's, as I know he'd impressed you. We were eleven in all. There were no flowers. Liszt's 'Bénédiction' on the way in, Elgar cellos on the way out. Regrettable that we had to sit there in our masks, but there was no way round it. Stanley Baxter spoke about you and just about managed to get through it. Maggie Smith did the reading, Revelation 21, quite beautifully. Barbara offered to do 'Sparrows Can't Sing' but, considering your feelings towards birds, we thought it inappropriate. Drinks at the Five Bells afterwards, then home.

    I know that you were never totally convinced about us. You made that obvious. A circle that was never fully squared. Too different in too many ways. But if that were true, I doubt I'd be feeling quite this empty and hurt. You weren't what I'd pictured for myself, believe me. Not by a long chalk. I never imagined I'd allow myself to be called an 'idiotic shit' and an 'uncouth nance', not in public anyway. I never thought I'd be content to be with an old man who would slam the door in my face and get his cleaner to tell me to sod off. But then I never thought I could laugh so helplessly, think so deeply, or be so excited to see someone to such a giddy extent. Maybe your name and position got in the way more than it ought to have. Maybe your lone wolf lifestyle had built a shell too thick to crack, I don't know. It doesn't matter now. All that matters is that I loved you — and I think, in your own way, you loved me.

    There are so many letters and cards. It's a strange thing, to write to someone who's just died, but they've done it, in their hundreds. Instinct, I suppose. The need to do something, anything. I know the feeling.

    Thank you for leaving me your watch. You were right, it does suit me. It has just ticked past twelve and I can hear them singing outside the pub. Welcoming in '93. A fresh start for all of us.

Happy new year, and God bless.
Love,
Rupert.

ACKNOWLEDGEMENTS

In writing an alternative history that straddles a speculative line between the flatly legitimate and the absurdly invented, there are two principal strings of inspiration which, in my view, have to be plucked most vigorously: those of imagination and research. These are key, of course, in a majority of literary pursuits, but mingling the strains – or harmonising fact and fiction, so that one can't be readily distinguished from the other – is vital for an outlandish plot to ring true. For the duration of this particular endeavour, I can say (without too much immodesty) that I handled the imagination side of things myself. The research part, however, was predominantly realised due to the goodwill and patience of various accommodating individuals, either by their sharing of private recollections, or by the opening of doors so that unmediated study of source material was practicable. These people deserve huge credit in helping me achieve my aims. By the same token, it's irrefutable that an enterprise such as compiling a book can only ever come to fruition by dint of the encouragement and succour of well-wishers and confidants. Having spurred me on and bucked me up when spirits needed lifting, I should like to recognise those kind souls here too.

Above all, I want to thank Adam Endacott – author of *The Kenneth Williams Companion*, and notable authority on the subject – for his reassurance and prudent guidance throughout the creative process. Not only has his endorsing of my work been personally fortifying, but his suggestions and counsel have proved invaluable in bringing the project to a conclusion. What's more, as a consequence of my affiliation with Adam, I have felt genuinely welcomed by the loyal circle of Williams' associates and devotees, who from the beginning embraced my venture with broadmindedness and enthusiasm. Foremost among this group are Kenneth's close chums Michael Whittaker and Paul Richardson. Their willingness to indulge in reminiscence at length in order to add body to my words demonstrates remarkable generosity, and accordingly I will always be grateful to this pair of amiable and magnanimous gentlemen. I must also highlight the contribution of Wes Butters, whose meticulous scrutiny of the text reinforced my drive for an authentic-feeling narrative, and of Gyles Brandreth, who recounted such uproarious anecdotes one couldn't fail to be galvanised. Others in the community that have aided me in shaping this volume include Nick Lewis, Peter Cadley, Kenneth's godson Robert Chidell, the Rev'd Canon Dr Mark Oakley, Vincenzo Catapano, John Lahr, David Benson and Morris Bright MBE – I am obliged to each of them for their assistance.

In terms of facilitating documentary investigation, I am indebted to Greg Buzwell and Helen Melody of the British Library, whose efforts made it possible for me to extensively examine original diaries and letters from the Williams archive. Perusal of these – particularly examples dating to the very end of Kenneth's life – helped me enormously in forming a faithful tone with which to begin my manuscript, smoothing the transition from reality to fantasy, from truth to parody. I feel privileged to have been granted access to this unique and treasured collection. Equally cooperative were Sebastian Cody and Laura Cook of Open Media; I'm greatly appreciative of their ebullient readiness to take unexpected trips down memory lane.

It goes without saying that my family have bestowed the bulk of the moral support I've required during this journey, along with friends (both long-standing and new-found) whose sustained championing and thoughtful advice have seen me through. But it's my father, Keith Holland, that deserves singular praise. His unswerving belief in me – not solely in the course of this undertaking, but every day of my life – has instilled an inner confidence and resolve that has carried me over many a hurdle, at all times assured of his steadfast backing. I shall be forever beholden to him, and my late mother, for the sacrifices made so that I might succeed.

Lastly, it would be preposterous if I didn't affirm my abiding respect and admiration for the person who sparked this off, both as a legendary entertainer and a truly fascinating human being, the *fantabulosa* Kenneth Williams. Still a toddler when he passed away, I never met him, nor did I know a great deal about him when I was young, beyond the characters I saw him portray in films on wet Sunday afternoons; the flared nostril grotesques, the uptight neurotics, the hysterically camp show-offs. Though a fan of his comedy, and curiously drawn to the peculiar, waspish guise he often displayed, it wasn't until I bought a copy of his published diaries in my early

Acknowledgements

teens that I became profoundly hooked. That unputdownable tome, an 800-page doorstop comprising excerpts from the forty-three journals he left behind, was the best book I'd ever read. Scrupulously edited by Russell Davies, this beguiling window into an actor's mind – the ultimate record of the conflict between austere privacy and inescapable fame – remains my unrivalled favourite. I'll admit, it's audacious of me to presume I have even the slightest ability to fabricate a convincing continuation to this extraordinary chronicle of a lifetime. Yet, ultimately, all I ever wanted to do was devise a world where Kenneth Charles Williams carried on, his existence and mine overlapping just that little bit more... As I can't thank him in person, I hope I have demonstrated my gratitude with this heartfelt homage.

Bill Holland,
November 2024